SECRETS OF ACTING
SHAKESPEARE

SECRETS OF ACTING
SHAKESPEARE
THE ORIGINAL APPROACH

PATRICK TUCKER

ROUTLEDGE/A Theatre Arts Book
New York and London

To Cue Script actors everywhere

Published in 2002 by
Routledge
29 West 35th Street
New York, NY 10001

Published in Great Britain by
Routledge
11 New Fetter Lane
London EC4P 4EE

Routledge is an imprint of the Taylor & Francis Group.
Copyright © 2002 by Routledge

Printed in the United States of America on acid-free paper.

10 9 8 7 6 5 4 3 2 1

Library of Congress Cataloguing-in-Publication Data

Tucker, Patrick, 1941–
     Secrets of acting Shakespeare: the original approach / by Patrick Tucker.
         p. cm.
     Includes bibliographical references and index.
     ISBN 0-87830-148-8 (hb.) — ISBN 0-87830-095-3 (pbk.)
         1. Shakespeare, William, 1564–1616—Dramatic production. 2. Acting. I. Title
PR3091.T83 2001
     792.9'5—dc21   2001019664

CONTENTS

PREFACE

Four hundred years ago a bunch of actors presented the plays of Shakespeare in daylight performances, working from Cue Scripts, with no group rehearsals, and no director, and working to a schedule that saw them in any one week putting on a different play every day. By modern standards it seems impossible, so what was their secret?

This book investigates the conditions and techniques of the Elizabethan companies, and uses these to come up with conclusions that are invaluable to everyone concerned, from professional actors and scholars, to acting students and high school English classes, and to all of those who take delight in having new insights into the genius of Shakespeare.

The journey I have made to this point has been possible only with the help and support of many people, and thanks are due to:

The faculty of Boston University, who not only admitted this English physicist to its MFA theatre directing program in the 1960s but gave me a full-tuition scholarship as well.

John Barton at the Royal Shakespeare Company, who when I was his assistant director in the 1970s taught me how the text was paramount (even though he would disagree with me about which text that was).

Peter Layton and his Drama Studio London, who gave me room and license to put Cue Scripts into practice with its graduate acting program for the past twenty years.

Christine Ozanne, my beloved partner, who sold the idea to professional actors so well that they wanted to do it for themselves; and has helped immeasurably with all my Shakespeare work, the Original Shakespeare Company, and this book.

Gillian McCutcheon, who decided that something had to be done, and made her front room available for the first series of verse classes I gave to working actors.

Graham Pountney, who came in with the two of us to form and run the OSC in the early 1990s.

Don Shipley of the World Stage Festival in Toronto, who invited us over to train its actors and present a production in Canada—and then invited us back.

Diana Denley of Shakespeare's Globe Centre in Australia, who invited us over to Sydney to work with its actors in workshops and to put on a production with three different casts.

Akram Massarweh of the Jerash Festival in Jordan, who for four years kept inviting the OSC back to perform on its 2,500-year-old Artimes Temple steps.

Mark Rylance of Shakespeare's Globe, who for its first three seasons invited us to put on sold-out performances of three different plays.

Tiffany Stern, who believed in her Uncle Patrick's ideas and did the proper scholastic work on it all, culminating in her successful thesis and book—and so ruined my claim that no one had done any research into how they rehearsed in Shakespeare's day; she also burrowed into my manuscript and attempted to keep me intellectually honest.

All the actors, professional and student, who have over the years been willing to risk reputation and nerve by acting without the usual security blankets of given moves, stage business, and character to put the ideas and techniques discussed in this book into such glorious practice.

INTRODUCTION

The book that follows is in several sections, which you can read in any order.

At first I deal with the background to my investigations, and the evidence I have found for it. THE PERFORMANCES gives an account of the developing journey we have made working this way with the Original Shakespeare Company, with lots of examples and illustrations. THE SECRETS section goes straight to what you do when approaching Shakespearean text, and THE OSC CHECKLIST is a collection of the practical acting notes we have accumulated.

All the Shakespearean quotations are taken from the First Folio text, including its spelling, capitalization, punctuation, and lineage. The reason will become clear if you venture into THE FOLIO sections. This is the most troublesome area, primarily because not all of you will have access to a First Folio or, if you do, your lecturer/teacher/director will not necessarily like you to use it. I have made this book valid whether you do or do not use the Folio, but I cannot hide my admiration for it. Suffice it to say, in bold terms, that in the thousands and thousands of Shakespeare lines I have worked on in speeches, scenes, and full-length plays, I have always (repeat <u>always</u>) found that the Folio text improves and helps matters. I realize this is not evidence, just opinion, so I will leave further discussion for that particular section, where you may pass over it should you be so inclined or lack access to the Folio. It is easily available on the Internet, however, and I know of a growing number of actors who consult it to get their additional clues, and then <u>do not tell anyone where they got the ideas from</u>. (What a good, tactful idea.)

I have tried where possible to give examples of what I am talking about, but I must insist that it is all my own opinion, and referring to someone else does not necessarily imply that they agree with everything I have discovered and come up with in the twenty-five years I have been examining and experimenting with these ideas.

In other words, where this is helpful, be my guest, and if you disagree with any bit, I shall happily accept equal blame.

THE QUESTION

The Shakespeare Problem

You have to act a character.
You have to prepare an essay on a character.
You have to teach a class about a character—or a play.

The Shakespeare Delight

You want to understand the inner workings of a character.
You want some insight into what Shakespeare intended.
You want to prepare yourself before seeing a wonderful production of a play.

The Solution?

You go to a book, and read it. You turn the pages, flicking backward and forward, comparing and contrasting various passages.

You read each scene, trying to work out what is going on, and working out what you would do in those given circumstances.

Remembering some lecture or essay, you try to match up what you were told is going on with what you perceive from the story is going on.

All these solutions are understandable, seemingly logical—and so very different from what would have happened in Shakespeare's day.

The Original Solution

Elizabethan actors would not go to a book, flicking the pages back and forth; would not work out what was going on from the situation. They would go to their scroll, where they would read just their own lines, where it is not easy to compare Act One with Act Five; where the situation can only be guessed at, and where they only had their own lines to give them guidance as to the character, the play, and the unknown situation.

Looking at a scroll for just one character is a very different and liberating experience from looking at the pages of a book.

This book addresses all the differences that such an approach brings, and the delights and insights that can follow such a seemingly old-fashioned approach.

A modern film or television script is not written for the general public but for working professionals, who will understand the shortcuts and abbreviations used by their fellow workers. In screen work, therefore, those in the know will use such terms as VO and POV, knowing that they will be understood by those reading the script as indicating "voice-over" and "point of view." One television company regularly uses TIC in their scripts at the start of certain speeches; only those who work for the company, including writers, directors, actors, and technicians, know that this stands for "tongue in cheek."

In the same way, the Elizabethan playwrights wrote shorthand instructions into their scripts for those who were going to use them—the actors—and this book addresses what these instructions were.

THE RESEARCH

Starting Off

This journey started for me at a committee meeting about the rebuilding of Shakespeare's Globe in London in the mid 1980s.

Some years earlier Sam Wanamaker, the leader and inspiration of this rebuilding, had seen my production of *Cymbeline* for the Berkeley Shakespeare Festival, and since it was a performance that went on in the afternoon without any lighting and in the open air (and I presume he liked it), he asked me to join the theatre committee of the Globe.

I started my journey at the meeting of an advisory council that was to discuss what should be built on the site we hoped to have in London by the river Thames; I was the theatre committee representative. We all knew that we wanted to build a Globe, but debate raged over what else should be on the site. Should there be a property store? A costume shop? Storage spaces? A rehearsal room? As to this last, they looked to me for advice, as it was apparent that building a rehearsal room would take up precious space. Could it be justified? Obviously, I told them, this would depend on how long it would be used each year, and that would depend on how many productions were to be put on, and how long they would rehearse.

We knew we wanted to put on four main productions a year, so now the problem was how long each would occupy the proposed rehearsal room. "How long should we rehearse?" I was asked, and since I was in my committee mode, I replied that since we were rebuilding the Globe and hoping to replicate some of the original conditions in which these great plays were first performed, perhaps we should rehearse for the same length of time that the Elizabethans did.

There was silence. I broke it by asking the professor sitting opposite me, "How long did they rehearse in Shakespeare's time?" He paused, and then prevaricated, and eventually came up with "ten days." His groundbreaking books on Shakespearean productions had obviously not covered this point. The chairman of the meeting was an Elizabethan stage authority, so I asked him the same question—yet got the same uncertain reply, ending with a vague "two weeks."

I was the only theatre person present, and yet it was obvious that the experts not only did not know the answer to the question but—far more revealing—had never even thought of the question. I could not wait to get back home and look up "rehearsal" in my Shakespeare books. A foolish thought, for the word did not occur—and even though this now forced me to read those books I had bought to "read at a later date" (as we all do), I could find no reference in indexes or anywhere to any discussion of this most vital point.

For a professional director undertaking a project, how long you have to rehearse makes a huge difference to the type and style of production, and to the eventual results. Yet there I was presented with the possibility that the academic world had never addressed the problem with regard to Shakespeare's writings.

Rehearsals

Let us talk about rehearsing a play, and how long it should take.

Now, I have rehearsed plays in a week, in two weeks, in three weeks, in five weeks, over three months—and not at all. Each has its pluses and minuses.

One Week (Weekly Rep, Mostly the 1950s and '60s)

To rehearse a play in a week—as in weekly rep—is not as awful as it sounds. You have time to rehearse each bit—once. Everyone knows of the time restriction, so rehearsals are strictly focused on the matter in hand: where do we stand, where do we enter, what do we do. The quality of acting is surprisingly high, as rehearsals tend to be limited to practical matters, leaving the interpretive side to the actors themselves. There is a regular company of actors, who are in every play, with extra actors brought in (for a "special week"), if the play demands a cast larger than the regular company.

It goes like this. The play you have prepared opens on a Monday night, and at the end during the curtain call the lead actor steps forward with a speech along the lines of: "We are glad you enjoyed tonight's performance of *Blithe Spirit*. Next week, we are presenting that exciting thriller by Agatha Christie, *The Spider's Web*." The other actors smile at the audience, secretly worrying that they have not even had the time to read the play and see what they are to be challenged with.

On Tuesday morning the director goes through *The Spider's Web* once, giving moves and agreeing on stage business. Most often, the decision has been made to use the same set design as in the copy of the play (French's Acting Edition, of course), and so all the moves noted in that edition can be used by the actors. Tuesday afternoon is taken up by the actors learning Act One, and on Tuesday evening they all perform *Blithe Spirit* again.

On Wednesday morning, the actors and director go through Act One with all lines learned. There is time to go through each moment once or twice, with reaction from the director, and then move on to the next. The morning ends with a run-through of Act One. In the afternoon, the actors learn Act Two, and of course perform in the evening.

Thursday is the same as Wednesday, going through Act Two with lines learned, except that there is probably a matinee performance in the afternoon, and so the actors have to fit in learning Act Three around their performance commitments for the rest of the day.

Friday morning is Act Three with no books, and often on Friday afternoon there would be a run-through of the complete play, with time for a few concise notes from the director before breaking to get ready for another performance of *Blithe Spirit* that evening.

Saturday morning is a second run-through of the whole play, with a break before the later matinee where you might find some time for personal shopping. On Sunday the actors have a day off, except that being responsible for their own costumes, they often spend it adapting a dress, ironing a shirt, and worrying that the regular audience might spot that they have already worn that particular outfit several times that season.

Monday morning sees the "technical" of the play, working out how to negotiate the new set, where to put one's hand to pretend that you are turning the light on, and the like. On Monday afternoon there is a dress rehearsal, again with time for a few quick notes from the director before getting ready for the first night of *The Spider's Web*. At the curtain call, the lead actor steps forward with a speech along the lines of: "We are glad you enjoyed tonight's performance of *The Spider's Web*. Next week, we are presenting that wonderful classic by Terence Rattigan, *Separate Tables*." The other actors smile at the audience, secretly worrying that they have not even had time to read the play and see what they are to be challenged with.

And so on for as long as the season lasts, sometimes up to twenty-six weeks.

Two Weeks (Fortnightly Rep, the 1960s and '70s)

This is the most unsatisfactory of rehearsal times. You have enough time to go through the play, and you also have just enough time to discover what extras you could bring to it, but not enough time to put this into practice.

The actors and director do not want to slavishly follow the moves in the French's Acting Edition, but there is so little time to add the embellishments and refinements. Rehearsals tend to be all day, with the actors learning their lines during rehearsal and over the one free weekend. Actors being actors will leave their learning to the last moment, using timeworn phrases like "I cannot learn my lines until I know my moves and character," and the dress rehearsal is often marked by a conspicuous amount of prompting.

Three Weeks (1970s Onward)

This used to be the normal rehearsal time for repertory theatre companies, and sometimes even for major West End productions as well. In the first week of rehearsal the play is blocked—that is, all moves and bits of stage business worked out—and talked through. In the second week, the actors go through the play without book (where possible), and the scenes are individually worked and commented on. In the third week, this process is completed, and then the play is run several times, enabling the director to give notes on the whole arc of the play, the development of the individual characters, and the play's overall impact.

If the necessary work is done in time, then in the third week time can be spent on refining a difficult moment or rehearsing a very tricky piece of staging.

Longer Rehearsal Periods

There is a growing tendency for longer periods of rehearsal, with directors even claiming that a production cannot have any quality without the "necessary six weeks of rehearsal." The actors get down to such exciting activities as bonding and amateur psychology; in a recent production at the rebuilt Shakespeare's Globe, all the actors were given a ball of clay from which they had to make their own personal temple or god and worship it. This was for a production of *The Winters Tale*, where alas there seemed no obvious result from this questionable use of rehearsal time. Mind you, this was also a production whose director for some rehearsals insisted that the actors rehearse nude—not because they would do so in the final production but to make sure they were "honest" with each other. To be truthful, the actors honestly hated this idea.

Directors fill rehearsal time, but now it is not always concerned with direct work on the play, and the belief has grown that the <u>process</u> of rehearsal is important in itself, rather than the <u>result</u> that the audience experiences.

Some wonderful productions do come out of these longer production times, as theatre artists aim for total experiences involving many varied theatrical elements, but these are weakened by the self-indulgence that the luxury of extra time can foster. I understood therefore that writers would incorporate into their writings their knowledge of how long the eventual play would be rehearsed. Chekhov knew that Stanislavsky would rehearse his plays for three months or so, which might explain some of his elliptical phrases and thoughts: after all, he knew that the actor would have plenty of time to investigate and inhabit the role. A writer on a daily television drama knows that an actor will in all probability pick up the script upon finishing a day's work, ready to act the next day, and so there is very little time for the actor to do other than perform the lines in the manner of day in, day out typecasting.

In fact, with the time and money pressures on television and film production, rehearsal time has all but disappeared, and to compensate, more time is spent on preparing the script. The better the script, the easier it is to come up with wonderful performances. All actors will admit that their best performances on screen are attributed to the work of the scriptwriter, and all want to work with the best writers there are.

Preparations in Shakespeare's Time

And what was in Shakespeare's mind when he wrote his plays, what was his perception of how his plays should be prepared? It became quite a quest, searching out books in libraries and trying to track down references to such an important aspect of Shakespearean production.

As you can guess from the very fact of this book, I found nothing—there is nothing (well, until the very recent book by Dr. Tiffany Stern)—and I had to start assembling the evidence myself. So many people, when they did touch on the subject, would immediately make the assumption that the plays were prepared the way they are today, and would make careless references to actors perhaps even being directed by Shakespeare himself.

The first objective was to learn what the original theatre companies four hundred years ago put on, how many plays, how often they did new productions, and what was the gap between performances of the same play. The information is easy to get hold of. Although there are no complete records of what was performed at the Globe in London, next door in the Rose Theatre, Philip Henslowe, the manager, had kept a record of plays presented, bills paid, and so on, and this "Henslowe's Diary" is a revelation, and full of extraordinary information.

I chose 1595 as a date by which Shakespeare himself might have begun writing, and I started digging around. I found that the Elizabethan companies presented an enormous number of plays in a short time. It was quite common to have over twenty plays in repertoire and to put on six different plays in the six days of one week. Plays would drop in and out of the repertoire at short notice, and companies would introduce new plays into their repertoire at an average of one every two weeks.

Although we have a sketchy idea of the plays performed by the Lord Chamberlain's Men, the company Shakespeare was a shareholder in, we do know that they would take up to twenty productions to Hampton Court for the Christmas festive season, and their pattern of work would seem to be similar to that recorded by Philip Henslowe.

There was a gap between 27 June and 24 August (eight weeks). The company then played continuously for twenty-seven weeks (including Christmas Day) until 1 March, with a break of six weeks until starting again on 12 April 1596 (Easter Monday).

THE ROSE THEATRE, AUTUMN 1595

DATE		NAME OF PLAY	NEW PLAY?	NO. OF DAYS TO: LAST PERF	NEXT PERF
Monday	Aug. 25	The knacke to know a nonest man		58	24
Tuesday	Aug. 26	The wisman of wescheaster		76	13
Wednesday	Aug. 27	The weacke		65	7
Thursday	Aug. 28	Longe mege		70	16
Friday	Aug. 29	Longe shanke	YES		11
Saturday	Aug. 30	The seage of london		169	21
Monday	Sept. 1	1st pte of herculos		81	22
Tuesday	Sept. 2	2nd pte of herculos		81	22
Wednesday	Sept. 3	The vii dayes of the weacke		7	9

Thursday	Sept. 4	Olempeo and hengenyo		88	24
Friday	Sept. 5	Cracke me this nutte	YES		7
Saturday	Sept. 6	Valia and antony		78	40
Monday	Sept. 8	The wise man		13	22
Tuesday	Sept. 9	Longshancke		11	22
Wednesday	Sept. 10	Doctor fostes		97	17
Thursday	Sept. 11	Cracke me this nutte		6	14
Friday	Sept. 12	The vii dayes		9	10
Saturday	Sept. 13	Longe mege		16	21
Monday	Sept. 15	1st pte of tamberlen		117	58
Tuesday	Sept. 16	Godfrey of bullen		122	?
Wednesday	Sept. 17	The worldes tragedy	YES		9
Thursday	Sept. 18	The Knacke		24	121
Friday	Sept. 19	The frenshe Doctor		87	293
Saturday	Sept. 20	The sege of london		21	115
Monday	Sept. 22	The vii dayes		10	15
Tuesday	Sept. 23	1st pte of herculos		22	19
Wednesday	Sept. 24	2nd pte of herculos		22	19
Thursday	Sept. 25	Cracke me this nutte		14	4
Friday	Sept. 26	The worldes tragedy		9	11
Saturday	Sept. 27	Docter fostes		17	140
Monday	Sept. 29	Crack me this nutte		4	9
Tuesday	Sept. 30	The wiseman		22	7
Wednesday	Oct. 1	Longe shancke		22	20
Thursday	Oct. 2	The Desgysses	YES		8
Friday	Oct. 3	Olempeo		29	51
Saturday	Oct. 4	Longe mege		21	394
6 weeks		36 performances			
42 days		17 different plays	4 new		

As we look at each week, the first startling piece of information is that they would perform six different plays in six days. Week in, week out, six plays in six days. The second main thing to notice is that there are large gaps between performances. On 1 and 2 September, they did performances of both parts of *Hercules*, plays they had not performed for eighty-one days, or nearly three months. I wondered how the actors could keep all those lines in their heads over such a long period, because although modern actors can keep a number of plays in repertoire in their heads, these are all plays they perform regularly, with a long preparation and rehearsal period.

Now look at the new plays. Ah yes, there is the two-week gap between presentations of new plays, which must be where those professorial estimations came from, but in the interim, the actors have to perform many other plays, some of which have not been done for ages. *Cracke me this nutte* looks to have been a hit, coming back quickly into the repertoire, but the text for it has now alas gone for good, and all we have for it is its title.

From a look at the schedule, it seems as if an actor's life would consist of relearning lines in the mornings and performing in the afternoons, with no time left for what we call rehearsal—which made putting on a play very puzzling. At most they would have had time for a quick technical rather than a textual get-together, just like the one *Peter Quince* puts his actors through. Even today, you would be given more rehearsal time for a Shakespeare play than for one by Arthur Miller or Alan Ayckbourn.

To recap: Henslowe's Diary reveals that in the thirty days of September 1595 they put on twenty-six performances of sixteen different full-length plays. These included a performance of *Doctor Faustus,* the next performance of which was in February 1596, 140 days later, by which time the Rose had presented 107 performances of twenty-one different plays. And this February performance of *Faustus* was the day after the first performance of *The Blind Beggar of Alexandria.*

If these are the conditions that an original company worked under, and if they themselves did not seem to have time for "rehearsal," then what would happen if this process were applied to the modern actor? I have found the results to be startling and gratifyingly refreshing.

We need to understand first what a play in Shakespeare's England consisted of. The only full copies of a play were at the time called "the book," or "boke," roughly equivalent to (though not the same as) a modern prompt book, which was kept under close guard. The reason for this was that the play was the property of the Company, and they were guarded against unscrupulous members of the Company memorizing or copying bits of the play out, and giving it to rival companies or printers. In purely practical terms, it was also very time consuming (and expensive both in buying the paper and paying a scribe) to write out a complete script, and was considered entirely unnecessary for an actor who may have only a few lines.

The hired actor (a hireling) therefore would never read the whole play, and even the shareholders would have had the complete play read to them only once by the playwright some time before. Instead of receiving a full copy of the play, then, the actor would be presented with a script containing just his own lines, plus the cue words before each speech, wound in a roll on a piece of wood (hence, "Here's your role for tonight"?), and he would have to read and learn it in sequence from his character's first entrance. I shall use the term "Cue Script" for this, as our modern equivalent of what was in those days called a "part," and later a "length"; as the cues are an intrinsic part of my argument, I shall stick with the former. The only other words on the Cue Script apart from the actor's own would be the last three or four words of speeches immediately preceding his: the cue line.

The only extant copy of a professional theatre actor's Cue Script from the Renaissance theatre is to be found in the treasure house of Dulwich College with the papers of Philip Henslowe, and there we can see that, indeed, the actor was not given the full story of each scene, but just what he himself said. (There is another Cue Script elsewhere, but it is a University one from the 1620s and very different in appearance—and we are here dealing with the professional theatre.)

Many radical changes flow from this understanding that the actors worked only on their own lines. Here is some of the Cue Script from Henslowe's papers for the part of *Orlando* from Robert Greene's *Orlando Furioso*:

CUE SCRIPT FOR ORLANDO

_____ my Lord
come hether Argalio, Vilayne behold these lynes
see all these trees, carved with true love knottes
wherin are figured Medor and Angelica.
what thinkst thou of it
_____ is a woeman
and what then
_____ some newes
what messenger hath Ate sent abrode
with Idle lookes to listen my lament
sirha who wronged happy nature thus
to spoyle thes trees with this Angelica
yet in hir name Orlando they are blest.
_____ folow love
As follow love, darest thou disprayse my heaven

And here is the equivalent that I have prepared from the full text, which would be for the entire part of *Lady Macduffe* from the play *Macbeth*:

CUE SCRIPT FOR LADY MACDUFFE

ENTER MACDUFFES WIFE, HER SON, AND ROSSE.

What had he done, to make him fly the Land?
_____ patience Madam.
He had none:
His flight was madnesse: when our Actions do not,
Our feares do make us Traitors.
_____ wisedome, or his feare.
Wisedom? to leave his wife, to leave his Babes,
His Mansion, and his Titles, in a place

From whence himselfe do's flye? He loves us not,
He wants the naturall touch. For the poore Wren
(The most diminitive of Birds) will fight,
Her yong ones in her Nest, against the Owle:
All is the Feare, and nothing is the Love;
As little is the Wisedome, where the flight
So runnes against all reason.

_____ Blessing upon you.

Father'd he is,
And yet hee's Father-lesse.

_____ my leave at once.

    EXIT ROSSE.

Sirra, your Fathers dead,
And what will you do now? How will you live?

_____ Birds do Mother.

What with Wormes, and Flyes?

_____ and so do they.

Poore Bird,
Thou'dst never Feare the Net, nor Lime,
The Pitfall, nor the Gin.

_____ all your saying.

Yes, he is dead:
How wilt thou do for a Father?

_____ for a Husband?

Why I can buy me twenty at any Market.

_____ to sell againe.

Thou speak'st withall thy wit,
And yet i'faith with wit enough for thee.

_____ Traitor, Mother?

I, that he was.

_____ is a Traitor?

Why one that sweares, and lyes.

_____ Traitors, that do so.

Every one that do's so, is a Traitor,
And must be hang'd.

_____ that swear and lye?

Every one.

_____ Who must hang them?

Why, the honest men.

_____ and hang up them.

Now God helpe thee, poore Monkie:
But how wilt thou do for a Father?
_____ a new Father.
Poore pratler, how thou talk'st?
_____ abide no longer.

EXIT MESSENGER.

Whether should I flye?
I have done no harme. But I remember now
I am in this earthly world: where to do harme
Is often laudable, to do good sometime
Accounted dangerous folly. Why then (alas)
Do I put up that womanly defence,
To say I have done no harme?
What are these faces?
_____ is your Husband?
I hope in no place so unsanctified,
Where such as thou may'st finde him.
_____ away I pray you.

EXIT CRYING MURTHER.

As you can see, the actor knows what he has to say but does not know the context or the situation (very similar to a modern actor today working in film or television). The preceding then is the complete information the actor would have for preparing the part of *Lady Macduffe*, with apparently no group rehearsal either. At this point, I was convinced I was on a fool's errand, since such conditions seemed impossible.

I have decided, after a lot of trial and error, to make the cue line consistently a double iamb where possible (di-dum, di-dum). At first I had standardized on a three-word cue, but then some cue lines were very long and others impossibly short, and I found that the actors picked up double iambic cue lines better than any other form—and this seems to have been followed in the University Cue Script I mentioned much earlier.

There was a third element to a play, apart from the book or boke, and the individual Cue Scripts, and that is the Platt.

On the day of performance at an Elizabethan theatre there would be a Platt (or plot) hanging in the wings, which would outline briefly what happened in each scene, who was in it, and who played the parts. Accompanying is a copy of *The Platt of The Second parte of the Seven Deadlie Sinnes*, probably from about 1590, the original being about two feet wide and three feet long with a square hole in the middle (for hanging up on a peg back stage?).

The original of this Platt is, again, in Dulwich College. On it one can see that the names of the Company shareholders were denoted by a "Mr" (Mr Brian), the hired men were identified by just their surnames with initial or first name (J Duke, Ro Pallant), and the apprentice boys were referred to by their nicknames (Saunder, Harry, Kitt). Richard Burbadge was in this company, as his group had joined forces with the Rose actors for this time, although when they went on tour in 1593, the plague having shut the London theatres, he was no longer with them. By 1595, Burbadge was with the Lord Chamberlain's Men, and stayed to become their leading actor.

The Platt of The Second parte of the Seven Deadlie Sinnes

A tent being plast one the stage for Henry the Sixt. he in it A sleepe to him The Leutenant A purcevaunt R Cowly Jo Duke and 1 wardere R Pallant: to them Pride Gluttony Wrath and Covetousnes at one dore. at another dore Envie. Sloth and Lechery. The Three put back the foure. and so Exeunt

Henry Awaking Enter A Keeper J Sincler to him a servaunt T Belt. to him Lidgate and the Keeper. Exit then enter againe. Then Envy passeth over the stage. Lidgate speakes

A Senitt. Dumb show.
Enter King Gorboduk with 2 Counsailers. R Burbadge Mr Brian. Th Goodale. The Queene with Ferrex and Porrex and som attendaunts follow. Saunder. W Sly. Harry. J Duke. Kitt. Ro Pallant. J Holland After Gordbeduk hath Consulted with his Lords he brings his 2 sonns to to severall seates. They enving on on other Ferrex offers to take Porex his Corowne. he draws his weapon. The King Queen and Lords step between them. They Thrust them away and menasing ech other exit. The Queene and Lords depart Hevilie. Lidgate speaks

Enter Ferrex Crownd with Drum and Coulers and soldiers one way. Harry. Kitt. R Cowly John Duke. to them At another dore. Porrex drum and Collors and soldiers W Sly. R Pallant. John Sincler. J Holland.

Enter Queene. with 2 Counsailors. Mr Brian. Tho Goodale. to them Ferrex and Porrex severall waies with Drums and Powers. Gorboduk entreing in The midst between. Henry speaks

Alarum with Excurtions After Lidgate speakes

Enter Ferrex and Porrex severally Gorboduke still following them. Lucius and Damasus Mr Bry T Good.

Enter Ferrex at one dore. Porrex at an other. The fight. Ferrrex is slayn. to them Videna the Queene to hir Damasus. to him Lucius.

Enter Porrex sad with Dordan his man. R P. W Sly. to them the Queene and A Ladie Nick. Saunder. And Lords R Cowly Mr Brian. to them Lucius Running

Henry and Lidgat speaks Sloth Passeth over.

Enter Giraldus Phronesius Aspatia Pompeia Rodope R Cowly Th Goodale. R Go. Ned. Nick.

Enter Sardinapalus Arbactus Nicanor and Captaines marching. Mr Phillipps Mr Pope R Pa. Kit J Sincler. J Holland.

Enter A Captaine with Aspatia and the Ladies Kitt.

Lidgat speakes

Enter Nicanor with other Captaines R Pall. J Sincler. Kitt. J Holland. R Cowly. to them Arbactus. Mr Pope. to him Will Foole. J Duke. to him Rodopeie. Ned. to her Sardanapalus Like A woman with Aspatia Rodope Pompeia Will Foole to them Arbactus and 3 musitions Mr Pope J Sincler. Vincent R Cowly to them Nicanor and others R P. Kitt

Enter Sardanapa. with the Ladies to them A Messenger. Th Goodale. to him Will Foole Running. Alarum.

Enter Arbactus pursuing Sardanapalus and the Ladies fly. After Enter Sarda with as many Jewels robes and Gold as he can cary.

Alarum.

Enter Arbactus Nicanor and The other Captains in triumph. Mr Pope. R Pa. Kitt. J Holl. R Cow. J Sinc.

Henry speaks and Lidgate. Lechery passeth over the stage.

Enter Tereus Philomele Julio and others R Burbadge. R Goughe. R Pallant. J Sincler. Kit.

Enter Progne Itis and Lords Saunder. Will. J Duke. W Sly Hary.

Enter Philomele and Tereus to them Julio

Enter Progne Panthea Itis and Lords. Saunder. T Belt. Will. W Sly. Hary. Th Goodale. to them Tereus with Lords. R Burbadge. J Duke R Cowly.

A Dumb show. Lidgate speakes

Enter Progne with the Sampler to her Tereus from Hunting with his Lords to them Philomele with Itis hed in a dish. Mercury Comes and all vanish. to him 3 Lords Th Goodale Hary W Sly.

Henry speaks. to him Leiutenant Pursevaunt and warders R Cowly J Duke. J Holland. John Sincler. to them Warwick. Mr Brian.

Lidgate speaks to the Audiens and so Exitts.

Finis

The existence of these artifacts then suggest that there was no rehearsal in the modern sense of the word and no complete understanding of the play, but that the actor would go on stage informed by his Cue Script, and the Platt backstage; such an impossibility should be tested, and so it was that I started to see how this would work out in practice.

If there were no rehearsals as such, there was also no director, and no way the author could inform the actors how to perform except through the text itself. Many times, a re-placement actor would be put on in a play in a hurry, such as when an apprentice actor's voice would break. On at least one famous occasion, the company put on a perfor-mance of *King Richard the Second* at very short notice, indeed not having performed it for years, at the request of the Essex conspirators in 1601. They were hoping for back-ing from the citizens of London to overthrow Queen Elizabeth, and thought that a play showing the deposition of a sovereign might help their cause. (It didn't). The text itself, then, must contain many useful and important clues to stage moves, stage business, character, and mood.

So how would an actor playing a major part like *Faustus* or *Mephistopheles* be able to prepare the role after a long break, which was by no means atypical? The only way we can fit the known facts into a timetable would be if after a performance, the actor took his "role"—or rolls—for the next day to learn or relearn the lines and cues as fully as possible. Since actors' wages were unlikely to have allowed them to buy expensive can-dles, there would be precious little light to study a role/roll in the evening hours. The actor would have to get up with the sun, and divide his time in the morning between learning his lines, getting ready for the performance, and attending any necessary prepa-rations such as for dances and fights. There would not be time for rehearsal the way we understand the word. All evidence shows that the actors spent most evenings in the tav-erns, but even there the light would be provided by rush candles—very dim and smoky and very hard to read by.

There is one reference to rehearsal in Henslowe's Diary, stating that actors would be fined if they were late for rehearsal, but the very word "rehearsal" had a different mean-ing then than it does today.

In the works of Shakespeare himself, "rehearse" means "repeat" or "recite," as in its use by *Launce* in *The Two Gentlemen of Verona*:

LAUNCE:
> Stop there: Ile have her: she was mine, and not
> mine, twice or thrice in that last Article: rehearse that
> once more.

or again from the same play, with *Valentine's*:

VALENTINE:
> For that which now torments me to rehearse;
> I kil'd a man,

In court records we can read that the Lord Chamberlain "rehearsed" several plays in a day—just as in fact *Philostrate* claims at the end of *A Midsommer Nights Dreame*, and this would have been a "re-hearing" of the plays (to make sure there was no salacious material in it to offend the monarch), <u>not</u> the modern idea of a going through and discussion type of meeting.

The references to "rehearsal" then have more to do with a public hearing of the complete text than with the "can you move down left crying silently?" approach of the present day.

In the morning, therefore, there must have been a *Piramus* and *Thisby* type of meeting for all those actors in the afternoon's performance, dealing with the immediate entrances and exits of the play to be done that day, together with any dances and fights. There would be no time for "interpretation" or discussion and probably no time for going through the play even once. During this period, the actor would have to complete his memorization and make sure that any costumes and properties needed for his roles had been sorted out (possibly done by the Book-Holder).

At performance time, the actor would "go on," probably after consulting the Platt as to when to enter. He would also have to check the Platt to see if he was down to play any extras, lords, servants, and so on. Onstage, he would have to pay close attention to the other characters' lines to recognize his cue line—and then speak. If he had different roles to play, he would be very busy indeed. In *The Second parte of the Seven Deadlie Sinnes*, one unfortunate actor, Richard Cowly, is set down to play in order: *Leutenant; Soldier; Lord; Giraldus; Captaine; Musition; Captaine; Lord; Leutenant*. His afternoon must have been a confusion of costume and prop changes—no time for him to stand in the wings and get an idea of what the play was about.

I believe, from the experience of putting on plays this way, that the preceding paragraph describes what the actors would have done. Certainly, when I started to put a Platt up backstage, the actors were often to be found gazing at it, getting a picture of where they were in the play and what entrance they had to do next.

There are understandably many contemporary references to the fact that the prompter or Book-Holder (who I believe sat on the stage itself) was sometimes heard more often than the actors! This shows that the actors were of course intended to know all their lines, and being "out" meant you had temporarily forgotten them, as *Viola* says to *Olivia*:

VIOLA:
I can say little more then I have studied, and that
question's out of my part.

and as *Olivia* replies:

OLIVIA:
Have you any Commission from your Lord, to
negotiate with my face: you are now out of your Text:

Parts Played in One Afternoon

The original actors would play many different roles in one afternoon's performance.

Here is a list of who played what part, in which order, at the performance of *The Second parte of the Seven Deadlie Sinnes* as noted in Henslowe's papers. This is extracted from the Platt, with a few educated guesses as to some of the casting.

Sharers

Mr George Brian	Counsailer; Damasus; Lord; Warwick.
Mr Augustine Phillips	Sardanapalus.
Mr Thomas Pope	Arbactus.

Hired men

T. Belt	Servaunt; Panthea.
Richard Burbadge	King Gorboduk; Tereus.
Richard Cowly	Leutenant; Soldier; Lord; Giraldus; Captaine; Musition; Captaine; Lord; Leutenant.
John Duke	Persevaunt; Attendant; Soldier; Will Foole; Lord; Persevaunt.
Thomas Goodale	Counsailer; Lucius; Phronesius; Messenger; Lord.
Robert Gough	Covetousness; Aspatia; Philomele.
John Holland	Gluttony; Attendant; Soldier; Captaine; Warder.
Robert Pallant	1st Wardere; Attendant; Soldier; Dordan; Nicanor; Julio.
John Sincler	Keeper; Soldier; Captaine; Musition; Captaine; Lord; Wardere.
William Sly	Porrex; Lord.

Apprentices

Harry	Ferrex; Lord.
Kitt	Sloth; Attendant; Soldier; Sloth; Captaine; Lord.
Ned	Lechery; Rodope; Lechery.
Nick	Wrath; Lady; Pompeia.
Saunder	Pride; Videna the Queene; Progne.
Vincent	Musician.
Will	Envy; Itis.
?	Henry the Sixt
?	Lidgate

THE EVIDENCE

The Tomb Scene from *The Tragedie of Romeo and Juliet*

Let us put these thoughts into practice, and examine a scene in the light of Cue Script, rather than of situation. This is a scene that unravels itself in a very different way when acted with Cue Scripts, performed from the lines and not from the perceived situation.

First, read the scene, and think what may be going on:

EXIT FRIER AND BALTHAZAR.

JULIET:
    Go get thee hence, for I will not away,
    What's here? A cup clos'd in my true loves hand?
    Poyson I see hath bin his timelesse end
    O churle, drinke all? and left no friendly drop,
    To helpe me after, I will kisse thy lips,
    Happlie some poyson yet doth hang on them,
    To make me die with a restorative.
    Thy lips are warme.
       ENTER PAGE AND WATCH.

CHIEF WATCH:
    Lead Boy, which way?

JULIET:
    Yea noise?
    Then ile be briefe. O happy Dagger.
    'Tis in thy sheath, there rust and let me die
       KILS HERSELFE.

PAGE:
    This is the place,
    There where the Torch doth burne

CHIEF WATCH:
    The ground is bloody,
    Search about the Churchyard.
    Go some of you, who ere you find attach.
    Pittiful sight, here lies the Countie slaine,
    And *Juliett* bleeding, warme and newly dead

Who here hath laine these two dayes buried.
Go tell the Prince, runne to the *Capulets,*
Raise up the *Mountagues,* some others search,
We see the ground whereon these woes do lye,
But the true ground of all these piteous woes,
We cannot without circumstance descry.
    ENTER SECOND WATCH WITH ROMEO'S MAN.
SECOND WATCH:

Here's *Romeo's* man,
We found him in the Churchyard.
CHIEF WATCH:

Hold him in safety, till the Prince come hither.
    ENTER FRIER, AND ANOTHER WATCHMAN
    CARRYING A MATTOCKE AND SPADE.
THIRD WATCH:

Here is a Frier that trembles, sighes, and weepes
We tooke this Mattocke and this Spade from him,
As he was comming from this Church-yard side.
CHIEF WATCH:

A great suspition, stay the Frier too.
    ENTER THE PRINCE.
PRINCE:

What misadventure is so earely up,
That calls our person from our mornings rest?
    ENTER CAPULET AND HIS WIFE.
CAPULET:

What should it be that they so shrike abroad?
LADY CAPULET:

O the people in the streete crie *Romeo.*
Some *Juliet,* and some *Paris,* and all runne
With open outcry toward our Monument.
PRINCE:

What feare is this which startles in your eares?
CHIEF WATCH:

Soveraigne, here lies the Countie *Paris* slaine,
And *Romeo* dead, and *Juliet* dead before,
Warme and new kil'd.
PRINCE:

Search,
Seeke, and know how, this foule murder comes.
CHIEF WATCH:

Here is a Frier, and Slaughter'd *Romeos* man,

With Instruments upon them fit to open
These dead mens Tombes.

CAPULET:

O heaven!
O wife looke how our Daughter bleedes!
This Dagger hath mistaine, for loe his house
Is empty on the backe of *Mountague,*
And is misheathed in my Daughters bosome.

LADY CAPULET:

O me, this sight of death, is as a Bell
That warnes my old age to a Sepulcher.

    ENTER MOUNTAGUE.

PRINCE:

Come *Mountague*, for thou art early up
To see thy Sonne and Heire, now early downe.

MOUNTAGUE:

Alas my liege, my wife is dead to night,
Griefe of my Sonnes exile hath stopt her breath:
What further woe conspires against my age?

PRINCE:

Looke: and thou shalt see.

MOUNTAGUE:

O thou untaught, what manners in is this,
To presse before thy Father to a grave?

PRINCE:

Seale up the mouth of outrage for a while,
Till we can cleare these ambiguities,
And know their spring, their head, their true descent,
And then will I be generall of your woes,
And lead you even to death? meane time forbeare,
And let mischance be slave to patience,
Bring forth the parties of suspition.

FRIER LAWRENCE:

I am the greatest, able to doe least,
Yet most suspected as the time and place
Doth make against me of this direfull murther:
And heere I stand both to impeach and purge
My selfe condemned, and my selfe excus'd.

PRINCE:

Then say at once, what thou dost know in this?

FRIER LAWRENCE:

I will be briefe, for my short date of breath

Is not so long as is a tedious tale.
Romeo there dead, was husband to that *Juliet*,
And she there dead, that's *Romeos* faithfull wife:
I married them.

> THE SCENE CONTINUES, BUT WE END HERE.

Now, as we read it, we start to imagine how we would feel in these circumstances, and put this into the scene. When does the *Chief Watch* notice the newly dead *Juliet*? Does *Lady Capulet* rush to the body and mourn over it? How does *Mountague* deal with all those *Capulets* when he enters? What do all the characters <u>do</u> to theatricalize this scene?

Let us look at the lines again, and this time I have written in certain conclusions from the individual texts, not from an overview of the scene:

> EXIT FRIER AND BALTHAZAR.

JULIET:

Go get thee hence, for I will not away,
What's here? A cup clos'd in my true loves hand?
Poyson I see hath bin his timelesse end
O churle, drinke all? and left no friendly drop,
To helpe me after, I will kisse thy lips,
Happlie some poyson yet doth hang on them,
To make me die with a restorative.
Thy lips are warme.

> ENTER PAGE AND WATCH.

CHIEF WATCH:

Lead Boy, which way?

JULIET:

Yea noise?
Then ile be briefe. O happy Dagger.
'Tis in thy sheath, there rust and let me die

> KILS HERSELFE.

PAGE:

This is the place,
There where the Torch doth burne

Juliet has just woken up in the tomb, to find her husband *Romeo* dead, with *Paris* dead nearby, and the *Frier* leaving. The others have already started to leave the stage, so the first line is shouted after them.

All her business is in her lines, of kissing, finding the poison, and then the dagger.

And why do they not see *Juliet* in the tomb? Because she is inside the tomb, they are outside, and there must be an entrance (a portable entrance such as they would have for a cave, so maybe the actors have to stoop to get through it). There are definitely two acting areas that the audience can see for this scene— inside and outside the tomb.

Tis in thy sheath, there rust and let me die is changed by Editors to *This is thy sheath, there rest and let me die*; I find no need for this.

Saying *there where the Torch doth burne* and not *here where . . .* shows that any lighting is at a distance, and therefore they are <u>all in the dark</u> (and so cannot see *Juliet* until the author tells them to).

CHIEF WATCH:

    The ground is bloody,
    Search about the Churchyard.
    Go some of you, who ere you find attach.

I have done this scene with students, professionals, actors from the RSC—and they always deliver this line as if you can tell just by looking <u>at night</u> that the patch on the floor is blood on the ground. The acting instruction? In order to <u>know</u> the ground is bloody, the *Chief Watch* has to check it out, smell it, taste it even? By his having to stoop to get through the tomb entrance, his face is interestingly brought close to the "blood" and the swords left behind.

    Pittiful sight, here lies the Countie slaine,

How does the *Chief Watch* know that *Paris* is slain? Obviously, again he has to check it out (he might after all only be wounded and unconscious).

    And *Juliett* bleeding, warme and newly dead
    Who here hath laine these two dayes buried.

Warme? Again, there are absolute instructions to the *Chief Watch* as to how to behave, to check the body of *Juliet*.

    Go tell the Prince, runne to the *Capulets,*
    Raise up the *Mountagues,* some others search,

He speaks to others, yet there is no one else onstage; these instructions need therefore to be shouted out to the other members of the *Watch* who are elsewhere.

    We see the ground whereon these woes do lye,
    But the true ground of all these piteous woes,
    We cannot without circumstance descry.

And here he goes in for wordplay (a pun on the word *ground.*) When do people get witty and clever? Often when they are nervous and ill at ease.
The verbal puns help to show the inner feelings, and since he is onstage with dead bodies, he needs to address this to the audience.

    ENTER SECOND WATCH WITH ROMEO'S MAN

SECOND WATCH:

    Here's *Romeo's* man,
    We found him in the Churchyard.

CHIEF WATCH:

    Hold him in safety, till the Prince come hither.

This simple instruction is essential if the center of the stage is not to get cluttered up. Here—and later—the *Chief Watch* tells the others to take the smaller roles to one side.

    ENTER FRIER, AND ANOTHER WATCHMAN
    CARRYING A MATTOCKE AND SPADE.

THIRD WATCH:

Here is a Frier that trembles, sighes, and weepes
We tooke this Mattocke and this Spade from him,
As he was comming from this Church-yard side.

CHIEF WATCH:

A great suspition, stay the Frier too.

ENTER THE PRINCE.

PRINCE:

What misadventure is so earely up,
That calls our person from our mornings rest?

ENTER CAPULET AND HIS WIFE.

CAPULET:

What should it be that they so shrike abroad?

LADY CAPULET:

O the people in the streete crie *Romeo,*
Some *Juliet,* and some *Paris,* and all runne
With open outcry toward our Monument.

PRINCE:

What feare is this which startles in your eares?

CHIEF WATCH:

Soveraigne, here lies the Countie *Paris* slaine,

And *Romeo* dead, and *Juliet* dead before,
Warme and new kil'd.

PRINCE:

Search,
Seeke, and know how, this foule murder comes.

CHIEF WATCH:

Here is a Frier, and Slaughter'd *Romeos* man,
With Instruments upon them fit to open
These dead mens Tombes.

The Third Watch can help by wiping a tear from the Frier's face (since he knows what is in his own lines).

So the *Frier* is also cleared from stage center.

The *Prince* need not worry about delivering these lines in the presence of the dead bodies. These pompous lines cover his entrance onstage to his entrance into the tomb.

It can be seen that both the *Capulets* have no instructions in their lines to "see" the corpse of *Juliet*—not yet. They too have to get from their entrance onstage to the tomb.

The use of the word *here* rather than *there* tells the *Chief Watch* to go up to *Paris.*

A crucial point. This is the very first time that the *Chief Watch* has mentioned *Romeo*—so this is the first time he actually sees him, and reacts to his death.

It is also crucial that the *Capulets,* hearing that their daughter is warm, newly dead, say and do nothing.

Again, the *Chief Watch* is directed by his lines to move around the stage.

CAPULET:

O heaven!

O wife looke how our Daughter bleedes!

This Dagger hath mistaine, for loe his house

Is empty on the backe of *Mountague,*

And is misheathed in my Daughters bosome.

LADY CAPULET:

O me, this sight of death, is as a Bell

That warnes my old age to a Sepulcher.

ENTER MOUNTAGUE.

PRINCE:

Come *Mountague*, for thou art early up

To see thy Sonne and Heire, now early downe.

MOUNTAGUE:

Alas my liege, my wife is dead to night,

Griefe of my Sonnes exile hath stopt her breath:

What further woe conspires against my age?

PRINCE:

Looke: and thou shalt see.

MOUNTAGUE:

O thou untaught, what manners in is this,

To presse before thy Father to a grave?

PRINCE:

Seale up the mouth of outrage for a while,

Till we can cleare these ambiguities,

And know their spring, their head, their true descent,

And then will I be generall of your woes,

And lead you even to death? meane time forbeare,

And let mischance be slave to patience,

Bring forth the parties of suspition.

FRIER LAWRENCE:

I am the greatest, able to doe least,

Yet most suspected as the time and place

Doth make against me of this direfull murther:

And heere I stand both to impeach and purge

My selfe condemned, and my selfe excus'd.

PRINCE:

Then say at once, what thou dost know in this?

FRIER LAWRENCE:

I will be briefe, for my short date of breath

Is not so long as is a tedious tale.

The simple lines given to the *Capulets* correspond to the simple things *we* say when suddenly hearing horrific news.

To justify the line, he has to make sure he can see the back of *Romeo* and the empty sheath, turning him over if necessary.

A play on words *early up/early down* shows the *Prince* to be nervous, or trying to lighten the dreadful situation.

And now the *Prince* has no more wordplay, and gives the news simply.

This simple line brings *Mountague* down to the corpses, sharing space and attitude with the *Capulets*.

Romeo there dead, was husband to that *Juliet,*
And she there dead, that's *Romeos* faithfull wife:
I married them.
    ENDS.

> And here the use of the word *there dead* tells the *Frier* that he is to illustrate at a distance.

One main thing to notice is that the actors are told <u>when</u> they are to react to an event or situation, and that these reactions correspond to our knowledge of human behavior, including our own.

When we hear terrible news, when we are almost killed by a passing car, what happens is that we are inarticulate, we utter nothing, or just a few simple words. It is only after a gap in time that we start talking about it, and quite some time later that we can hold forth on it. Many are the jokes and puns at funerals.

When news of Princess Diana's death spread, people said very little, short little simple words of disbelief and despair; at her funeral, we had wonderful examples of oratory and passion: emotion in recollection.

This is because articulate speech—clever speech—is possible when we are remembering an emotion, not the moment when we first experienced it. This is our knowledge of real life and how we behave, and I suggest that Shakespeare knew and wrote this way too. Those great articulate speeches are the character's <u>remembering</u> the emotion, not the actual moment of emotion itself.

This explains why so many of the great speeches have gone wrong, become unintelligible or even boring, because the actor is trying to say the clever witty speech <u>with</u> emotion, rather than responding to what we all know from our private lives, which is that the further away from the event we get, the more eloquent we become.

Rosalind, Celia—and the Duke

Information about moves and stage business, as in *Romeo and Juliet*, is obvious to see. Perhaps a little less obvious at first but an absolutely crucial tool for understanding how to unlock the scripts is understanding that changes of title or of address give fascinating and accurate insights into the relationships between the characters. I have chosen the best example of this I know, in the scene from *As you Like it* when *Rosalind*'s uncle comes in to banish her from his court.

This is a crucial scene for seeing what the text leads to, rather than an assumed idea about the scene from the situation. So often, in productions of this play, we see the *Duke* come storming on in a rage, at which we conclude he is angry, and then have to watch the scene played out of his banishing *Rosalind* with that assumption in mind. The text and a precise playing of it lead to a much more subtle and interesting interpretation, as well as clearly giving the actors help and instructions all the way through:

CELIA:

Is it possible on such a sodaine,

you should fall into so strong a liking with old Sir

Roulands yongest sonne?

ROSALIND:

The Duke my Father lov'd his Father deerelie.

CELIA:

Doth it therefore ensue that you should love his

Sonne deerelie? By this kinde of chase, I should hate

him, for my father hated his father deerely; yet I hate

not *Orlando*.

ROSALIND:

No faith, hate him not for my sake.

CELIA:

Why should I not? doth he not deserve well?

ENTER DUKE WITH LORDS.

ROSALIND:

Let me love him for that, and do you love him

Because I doe. Looke, here comes the Duke.

CELIA:

With his eies full of anger.

DUKE:

Mistris, dispatch you with your safest haste,

And get you from our Court.

ROSALIND:

Me Uncle.

DUKE:

You Cosen,

Within these ten daies if that thou beest found

So neere our publike Court as twentie miles,

Thou diest for it.

ROSALIND:

I doe beseech your Grace

Let me the knowledge of my fault beare with me:

If with my selfe I hold intelligence,

Celia, the daughter of the usurping *Duke*, and *Rosalind*, daughter of the true *Duke* and brother to the usurper, are alone on stage.

Speaking in prose at first, the two girls are not in a heightened state.

The *Duke* enters, a fact which *Rosalind* cannot ignore (although some do, or go along with Editors who unhelpfully move this entrance to a more "practical" place); her next lines are then spoken in the knowledge that the *Duke* is onstage, but she is ignoring him and his retinue.

The *Duke* addresses *Rosalind* impersonally.

She replies in the most personal family tones, maybe even showing this with a hug or embrace. He replies with the impersonal *you*, but an acknowledgment of their family relationship. Crucially, he now changes into the intimate *thee*, which implies that these words are for her ears alone, not for those of the attending court.

She starts to speak in poetry, and goes to a formal *Grace* at first, probably accompanied by a

Or have acquaintance with mine owne desires,
If that I doe not dreame, or be not franticke,
(As I doe trust I am not) then deere Uncle,
Never so much as in a thought unborne,
Did I offend your highnesse.

DUKE:
Thus doe all Traitors,
If their purgation did consist in words,
They are as innocent as grace it selfe;
Let it suffice thee that I trust thee not.
ROSALIND:
Yet your mistrust cannot make me a Traitor;
Tell me whereon the likelihoods depends?
DUKE:
Thou art thy Fathers daughter, there's enough.

ROSALIND:
So was I when your highnes took his Dukdome,
So was I when your highnesse banisht him;
Treason is not inherited my Lord,
Or if we did derive it from our friends,
What's that to me, my Father was no Traitor,
Then good my Leige, mistake me not so much,
To thinke my povertie is treacherous.

CELIA:
Deere Soveraigne heare me speake.
DUKE:
I Celia, we staid her for your sake,
Else had she with her Father rang'd along.
CELIA:
I did not then intreat to have her stay,
It was your pleasure, and your owne remorse,
I was too yong that time to value her,
But now I know her: if she be a Traitor,
Why so am I: we still have slept together,
Rose at an instant, learn'd, plaid, eate together,

---

deep curtsy, but emboldened by the way it is going, slips back to an intimate *Uncle*, maybe getting up and trying to embrace him again, but realizes that this is going nowhere, and reverts to a completely formal *highnesse*.

His response is to make a public declaration of her treachery, followed by intimate words to her.

She replies to his *thee* with a formal *your*.

He is still reasoning with her on an intimate, maybe private level.

Her reply is a formal, almost legalistic appeal to the rest of the court.

She then uses the most formal address of all, *my Leige*, which is often accompanied by completely abasing oneself on the floor, since it acknowledges the recipient has power of life and death over the prostrate speaker of it.

Celia joins in the argument, but addresses her father as *Soveraigne*, so appealing to him as a subject, not a daughter.

Her argument is in *you* terms, and so heard by all on stage.

And wheresoere we went, like *Junos* Swans,
Still we went coupled and inseperable.

DUKE:

She is too subtile for thee, and her smoothnes;
Her verie silence, and her patience,
Speake to the people, and they pittie her:
Thou art a foole, she robs thee of thy name,
And thou wilt show more bright, and seem more vertuous
When she is gone: then open not thy lips
Firme, and irrevocable is my doombe,
Which I have past upon her, she is banish'd.

Her father replies in *thee* terms, so perhaps taking her to one side, arguing with her privately.

CELIA:

Pronounce that sentence then on me my Leige,
I cannot live out of her companie.

Celia now uses the most formal address, *my Leige*, which links her with *Rosalind*, maybe even joining her on the floor.

DUKE:

You are a foole: you Neice provide your selfe,
If you out-stay the time, upon mine honor,
And in the greatnesse of my word you die.

EXIT DUKE, ETC.

The *Duke* reverts to the formal *you*, repeating a line he had previously used *thee* in, and so distancing himself from his rebellious daughter in front of the court. Although he uses *you* to *Rosalind*, he still reminds everyone of their relationship, with *Neice*.

CELIA:

O my poore *Rosaline,* whether wilt thou goe?
Wilt thou change Fathers? I will give thee mine:
I charge thee be not thou more griev'd then I am.

ROSALIND:

I have more cause.

ENDS.

Celia, of course, goes to the intimate *thee* to comfort *Rosalind*.

It is expensive and boring to put extra actors upon a stage, and often they are left out. This scene has often been played just between the three principals, but as you can see, the Lords in this scene are crucial, showing up the differences between the public pronouncements and the private moments.

The inner movement of the scene is plainly shown, with all the characters having their relationships defined by the title with which they address each other and the varying use of *thee* and *you*. I have to confess that it was only after about five years of working from Cue Scripts that I realized the magnitude of this simple clue, of the difference between the two words, and how Shakespeare uses it to define such differences.

I am aware that there is debate as to the exact significance of the differences, since about this time in the history of language, there was a shift going on between the two, with *thee* ending up being used on more formal occasions. But at the beginning of Shakespeare's writing career the change between *you/thee* was more along the public/private, outgoing/intimate, far away/very close lines, and I feel it is safe to say that he did not write anything at random and that if he used one word rather than another, it was a choice that we need to respond to and take its significance into account.

In all the plays I have worked on, together with all the hundreds of scenes I have re-worked, I have always found these gear changes between *you* and *thee*, and in fact all the changes of title and address, to be theatrically valid and have a significant impact on the meaning and playing of the scene.

Viola, the Captaine—and the Saylors

We have seen from the *tomb scene* how the language contains acting notes about moves and stage business, and from *Rosalind, Celia—and the Duke* how the language contains intricate information about the changing attitudes and relationships by the changing modes of address. What about more basic ideas and thoughts? Have a look at the second scene of *Twelfe Night*, where we first meet *Viola*:

ENTER VIOLA, A CAPTAINE, AND SAYLORS.

VIOLA:
    What Country (Friends) is this?
CAPTAINE:
    This is Illyria Ladie.
VIOLA:
    And what should I do in Illyria?
    My brother he is in Elizium,
    Perchance he is not drown'd: What thinke you saylors?
CAPTAINE:
    It is perchance that you your selfe were saved.
VIOLA:
    O my poore brother, and so perchance may he be.
CAPTAINE:
    True Madam, and to comfort you with chance,
    Assure your selfe, after our ship did split,
    When you, and those poore number saved with you,
    Hung on our driving boate: I saw your brother
    Most provident in perill, binde himselfe,
    (Courage and hope both teaching him the practise)
    To a strong Maste, that liv'd upon the sea:
    Where like *Orion* on the Dolphines backe,

I saw him hold acquaintance with the waves,
So long as I could see.

So what is going on ere? Should we tell *Viola* she is obviously wet and cold, and up-set about her missing brother? Should we tell the *Captaine* that he ought to be careful and considerate to this young woman? Perhaps we can only have the *Captaine* onstage, so saving the cost of the extra actors and their costumes playing the *Saylors*?

All this is taking the information about acting from what might be going on, so now let us look at the language itself, and see what happens:

ENTER VIOLA, A CAPTAINE, AND SAYLORS.	I believe that the plays work, so if the *Saylors* are mentioned, then I believe they are needed.
VIOLA: What Country (Friends) is this?	A simple question to the others on stage with her; but could Shakespeare have given her information that she was cold and wet? Yes. Did he? No.
CAPTAINE: This is Illyria Ladie.	A simple answer? Not when the first three words assonate with each other with the "i" sound, the last two words repeat the "l" sound, and the structure is formal.
VIOLA: And what should I do in Illyria? My brother he is in Elizium, Perchance he is not drown'd: What thinke you saylors?	To which *Viola* replies with a joke, a pun on the words *Illyria* and *Elizium* (which is the classical Greek term for their version of heaven). She then speaks to the *Saylors* and, by so doing, will inevitably get herself surrounded by men.
CAPTAINE: It is perchance that you your selfe were saved.	The *Captaine* replies, and he repeats the word *perchance* that she has just used.
VIOLA: O my poore brother, and so perchance may he be. CAPTAINE: True Madam, and to comfort you with chance, Assure your selfe, after our ship did split, When you, and those poore number saved with you, Hung on our driving boate: I saw your brother Most provident in perill, binde himselfe, (Courage and hope both teaching him the practise)	Nothing daunted, *Viola* repeats the word back at him. He repeats a variation on the word again: *chance*. And if he obeys *Hamlet*'s instruction to the Players: *Sute the Action to the Word, the Word to the Action* and puts his arm round her on *comfort*, then the little battles

To a strong Maste, that liv'd upon the sea:
Where like *Orion* on the Dolphines backe,
I saw him hold acquaintance with the waves,
So long as I could see.

between them, and the single woman surrounded by men, might well explain why it is that *Viola* decides to dress as a man, and the scene is about one of the topics of the play, not a treatise on wet and cold.

I believe, from the experiences I have had working on all these speeches and parts, that Shakespeare would know that to perform a role in a very short space of time, you need as much help as you can get. The best place to give that help is with the first speeches that you have, which is where you are looking for a clue and hint as to your character. So this beginning of *Twelfe Night* is much more interesting and revealing than just a variation of how it might be done: it is a fundamental question of taking character and interpretation from the lines that Shakespeare has given you, not from the situation.

So much modern acting is based on the idea that if only we can work out what is going on, and then work out how we ourselves would respond to that, then if we put all that into our acting, we will come over as truthful and real. Alas, this is not so for classic plays, where the writing is not based on some form of naturalism but on another basis altogether—on language as a communication, on poetry as a form of subtext, and on the whole affecting an audience the way a wonderful painting or piece of music might, as a complete experience, not as a simple slice of life.

To reduce Shakespearean characters to our own level is to remove from them their universal appeal and complexity, and to make the play so specific to our interpretation that it speaks to a small part of our lives, rather than to the grandeur of the human condition.

Oh dear, that was a bit high flown. Back to practical matters, and on to the next section.

Original Elizabethan Language

I am often told that Shakespeare wrote the way he did because that was the way they spoke in those days. He is hard to understand because we no longer speak that way, with the odd use of words, strange language, and the huge vocabulary that they had back then.

This always puzzled me, because I knew that Shakespeare had introduced or invented many new words in the English language, so however hard it might be for us, it must have been much harder for an Elizabethan who had <u>never</u> heard that word or phrase before.

Eventually, after one too many "they spoke in a more complicated way 400 years ago," I decided to look it all up, and found to my surprise that they did <u>not</u>, in fact, have all that complicated language, vocabulary, or structure.

I wanted to find out what they actually said to each other, and I started with law reports, since they have to be what the people were saying in court:

JUNE 1564:

This capon being delivered, they fell in talk. The said Wignoll said to the said John Lewis in this wise: "Fye for shame, Lewis, being an old man wilt not leave thy pilfering? For thirty years past my father took a hand-saw out of thy house." Then said Lewis, "I pray you end this matter and I will never do so more."

No problem there, and easy to get hold of. Where else could I find ordinary language? Diaries or memorandums; what people were thinking that day; written down, but not to be published:

JOHN MANNINGHAM, MARCH 13, 1602:

Upon a tyme when Burbidge played Rich. 3. there was a citizen grewe soe farr in liking with him, that before shee went from the play shee appointed him to come that night unto hir by the name of Ri: the 3. Shakespeare overhearing their conclusion, went before, was intertained, and at his game ere Burbidge came. Then message being brought that Rich. the 3d. was at the dore, Shakespeare caused returne to be made that William the Conquerour was before Rich. the 3. Shakespeares name William.

Again, although the spelling may be a bit unusual, the whole thing is still very <u>accessible</u>. Another two:

DR SIMON FORMAN, APRIL 20, 1610:

In Mackbeth at the glob 1610 the 20 of Aprill, Saturday. ther was to be observed firste howe Mackbeth and Bancko 2 noble men of Scotland Ridinge thorowe a wod the strode befor them 3 women feiries or Nimphes And Saluted Mackbeth sayinge .t. 3 tymes unto him. haille mackbeth. king of Codon for thou shalt be a kinge but shalt beget No kinges &c. then said Bancko what all to mackbeth And nothing to me. yes said the nimphes haille to thee Banko thou shalt beget kinges. yet be no kinge And so they departed & cam to the Courte of Scotland to Dunkin king of Scotes and it was in the dais of Edward the Confessor. And Dunkin bad them both kindly wellcom.

"CRUDITIES" THOMAS CORYAT, 1611 (AN ENGLISHMAN IN VENICE):

I was at one of their Play-houses where I saw a Comedie acted. The house is very beggarly and base in comparison of our stately Play-houses in England: neyther can their Actors compare with us for apparell, shewes and musicke. Here I observed certaine things that I never saw before. For I saw women acte, a thing that I never saw before, though I have heard that it hath beene sometimes used in

London, and they performed it with as good a grace, action, gesture, and what-soever convenient for a Player, as ever I saw any masculine Actor.

Incidentally, the implication of the preceding entry is that women actors on the stage in London were not completely unknown—and it was known that sometimes women dressed up as men in order to go about at night, one even ending up as a famous high-wayman. (I wonder if any girl dressed up as a boy in order to be able to act? I shall leave that territory to *Shakespeare In Love*.)

Going back to the time well before Shakespeare was born, here is a letter to one Lady Lisle:

LORD EDMUND HOWARD TO LADY LISLE, 1535:

To the ryght honerable the Vycountes lysle this be delyverd has post hast hast for thy lyffe.

Madame, so it is this nyght after mydnyght takyn your medysyne, for the whych I heartily thanke you, for it hath done me mych good, and hathe causyd the stone to breake, so that now I voyd mych gravyll. But for all that, your sayd me-dysyne hath done me lytyll honestie, for it made me pys my bed thys nyght, for the whych my Wyffe hathe sore betyn me, and saying it is chyldryns parts to bepys ther bed. Ye have made me such a pysser that I dare not this daye go abrode, wherfore I beseche you to make myne exkouse to my Lord and Master Tresurer, for that I shall not be with you this daye at dynner. Madame, it is showyd me that a wyng or a leg of a storke, if I eat theroff, wyll make me that I shall nevyr pysse more in bed, and though my body be simple yet my tong shalbe evyr good, and specially when it spekyth of women; and sithynce suche a me-dysyn wyll do suche a gret curre god send me a pece theroff.

Of course, we can laugh at this letter, but that is the point; we understand it so well that it is completely open, and there are no great terrors or problems in understanding it.

Another worrying letter, which shows that in Shakespeare's time, plays were not re-garded as anything of note:

SIR THOMAS BODLEY TO THOMAS JAMES, KEEPER OF HIS LIBRARY,
1ST JANUARY 1611

Sir, I would you had forborne to catelogue our London books, until I had been privy to your purpose. There are many idle books, and riff-raffs among them, which shall never come to the library, and I fear me that little, which you have done already, will raise a scandal upon it, when it shall be given out by such as would disgrace it, that I have made up a number with almanacs, plays, and proclamations: of which I will have none, but such as are singular.

Sir Thomas Bodley to Thomas James, Keeper of His Library, 4th January 1611

I can see no good reason to alter my opinion for excluding such books as almanacs, plays, and an infinite number, that are daily printed, of very unworthy matters and handling, such as, methinks, both the keeper and the underkeeper should disdain to seek out, to deliver unto any man. Haply some plays may be worth the keeping: but hardly one in forty.

Sir Thomas Bodley kept his word, so the famous Bodleian Library in Oxford contained no early copies of Shakespeare's plays. They could have gone out and bought copies of *The Tragedie of Romeo and Juliet, Henry the Fift*, or *The Tragedie of Hamlet*, but, no, they were considered "idle books," and "riff-raffs" and were not to grace the shelves of so noble a library.

His meaning in his letters is, of course, blindingly clear, the language being completely accessible.

Here is a letter written by Edward Alleyn himself, the famous Elizabethan actor of the Rose Theatre, again taken from his papers kept at Dulwich College, containing all sorts of gossip, news, and advice—and nothing about "rehearsals":

Edward Alleyn on Tour with the Lord Strange's Men, to His Wife Joan; 1 August 1593

My good sweett mouse I comend me hartely to you And to my father my mother & my sister bess hoping in god thought the siknes beround about you yett by his mercy itt may escape your house which by the grace of god it shall therfor use this corse kepe your house fayr and clean which I knowe you will and every evening throwe water before your dore and in your bakcsid and have in your windowes good store of rwe and herbe of grace and with all the grace of god which must be obtayned by prayers and so doinge no doubt but the Lord will mercyfully defend you:

now good mouse I have no newse to send you but this thatt we have all our helth for which the Lord be praysed I reseved your Letter att bristo by richard couley for the wich I thank you I have sent you by this berer Thomas popes kinsman my whit wascote because it is a trobell to me to cary it reseave it with this Letter And lay it up for me till I com if you send any mor Letters send to me by cariers of shrowsbery of to west chester or to york to be keptt till my Lord stranges players com and thus sweett hartt with my harty comendacions to all our frends I sess from bristo this wensday after saint Jams his day being redy to begin the playe of hary of cornwall mouse do my harty comendacions to mr grigs his wif and all his houshold and to my sister phillyps.

Your Loving housband E Alleyn

mouse you send me no newes of any things you should send of your domestycall matters such things as hapens att home as how your distilled watter proves or this or that or any thing what you will.

(in margin:)

and Jug I pray you lett my orayngtawny stokins of wolen be dyed a very good blak against I com hom to wear in the winter you sente me nott word of my garden but next tym you will but remember this in any case that all that bed which was parsley in the month of september you sowe itt with spinach for then is the tym: I would do it my self but we shall nott com home till allholand tyd and so swett mouse farwell and broke our Long Jorney with patienc.

Maybe, I thought, the literature of the time would show me those complex phrases and the difficult language that I was promised filled up so many Elizabethan speeches. Here is an extract from a novel (one of the first) from that time:

THE UNFORTUNATE TRAVELLER: THOMAS NASHE, 1594:

Therewith he flew upon her, and threatned her with his sword, but it was not that he meant to wound her with. He graspt her by the ivorie throat, and shooke her as a mastiffe would shake a yong beare, swearing and staring he would teare out her weasand if shee refused. Not content with that savage constraint, he slipt his sacriligius hand from her lilly lawne skinned necke, and inscarft it in her long silver lockes, which with strugling were unrould. Backward he dragd her even as a man backwarde would plucke a tree downe by the twigs, and then like a traitor that is drawen to execution on a hurdle, he traileth her up and down the chamber by those tender untwisted braids, and setting his barbarous foote on her bare snowy breast, bad her yeld or have her winde stampt out. She cride, stamp, stifle me in my haire, hang me up by it on a beame, and so let me die, rather than I should goe to heaven with a beame in my eye. No quoth he, not stampt, nor stifled, nor hanged, nor to heaven shalt thou go till I have had my wil of thee thy busie armes in these silken fetters Ile infold. Dismissing her haire from his fingers, and pinnioning her elbowes therwithall, she strugled, she wrested, but all was in vaine. So strugling, and so resisting, her jewels did sweate, signifying there was poison comming towards her. On the hard boords he threw her, and used his knee as an iron ramme to beat ope the two leavd gate of her chastitie. Her husbands dead bodie he made a pillow to his abhomination. Conjecture the rest, my words sticke fast in the myre and are cleane tyred, would I had never undertooke this tragicall tale.

Well, that reads like the sort of book you can buy at your local supermarket, the only problem being the word *weasand* (which is the voice box.)

So the language they used at the time seems much closer to our own than I had imagined, and that means that the language of Shakespeare would have been as extraordinary to them as it is to us. And the complexity and richness he uses are means of communicating with his actors and his audience, not just a reflection of natural Elizabethan speech.

THE EXPERIMENT

Geiger

Now for a brief word about scientific method.

When there are a series of facts that need explaining, any number of solutions can present themselves—these are called hypotheses. Any particular hypothesis has to be tested in every circumstance, under all conditions, and if it still holds up even in extreme conditions, it stops being a hypothesis and is called a theory.

The young Hans Geiger was asked by his professor to carry out an experiment involving firing some alpha rays at a thin sheet of gold. The professor wanted to know if the beams would be deflected by the foil, but he believed that this was the equivalent of firing a fifteen-inch shell at a piece of tissue paper. So the deflections would be very small, and the detectors should therefore be almost in a straight line behind the thin sheet.

He was furious to discover that Geiger had surrounded the experiment with detectors in a large circle, feeling this was a waste of time and money, but Geiger quite simply said that if you are going to do an experiment, you should do it completely, even if you yourself think that nothing could happen. History records that Geiger detected particles being deflected at huge angles, some of them almost straight back from the gold sheet, thus completely destroying the shell and tissue paper belief and allowing Ernest Rutherford to develop his theory about an atom having a tiny nucleus.

If you are going to experiment, then do it completely, even if you yourself think that what you are doing is pointless and could not possibly work. Hans Geiger was probably as surprised as his professor—and I have been surprised how well Cue Script productions work in practice.

Thank you, Hans.

Cue Script Productions

So the evidence in our case is that the actors in those far-off days did not read the play as a whole and did not have time for more than minimal group rehearsals. How on earth then did they put on full-length, fully mounted—and well-received—productions?

I decided to try the experiment of giving out Cue Scripts to actors and having them act from their own lines with no rehearsal. At first I did this with graduate acting students, and found to my utter astonishment that the experiment worked well—that all the scenes I could come up with could be acted, and acted well, just from Cue Scripts.

My partner, Christine Ozanne, a professional actress, then got other professional actors interested, and one of them opened up her house for Sunday meetings. She invited some actors in to try to put these principles into practice and learn how to extract from an individual script all the necessary information that actors need to present a part.

Together with another of these actors, Christine and I founded the **Original Shakespeare Company**, which is devoted to presenting full-length plays in this manner.

This next section is a record of the Original Shakespeare Company's productions—but not an exact or laborious "this is what we did next" sequence. This will be a record of the journey we have made in forming and running the company, and of all the discoveries we have made in doing full-length plays, discoveries directly resulting from putting on a Cue Script production, with the preparation restricted to one-on-one verse sessions and a simple full-company meeting to settle entrances and exits.

We started by just sending the actors their Cue Scripts and telling them on the day where they came from and went to. It soon became apparent that the actors needed to tell each other certain things. For example, *King Lear* wanted someone to hand him the map when he stuck his hand out, so we invented a time when the actors could do this, and named it Burbadge time. We made this tribute to the leading actor in the Lord Chamberlain's Men, Richard Burbadge (often written Burbage), because we were sure that if he wanted something done to facilitate his performance, it would indeed be done. I took advantage of this time to give the actors their entrances and exits.

At first I would laboriously give them each entrance and exit—stage left, stage right, through the audience, and sometimes the actors would suggest changes, like the *Duke's* wanting to enter up center, and the change was always allowed, since this session was essentially traffic control. I found that instead of giving specific entrances, I could give general ones, such as "The *Capulets* always enter stage left; the *Mountagues* stage right; *Prince* stage right; and *Frier Lawrence* stage left." This association of an entrance with a general thought works well, and actors are able to remember it.

This Burbadge lasts between one and one and a half hours. Interestingly, one academic, positive that I was wrong about "no rehearsal," brought me a copy of her paper that "proved" it. She had analyzed the companies working in France during the same historical period, and there was a list of the plays rehearsed, and so "the actors would have the lines and moves of many plays in their heads." Her research showed that the actors "rehearsed" one play at midday, another at 1:00 P.M., and yet another at 2:00 P.M. A "rehearsal" of an hour is only just enough to give entrances and exits, with no time at all to give detailed or even general moves—and matches with the length of my Burbadges. Just to go through a play once will, of course, take as long as the running time, and that is without input, notes, and reworkings.

My actors varied in their experience both of verse work and of actual theatre performances, so I started early on meeting each actor and going over the assigned lines. This led to one of the most powerful weapons that the OSC has in preparing its productions:

the verse nursing session. Each actor comes to me for a one-on-one verse session, and often the Book-Holder is present, needing to know how the actor is doing and which lines are a little bit dodgy. (I am using Book-Holder to describe what modern theatre calls the prompter; in our productions the Book-Holder is much more part of the action.) The actors go over all their lines with only their cues being given to them, and they are <u>never</u> told how to act, and certainly not given any attitudes of emotions, but are simply challenged with "Have you found this clue?" and—crucially—"What are you going to do about it?"

A verse nurse session has become the time when the actor is confronted with the clues given in the rest of this book, and asked to wonder why, at this particular time, his character changes from poetry to prose, or from complex to simple language, and, the glory of it all, why they are changing from *you* to *thee*. It is in these sessions that the actors find their characters take hold, and get the framework their acting will fit into.

This process is one of actor empowerment, and it is increasingly rare these days for them to have such an input. In this modern age of acting, where actors working for the big or small screen can be told not just where and when to move but also the minutest facial expression, the actor can feel just like another piece of scenery. Even in the theatre, productions are becoming more technically complex, with the actors again slotted into preconceived patterns. One of my actors in Canada best summed it up when he said that the actors' imagination was an underused resource. You are, he said, cast in a role, read it, and come up with all sorts of ideas and thoughts—for to be creative is one of the reasons why you became an actor in the first place. On the first day of rehearsal, you take one look at the model of the set, one look at the costume designs, and realize that your input is not really required at all. Many the actor who has worked on and rehearsed a part discovers too late that the assigned costume is based on a different concept from the one the artist has come up with from rehearsals.

The Elizabethans would end their performances with a dance or jig, and for some while this confused me, since such an event might seem inappropriate for a serious play. However, since they did, I felt we should, and we started to end our performances with the full cast singing the Company song, "Pass Time with Good Company," an authentic piece from the period. There still seemed something missing, and so I devised the Company dance as well, based on a pavane, and once we started doing it, I saw why they ended a performance in the old days with such a thing.

In modern theatre, when the play ends, there is a moment of transition, where the actors hover between the part they have just played and their own persona: the curtain call. This is when we can start to adjust from seeing them as their character, and seeing them as themselves, and to get to this moment, either there is a blackout or a curtain swishes down. The play ends, we have the transformation moments—and confirmation of approval (we hope)—and then the event is at an end. In the open air, in daylight, and on the Elizabethan stages, there is neither a blackout nor a curtain, so how do you go from the world of the play back to the everyday world? How can the dead suddenly get up from the stage floor and become the original actor? It became obvious to me that the finale dance is just that transforming moment that a modern curtain call is, allowing the dead to rise up and the actors to be acknowledged.

This dance must be taught to the actors, as must any songs to be sung, or fights to happen, and so these are gone over with the actors in two or three afternoon meetings prior to the performance of a new play by the OSC. We also make it an opportunity for the actors to check their costumes.

Costume is a major area where productions and directors signal to the audience the significance and idea of a character, and I did not want this to color the work my actors were coming up with from the text. I remember when I was at Stratford-upon-Avon, a wonderful actor preparing the part of *Pandulph* in *King John*, and quite mesmeric in the final run-through, got his costume that included a twenty-foot cloak. His whole performance changed into the task of maneuvering this hazard about the stage and through the entrance, and the interest and subtlety of the performance disappeared, never to come back.

I realized that since the actors know what they are playing, they themselves should be in charge of the image they present. I am sure that the original actors did this, and from what we can gather, they would tend to wear contemporary sixteenth- or seventeenth-century costumes, and then augment them. The picture of actors performing in *Titus Andronicus* that has come down to us has them in Elizabethan costumes, with bits of Roman togas thrown on top. When we started, I would ask a costumier to bring in many different costumes, and then let the actors choose what was appropriate for themselves. No style was ever announced, and sometimes there would be a complete eclectic mix on stage with costumes ranging from the medieval to a twentieth-century smoking jacket. It always looked right, actually looked designed, because these costume decisions came from those who were to perform the part, and that was the image they felt illustrated what they were feeling about the part.

When it came to performing at the rebuilt Globe, however, I had seen from previous productions that modern costumes and the Globe stage just did not fit happily with each other, and I felt we needed to reflect that in our presentation. A wonderful costumier, Ellie Cockerill, came on board and devised a simple basic costume for the men and women that was capable of much adjustment and change, and we instigated a policy where we costumed the actor, not the character. Various sizes had been made, and these were allotted to the actors playing the parts, who were then responsible for any embellishments and changes. This has led to a whole series of wonderful costume ideas and themes, all executed by the actors themselves. Specialist costumes, such as for monks or soldiers, would of course be provided by us.

Our own *Pandulphe*, for example, felt that his cardinal's gown was not sufficiently magnificent for his idea of the role, and so he spent many happy hours sewing on extra buttons and making a huge decorated white collar. Our *Mercutio* devised his own brand of extravagance onto his basic costume, and spent his own time making his visual image match the one he was going to act.

One of my actors was in a small role at the Royal National Theatre, and understudying a main part. The day came when the principal actor fell ill, and he was called upon to take over the role. Considering that he was far younger than the other actor, and for the part he was playing, he decided he would wear a pair of spectacles to give his performance a little more age and gravitas. This caused mayhem backstage: he was told he could not change his costume without permission of the designer, who was out of the country. The assistant designer was unavailable, as was the director and assistant director, but he was still forbidden to do what he knew would make that day's performance better. All this fuss and worry was about an actor actually making an artistic decision for himself—and all for a pair of spectacles.

When Sam Wanamaker first saw a production of mine, and invited me to join the Globe project, I was a bit sad that he had only seen my production at a daylight matinee, and missed all the wonderful lighting effects that the evening audiences saw. It then became clear that this was precisely what he was interested in—productions telling stories without the "help" of lighting to focus the audience's attention on different parts of the stage. The original actors at the Globe would have had to guide where the audience looked by the force of their performances, and that is what we decided to do with all the OSC productions.

We always kept the house lights on, and sometimes installed extra lights, to make sure that the actors could see the audience, and that the audience would always know that they could be seen. This has an extraordinarily powerful theatrical result. In our modern times, for most productions the audience sit in the dark, and the actors are up there on stage in the light—the event is very much divided into Us and Them. This is, however, quite a recent development, and for much of the history of theatre, audiences were very much seen by their actors. The effect is that the actors and audience share just one space, and together they explore and enjoy the discoveries and ideas of the play, and all our productions have been presented in this manner. As one of my actors excitedly told me after one of our performances: "It is just Us and Us out there, not Us and Them."

All the time I have been working on these plays, and making these discoveries, I have been inspired and helped by that essential ingredient to any experiment, willing and talented source material: in this case the actors. It is they who have had the courage to step out onto a stage not knowing where their journey would end, and the willingness to make fools of themselves, risking their professional reputations on a project that frankly sounds crazy when first presented: to be in a full-length play, where you do not read it, there is no rehearsal for it, and you do not know what will be said to you until the actual moment of performance in front of an audience. That is why this book is dedicated to them, and that is why each presentation has the cast list of these brave thespians included in the text.

THE PERFORMANCES

The Original Shakespeare Company Productions

When I have made other discoveries from these plays from scene study work, I have included these in the discussion of the individual play that was performed by the OSC.

As each presentation is discussed, it has nearby the first page of the Platt that served as our program for the event. This both gives you an idea of what the actors were working from and lets you know just who these brave souls were, striding out onto the stage without quite knowing what was to happen next. If there were cast changes between performances, then I have included the different Platts for that presentation.

I remember when we were first in Jordan, one of my most experienced actors seemed a little nervous. When I talked to him about it, it turned out that although he had performed for me many times, and had done numerous demonstrations, workshops, and scene studies, this was the first time he had ever done a full-length play this way—and the prospect of embarking on a two- to three-hour journey across a tightrope without any safety harness or railings was very daunting.

I told him I just knew he would do really well—and so he did. And to him and to all the actors inscribed here goes my admiration and unbounded thanks.

As He Liked It, May 1990

The Save the Rose Campaign needed to raise funds for their failed court action, trying to stop Margaret Thatcher's government from allowing the only Elizabethan theatre that had been discovered to be covered up under a high-rise office block. They failed, and the Rose now slumbers under a covering of sand beneath the building; as a sop to the protesters, a hall was built over the sand, and, if and when many millions of pounds have been raised to excavate and preserve the remains, they may be seen again.

This was followed by John Major's conservative government allowing (in one of its last acts before being kicked out of office) the site of the original Globe Theatre to be completely built over. As it was put to the protesters, this would give archaeologists something to do in two hundred years' time, when it may be possible to excavate and really find out how the Globe was built. The humiliation of the government in the election was no consolation for this cultural barbarism.

To raise the funds, Peter Woodward and Julia Goodman decided to have a series of Shakespeare scenes performed by as many stars as they could get, at the Haymarket

Theatre in London's West End, and they had heard about my Shakespeare Cue Script Scenes. My contribution was therefore to make it a Cue Script evening. Actors would collect their scripts (choosing how many lines they wanted to be challenged with) and come over to my house to go over their lines. The extra fillip for the evening was that they were not to know who they were acting with until the actual performance.

The Platt of As He Liked It

A Presentation for the Campaign to Save the Rose, Haymarket Theatre, London at 8:00 pm on Sunday 13th May, 1990

Platt One

Enter two Centinels, Barnardo and Francisco: (TIMOTHY BENTINCK; LISA SADOVY). Enter Horatio and Marcellus: (DEREK SMITH; BARRIE RUTTER). Enter the Ghost: (STEPHEN MOORE). Exit the Ghost. They sit down. Ends.

Set the rock.
Enter Ferdinand: (SAM WEST) bearing a log. Enter Miranda: (ANNE ATKINS) and Prospero hiding behind to overhear: (JAMES FOX). The lovers exit. Exit Prospero. Strike the log and rock.

Enter the old Dutchesse of Yorke, with the son and daughter of Clarence: (SHEILA ALLEN; OLIVER McCUTCHEON; NAOMI KERBEL). Enter Queene Elizabeth, with her haire about her eares: (HELEN ALEXANDER), Rivers and Dorset after her: (OLIVER HADEN; STEPHEN MOORE). Ends.

Enter Demetrius: (CHRIS LINEHAM), Helena following him: (JULIA GOODMAN).

Platt Two

Enter the Princesse of France, with her three attending ladies: (GILLIAN McCUTCHEON; MARGARET COURTENAY; SUSANNAH YORK; MELANIE SCHINAZI); with them Boyet and Lord: (SIMON CLARK; PAT McDONALD). Ends.

Manet Isabella: (MEG DAVIES) and her brother Claudio: (NICHOLAS CLAY). Ends.

Enter Viola: (SALLY COOKSON), a Captaine and Saylors: (BRADLEY LAVELLE). Viola gives the Captaine a bag of gold. Exeunt.

Set the chair.
Enter Juliet: (SERENA GORDON). Enter the Nurse, footsore: (JACK SHEPHERD). Exeunt. Strike the chair.

Interval.

Platt Three

Enter Joane de Puzel: (ANNE ATKINS), driving Englishmen before her. Exeunt. Then enter Talbot: (PETER WOODWARD). Enter Puzel. They fight. They fight againe. A short Alarum: then enter the Towne with Soldiers. Exit Puzel. A short Alarum. Alarum. Here another skirmish. Exit Talbot. Alarum, Retreat, Flourish.

Set the chair.
Enter Hermione, Mamillius and Ladies: (CIARAN MADDEN; OLIVER MANN; KAREN COOPER; SOPHIE REISSNER). Ends.

Enter Antipholis and Dromio of Syracuse, and a Marchant: (RALPH FIENNES; PAT McDONALD; BERNARD BRESSLAW) The Marchant gives a bag of money to Antipholis. Exit Dromio of Syracuse with the money. To Antipholis, Dromio of Ephesus: (DAVID DELVE). Exit Dromio of Ephesus. Exit Antipholis.

Set the Tower.
Enter Lady Macbeth: (VIVIEN HEILBRON). Enter Macbeth above, with bloody daggers: (ART MALIK). He descends to her. Exit Lady Macbeth with the daggers. Knocke within. Enter Lady Macbeth with bloody hands. Knocke. Knocke. Exeunt. Strike the Tower.

Platt Four

Alarum and Excursions. Enter Jone De Pucel: (JILL BENEDICT). Thunder. Enter the Fiends. Exit the Fiends. Exit Jone.

Manet Lucentio and his servant Tranio: (GREG HICKS; CAMPBELL GRAHAM). They exchange clothes. To them, Biondello: (ALAN COX). Exeunt.

Enter Antipholus of Syracuse: (GARY WILMOT), wearing a gold chain. To him, Dromio of Syracuse with the bag of gold: (GRAHAM POUNTNEY). To them, a Curtizan: (PRUNELLA SCALES). Exeunt Antipholus and Dromio. Exit Curtizan.

Set the tomb. Set on the tomb the body of Juliet, with dagger. Set on the tomb the body of Romeo. Set the body of Paris.
Enter Page and three members of the Watch: (TERRY DOUGHERTY; MELANIE HILL; NICHOLAS COURTNEY). Exit some of the Watch. Enter Second Watch with Balthazar. Enter Frier, and Third Watch: (JONATHAN MORRIS). Enter the Prince: (DERMOT CROWLEY). Enter Capulet: (RONALD FORFAR), with his Wife: (JEAN BOHT). Enter Montague: (RODNEY BEWES). Ends.

Finis.

Producers:	PETER WOODWARD AND JULIA GOODMAN
Introduction:	DAME PEGGY ASHCROFT
Book-Holder:	CHRISTINE OZANNE
Presenter:	PATRICK TUCKER

I do not think I have ever come across such a nervous group of actors, but the evening was a stunning success—and the final proof to me that this way of working was not only feasible, but a valid modern production technique.

The scenes were astonishing. As one of the actors said to me, "We are doing things out there on stage that normally take four or five weeks to achieve in rehearsal." There were mistakes—and for this we had the Book-Holder on stage, Christine taking up the first of many appearances in this spot. But the audience was more than willing to forgive the rough edges in order to get the spontaneous and exciting acting.

The scene between *Isabella* and *Claudio*, for example, was prepared from the following Cue Scripts:

CUE SCRIPT FOR ISABELLA

                          _____ what's the comfort?

Why,
As all comforts are: most good, most good indeede,
Lord *Angelo* having affaires to heaven
Intends you for his swift Ambassador,
Where you shall be an everlasting Leiger;
Therefore your best appointment make with speed,
To Morrow you set on.

                          _____ no remedie?

None, but such remedie, as to save a head
To cleave a heart in twaine:

                          _____ is there anie?

Yes brother, you may live;
There is a divellish mercie in the Judge,
If you'l implore it, that will free your life,
But fetter you till death.

                          _____ Perpetuall durance?

I just, perpetuall durance, a restraint
Through all the worlds vastiditie you had
To a determin'd scope.

                          _____ in what nature?

In such a one, as you consenting too't,
Would barke your honor from that trunke you beare,
And leave you naked.

                          _____ me know the point.

Oh, I do feare thee *Claudio*, and I quake,
Least thou a feavorous life shouldst entertaine,
And six or seven winters more respect
Then a perpetuall Honor. Dar'st thou die?

The sence of death is most in apprehension,
And the poore Beetle that we treade upon
In corporall sufferance, finds a pang as great,
As when a Giant dies.

_____ it in mine armes.

There spake my brother: there my fathers grave
Did utter forth a voice. Yes, thou must die:
Thou art too noble, to conserve a life
In base appliances. This outward sainted Deputie,
Whose setled visage, and deliberate word
Nips youth i'th head, and follies doth emmew
As Falcon doth the Fowle, is yet a divell:
His filth within being cast, he would appeare
A pond, as deepe as hell.

_____ prenzie, *Angelo*?

Oh 'tis the cunning Liverie of hell,
The damnest bodie to invest, and cover
In prenzie gardes; dost thou thinke *Claudio*,
If I would yeeld him my virginitie
Thou might'st be freed?

_____ it cannot be.

Yes, he would giv't thee; from this rank offence
So to offend him still. This night's the time
That I should do what I abhorre to name,
Or else thou diest to morrow.

_____ Thou shalt not do't.

O, were it but my life,
I'de throw it downe for your deliverance
As frankely as a pin.

_____ deere *Isabell*.

Be readie *Claudio*, for your death to morrow.

_____ it is the least.

Which is the least?

_____ Oh *Isabell*.

What saies my brother?

_____ a fearefull thing.

And shamed life, a hatefull.

_____ we feare of death.

Alas, alas.

_____ becomes a vertue.

Oh you beast,
Oh faithlesse Coward, oh dishonest wretch,

Wilt thou be made a man, out of my vice?
Is't not a kinde of Incest, to take life
From thine owne sisters shame? What should I thinke,
Heaven shield my Mother plaid my Father faire:
For such a warped slip of wildernesse
Nere issu'd from his blood. Take my defiance,
Die, perish: Might but my bending downe
Repreeve thee from thy fate, it should proceede.
Ile pray a thousand praiers for thy death,
No word to save thee.
_____ me *Isabell*.
Oh fie, fie, fie:
Thy sinn's not accidentall, but a Trade;
Mercy to thee would prove it selfe a Bawd,
'Tis best that thou diest quickly.
_____ me *Isabella*.
Ends.

As you can see, she starts off with very florid, complex language, then gets simpler and shorter for a while, ending with long but straightforward speeches.

CUE SCRIPT FOR CLAUDIO

Now sister, what's the comfort?
_____ Morrow you set on.
Is there no remedie?
_____ a heart in twaine.
But is there anie?
_____ fetter you till death.
Perpetuall durance?
_____ determin'd scope.
But in what nature?
_____ leave you naked.
Let me know the point.
_____ a Giant dies.
Why give you me this shame?
Thinke you I can a resolution fetch
From flowrie tendernesse? If I must die,
I will encounter darknesse as a bride,
And hugge it in mine armes.
_____ as deepe as hell.
The prenzie, *Angelo*?

_____ Thou might'st be freed?

Oh heavens, it cannot be.

_____ thou diest to morrow.

Thou shalt not do't.

_____ frankely as a pin.

Thankes deere *Isabell*.

_____ your death to morrow.

Yes. Has he affections in him,

That thus can make him bite the Law by th'nose,

When he would force it? Sure it is no sinne,

Or of the deadly seven it is the least.

_____ Which is the least?

If it were damnable, he being so wise,

Why would he for the momentarie tricke

Be perdurablie fin'de? Oh *Isabell*.

_____ saies my brother?

Death is a fearefull thing.

_____ life, a hatefull.

I, but to die, and go we know not where,

To lie in cold obstruction, and to rot,

This sensible warme motion, to become

A kneaded clod; And the delighted spirit

To bath in fierie floods, or to recide

In thrilling Region of thicke-ribbed Ice,

To be imprison'd in the viewlesse windes

And blowne with restlesse violence round about

The pendant world: or to be worse then worst

Of those, that lawlesse and incertaine thought,

Imagine howling, 'tis too horrible.

The weariest, and most loathed worldly life

That Age, Ache, perjury, and imprisonment

Can lay on nature, is a Paradise

To what we feare of death.

_____ Alas, alas.

Sweet Sister, let me live.

What sinne you do, to save a brothers life,

Nature dispenses with the deede so farre,

That it becomes a vertue.

_____ word to save thee.

Nay heare me *Isabell*.

_____ thou diest quickly.

Oh heare me *Isabella*.

Ends.

Isabella starts off with quite complex language but then gets much simpler. The reverse is true of *Claudio*. He starts off with simple, "to the point" questions and then gets much more complex toward the end. These notable differences, which only really become clear when the intervening lines of other characters are taken out, give the actors a different instruction as to how they might approach the scene. In the performance at the Haymarket this was triumphantly acted by Meg Davies and Nicholas Clay.

The scene from *The Tempest* with *Ferdinand* talking to *Miranda* was a revelation, for it is full of sexual innuendos and double entendres (remembering that "will" also means sexual desire, as well as the naughty parts themselves: *for my good will is to it, And yours it is against.*):

MIRANDA:
　　Alas, now pray you
　　Worke not so hard: I would the lightning had
　　Burnt up those Logs that you are enjoynd to pile:
　　Pray set it downe, and rest you: when this burnes
　　'Twill weepe for having wearied you: my Father
　　Is hard at study; pray now rest your selfe,
　　Hee's safe for these three houres.
FERDINAND:
　　O most deere Mistris,
　　The Sun will set before I shall discharge
　　What I must strive to do.
MIRANDA:
　　If you'l sit downe
　　Ile beare your Logges the while: pray give me that,
　　Ile carry it to the pile.
FERDINAND:
　　No precious Creature,
　　I had rather cracke my sinewes, breake my backe,
　　Then you should such dishonor undergoe,
　　While I sit lazy by.
MIRANDA:
　　It would become me
　　As well as it do's you; and I should do it
　　With much more ease: for my good will is to it,
　　And yours it is against.
PROSPERO:
　　Poore worme thou art infected,
　　This visitation shewes it.
MIRANDA:
　　You looke wearily.

FERDINAND:

    No, noble Mistris, 'tis fresh morning with me
    When you are by at night: I do beseech you
    Cheefely, that I might set it in my prayers,
    What is your name?

MIRANDA:

    Miranda, O my Father,
    I have broke your hest to say so.

FERDINAND:

    Admir'd *Miranda*,
    Indeede the top of Admiration, worth
    What's deerest to the world: full many a Lady
    I have ey'd with best regard, and many a time
    Th'harmony of their tongues, hath into bondage
    Brought my too diligent eare: for severall vertues
    Have I lik'd severall women, never any
    With so full soule, but some defect in her
    Did quarrell with the noblest grace she ow'd,
    And put it to the foile. But you, O you,
    So perfect, and so peerlesse, are created
    Of everie Creatures best.

MIRANDA:

    I do not know
    One of my sexe; no womans face remember,
    Save from my glasse, mine owne: Nor have I seene
    More that I may call men, then you good friend,
    And my deere Father: how features are abroad
    I am skillesse of; but by my modestie
    (The jewell in my dower) I would not wish
    Any Companion in the world but you:
    Nor can imagination forme a shape
    Besides your selfe, to like of: but I prattle
    Something too wildely, and my Fathers precepts
    I therein do forget.

FERDINAND:

    I am, in my condition
    A Prince (*Miranda*) I do thinke a King
    (I would not so) and would no more endure
    This wodden slaverie, then to suffer
    The flesh-flie blow my mouth: heare my soule speake.
    The verie instant that I saw you, did
    My heart flie to your service, there resides

To make me slave to it, and for your sake
Am I this patient Logge-man.

MIRANDA:

Do you love me?

FERDINAND:

O heaven; O earth, beare witnes to this sound,
And crowne what I professe with kinde event
If I speake true: if hollowly, invert
What best is boaded me, to mischiefe: I,
Beyond all limit of what else i'th world
Do love, prize, honor you.

MIRANDA:

I am a foole
To weepe at what I am glad of.

PROSPERO:

Faire encounter
Of two most rare affections: heavens raine grace
On that which breeds betweene 'em.

FERDINAND:

Wherefore weepe you?

MIRANDA:

At mine unworthinesse, that dare not offer
What I desire to give; and much lesse take
What I shall die to want: But this is trifling,
And all the more it seekes to hide it selfe,
The bigger bulke it shewes. Hence bashfull cunning,
And prompt me plaine and holy innocence.
I am your wife, if you will marrie me;
If not, Ile die your maid: to be your fellow
You may denie me, but Ile be your servant
Whether you will or no.

The bigger bulke it shewes indeed for this patient *Logge-man*, and the actors' assumption that this was a simple virginal scene from their knowledge of what they thought it was about had to be adjusted by what they actually said. And the delightful result is that although these two young people on stage were talking in sexual imagery, it only made them seem the more innocent and naive about the real world: they did not have to <u>play</u> innocent and naive.

Juliet came out for her *Gallop apace* scene, and only discovered, when he entered, that the *Nurse* was being played by a man. Her "Oh no" could be heard all around the auditorium, but the scene itself was magical, both funny and moving.

Macbeth had quite a time chasing *Lady Macbeth* round the stage, as he was only too anxious to get rid of the daggers in his hands. She, of course, was resisting taking them because she knew too well that there was a moment in <u>her</u> script that told her when to get them: *Give me the Daggers*, and certainly did not want them in advance of the line. We were all learning valuable lessons: that Shakespeare had solved the acting problems in the text, and it was up to us to trust him.

The fight scene was done with the minimum of preparation or rehearsal—twenty minutes—and it played well, and was very spontaneous and exciting (not surprising, really—wielding swords about without hours and hours of careful practice). This spontaneity showed itself best of all in the *Macbeth* scene, where the dramatic tension was part "what is it about?" and part "will he remember the lines?"—at all times <u>adding</u> to the theatricality of what was going on.

The scene between *Jone de Pucell* and the *Fiends* was enlivened by getting members of the audience to be the *Fiends*, each being given a Cue Script of what they were to do.

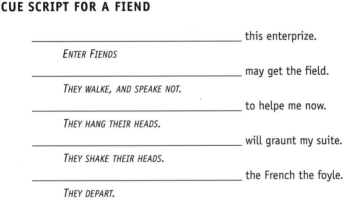

CUE SCRIPT FOR A FIEND

_____ this enterprize.

ENTER FIENDS

_____ may get the field.

THEY WALKE, AND SPEAKE NOT.

_____ to helpe me now.

THEY HANG THEIR HEADS.

_____ will graunt my suite.

THEY SHAKE THEIR HEADS.

_____ the French the foyle.

THEY DEPART.

Even here, with no preparation, the *Fiends* were strangely effective as they wandered about the stage slowly shaking their heads as *Jone* tried to get them to help her. It was a far more moving and poignant scene than a recent one I saw where the *Fiends* were represented just by flashing lights. Real *Fiends* were scripted, and the real bodies circling but not helping her were a plain indication of how *Jone* had lost her potency.

We ended the evening with the tomb scene from *Romeo and Juliet*, which I devoted a whole section to earlier, and a curtain call I had arranged from Cue Scripts, with all the actors coming on as Julia gave a speech. They didn't know when their cue to come on was going to be until they heard the three-word cue. It was a lot of fun, worked very efficiently, and proved the point yet again that if the different parts are prepared in the knowledge of how they are to be performed, then complex theatrical events can be done with no preparation. It reminded me of a wonderful evening of Korean drumming I attended in Seoul, where over two hundred drummers played together, rhythms and tempi rising and falling. Talking afterward to the master drummer, who controlled it all from his huge drum, I asked him how long they had rehearsed. They do not rehearse at all, I was amazed to hear, and when I asked him how this was possible given the complexities of the performance, he said, "I tell them all before the performance, listen to the spirit of the Drum!"

We Cue Scripters all went home from the Haymarket on a high, knowing that we had tapped into something special.

A Midsommer Nights Dreame (scenes), September 1991

We decided to try out the first four scenes of *A Midsommer Nights Dreame* using our Cue Script techniques with our own trained actors. We had expanded our actor base and were keen for the people at the Globe to see our work, as we felt that trying to replicate original conditions of rehearsal and presentation should be the very thing that the reconstructed Globe would be concerned with, and interested in.

The Platt of the first four Scenes of
A Midsommer Nights Dreame
An OSC Presentation at the Bear Gardens, London
on Sunday 29th September, 1991

I-1: Enter Theseus, Duke of Athens: (JOHN CORDING), with his bride-to-be Hippolita Queene of the Amazons: (JILL BENEDICT). To them, Egeus: (JEROME WILLIS), and his daughter Hermia: (FELICITY DUNCAN), and Lysander, and Demetrius: (LEWIS HANCOCK; GRAHAM POUNTNEY). Lysander and Demetrius stand forth. Exeunt all but Lysander and Hermia. To them Helena: (JULIETTE GRASSBY). Exit Hermia. Exit Lysander. Exit Helena.

I-2: Enter Quince the Carpenter, Snug the Joyner, Bottome the Weaver, Flute the bellowes-mender, Snout the Tinker, and Starveling the Taylor: (HUGH WALTERS; GILLIAN MCCUTCHEON; NICHOLAS DAY; OLIVER MCCUTCHEON; SALLY MATES; ELLEN SHEEAN). Quince gives out the scrolls. Exeunt.

II-1: Enter a Fairie at one doore: (CAMILLA VELLA), and Robin Goodfellow, known as Pucke, at another: (VIVIEN HEILBRON). Enter the King of Fairies, Oberon: (MARTIN BELVILLE) at one door with his traine: (CAROLINE SPIERS; RUTH HURST; SIOBHAN STAMPE), and the Queen of Fairies, Tytania: (MEG DAVIES) at another with her traine: (LISA BURGETT; HELEN HIGHAM; ELLA KENYON; CANDIDA HALTON). Exeunt the Queen with her traine. Exit Pucke. Enter Demetrius, Helena following him, the King being invisible. Exit Demetrius, Helena following. To the King, Pucke with the flower. Exeunt.

Repeated Scene:
II-1: Manet Oberon: (BEN COLE). Enter Demetrius: (BRADLEY LAVELLE), Helena following him: (JUDY HOPTON), the King being invisible. Exit Demetrius, Helena following. To the King, Pucke with the flower: (HELEN HIGHAM). Exeunt.

Ends.

Book-Holder: CHRISTINE OZANNE
Presenter: PATRICK TUCKER

I had decided that as a demonstration, the actors could choose whether to be in costumes or not, so I provided a heap of costumes for them to pick and choose from. My *Tytania* had decided that she would in fact not wear a costume, but then, as she spied her *Oberon* picking out a rather splendid garment, she quietly went about creating her own imaginative vision.

I was learning a valuable lesson: actors need to costume themselves in the knowledge of what the others are wearing, and when they do, a strange consistency comes over the group, with a result that looks as if a costume designer had decided the whole lot.

Going onstage with costumes they themselves approve of, and often have worked on, my actors are able to marry the ideas in their heads with the visual image that will come over to the audience; not a revolutionary idea, but contrary to popular modern thinking, wherein the actor is so often regarded as more a marionette than a creative partner.

The little scenes played well, and in particular our *Tytania*, an experienced sexy actress, found herself with a rather young *Oberon* and performed her first speech to him as she idly ground her rear into his groin:

TYTANIA:
>These are the forgeries of jealousie,
>And never since the middle Summers spring
>Met we on hil, in dale, forrest, or mead,
>By paved fountaine, or by rushie brooke,
>Or in the beached margent of the sea,
>To dance our ringlets to the whistling Winde,
>But with thy braules thou hast disturb'd our sport.
>Therefore the Windes, piping to us in vaine,
>As in revenge, have suck'd up from the sea
>Contagious fogges: Which falling in the Land,
>Hath everie petty River made so proud,
>That they have over-borne their Continents.
>The Oxe hath therefore stretch'd his yoake in vaine,
>The Ploughman lost his sweat, and the greene Corne
>Hath rotted, ere his youth attain'd a beard:
>The fold stands empty in the drowned field,
>And Crowes are fatted with the murrion flocke,
>The nine mens Morris is fild up with mud,
>And the queint Mazes in the wanton greene,
>For lacke of tread are undistinguishable.
>The humane mortals want their winter heere,
>No night is now with hymne or caroll blest;
>Therefore the Moone (the governesse of floods)
>Pale in her anger, washes all the aire;

That Rheumaticke diseases doe abound.
And through this distemperature, we see
The seasons alter; hoared headed frosts
Fall in the fresh lap of the crimson Rose,
And on old *Hyems* chinne and Icie crowne,
An odorous Chaplet of sweet Sommer buds
Is as in mockry set. The Spring, the Sommer,
The childing Autumne, angry Winter change
Their wonted Liveries, and the mazed world,
By their increase, now knowes not which is which;
And this same progeny of evills,
Comes from our debate, from our dissention,
We are their parents and originall.

The impact on the actor/*Oberon*, and the knowledge that he had no idea just how long this exquisite torture was to continue, as each bawdy element was punctuated, gave an immediacy and passion (and humor) to the scene that I had not seen before, and the whole presentation was full of fun, mad moments, and agonizing truth.

Bottome had privately arranged that in the bag of scrolls there should be a particularly long one, and so when *Peter Quince* gave them out, he grabbed it, allowed it to open out completely, and furiously began to count his lines. The audience laughed, and his fellow actors laughed, and I had another insight. Normally, in a rehearsed moment, although the fellow actors would have found this funny, they would have prepared "their" character's responses, and so in performance they would have scowled, been angry, and so on, at *Bottome's* arrogance. Here, their natural response seemed completely appropriate, and added to the audience's enjoyment, since they could tell this was a completely truthful moment.

I started double casting, and had the same scene done by a different group of actors, since I was fascinated to know how differently the scenes would come over, and if they would somehow alter the author's intent. Each of the scenes played well, each was very different, and yet the suspicion was there that the final effect was the same. I knew that this must be followed up later, as a way of exploring the consequences of taking acting notes from text and not context, and because it gave more opportunities to the many actors that wanted the experience of being responsible for their performances.

The audience, which had many friends and supporters but alas few from the Globe, responded very well, and we knew we must continue this brave experiment.

The Comedie of Errors (abridged), December 1991

This was to be our first public presentation of what we did, and it was to be a mixture of the bulk of the play, followed by an explanatory workshop to be presented at a London theatre, the Mermaid. The whole thing was to be filmed by Forge Productions, who shared this belief of ours that somewhere, somehow, a program could and should be made out of this work.

The first problem that arose was in casting, as we did not really have actors identi-

---

The Platt of The Comedie of Errors (1000 Lines)

An OSC Presentation at the Mermaid Theatre, London
at 7:30 pm on Thursday 12th December, 1991

Actus Primus.   Enter the Duke of Ephesus, with Egeon, the Merchant of Siracusa, Jaylor, and other attendants. Exeunt, Egeon being taken to prison.

Actus Primus, Scena Secunda.
Enter Antipholus of Siracuse: (NICHOLAS DAY), his servant Dromio of Siracuse:(RICHARD CORDERY), and the First Marchant: (NICHOLAS HUTCHISON), who gives S.Antipholus a bag of money. Exit S.Dromio with the bag of money. Exit the Marchant. Enter Dromio of Ephesus: (HUGH WALTERS), inviting S.Antipholus home to dinner. He gets beaten. Exit E.Dromio. Exit S.Antipholus.

Actus Secundus.
Enter the wife to Antipholus of Ephesus, Adriana: (MEG DAVIES), with her sister Luciana : (ELIZABETH COUNSELL). Enter Dromio of Ephesus. Exit E.Dromio. Exeunt.

Enter S.Antipholus. Enter Dromio of Siracusia. S.Antipholus beats S.Dromio. To them, Adriana and Luciana. Exeunt, S.Antipholus being taken home by Adriana for dinner.

Actus Tertius.
[SET THE GATE] Enter Antipholus of Ephesus: (GRAHAM POUNTNEY), his man Dromio, Angelo the Goldsmith: (ROBIN BOWERMAN), and Balthaser the Merchant: (GREG HICKS). They arrive at E.Antipholus gate - which is locked. Enter S.Dromio within, who bars entrance to E.Antipholus, since an Antipholus is already inside. To S.Dromio, Luce: (GILLIAN MCCUTCHEON), who also refused entrance to E.Antipholus. To S.Dromio Adriana, complaining of the noise. She also refuses entrance to E.Antipholus. Exit Adriana with Luce. Exit S.Dromio. Exeunt. [RE-SET THE GATE].

Enter Luciana, with Antipholus of Siracusia. He wooes her. Exit Luciana. Enter Dromio of Siracusia. Exit S.Dromio, to find passage on a ship for them to escape. Enter Angelo the Goldsmith with the Chaine, which he gives to Antipholus, expecting payment later. Exit Angelo. Exit S.Antipholus.

Actus Quartus.
Enter the Second Merchant: (LEWIS HANCOCK), Angelo the Goldsmith, and an Officer: (TERENCE DOUGHERTY). Enter Antipholus and Dromio of Ephesus, coming from the Courtezan's house. Exit E.Dromio to get a rope. The Goldsmith asks for the money for the Chaine. Enter Dromio of Siracuse from the Bay, with news of a ship. E.Atipholus is taken in custody to prison by the Officer, Goldsmith and Second Merchant. Exit S.Dromio.

Enter Adriana and Luciana. To them, S.Dromio to get money to bail out Antipholus. Exit Luciana to get the purse. Enter Luciana with the purse. Exeunt, S.Dromio exits taking the purse.

Enter Antipholus of Siracusia. To him, S.Dromio with the money. To them, the Courtezan: (FENELLA FIELDING). Exeunt S.Antipholus and S.Dromio, fearing that the Courtezan is a Witch. Exit the Courtezan.

Enter Antipholus of Ephesus in the custody of the Jailor. Enter Dromio of Ephesus with the rope. E.Dromio is beaten for not bringing the money. Enter Adriana, Luciana, the Courtezan, and a Schoole-master called Pinch. E.Antipholus beats E.Dromio again, then strikes Pinch. Enter three or foure, and offer to bind E.Antipholus - he strives. Pinch and the others bind and take off E.Antipholus and E.Dromio. Manet Officer, Adriana, Luciana and the Courtezan. Enter Antipholus of Siracuse with his Rapier drawn, and Dromio of Siracuse. They all runne about. Exeunt omnes, as fast as may be, frightened. Manet Antipholus and Dromio of Siracuse. Exeunt.

Actus Quintus. Enter the Second Merchant and the Goldsmith. Enter Antipholus and Dromio of Siracuse againe. The Merchant and S.Antipholus draw on each other. Enter Adriana, Luciana, the Courtezan, and others. Exeunt S.Antipholus and S.Dromio to the Priorie for sanctuary. Enter the Lady Abbesse. Exit the Abbesse, refusing to give up S.Antipholus and S.Dromio. Enter the Duke of Ephesus, and Egeon the Merchant of Siracuse, with the headsman, and other officers. To Adriana a Messenger, with news that E.Antipholus has broken loose. Cry within. Enter Antipholus and Dromio of Ephesus, craving justice from the Duke. Exit one to the Abbesse, to resolve the confusions. Egeon is not recognised by "his" son Antipholus. Enter the Abbesse with Antipholus and Dromio of Siracuse. All gather to see them. Exeunt omnes. Manet the two Dromio's and the two brothers Antipholus. Exit S.Antipholus with E.Antipholus. Exeunt S.Dromio and E.Dromio.

FINIS.

With grateful thanks to Gillian Wilson, BATCO, Emma Coats, Stephen Parker, Maggie Scobie, and Suki Turner.

Filming	Forge Productions
Music	Terrence Dougherty
Presenter	Patrick Tucker
Book-Holder	Christine Ozanne

cal enough to play the two sets of twins. I suddenly realized that this was modern think-ing, and that, instead, I should go back to that imagined company that first put on the play. Would the original players have had two clowns who looked alike? The answer is obvious, they would have had two entirely different looking clowns, so that is what I should do. I therefore cast the two identical *Dromios* with one actor who was large and 6'5" (1.95m), and the other a lightweight 5'7" (1.70m).

It then made perfect sense. After all, in every production where a girl is dressed up as a boy, we, the audience, always know she is a girl. We are not fooled, but the charac-ters on stage act as if they are. In *The Comedie of Errors*, as long as the characters on stage believed that the twins were identical, then all would be well.

In performance this gave some superb theatrical bonuses. Instead of the audience wondering "which one is this?" at the start of the scene, they always knew, and so could enjoy the confusion on the stage even more, as they themselves were not confused. No one mentioned that the twins did not in fact look alike, but the sigh of pleasure from the audience as the "wrong" one came onstage and they looked forward to the resulting mayhem taught me, as audiences always do, that the joy is in the eye of the beholder, not in some spurious "reality" that fools no one and sometimes just confuses. The audi-ence, being in on the joke at all times, relaxed and enjoyed themselves.

After the performance, an actor in the audience came backstage and said that it was a wonderful choice to cast different-looking actors as the twins. He had once played an *Antipholus*, and the director had reprimanded him for wearing a small earring when the other actor was not; his instruction had been to be as alike as possible. Now the actor saw that the confusion was in the language, not in looking alike.

The show went very well, and in particular the rather difficult *Dromio* comedy routine describing the kitchen wench in geographical terms played to as many laughs as I have ever heard:

ANTIPHOLUS:
  In what part of her body stands *Ireland*?
DROMIO:
  Marry sir in her buttockes, I found it out by
  the bogges.
ANTIPHOLUS:
  Where *Scotland*?
DROMIO:
  I found it by the barrennesse, hard in the palme
  of the hand.
ANTIPHOLUS:
  Where *France*?
DROMIO:
  In her forhead, arm'd and reverted, making
  warre against her heire.

ANTIPHOLUS:
  Where *England*?
DROMIO:
  I look'd for the chalkle Cliffes, but I could find
  no whitenesse in them. But I guesse, it stood in her chin
  by the salt rheume that ranne betweene *France*, and it.
ANTIPHOLUS:
  Where *Spaine*?
DROMIO:
  Faith I saw it not: but I felt it hot in her breth.
ANTIPHOLUS:
  Where *America,* the *Indies*?
DROMIO:
  Oh sir, upon her nose, all ore embellished with
  Rubies, Carbuncles, Saphires, declining their rich As-
  pect to the hot breath of Spaine, who sent whole Ar-
  madoes of Carrects to be ballast at her nose.
ANTIPHOLUS:
  Where stood *Belgia,* the *Netherlands*?
DROMIO:
  Oh sir, I did not looke so low.

Richard Cordery, playing *Dromio,* invested every line with an illustration as he lugubriously told the sad tale, and Nick Day, playing *Antipholus,* suddenly realized his role was to be the feed guy, and played it like a comedy routine between Abbott and Costello. It was also spontaneous and funny because Nick had no idea what replies were going to be given to his feed lines, and so his amused then hilarious response was completely real, and very theatrically effective. For me as a director it was salutary that unrehearsed-by-me actors should get such a tremendous response from the audience.

Two of my actors came to me rather shamefacedly afterward and confessed that just before the show they had run their scene through, because they were so worried about forgetting their lines. But they wished they had not. They had enjoyed the discovery of the scene backstage, and then had the choice onstage of either repeating what they had just discovered or trying to rediscover it. Neither solution worked well, and it explained to me why that scene had not gone as well as I had hoped. The actors' wish that they had <u>not</u> gone through the scene first was confirmation that putting plays on this way demanded a different approach from us all.

Following our experience at the Haymarket, we put into practice our belief that the prompter (or Book-Holder, the original designation sometimes used) should be onstage as part of the presentation. Partly this was to remind the audience that they were seeing a production based on a different premise, but it was also done out of sheer practicality.

A short time before I had directed a student *Twelfe Night*, and had only given the students Cue Scripts to work from. This had the hugely beneficial result of them concentrating on their own lines and not worrying about others—or even imagining how they themselves would play the role. I had rehearsed the play normally, and all went very well, until the second performance. At a crucial moment, *Fabian* leapt from the tree with unusual vigor, landing on top of the cassette player that was standing by to play essential music. Realizing his error, he disappeared into the wings to find a replacement, and so was "off" when his next line was to be spoken.

The play quickly ground to a halt. Normally, when something goes wrong, the actors onstage can "look" in their heads at the script they had all studied, "see" what is missing or left out, and cope with ad-libs and "made-up" lines until they all get back on track. I suddenly realized that working from Cue Scripts meant that the pattern they all had in their heads was useless: they had no idea if their next line was to be said now or in a few pages' time. Doing Cue Script work, therefore, absolutely demanded the use of a prompter, so that if things went wrong, there was someone to bring them back together.

At the Mermaid the Book-Holder was Christine, and she found that her job was not just to keep the actors on track, but sometimes to be a confirming face that said, "Yes, it is your time to speak," or to correct a cue line, for if the wrong cue is given, the next actor cannot speak his lines, as he is waiting for a precise three- or four-word cue.

We put the prompt desk downstage left, where Christine could see and be seen by the actors, and that is where our Book-Holder has stayed. Everything points to this being the original method of putting on plays. After all, in the nineteenth century, theatres were built with specific prompt boxes down stage center, and they are still in use in the operatic world. Seeing a prompt being given oddly makes it more acceptable, as the audience knows exactly what is going on, just as at a concert when the audience sees the conductor bringing in the trumpets on cue and accepts this as natural.

Modern practice has suggested that actors should always get themselves out of trouble, but acting in iambic pentameter puts a strange discipline on all this. (Enter an actor, late for his cue; "Where hast thou been?" improvised the onstage actor, thus precipitating a real crisis as the "late" actor attempted to deliver a reply in verse.)

For the second part of the evening, I took some of the scenes and reworked them, showing the audience that, for example, getting *Adriana* to <u>really</u> want to repeat her *that never*'s gave a wonderful lift and build to the speech:

ADRIANA:
I, I, *Antipholus*, looke strange and frowne,
Some other Mistresse hath thy sweet aspects:
I am not *Adriana*, nor thy wife.
The time was once, when thou un-urg'd wouldst vow,
That never words were musicke to thine eare,
That never object pleasing in thine eye,

That never touch well welcome to thy hand,
That never meat sweet-savour'd in thy taste,
Unlesse I spake, or look'd, or touch'd, or carv'd to thee.

She made each *That never* louder than the one before, giving the speech an amazing build and passion. The same use of building on a verbal conceit came from Nick as *Antipholus*:

S.ANTIPHOLUS:
There's not a man I meete but doth salute me
As if I were their well acquainted friend,
And everie one doth call me by my name:
Some tender monie to me, some invite me;
Some other give me thankes for kindnesses;
Some offer me Commodities to buy.
Even now a tailor cal'd me in his shop,
And show'd me Silkes that he had bought for me,
And therewithall tooke measure of my body.
Sure these are but imaginarie wiles,
And lapland Sorcerers inhabite here.

The repetition of the word me, and building on it, gave Nick one of the best audience reactions of the evening.

The results of the night's work were a determination to present full-length plays this way and a promotional tape that went the rounds but has never yet found a home.

The Merchant of Venice (scenes), April 1993

The base of the rebuilt Globe was starting to rise, and I very much wanted to see how our work would match the building. I was also interested in seeing how two different groups would interpret the same scenes. I planned therefore to present four scenes from *The Merchant of Venice* with two different casts, the one not seeing the other perform.

One of the *Nerrissa*s became unavailable, so with that one exception, we did two versions on a stage that was the base of the Globe. The results were extraordinarily revealing, in that each group performed differently, but, more important, the main parts were interpreted differently.

The first *Shylocke* was performed in a rage (partly spurred by the *Solanio* continually repeating his line when he heard the "same" cue, even though the Cue Script only indicated it should be said once—a lesson there), and the other *Shylocke* from the same text found a quiet confidence and authority. The first *Portia* was amused and amusing, the second a passionate advocate.

The extraordinary result was that the scenes were very different, and yet they had the same effect on the audience. In both cases, the audience responded to the trial by finding sympathy for *Shylocke* at the end and deeming the Christians unsympathetic and manipulative. So although the performances were different, the eventual theatrical result was the same.

GRATIANO:
Beg that thou maist have leave to hang thy selfe,

Partial Platts

*An OSC Presentation for Shakespeare's Globe Birthday Festival
at 2:30 pm on Tuesday 27th April, 1993*

Presenter: *Patrick Tucker*   *Keeper of the Book:*   *Christine Ozanne*

The Partial Platt of Richard the Third

Enter old Queene Margaret: (CAROLYN JONES). She hides. Enter the Dutchesse of Yorke: (JUDITH PARIS) and Queene Elizabeth: (LISA BOWERMAN). They sit down and mourne. Queene Margaret comes forward.   ENDS.

The Pink Platt of The Merchant of Venice	The Purple Platt of The Merchant of Venice
Enter Shylocke: (NICHOLAS DAY), and Solanio: (ANTHONY BARNETT), and Anthonio: (PAUL ALEXANDER), and the Jaylor: (GARTH NAPIER JONES). Exit Shylocke. Exeunt.	Enter Shylocke: (RICHARD CORDERY), and Solanio: (JUSTIN BUTCHER), and Anthonio: (STEPHEN LIND), and the Jaylor: (LEWIS HANCOCK). Exit Shylocke. Exeunt.
Enter Portia: (MEG DAVIES), Nerrissa: (SONIA RITTER), Lorenzo: (OLIVER SENTON), Jessica: (SARAH FINCH), and a man of of Portia's: (JUSTIN BUTCHER). Exeunt Lorenzo and Jessica. Exit Balthaser with a letter for a Doctor Belario. Exeunt.	Enter Portia: (ELIZABETH COUNSELL), Nerrissa: (SONIA RITTER), Lorenzo: (CALLUM COATES), Jessica: (KERRY OWEN), and a man of of Portia's: (ANTHONY BARNETT). Exeunt Lorenzo and Jessica. Exit Balthaser with a letter for a Doctor Belario. Exeunt.
Enter: Clowne: (GLEN KINCH) and Jessica. Enter Lorenzo. Exit Clowne. Exeunt.	Enter: Clowne: (MARK WAGHORN) and Jessica. Enter Lorenzo. Exit Clowne. Exeunt.
Enter the Duke: (HUGH WALTERS), the Magnificoes, Anthonio, Bassanio: (DAVID JARVIS), Gratiano: (LEWIS HANCOCK), and others. Enter Shylocke. Enter Nerrissa dressed as a lawyer's clerk. She gives a letter to the Duke. Enter Portia dressed as Balthazar, a lawyer. Shylocke has balances ready, to weigh the flesh, and a knife to cut with. Exit Shylocke. Exit Duke and his traine. Exeunt Portia and Nerrissa. Exit Gratiano after them, to give them the wedding ring. Exeunt.	Enter the Duke: (DOMINIC BORRELLI), the Magnificoes, Anthonio, Bassanio: (NICHOLAS HUTCHISON), Gratiano: (GARTH NAPIER JONES), and others. Enter Shylocke. Enter Nerrissa dressed as a lawyer's clerk. She gives a letter to the Duke. Enter Portia dressed as Balthazar, a lawyer. Shylocke has balances ready, to weigh the flesh, and a knife to cut with. Exit Shylocke. Exit Duke and his traine. Exeunt Portia and Nerrissa. Exit Gratiano after them, to give them the wedding ring. Exeunt.
Enter Portia and Nerrissa. To them, Gratiano with the ring, which he gives to Portia. Exeunt.	Enter Portia and Nerrissa. To them, Gratiano with the ring, which he gives to Portia. Exeunt.
Interval of 15 minutes.	Finis.

And yet thy wealth being forfeit to the state,
Thou hast not left the value of a cord,
Therefore thou must be hang'd at the states charge.
DUKE:
That thou shalt see the difference of our spirit,
I pardon thee thy life before thou aske it:
For halfe thy wealth, it is *Anthonio's*
The other halfe comes to the generall state,
Which humblenesse may drive unto a fine.
PORTIA:
I for the state, not for *Anthonio.*
SHYLOCKE:
Nay, take my life and all, pardon not that,
You take my house, when you do take the prop
That doth sustaine my house: you take my life
When you doe take the meanes whereby I live.
PORTIA:
What mercy can you render him *Anthonio?*
GRATIANO:
A halter *gratis*, nothing else for Gods sake.
ANTHONIO:
So please my Lord the Duke, and all the Court
To quit the fine for one halfe of his goods,
I am content: so he will let me have
The other halfe in use, to render it
Upon his death, unto the Gentleman
That lately stole his daughter.
Two things provided more, that for this favour
He presently become a Christian:
The other, that he doe record a gift
Heere in the Court of all he dies possest
Unto his sonne *Lorenzo*, and his daughter.
DUKE:
He shall doe this, or else I doe recant
The pardon that I late pronounced heere.
PORTIA:
Art thou contented Jew? what dost thou say?
SHYLOCKE:
I am content.
PORTIA:
Clarke, draw a deed of gift.

SHYLOCKE:

> I pray you give me leave to goe from hence,
> I am not well, send the deed after me,
> And I will signe it.

DUKE:

> Get thee gone, but doe it.

GRATIANO:

> In christning thou shalt have two godfathers,
> Had I been judge, thou shouldst have had ten more,
> To bring thee to the gallowes, not to the font.
>> *EXIT SHYLOCKE.*

A problem that has consistently cropped up made its first appearance here. The bulk of the audience found the performances extraordinarily exciting and spontaneous (which to quite some extent they were) and enjoyed the dangerous performance energy and effects; a small part of the audience (and always the professional directors and the-atre manager sections) concentrated on the mistakes and thought they saw the audience enjoying only the errors. It was pointed out to me that this technique would work only with comedies, that such an approach would be unworkable with the tragedies, and I vowed to present just such a play when the members of the Company were ready for it.

A Midsommer Nights Dreame and The Merchant of Venice, June 1993

We were invited to present two plays for the Shakespeare Festival at the German Globe in Neuss, a prefabricated metal building in a little town just outside Düsseldorf (for the Germans had, of course, built their version of the Globe well before we in the UK got around to even thinking about it). They asked me what I had in my repertoire, I asked them what they wanted. After we had gone around this circle several times, I under-stood that the concept of putting on plays just for two performances was only in my own heart, so I offered *A Midsommer Nights Dreame* and *The Merchant of Venice*. Both were accepted with alacrity.

We were presented with the problem of assembling a complete company to do the two plays, and we had to arrange the production, get costumes and properties together, and work out what to do about a set and how to travel there. Actors who had taken part in my workshops and demonstrations were found, but it was only when they got onto the coach to travel to Germany and perform the next day that I realized a lot of them had never met one another before and in some cases did not even know one another's names.

Richard Cordery, who had been such a success as *Dromio*, was cast as *Pucke* and *Shy-locke* (probably the first time that particular double had been taken by the same actor), and when we got to Neuss, he spent a lot of time running round the building, working out how he could appear here, disappear there, and generally pop up in unexpected places. Unfortunately, in his eagerness he tripped and hurt his leg, and the injury got worse as curtain time approached. He came to me with a tale of woe: he could not walk. So I told him, "Alright, don't walk." That is what he did, staying on stage with a vast gesture that indicated he was invisible (and getting some very approving reactions from

---

The Platt of The Merchant of Venice
An OSC Presentation for the Festival im Globe Neuss, Germany
at 7:30 pm on Monday 14th June, 1993

I-1 Enter Anthonio, Salarino, Solanio: (STEPHEN LIND; GARTH NAPIER JONES; BEN COLE). Enter Bassanio, Lorenso, and Gratiano: (DAVID JARVIS; CALLUM COATES; LEWIS HANCOCK). Exeunt Salarino, and Solanio. Exit Gratiano and Lorenzo. Exeunt.

I-2: Enter Portia with her waiting woman Nerissa: (MEG DAVIES; SONIA RITTER). To them, a Servingman: (ELIZABETH COUNSELL). Exeunt.

I-3: Enter Bassanio with Shylocke the Jew: (RICHARD CORDERY). Enter Anthonio. Exit Shylocke. Exeunt.

II-1: Enter Morochus a tawnie Moore all in white: (DOMINIC BORRELLI) and three or foure followers accordingly: (), with Portia, Nerrissa, and their traine: (). Flourish of Cornets. Flourish of Cornets. Exeunt.

II-2: Enter Lancelet the Clowne alone: (GLEN KINCH). Enter old Gobbo his blind father: (HUGH WALTERS), with a Basket. Enter Bassanio with a follower or two: (ELIZABETH COUNSELL). Exit Clowne with old Gobbo. Exit Leonardo. Enter Gratiano. Exeunt.

II-3: Enter Jessica: (SARAH FINCH), daughter to Shylocke, and the Clowne. She gives him a letter for Lorenzo. Exit the Clowne. Exit Jessica.

II-4: Enter Gratiano, Lorenzo, Salarino, and Solanio. Enter Lancelet with a Letter. Lorenzo reads the letter. Clowne exits. Exeunt Salarino and Solanio. Exeunt.

II-5: Enter Shylocke, and his man that was the Clowne. To them Jessica. Shylocke gives her his keys. Exit Lancelet. Exit Shylocke. Exit Jessica.

II-6: Enter the Maskers, Gratiano and Salarino. Enter Lorenzo. Jessica appears above, dressed in boy's clothing. She throws down a casket of treasure, and descends. Enter Jessica. Exit Lorenzo, Salino, and Jessica. Enter Anthonio. Exeunt.

II-7: Enter Portia with Morrocho and both their traines: (). Flourish Cornets. The curtains are drawn to show the three Caskets. Morrocho chooses the gold casket, and Portia gives him the key. He discovers a skull's head, and a scroll, which he reads. Exit Morrocho with his traine. Exeunt.

II-8: Enter Salarino and Solanio. Exeunt.

II-9: Enter Nerrissa and a Serviture: (). They draw the curtains to reveal the caskets. Enter Arragon: (HUGH WALTERS), his traine: (), and Portia. Flourish Cornets. Arragon chooses the silver casket, and Portia gives him the key. He finds a picture and a scroll, which he reads. Exit Arragon and his traine. Enter a Messenger: (ELIZABETH COUNSELL). Exeunt.

III-1: Enter Solanio and Salarino. Enter Shylocke. They tease him. To them, a man from Anthonio: (GLEN KINCH). Enter Tuball: (DOMINIC BORRELLI). Exeunt Gentlemen. Tuball tells of Anthonio's ships all being lost. Exeunt.

Interval.

III-2: Enter Bassanio, Portia, Gratiano, and all their traine: (ELIZABETH COUNSELL; BEN COLE). Heere Musicke and a Song, whilst Bassanio comments on the Caskets to himselfe He chooses the lead casket, and finds Portia's portrait inside. He reads the scroll. Portia gives Bassanio a ring. Enter Lorenzo, Jessica, and Salerio. Salerio gives Bassanio a letter. Exeunt.

III-3: Enter Shylocke, and Solanio, and Anthonio, and the Jaylor: (DOMINIC BORRELLI). Exit Shylocke. Exeunt.

III-4: Enter Portia, Nerrissa, Lorenzo, Jessica, and a man of Portia's: (GARTH NAPIER JONES). Exeunt Lorenzo and Jessica. Exit Balthaser with a letter for a Doctor Belario. Exeunt.

III-5: Enter Clowne and Jessica. Enter Lorenzo. Exit Clowne. Exeunt.

IV-1: Enter the Duke: (HUGH WALTERS), the Magnificoes: (BEN COLE; ELIZABETH COUNSELL), Anthonio, Bassanio, Gratiano, and others. Enter Shylocke. Enter Nerrisssa dressed as a lawyer's clerk. She gives a letter to the Duke. Enter Portia dressed as Balthazar, a lawyer. Shylocke has balances ready, to weigh the flesh, and a knife to cut with. Exit Shylocke. Exit Duke and his traine. Exeunt Portia and Nerrissa. Exit Gratiano after them. Exeunt.

IV-2: Enter Portia and Nerrissa. To them, Gratiano with the ring, which he gives to Portia. Exeunt.

V-1: Enter Lorenzo and Jessica. Enter Stephano a Messenger: (ELIZABETH COUNSELL). Enter the Clowne, noisily. Exit Stephano, to arrange some music. Play musicke. Enter Portia and Nerrissa. Musicke. Musicke ceases. A Tucket sounds. Enter Bassanio, Anthonio, Gratiano, and their Followers. Portia gives the ring to Anthonio to be returned to Bassanio. Exeunt.

Finis.

Costumes	LUCY BENNETT
Assistant Book-Keeper	CRISPIN BUXTON
Presenter	PATRICK TUCKER
Book-Holder	CHRISTINE OZANNE

the audience: "<u>very</u> interesting interpretation"). Then I had the blinding realization that *Pucke*'s not being able to move did not spoil or change anything the other actors were doing. You see, since they did not know what he was going to do anyway, whatever he came up with was what they reacted to and totally accepted as his contribution to the show.

I know that a lot of times actors are prevented from doing things for fear of putting off a colleague or ruining a moment that had been worked over in rehearsal. But here in Neuss, whatever they did is what they did, and that was fine.

The next night, as *Shylocke*, Richard limped on with a stick, and <u>that</u> was fine also. His fellow actors were at all times reacting to what he was doing at that performance, not reacting to what they remembered him doing in a rehearsal, and this spontaneity is something that I value greatly and would love to put on in a longer run of performances.

Libby Counsell was playing *Tytania*, and she had been involved in the demonstration of *A Midsommer Nights Dreame* that I had done the year before. She came to me, worried about having to do all that sexy stuff that she had seen Meg Davies do. I reassured her that that was <u>Meg's</u> way of presenting the part, and that Libby's *Tytania* should be her own. The result was very different indeed (no rubbing of the groins here)—but equally sexy and effective in <u>Libby</u>'s way.

Nick Day was playing *Bottome*, and the night before we set out, he had phoned me to ask if I had got a sword for *Piramus* to use in the "play-within-the-play" at the end. Of course I had, but he wondered if I minded if he brought his own. This principle then arose: we should provide all the absolute necessities for a production, and if the actors want anything different, then the actors should provide it.

Nick duly produced a sword made out of a car aerial, so when he got to stab himself, the dagger was seen to go in, and in, and in—the audience wildly enjoying all this. At the start of the scene, he had placed a small prop on the prompt desk, so that he could pick it up for this moment. When the sword made its final thrust into the bosom of *Piramus*, he let go a long red ribbon that had been wound round a button:

BOTTOME:
   O wherefore Nature, did'st thou Lions frame?
   Since Lion vilde hath heere deflour'd my deere:
   Which is: no, no, which was the fairest Dame
   That liv'd, that lov'd, that lik'd, that look'd with cheere.
   Come teares, confound: Out sword, and wound
   The pap of *Piramus*:
   I, that left pap, where heart doth hop;
   Thus dye I, thus, thus, thus.
   Now am I dead, now am I fled, my soule is in the sky,
   Tongue lose thy light, Moone take thy flight,
   Now dye, dye, dye, dye, dye.

The ribbon jetted out of his chest as symbolic blood—and the audience let out a yell of laughter the like of which I had never heard before. The whole play came to a halt as the audience and actors roared together—another lesson for me: if something funny happens, it is truthful if the other characters on stage find this funny too. Also, because this was Nick's idea, planned and executed by him, it had a kind of artistic purity that gives one of those never-to-be-forgotten theatrical moments.

Ben Cole, playing *Snug*, did not hear his cue when he was to roar as the *Lyon* in the "play-within-the-play" at the end. In the script it is:

THISBY:

This is old *Ninnies* tombe: where is my love?

LYON:

Oh.

THE LION ROARES, THISBY RUNS OFF.

So he was prompted by Christine. Ben was so cross at missing his cue that he played *Snug* as being upset, and his *Lyon* roared and roared, rushing round the stage until a contrite prompter in the person of *Peter Quince* was able to console and calm him down. It was a wonderful combination of personal experience feeding a theatrical joy.

The *Mechanicals* present a problem with the theory of Cue Script acting, since their scene seems to indicate that there was rehearsal in those days. There was indeed—but for amateur actors. There are records of mummers plays being rehearsed over six months, and of times when several prompters were on stage, standing behind each actor and whispering their lines to them just before they should say them. A world of difference between amateur and professional theatre has always existed. After all, for many amateurs the rehearsal process is the enjoyable time and why they go in for it, while for a professional company, every moment spent rehearsing is time being paid for without generating any income. Many people feel that because they themselves need rehearsals before they perform, this is what all performers need. But the modern world of film and television has so developed that rehearsal is very much the exception. Most professional actors going to work in front of a camera bring to the screen what they themselves have privately prepared, and their work is not guided, but reacted to—just like the Elizabethans.

Demetrius starts off with very simple language:

DEMETRIUS:

Relent sweet *Hermia*, and *Lysander*, yeelde
Thy crazed title to my certaine right.

but when he is under the influence of the drug put upon him by *Pucke,* his language becomes more florid and complex:

DEMETRIUS:

> O *Helen*, goddesse, nimph, perfect, divine,
> To what, my love, shall I compare thine eyne!
> Christall is muddy, O how ripe in show,
> Thy lips, those kissing cherries, tempting grow!
> That pure congealed white, high *Taurus* snow,
> Fan'd with the Easterne winde, turnes to a crow,
> When thou holdst up thy hand. O let me kisse
> This Princesse of pure white, this seale of blisse.

Interestingly, the actor found that this complexity continues to the end, with lots of rhyming words and sounds—very different from his first speeches in the play:

DEMETRIUS:

> It seemes to mee,
> That yet we sleepe, we dreame.

and the audience saw that this was because once under the influence, *Demetrius* never comes out of it.

On the second day, getting ready for our *The Merchant of Venice*, the actress playing *Jessica* was very worried that she would not have enough time to change from her *Jessica* costume into her Page costume for running away with *Lorenzo*, so I ran just this bit of dialogue with the actors to check that she would be able to accomplish the change. Of course she could, and I never did this again; the original company of actors must have had these same problems, and there would have been enough lines written in by the Big Man himself to make sure that things would work seamlessly in a practical, theatrical sense.

The relationship between *Lorenzo* and *Jessica*, examined through Cue Scripts, is a fascinating one. When they have spoken to each other up at the balcony, it is in love terms, but once she joins him in flight his words change:

LORENZO:

> Beshrew me but I love her heartily.
> For she is wise, if I can judge of her,
> And faire she is, if that mine eyes be true,
> And true she is, as she hath prov'd her selfe:
> And therefore like her selfe, wise, faire, and true,
> Shall she be placed in my constant soule.
>   *ENTER JESSICA.*
> What, art thou come? on gentlemen, away,
> Our masking mates by this time for us stay.
>   *EXIT.*

By the rules of iambic pentameter, since there is a full line spoken by *Lorenzo,* there is no pause between his addressing her and the gentlemen. In performance, this led to his briskly addressing her and then marching offstage with his companions, leaving her to trail along behind them all. I was intrigued to see what would happen in the next scene.

The Platt of The Merchant of Venice
An OSC Presentation for the Festival im Globe Neuss, Germany
at 7:30 pm on Monday 14th June, 1993

I-1 Enter Anthonio, Salarino, Solanio: (**STEPHEN LOND; GARTH NAPIER JONES; BEN COLE**). Enter Bassanio, Lorenso, and Gratiano: (**DAVID JARVIS; CALLUM COATES; LEWIS HANCOCK**). Exeunt Salarino, and Solanio. Exit Gratiano and Lorenzo. Exeunt.

I-2: Enter Portia with her waiting woman Nerissa: (**MEG DAVIES; SONIA RITTER**). To them, a Servingman: (**ELIZABETH COUNSELL**). Exeunt.

I-3: Enter Bassanio with Shylocke the Jew: (**RICHARD CORDERY**). Enter Anthonio. Exit Shylocke. Exeunt.

II-1: Enter Morochus a tawnie Moore all in white: (**DOMINIC BORRELLI**) and three or foure followers accordingly: (), with Portia, Nerrissa, and their traine: (). Flourish of Cornets. Flourish of Cornets. Exeunt.

II-2: Enter Lancelet the Clowne alone: (**GLEN KINCH**). Enter old Gobbo his blind father: (**HUGH WALTERS**), with a Basket. Enter Bassanio with a follower or two: (**ELIZABETH COUNSELL**). Exit Clowne with old Gobbo. Exit Leonardo. Enter Gratiano. Exeunt.

II-3: Enter Jessica: (**SARAH FINCH**), daughter to Shylocke, and the Clowne. She gives him a letter for Lorenzo. Exit the Clowne. Exit Jessica.

II-4: Enter Gratiano, Lorenzo, Salarino, and Solanio. Enter Lancelet with a Letter. Lorenzo reads the letter. Clowne exits. Exeunt Salarino and Solanio. Exeunt.

II-5: Enter Shylocke, and his man that was the Clowne. To them Jessica. Shylocke gives her his keys. Exit Lancelet. Exit Shylocke. Exit Jessica.

II-6: Enter the Maskers, Gratiano and Salarino. Enter Lorenzo. Jessica appears above, dresssed in boy's clothing. She throws down a casket of treasure, and descends. Enter Jessica. Exit Lorenzo, Salino, and Jessica. Enter Anthonio. Exeunt.

II-7: Enter Portia with Morrocho and both their traines: (). Flourish Cornets. The curtains are drawn to show the three Caskets. Morrocho chooses the gold casket, and Portia gives him the key. He discovers a skull's head, and a scroll, which he reads. Exit Morrocho with his traine. Exeunt.

II-8: Enter Salarino and Solanio. Exeunt.

II-9: Enter Nerrissa and a Serviture: (). They draw the curtains to reveal the caskets. Enter Arragon: (**HUGH WALTERS**), his traine: (), and Portia. Flourish Cornets. Arragon chooses the silver casket, and Portia gives him the key. He finds a picture and a scroll, which he reads. Exit Arragon and his traine. Enter a Messenger: (**ELIZABETH COUNSELL**). Exeunt.

III-1: Enter Solanio and Salarino. Enter Shylocke. They tease him. To them, a man from Anthonio: (**GLEN KINCH**). Enter Tuball: (**DOMINIC BORRELLI**). Exeunt Gentlemen. Tuball tells of Anthonio's ships all being lost. Exeunt.

Interval.

III-2: Enter Bassanio, Portia, Gratiano, and all their traine: (**ELIZABETH COUNSELL; BEN COLE**). Heere Musicke and a Song, whilst Bassanio comments on the Caskets to himselfe He chooses the lead casket, and finds Portia's portrait inside. He reads the scroll. Portia gives Bassanio a ring. Enter Lorenzo, Jessica, and Salerio. Salerio gives Bassanio a letter. Exeunt.

III-3: Enter Shylocke, and Solanio, and Anthonio, and the Jaylor: (**DOMINIC BORRELLI**). Exit Shylocke. Exeunt.

III-4: Enter Portia, Nerrissa, Lorenzo, Jessica, and a man of Portia's: (**GARTH NAPIER JONES**). Exeunt Lorenzo and Jessica. Exit Balthaser with a letter for a Doctor Belario. Exeunt.

III-5: Enter Clowne and Jessica. Enter Lorenzo. Exit Clowne. Exeunt.

IV-1: Enter the Duke: (**HUGH WALTERS**), the Magnificoes: (**BEN COLE; ELIZABETH COUNSELL**), Anthonio, Bassanio, Gratiano, and others. Enter Shylocke. Enter Nerrisssa dressed as a lawyer's clerk. She gives a letter to the Duke. Enter Portia dressed as Balthazar, a lawyer. Shylocke has balances ready, to weigh the flesh, and a knife to cut with. Exit Shylocke. Exit Duke and his traine. Exeunt Portia and Nerrissa. Exit Gratiano after them. Exeunt.

IV-2: Enter Portia and Nerrissa. To them, Gratiano with the ring, which he gives to Portia. Exeunt.

V-1: Enter Lorenzo and Jessica. Enter Stephano a Messenger: (**ELIZABETH COUNSELL**). Enter the Clowne, noisily. Exit Stephano, to arrange some music. Play musicke. Enter Portia and Nerrissa. Musicke. Musicke ceases. A Tucket sounds. Enter Bassanio, Anthonio, Gratiano, and their Followers. Portia gives the ring to Anthonio to be returned to Bassanio. Exeunt.

Finis.

Costumes	**LUCY BENNETT**
Assistant Book-Keeper	**CRISPIN BUXTON**
Presenter	**PATRICK TUCKER**
Book-Holder	**CHRISTINE OZANNE**

GRATIANO:

    No, we shal nere win at that sport, and stake downe.

    But who comes heere? *Lorenzo* and his Infidell?

    What and my old Venetian friend *Salerio*?

      ENTER LORENZO, JESSICA, AND SALERIO.

BASSANIO:

    Lorenzo and *Salerio*, welcome hether,

    If that the youth of my new interest heere

    Have power to bid you welcome: by your leave

    I bid my verie friends and Countrimen

    Sweet *Portia* welcome.

The stage instructions are very clearly put in the First Folio, and I have to confess that the majority of Editors who change it to two lines earlier seemed to have a point, but I played it as written to see what would happen.

    What happens is that, out of the hearing of *Lorenzo* and *Jessica*, *Gratiano* indulges in a little anti-Semitism, and in the subsequent scene no one refers to poor lonely *Jessica* until at last *Gratiano* puts his prejudices aside:

GRATIANO:

    Nerrissa, cheere yond stranger, bid her welcom.

Incidentally, in the recent production of *The Merchant of Venice* at Shakespeare's Globe this moment caused a huge problem. With the entrance being taken earlier, *Gratiano* insisted that he would not be so pejorative in *Jessica*'s hearing, and a whole day of rehearsal was consumed with this issue, finally solved by cutting the line altogether. Would playing the original stage instruction have simplified and helped matters? It would certainly have been quicker.

    The playing of this moment emphasizes how the Christian world treats *Jessica* as a stranger, and this is followed up by more tensions, leading to the famous "romantic" scene in the garden:

    ENTER LORENZO AND JESSICA.

LORENZO:

    The moone shines bright. In such a night as this,

    When the sweet winde did gently kisse the trees,

    And they did make no noyse, in such a night

    Troylus me thinkes mounted the Trojan walls,

    And sigh'd his soule toward the Grecian tents

    Where *Cressed* lay that night.

JESSICA:

    In such a night

Did *Thisbie* fearefully ore-trip the dewe,
And saw the Lyons shadow ere himselfe,
And ranne dismayed away.

LORENZO:

In such a night
Stood *Dido* with a Willow in her hand
Upon the wilde sea bankes, and waft her Love
To come againe to Carthage.

JESSICA:

In such a night
Medea gathered the inchanted hearbs
That did renew old *Eson*.

LORENZO:

In such a night
Did *Jessica* steale from the wealthy Jewe,
And with an Unthrift Love did runne from Venice,
As farre as Belmont.

JESSICA:

In such a night
Did young *Lorenzo* sweare he lov'd her well,
Stealing her soule with many vowes of faith,
And nere a true one.

LORENZO:

In such a night
Did pretty *Jessica* (like a little shrow)
Slander her Love, and he forgave it her.

JESSICA:

I would out-night you did no body come:
But harke, I heare the footing of a man.

ENTER MESSENGER.

The joy here is that both the lovers are using images of <u>disastrous</u> love affairs that led to death or estrangement. Not one of the images, even though they are picking up each other's *In such a night*, is a positive affirmation of a successful love match; all are of mismatched and unhappy outcomes of two lovers. The beauty of the language has seduced many into considering this a soft affirmation of passion, but the individual actors, once alerted to the significance of the classical names they were invoking, both responded with a scene that was challenging, and aggressive to each other. The togetherness eventually comes, but only after *Portia*'s intervention and giving of good news. Callum Coates, playing *Lorenzo*, could not get over the fact that in each scene he played, he found he was nastier than he had imagined, ending up playing the part nothing like the way it had seemed to him at first—but being very effective with the audience.

Hugh Walters, the most experienced actor among us, came up with a delightful selection of characterizations for the two plays. He was very worried, however, about the younger members of the Company not having enough stage sense, and doing distracting business (or upstaging) during someone else's speeches. He need not have worried, for in a Cue Script presentation, because the actors do not know when their next line is to be said, they dare not do any distracting business for fear of missing their next line, and in fact the performances were very focused, with no annoying extraneous stage business at all.

When *Bassanio*, having just won the hand of *Portia*, receives a letter from his friend *Anthonio*, all color goes from his cheeks:

PORTIA:
> There are some shrewd contents in yond same Paper,
> That steales the colour from *Bassianos* cheeke,
> Some deere friend dead, else nothing in the world
> Could turne so much the constitution
> Of any constant man. What, worse and worse?
> With leave *Bassanio* I am halfe your selfe,
> And I must freely have the halfe of any thing
> That this same paper brings you.

Bassanio tells her of the plight of his friend, now in danger of being killed by *Shylocke* demanding the letter of his bond. She tells him to pay the debt himself:

PORTIA:
> Bid your friends welcome, show a merry cheere,
> Since you are deere bought, I will love you deere.
> But let me heare the letter of your friend.
> *Sweet* Bassanio, *my ships have all miscarried, my Creditors grow cruell, my estate is very low, my bond to the Jew is forfeit, and since in paying it, it is impossible I should live, all debts are cleerd between you and I, if I might see you at my death: notwithstanding, use your pleasure, if your love doe not perswade you to come, let not my letter.*

PORTIA:
> O love! dispach all busines and be gone.

Well, that is the way it is in the Folio, so Editors change it to *Bassanio* reading the letter, on the grounds that the speech heading was probably left off as *Portia* gets a second speech heading for her next line, and anyway she herself has said *let me heare the letter of your friend,* so it is logical that he should read it. It is also profoundly wrong.

In *The Merchant of Venice* there are four occasions when a letter is read out, the one we have just seen, and three others:

MORROCHO:

O hell! what have we here, a carrion death,
Within whose emptie eye there is a written scroule;
Ile reade the writing.

> *All that glisters is not gold,*
> *Often have you heard that told;*
> *Many a man his life hath sold*
> *But my outside to behold;*
> *Guilded timber doe wormes infold:*
> *Had you beene as wise as bold,*
> *Yong in limbs, in judgement old,*
> *Your answere had not beene inscrold,*
> *Fareyouwell, your suite is cold,*

MORROCHO:

Cold indeede, and labour lost,
Then farewell heate, and welcome frost:
Portia adew, I have too griev'd a heart
To take a tedious leave: thus loosers part.

ARRAGON:

What is here?

> *The fier seaven times tried this,*
> *Seaven times tried that judgement is,*
> *That did never choose amis,*
> *Some there be that shadowes kisse,*
> *Such have but a shadowes blisse:*
> *There be fooles alive Iwis*
> *Silver'd o're, and so was this:*
> *Take what wife you will to bed,*
> *I will ever be your head:*
> *So be gone, you are sped.*

ARRAGON:

Still more foole I shall appeare
By the time I linger here,
With one fooles head I came to woo,
But I goe away with two.
Sweet adue, Ile keepe my oath,
Patiently to beare my wroath.

BASSANIO:

Here's the scroule,
The continent, and summarie of my fortune.

> *You that choose not by the view*
> *Chance as faire, and choose as true:*
> *Since this fortune fals to you,*
> *Be content, and seeke no new.*
> *If you be well pleasd with this,*
> *And hold your fortune for your blisse,*
> *Turne you where your Lady is,*
> *And claime her with a loving kisse.*

BASSANIO:
> A gentle scroule: Faire Lady, by your leave,
> I come by note to give, and to receive,
> Like one of two contending in a prize
> That thinks he hath done well in peoples eies:
> Hearing applause and universall shout,
> Giddie in spirit, still gazing in a doubt
> Whether those peales of praise be his or no.
> So thrice faire Lady stand I even so,
> As doubtfull whether what I see be true,
> Untill confirm'd, sign'd, ratified by you.

As you can see, in each case the letter is followed by a speech given by the person who read out the letter, and in each case the new speech has been given a new heading. I think this is because the letters themselves having been written out, the actor did not have to memorize those bits, so a new speech was needed to pick up the lines after the reading out of the letter.

In fact, to be logical and consistent, the letter should <u>always</u> be given to *Portia* to read out, and when Meg Davies did it in Neuss, suddenly a whole new meaning came over the play. For *Portia* is reading out what may appear to be a love letter to her new partner, and the force of reading out *Sweet Bassanio* came over as the moment when she realizes that this is no ordinary friendship, and if she is to have that equal-shared relationship she had talked of earlier, she really needs to sort out the *Anthonio/Bassanio* relationship—which is exactly what she does in the rest of the play.

Having her read the letter is a powerful theatrical moment, consistent with how the rest of the play is printed, and is changed only to the detriment of the play itself.

The "problem" of putting on *The Merchant of Venice* is how to prevent it being used as fuel for any form of anti-Semitism. With the play's presentation in Germany, the issue just did not arise, even though there was no director with a thesis to make any particular point. The moment when *Shylocke* decides to go through with his bargain with *Anthonio* is when he is talking with *Tuball*:

SHYLOCKE:
> How now *Tuball*, what newes from *Genowa*? hast
> thou found my daughter?

TUBALL:

I often came where I did heare of her, but cannot finde her.

SHYLOCKE:

Why there, there, there, there, a diamond gone
cost me two thousand ducats in Franckford, the curse never fell upon our Nation till now, I never felt it till now,
two thousand ducats in that, and other precious, precious jewels: I would my daughter were dead at my foot,
and the jewels in her eare: would she were hearst at my
foote, and the duckets in her coffin: no newes of them,
why so? and I know not how much is spent in the search:
why thou losse upon losse, the theefe gone with so
much, and so much to finde the theefe, and no satisfaction, no revenge, nor no ill luck stirring but what lights
a my shoulders, no sighes but a my breathing, no teares
but a my shedding.

TUBALL:

Yes, other men have ill lucke too, *Anthonio* as I
heard in Genowa?

SHYLOCKE:

What, what, what, ill lucke, ill lucke.

TUBALL:

Hath an Argosie cast away comming from Tri-
polis.

SHYLOCKE:

I thanke God, I thanke God, is it true, is it true?

TUBALL:

I spoke with some of the Saylers that escaped
the wracke.

SHYLOCKE:

I thanke thee good *Tuball*, good newes, good
newes: ha, ha, here in Genowa.

TUBALL:

Your daughter spent in Genowa, as I heard, one
night fourescore ducats.

SHYLOCKE:

Thou stick'st a dagger in me, I shall never see my
gold againe, fourescore ducats at a sitting, fourescore ducats.

TUBALL:

There came divers of *Anthonios* creditors in my

company to Venice, that sweare hee cannot choose but
breake.

SHYLOCKE:

I am very glad of it, ile plague him, ile torture
him, I am glad of it,

TUBALL:

One of them shewed me a ring that hee had of
your daughter for a Monkie.

SHYLOCKE:

Out upon her, thou torturest me *Tuball*, it was
my Turkies, I had it of *Leah* when I was a Batcheler: I
would not have given it for a wildernesse of Monkies.

TUBALL:

But *Anthonio* is certainely undone.

SHYLOCKE:

Nay, that's true, that's very true, goe *Tuball*, fee
me an Officer, bespeake him a fortnight before, I will
have the heart of him if he forfeit, for were he out of Venice, I can make what merchandize I will: goe *Tuball*,
and meete me at our Sinagogue, goe good *Tuball*, at our
Sinagogue *Tuball*.

    EXEUNT.

In performance, in front of that German audience, it became obvious that it was
Tuball that was continually making the connection between *Shylocke*'s loss of his daughter and *Anthonio*'s loss of ships. Every time *Shylocke* went on one tack, *Tuball* sought to
connect the two. It became then a matter of honor and of personal revenge, and the
anti-Semitic element just was not relevant; a really interesting insight gained at the moment of performance, not thought out prior to the audience's experiencing the play.

We returned to England in an euphoric state—two plays in two days with no rehearsal—but we did agree that the actors needed more help with their verse work, and
from that presentation on, a regular meeting with each member of the cast to go over
the actor's lines was instituted. At these meetings, the actors are never told how to perform, or indeed whether the decisions they have made are valid or not. They are simply
reminded of the clues, with the injunction that if they have a clue, they must do something about it, and these sessions quickly became known as "verse nursing."

Incidentally, after I developed verse nursing, I discovered that in Shakespeare's time
actors sometimes had "instruction" when they worked with an instructor away from the
rest of the cast, so all I had come up with independently was standard Renaissance practice. But then, since I was presenting the plays in their manner, it is likely that we would
have ended up with similar approaches.

As you Like it, April 1994

The organizer of this festival in Canada was looking for some original theatrical event, and had heard of what we did through an obscure radio broadcast I had made after our *As He Liked It* project at the Haymarket in London. It soon became apparent that it would be financially impossible for us to bring a full company over from the UK, and I suggested instead that Christine and I should travel to Canada, train up a local company of actors, and present Cue Script performances of *As you Like it*.

It was a very new concept, and we were inventing how to do it as we went along.

A group of actors had been assembled, and the idea was for me to give them a workshop on Cue Script techniques and then coach them into a host of scenes that would be presented to an invited audience. From these performances, we would cast the production—with the exception of the part of *Rosalind* (the largest female Shakespearean role)—which had been precast with a major actress.

Julia Smith, who was playing *Celia*, had come to me with a problem. She says in her own lines:

CELIA:

Ile put my selfe in poore and meane attire,
And with a kinde of umber smirch my face,
The like doe you, so shall we passe along,
And never stir assailants.

She was not sure she would have time to give herself a nut-brown look as well as change her costume in the gap between leaving the court and arriving in the Forest of Arden. I assured her—as I have many actors since—that this would have been a problem for the Elizabethans too, and so I was sure that if she just did it, all would work out fine.

Indeed, in the performance she found she did <u>not</u> have time to complete her makeup change. So she arrived with *Rosalind* at the Forest of Arden still putting the brown makeup onto her arms—a delightful touch. The play continued, and toward the end, *Oliver*, to whom *Celia* is immediately attracted, comes on. As this happened, Julia took out her hanky and started trying to remove the brown from her arms and from the gaze of the infatuated *Oliver*. Yet another wonderful theatrical moment of truth and insight.

Julia also led me to another insight. In the main wooing scene between *Orlando* and *Rosalind*, *Celia* is also present, and in directed productions is either sent offstage, sent to sleep in a hammock, or otherwise taken out of the action. But this *Celia*, knowing that she had to speak, <u>but not knowing when</u>, followed the wooing couple around the stage like a puppy dog, and made the scene both funnier and more understandable, with everything they say to each other having such a close witness.

Amyens was played by Mark Burgess, who was as inventive an actor in these circumstances as I have ever found. When playing *Charles* in the first part of the play, he sported a patch over one eye and did the whole routine of "who was whom" to *Oliver*.

CHARLES:

There's no newes at the Court Sir, but the
olde newes: that is, the old Duke is banished by his yon-
ger brother the new Duke, and three or foure loving
Lords have put themselves into voluntary exile with

The Platt of As you Like it

An OSC Presentation for the du Maurier World Stage Festival, Toronto
at 8:00 pm on Friday 15th & Saturday 16th April, 1994

I-1: Enter Orlando and Adam: (ALBERT SCHULTZ; CHRISTOPHER KELK). Enter Oliver, elder brother to Orlando: (TED ATHERTON). Oliver strikes Orlando. Exit Orlando and Adam. To Oliver, Dennis his servant: (ROSS MANSON). To Oliver, Charles the wrestler: (MARK BURGESS). Exit Dennis. Exit Charles. Exit Oliver.

I-2: Enter Rosalind, daughter of the banished Duke, and Celia, daughter of Duke Frederick: (SEANA MCKENNA; JULIA SMITH). Enter the Clowne, Touchstone: (STEWART ARNOTT). Enter le Beau: (ROBERT DODDS). Flourish. Enter Duke Frederick: (GARY REINEKE), Lords: (ROBERT DODDS; PETER VAN WART), Orlando, Charles, and Attendants with the Mat: (JENNIFER DOYLE; KARYN DWYER; MICHAEL FRANKLIN; DEBORAH JACKSON; DAVE NICHOL). Charles and Orlando wrestle. Charles is thrown and defeated. Shout. Exeunt all but Celia, Rosalind and Orlando, Charles being carried out. Rosalind gives Orlando a chain from around her neck. Exit Rosalind and Celia. Enter Le Beau. Exit Orlando and Le Beau.

I-3: Enter Celia and Rosalind. Enter Duke Frederick with Lords. The Duke banishes Rosalind. Exit the Duke and Lords. Exeunt Rosalind and Celia.

II-1: Enter Duke Senior, Amyens: (THOMAS HAUFF; MARK BURGESS), and two or three Lords like Forresters: (TED ATHERTON; ROSS MANSON). Exeunt.

II-2: Enter Duke Frederick, with Lords. Exeunt.

II-3: Enter Orlando and Adam. Adam offers Orlando a bag of gold. Exeunt.

II-4: Enter Rosaline dressed as the page Ganimed, Celia dressed as Aliena, and the Clowne Touchstone. Enter Corin and Silvius, two shepherds: (PETER VAN WART; ROBERT DODDS). Exit Silvius. Touchstone calls out to Corin. Exeunt.

II-5: Enter Amyens, Jaques: (MICHAEL HANRAHAN) and others: (TED ATHERTON; MICHAEL FRANKLIN; DEBORAH JACKSON; ROSS MANSON; DAVE NICHOL). Amyens sings a Song. They all sing the Song. Jaques does a parody of the Song. Exeunt.

II-6: Enter Orlando, and Adam. Exeunt, Orlando carrying Adam.

II-7: Enter Duke Senior, Amyens, Lords, like Out-lawes. A meal is set out. Enter Jaques. To them Orlando, with his sword drawn. Exit Orlando. Enter Orlando with Adam. Amyens sings a Song as they eat. Exeunt.

Interval

III-1: Enter Duke Frederick, Lords, and Oliver. Exeunt, pushing out Oliver.

III-2: Enter Orlando, who fastens a poem to a tree. Exit Orlando. Enter Corin and Clowne. Enter Rosalind, reading a poem. Enter Celia with a writing, which she reads. Exit Clowne with Corin. Enter Orlando and Jaques, Rosalind and Celia hiding behind. Rosalind comes forward. Exit Jaques. Exeunt.

III-3: Enter Clowne, Audrey: (JENNIFER DOYLE), and Jaques observing from behind. Enter Sir Oliver Mar-text, a vicar: (CHRISTOPHER KELK). Jaques comes forward. Exeunt.

III-4: Enter Rosalind and Celia. To them, Corin. Exeunt.

III-5: Enter Silvius and Phebe: (KARYN DWYER). Enter behind, Rosalind, Celia and Corin. Rosalind comes forward. Exit Rosalind, Celia, and Corin. Exeunt Silvius and Phebe.

IV-1: Enter Rosalind, and Celia, and Jaques. Enter Orlando. Exit Jaques. Orlando woos Ganimed as Rosalind. Exit Orlando. Exeunt.

IV-2: Enter Jaques and Lords like Forresters: (TED ATHERTON; MARK BURGESS; MICHAEL FRANKLIN; DEBORAH JACKSON; ROSS MANSON; DAVE NICHOL). They sing a Song. Exeunt.

IV-3: Enter Rosalind and Celia. Enter Silvius with a letter. Exit Silvius. Enter Oliver with a bloody napkin. Rosalind faints. Exeunt.

V-1: Enter Clowne and Awdrie. Enter William, a former follower of Awdrie: (MARK BURGESS). Exit William. To them, Corin. Exeunt.

V-2: Enter Orlando with his arm in a scarf, and Oliver. Enter Rosalind. Exit Oliver. Enter Silvius and Phebe. Rosalind gives them commands. Exeunt.

V-3: Enter Clowne and Audrey. Enter two Pages: (MICHAEL FRANKLIN; DEBORAH JACKSON). They sing a Song. Exeunt.

V-4: Enter Duke Senior, First Forrester, Jaques, Orlando, Oliver, Celia. Enter Rosalinde, Silvius, and Phebe. Enter Rosalinde and Celia. Enter Clowne and Audrey. Enter Hymen: (GARY REINEKE), with Rosalind and Celia dressed as themselves. Still Musicke. They all sing the Wedding Song. To them, the Second Brother of Orlando: (ROSS MANSON). Exit Jaques. A Dance. Exit all but Rosalind. Rosalind delivers the Epilogue. Exit Rosalind.

Finis.

Musicians: MICHAEL FRANKLIN; DEBORAH JACKSON; DAVE NICHOL
Costumes: BONNIE DEAKIN
Book-Holder: CHRISTINE OZANNE

Stage Manager: SARAH JEAN BUTLER
Presenter: PATRICK TUCKER

him, whose lands and revenues enrich the new Duke,
therefore he gives them good leave to wander.

O no; for the Dukes daughter her Cosen so
loves her, being ever from their Cradles bred together,
that hee would have followed her exile, or have died to
stay behind her; she is at the Court, and no lesse beloved
of her Uncle, then his owne daughter, and never two Ladies loved as they doe.

On the first night Mark displayed their varying heights with his hand, raising or
lowering it for each character (as written, *Celia* is described as taller than *Rosalind*, a
note we had followed by casting a robust actress who towered over our *Rosalind*). On
the second night, he had been out front and removed the pictures of the actors from the
front of house, so when talking to *Oliver* about all the various people, he brought out
their photographs, matching the faces to his description perfectly. In this second performance, when it got to the fight, Mark, as *Charles*, suddenly removed his eye patch with
a triumphant cry and a big wink at the audience, as if he had been wooing *Orlando* into
a false sense of security.

Jaques has the problem of a well-known "purple passage":

JAQUES:
All the world's a stage,
And all the men and women, meerely Players;

I had verse nursed him, but he was not sure how it should be played. In performance,
he was onstage with the other *Foresters* when he started the speech. They all without exception marched downstage in a line and sat facing upstage, ready for *Jaques's* speech.
The audience reacted hugely to this joyous moment. It was as if *Jaques* always gave this
speech around this time of the day, and they were settling themselves down for it.

What had happened was that the actors had been trained by me to move downstage
whenever another actor had a long speech, so that they had someone downstage to talk
to and the audience would see them better. They concentrated on trying to do this, but
when it came to the purple passage, they all <u>knew</u> that here was such a speech, and all
set off downstage only to find they were doing it in unison. I asked them what would
they do in the second performance: Something different? Recreate the original one? As
always the solution was left to the actors, and so when the moment came they all
stopped, looked at one another, shrugged, and again marched downstage to hear *Jaques*,
Mark taking the opportunity of opening up his shoulder bag to distribute sweets and
gum first to his fellow actors and then to the audience. Again, the positive reaction to
this moment, with *Jaques* glowering at them to settle so he could do his speech, was a
delightful discovery and a pure theatrical moment.

JAQUES:

> All the world's a stage,
> And all the men and women, meerely Players;
> They have their *Exits* and their Entrances,
> And one man in his time playes many parts,
> His Acts being seven ages. At first the Infant,   Midline ending.
> Mewling, and puking in the Nurses armes:
> Then, the whining Schoole-boy with his Satchell
> And shining morning face, creeping like snaile
> Unwillingly to schoole. And then the Lover,   Another one.
> Sighing like Furnace, with a wofull ballad
> Made to his Mistresse eye-brow. Then, a Soldier,   And another.
> Full of strange oaths, and bearded like the Pard,
> Jelous in honor, sodaine, and quicke in quarrell,
> Seeking the bubble Reputation
> Even in the Canons mouth: And then, the Justice
> In faire round belly, with good Capon lin'd,
> With eyes severe, and beard of formall cut,
> Full of wise sawes, and moderne instances,
> And so he playes his part. The sixt age shifts   And another—no full stop/period
> Into the leane and slipper'd Pantaloone,   at the end of any verse line, al-
> With spectacles on nose, and pouch on side,   ways in the middle.
> His youthfull hose well sav'd, a world too wide,
> For his shrunke shanke, and his bigge manly voice,
> Turning againe toward childish trebble pipes,
> And whistles in his sound. Last Scene of all,   Yet again.
> That ends this strange eventfull historie,
> Is second childishnesse, and meere oblivion,
> Sans teeth, sans eyes, sans taste, sans every thing.   At the very end, we get the end of
> the thought at the end of the line.

The sentences end in the middle of lines, called midline endings, and the instruction to Michael Hanrahan had been to get on with it, to let the next thought crash into the finishing one. This was very effective, as it gave a drive to the speech, and it came over as if *Jaques* was only too eager to deliver his speech and not leave a gap for the other *Foresters* to get a word in edgewise.

Orlando was played by Albert Schultz, who, although a very busy actor at the time, brought to the part an amazing inventiveness. Arriving in the forest armed with a sword, he demanded food from the *Foresters*. They, holding bread and apples, immediately dropped them on the stage, where Albert proceeded to skewer them onto his sword like a gigantic kebab. When he had to pin a love letter to a tree, and could not find a convenient place, he stuck it to the Book-Holder's head.

In a scene with *Jaques*, he has a line:

ORLANDO:

He is drown'd in the brooke, looke but in, and
you shall see him.

Taking this as his cue, he played the scene taking off his shoes, using his shoelaces and stick as a makeshift rod, and "fished" off the front of the stage. *Jaques*, needing to exit over the front of the stage, removed his own shoes and "waded" through the river. Wonderful.

The two performances of *As you Like it* went by in a flash, and the Canadian actors all begged us to return and do more of this type of work.

As you Like it (scenes), King Lear (scenes), The Two Gentlemen of Verona (scenes), and Hamlet (scenes), November 1994

We were asked to present examples of our work over two weekends in the foyer of the Barbican Theatre as part of their *Everybody's Shakespeare* Festival, so I decided to present the first 600 lines or so of four different plays.

We started off with *As you Like it*, and got a crowded foyer sitting around our small stage for the presentation, numbers that were repeated for all four afternoons.

Our first presentation went down well with the audience, and the *Duke* came out and shouted angrily at *Rosalind* and *Celia*. I had not yet found the huge clue that is dis-

The Platt for the first 600 lines of As you Like it

An OSC Presentation for the Barbican Centre's "Everybody's Shakespeare"
at 2:00 pm on Saturday 5th November, 1994

I-1: Enter Orlando and Adam: (DAVID JARVIS; NIGEL HARRIS). Enter Oliver, elder brother to Orlando: (GRAHAM POUNTNEY). Oliver strikes Orlando, who puts him in a wrestler's grip. Exit Orlando and Adam. To Oliver, Dennis his servant: (SARAH DENY JONES). Enter Charles the wrestler: (DOMINIC BORRELLI). Exit Dennis. Exit Charles. Exit Oliver.

I-2: Enter Rosalind, daughter of the banished Duke, and Celia, daughter of Duke Frederick: (JUDITH PARIS; JUDY HOPTON). Enter the Clown, Touchstone: (NON VAUGHAN-THOMAS). Enter Le Beau: (LEWIS HANCOCK). Flourish. Enter Duke Frederick: (NIGEL HARRIS), Lords: (), Orlando, Charles, and Attendants: (). Charles and Orlando wrestle. Charles is thrown and defeated. All shout. Exeunt all but Celia, Rosalind and Orlando, Charles the wrestler being carried out. Rosalind gives Orlando a chain from around her neck. Exit Rosalind and Celia. Enter Le Beau. Exit Orlando and Le Beau.

I-3: Enter Celia and Rosalind. Enter Duke Frederick with Lords: (). The Duke banishes Rosalind. Exit the Duke and Lords. Exeunt Rosalind and Celia.

Book-Holder   CHRISTINE OZANNE
Presenter   PATRICK TUCKER

cussed at length in MODES OF ADDRESS, even though now it is so obvious. We were still concentrating on just making sure the plays worked on a simple level. But we did know that the play started as prose and only changed to poetry when the *Duke* reacts to the knowledge that *Orlando*, the son of his brother, has won the wrestling match, and when *Rosalind* and *Celia* react to *Orlando*, but for different reasons, and so we made sure the actors were acting with the appropriate background. As always, the effect was to heighten the theatricality at that moment.

When it came to the play of *King Lear*, one of my senior actresses said that she had always wanted to play *Edmund*, and so she did, and I decided to cast a female *Edgar* to accompany her. This idea of having actresses play male roles was an acknowledgment partly that my growing group of committed actors and actresses had an uneven balance in expectations of a good role, and partly that the original companies would have had young male roles played by fresh-faced, treble-voiced boy actors—and a modern twenty-year-old actor is not the same. It was to be six years before the logical outcome of this, a "Boys' Company" presentation, came about.

Edmund first appears in the scene when he is introduced to *Kent*, and at the end of the scene the Editors send him offstage with his father, before the entrance of *Lear* himself and the dividing of the property among his three daughters. Well, in the Folio there is no exit for *Edmund*, and so I left him there. *Edmund* therefore was a witness to the division and to the fact that *Cordelia's* share was given to her two elder sisters—and this suddenly made even better sense of *Edmund's* relationships with both of them in the rest of the play; it even made him into a bit of a gold digger.

When it came to his famous soliloquy:

The Platt for the first 600 lines of The Tragedie of King Lear

An OSC Presentation for the Barbican Centre's "Everybody's Shakespeare" at 2:00 pm on Sunday 6th November, 1994

I-1: Enter Kent, Gloucester: (GRAHAM POUNTNEY; EDMUND DEHN), and Edmond his Bastard son: (ELIZABETH COUNSELL). Sennet. Enter one bearing a coronet: (). Enter King Lear: (RICHARD CORDERY), Cornwall, Albany: (ROGER RINGROSE; SIMON PURSE), Lear's daughters Gonerill: (CAROLYN JONES), Regan: (ANNE MARIE SPEED), Cordelia: (JULIETTE GRASSBY), and attendants: (). Exit Gloucester. A map being brought to Lear, to divide his kingdom between his daughters. Lear takes Cordelia's share away from her. Exit Kent, banished. Flourish. Enter Gloster with France, and Burgundy: (NATASHA TAMAR; TESS DIGNAN); Attendants: (). Flourish. Exeunt all except France, Cordelia, Gonerill, Regan. Exit France and Cordelia. Exeunt.

I-2: Enter Edmund the Bastard, with a letter he has written pretending to be treason from Edgar. Enter Gloucester. Edmund hides the letter in his pocket. Exit Gloucester. Enter Edgar, legitimate younger brother to Edmund: (BARBARA MUSTON). Exit Edgar. Exit Edmund.

I-3: Enter Gonerill and her Steward: (LEWIS HANCOCK). Exeunt.

Book-Holder   CHRISTINE OZANNE
Presenter   PATRICK TUCKER

EDMUND:

> Thou Nature art my Goddesse, to thy Law
> My services are bound, wherefore should I
> Stand in the plague of custome, and permit
> The curiosity of Nations, to deprive me?

the lighter tone voice of the actress suited the piece very well; it was as if the very youth and immaturity of the character explained better just why he was so cruel and vicious. The *Bastard* parts of the speech played just as well with an actress too.

In the Folio the speech heading for *Cordelia* is "*Cor.*" and for *Cornwall* is "*Corn.*"; I was interested to see that the Editors give two speeches that <u>are</u> headed "*Cor.*" to the logical speaker: *Cornwall.* I, equally obviously, gave them back to *Cordelia* to prove to myself that the Folio was incorrect at this point, for I was sure that here the Editors were correct:

Kent.

> Now by *Apollo*, King
> Thou swear'st thy Gods in vaine.

Lear.

> O Vassall! Miscreant.

Alb.Cor.

> Deare Sir forbeare.

Kent.

> Kill thy Physition, and thy fee bestow
> Upon the foule disease, revoke thy guift,
> Or whil'st I can vent clamour from my throate,
> Ile tell thee thou dost evill.

Lea.

> Heare me recreant, on thine allegeance heare me;
> That thou hast sought to make us breake our vowes,
> Which we durst never yet; and with strain'd pride,
> To come betwixt our sentences, and our power,
> Which, nor our nature, nor our place can beare;
> Our potencie made good, take thy reward.
> Five dayes we do allot thee for provision,
> To shield thee from disasters of the world,
> And on the sixt to turne thy hated backe
> Upon our kingdome: if on the tenth day following,
> Thy banisht trunke be found in our Dominions,
> The moment is thy death, away. By *Jupiter*,
> This shall not be revok'd,

Kent.

Fare thee well King, sith thus thou wilt appeare,
Freedome lives hence, and banishment is here;
The Gods to their deere shelter take thee Maid,
That justly think'st, and hast most rightly said:
And your large speeches, may your deeds approve,
That good effects may spring from words of love:
Thus *Kent*, O Princes, bids you all adew,
Hee'l shape his old course, in a Country new.
   Exit.
Flourish. Enter Gloster with France, and Burgundy, Attendants.
Cor.
Heere's *France* and *Burgundy*, my Noble Lord.

It seems so logical that it should be *Cornwall* speaking, but in performance—I repeat, in performance—I discovered other effects. Each of the three sisters has been called forward for her father's inheritance, and after *Cordelia* has got her *nothing* she still has—according to these lines—more to say, so instead of retreating to the sides of the stage, she stays put. When *Kent* receives the anger of *Lear*, it is *Cordelia* and *Albany* who try to intercede, and later, when the others arrive, it is *Cordelia* who attempts to do all she can to keep in favor with her father, apart from giving in about her principle of loving. All I can report is that it played wonderfully well, was not confusing, and gave an extra insight into *Cordelia's* dilemma. For the record, the Quarto version does not have these lines at all, and so is no guide as to how it was intended to be spoken.

As an extra thought on *King Lear*, I was working with an actor on his text for *Edgar*, when I found in the following passage a great change between *thou* and *you* when *Edgar* is accompanying his blind father in disguise and, first of all, calls him *thy* and *thee*:

GLOUCESTER:
There is a Cliffe, whose high and bending head
Lookes fearfully in the confined Deepe:
Bring me but to the very brimme of it,
And Ile repayre the misery thou do'st beare
With something rich about me: from that place,
I shall no leading neede.
EDGAR:
Give me thy arme;
Poore Tom shall leade thee.
   EXEUNT.

The next time we see them, *Edgar* is addressing *Gloucester* with the more formal *you*, so I told my actor to speak differently, and so he did:

GLOUCESTER:

When shall I come to th'top of that same hill?

EDGAR:

You do climbe up it now. Look how we labor.

GLOUCESTER:

Me thinkes the ground is eeven.

EDGAR:

Horrible steepe.

Hearke, do you heare the Sea?

GLOUCESTER:

No truly.

EDGAR:

Why then your other Senses grow imperfect

By your eyes anguish.

And what he did not know was that *Gloucester*'s next line is:

GLOUCESTER:

So may it be indeed.

Me thinkes thy voyce is alter'd, and thou speak'st

In better phrase, and matter then thou did'st.

In other words, the change from *thee* to *you* was part of Shakespeare's precise plan to have *Edgar* appear different to blind *Gloucester*, and a reassuring proof that his use of these words was no accident or whim.

The Platt for the first 600 lines of The Two Gentlemen of Verona

An OSC Presentation for the Barbican Centre's "Everybody's Shakespeare" at 2:00 pm on Saturday 12th November, 1994

I-1: Enter Valentine and Proteus: (CALLUM COATES; DUNCAN LAW). Exit Valentine. Enter Speed: (ANNE ATKINS), the clownish servant to Valentine. Proteus gives him money. Exeunt.	II-1: Enter Valentine with a letter, and Speed with a glove. Enter Silvia: (VICKI ORMISTON), beloved of Valentine. Exit Silvia. Exeunt.
I-2: Enter Julia: (SONIA RITTER) and Lucetta: (SARAH FINCH), her waiting woman. Lucetta offers a letter to Julia. Exit Lucetta. Enter Lucetta, dropping and picking up the letter. Julia takes and tears the letter. Exit Lucetta. To Julia, Lucetta. Exeunt.	II-2: Enter Protheus and Julia. They exchange rings. Exit Julia suddenly. To Protheus, Panthino. Exeunt.
I-3: Enter Antonio father to Protheus, and Panthino: (KATE BESWICK; OLIVER SENTON). Enter Proteus with a letter. Exeunt Antonio and Panthino. Re-enter Panthino. Exeunt.	Book-Holder / Presenter CHRISTINE OZANNE / PATRICK TUCKER

I chose *The Two Gentlemen of Verona* because it has the reputation of being somewhat "difficult," with the comic exchanges at the start being very unfunny. To my—and I trust the audience's—delight the first scenes played brilliantly, getting huge reactions from the audience and giving us the determination to do the full play sometime. I had cast a woman as *Antonio*, but I found that although actresses work very well playing boys or youths, their playing men does not work so well.

There is a lovely little scene, when *Julia* is saying goodbye to *Protheus*, where there is no exit in the Folio script, and so the Editors send her off at the end of his *Julia, farewell*. But by playing the original:

PROTHEUS:
Why then wee'll make exchange;
Here, take you this.
JULIA:
And seale the bargaine with a holy kisse.
PROTHEUS:
Here is my hand, for my true constancie:
And when that howre ore-slips me in the day,
Wherein I sigh not (*Julia*) for thy sake,
The next ensuing howre, some foule mischance
Torment me for my Loves forgetfulnesse:
My father staies my comming: answere not:
The tide is now; nay, not thy tide of teares,
That tide will stay me longer then I should,
Julia, farewell: what, gon without a word?
I, so true love should doe: it cannot speake,
For truth hath better deeds, then words to grace it.
PANTHION:
Sir *Protheus*: you are staid for.
PROTHEUS:
Goe: I come, I come:
Alas, this parting strikes poore Lovers dumbe.
    EXEUNT.

She stands there, cannot speak, and really theatricalizes the *this parting strikes poore Lovers dumbe.*, and they go offstage without the comforting kiss and cuddle they frequently get, and the awkwardness of the two is echoed in what happens for the rest of the play.

For the play of *Hamlet*, the start is simple enough:

ENTER BARNARDO AND FRANCISCO TWO CENTINELS.

So since there was no "enter at one door, enter at another," which we know is printed elsewhere, I made sure that the two actors entered together. The result is surprising: the scene becomes very funny, as well as clearly setting up a situation where the actors cannot "see" one another, as good a way of convincing an audience watching in the midday sun that this is a night time, misty scene:

ENTER BARNARDO AND FRANCISCO TWO CENTINELS.

BARNARDO:

Who's there?

FRANCISCO:

Nay answer me: Stand and unfold your selfe.

BARNARDO:

Long live the King.

FRANCISCO:

Barnardo?

BARNARDO:

He.

FRANCISCO:

You come most carefully upon your houre.

BARNARDO:

'Tis now strook twelve, get thee to bed *Francisco.*

The two actors enter within a foot of one another, but they cannot see who is speaking.

Francisco can now come over to where *Barnardo* is standing.

𝕿𝖍𝖊 𝕻𝖑𝖆𝖙𝖙 𝖋𝖔𝖗 𝖙𝖍𝖊 𝖋𝖎𝖗𝖘𝖙 600 𝖑𝖎𝖓𝖊𝖘 𝖔𝖋 𝕿𝖍𝖊 𝕿𝖗𝖆𝖌𝖊𝖉𝖎𝖊 𝖔𝖋 𝕳𝖆𝖒𝖑𝖊𝖙

An OSC Presentation for the Barbican Centre's "Everybody's Shakespeare" at 2:00 pm on Sunday 13th November, 1994

I-1: Enter Barnardo and Francisco: (**BEN COLE; MARTIN MCGLADE**), two Centinels. Enter Horatio and Marcellus: (**PHILIP BIRD; CAMILLA EVANS**) to take the Watch. Exit Francisco. Enter Ghost: (**JOHN CATER**). Ghost is offended, and stalks away. Exit Ghost. Enter Ghost againe. The cocke crowes, Ghost starts at it. Exit Ghost. Exeunt.	I-3: Enter Laertes and Ophelia. To them, Polonius to give counsel. Exit Laertes. Exeunt.
I-2: Enter Claudius King of Denmark: (**RICHARD CORDERY**), Gertrude the Queene: (**GILLIAN MCCUTCHEON**), Hamlet (dressed in black): (**MICHAEL MALONEY**), Polonius, Laertes: (**NICHOLAS DAY; JONATHAN ROBY**), and his Sister Ophelia: (**KERRY OWEN**), Lords, Attendants: (). Enter to the Court, Voltemand and Cornelius as Ambassadors to Norway: (**NATASHA TAMAR; TESS DIGNAN**). Exeunt. Manet Hamlet. To him, Horatio, Barnardo, and Marcellus. Exeunt. Manet Hamlet. Exit Hamlet.	
	Book-Holder **CHRISTINE OZANNE**
	Presenter **PATRICK TUCKER**

FRANCISCO:

For this releefe much thankes: 'Tis bitter cold,

And I am sicke at heart.

BARNARDO:

Have you had quiet Guard?

FRANCISCO:

Not a Mouse stirring.

BARNARDO:

Well, goodnight. If you do meet *Horatio* and

Marcellus, the Rivals of my Watch, bid them make hast.

ENTER HORATIO AND MARCELLUS.

FRANCISCO:

I thinke I heare them. Stand: who's there?

The other two characters march onto the stage. Of course *Francisco* can hear them—the point is that he cannot see them and is not certain exactly where they are.

HORATIO:

Friends to this ground.

MARCELLUS:

And Leige-men to the Dane.

Their voices confirm they are friends.

FRANCISCO:

Give you good night.

MARCELLUS:

O farwel honest Soldier, who hath reliev'd you?

O farwel indicates that *Marcellus* is shouting into the gloom.

FRANCISCO:

Barnardo ha's my place: give you goodnight.

EXIT FRANCISCO.

MARCELLUS:

Holla *Barnardo*.

Another *Holla*, indication that he is shouting at those he cannot see.

BARNARDO:

Say, what is *Horatio* there?

HORATIO:

A peece of him.

He has heard the voice, but not yet seen him.

BARNARDO:

Welcome *Horatio*, welcome good *Marcellus*.

Now he is close enough to welcome them personally.

MARCELLUS:

What, ha's this thing appear'd againe to night.

BARNARDO:

I have seene nothing.

And played correctly, this gets a nice laugh, since he has in fact seen nothing from the start of proceedings, due to the theatrical darkness and mist.

I presented the beginnings of plays because the actors will have no more or less information doing these scenes than they would have doing the entire play, and also because I believe that Shakespeare being a very practical man of the theatre carefully defines each character when they first come on, so that the actor preparing the role has a good guide for the rest of the play.

Measure, For Measure (scenes), May 1995

Dr. Peter Holland of Cambridge University (and now Professor of The Shakespeare Institute in Stratford) had seen some of our presentations for *Everybody's Shakespeare* at the Barbican, and as a result in 1995 he asked us to give a presentation to the undergraduates studying English up at Cambridge. We devised a workshop that dealt with all the main *Isabella/Angelo/Claudio* scenes, interspersed with an explanation of how and why we worked in the original way. This went down so well, and got such an enthusiastic response from the students, that we went back there for the next five years, with differing casts, presenting the same material.

The scenes were particularly interesting, and threw up all sorts of ideas and interpretations. For example, in the scene where *Lucio* tells *Isabella* of her brother's plight, there is a nun present, *Francisca*:

ENTER ISABELL AND FRANCISCA A NUN.
ISABELLA:
And have you *Nuns* no farther priviledges?

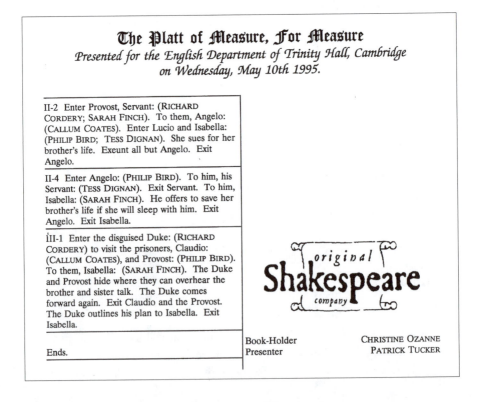

The Platt of Measure, For Measure
Presented for the English Department of Trinity Hall, Cambridge on Wednesday, May 10th 1995.

II-2 Enter Provost, Servant: (RICHARD CORDERY; SARAH FINCH). To them, Angelo: (CALLUM COATES). Enter Lucio and Isabella: (PHILIP BIRD; TESS DIGNAN). She sues for her brother's life. Exeunt all but Angelo. Exit Angelo.

II-4 Enter Angelo: (PHILIP BIRD). To him, his Servant: (TESS DIGNAN). Exit Servant. To him, Isabella: (SARAH FINCH). He offers to save her brother's life if she will sleep with him. Exit Angelo. Exit Isabella.

III-1 Enter the disguised Duke: (RICHARD CORDERY) to visit the prisoners, Claudio: (CALLUM COATES), and Provost: (PHILIP BIRD). To them, Isabella: (SARAH FINCH). The Duke and Provost hide where they can overhear the brother and sister talk. The Duke comes forward again. Exit Claudio and the Provost. The Duke outlines his plan to Isabella. Exit Isabella.

Ends.

original Shakespeare *company*

Book-Holder   CHRISTINE OZANNE
Presenter   PATRICK TUCKER

The Platt of Measure, For Measure

Presented for the English Department of Selwyn College, Cambridge on Wednesday, May 7th 1997.

I-1 Enter Vincentio Duke of Vienna, Escalus an ancient Lord: (), Lords: (). Enter Angelo, the Deputie: (). Exit Duke. Exeunt.

I-2 Enter Lucio a fantastique, and two other Gentlemen: (). Enter Mistres Over-don, a Bawd: (). Exeunt Lucio and two Gentlemen. Enter Pompey the Clowne: (). Exeunt.

I-3 Enter Provost, Claudio: (), Juliet: (), Officers, Lucio, second Gentleman. Exeunt.

I-4 Enter Duke and Frier Thomas: (). Exeunt.

I-5 Enter Isabella sister to Claudio and Francisca a Nun: (JENNIFER BURGESS; NATASHA TAMAR). Lucio calls from within: (JONATHAN ROBY). Enter Lucio. Exeunt.

II-1 Enter Angelo, Escalus, and servants, Justice: (). Enter Provost. Exit Provost. Enter Constable Elbow: () and Officers: () with Froth: () and the Clowne. Exit Angelo. Exit Froth. Exit the Clowne. Exeunt.

II-2 Enter Provost, Servant: (MICHAEL ELLIOTT; NATASHA TAMAR). To them, Angelo: (CALLUM COATES). Enter Lucio and Isabella: (JONATHAN ROBY; JENNIFER BURGESS). She sues for her brother's life. Exeunt all but Angelo. Exit Angelo.

II-3 Enter Duke (disguised) and Provost. Enter Juliet: (). Exit Duke. Exeunt.

II-4 Enter Angelo: (CALLUM COATES). To him, his Servant: (JENNIFER BURGESS). Exit Servant. To him, Isabella: (NATASHA TAMAR). He offers to save her brother's life if she will sleep with him. Exit Angelo. Exit Isabella.

III-1 Enter the disguised Duke, Claudio: (MICHAEL ELLIOTT; JONATHAN ROBY), and Provost: (CALLUM COATES). To them, Isabella: (NATASHA TAMAR). The Duke and Provost hide where they can overhear the brother and sister talk. The Duke comes forward again. Exit Claudio and the Provost. The Duke outlines his plan to Isabella. ENDS. *Exit Isabella. Enter Elbow, Clowne, Officers. Enter Lucio. Exeunt Elbow, Clowne, Officers. Exit Lucio. Enter Escalus, Provost, Mistresse Overdone with Officers. Exeunt Officers with Mistresse Overdone. Exeunt Escalus and Provost. Exit Duke.*

Interval

IV-1 Enter Mariana, and Boy singing: (). Enter Duke. Enter Isabella. Exit Mariana with Boy. Enter Mariana. Exit Isabella and Mariana. Enter Isabella and Mariana. Exeunt.

IV-2 Enter Provost with warrant and the Clowne. Enter Abhorson the executioner: (). Exit Provost. Enter Provost. Exit Abhorson and the Clowne. Enter Claudio. Exit Claudio. Enter the disguised Duke. Enter a Messenger with a letter: (). Exit Messenger. Exeunt.

IV-3 Enter Clowne. To him, Abhorson. Barnadine calls from within: (). Enter Barnadine. Enter the disguised Duke. Exit Barnadine, enter Provost. Exeunt Abhorson and the Clowne. Exit Provost. To the Duke, Provost with the head of Ragozine. Exit Provost. Isabella calls from within. To them, Isabella. To them, Lucio. Exeunt.

IV-4 Enter Angelo and Escalus. Exit Escalus. Exit Angelo.

IV-5 Enter Duke with letters and Frier Peter: (). To them, Varrius: (). Exeunt.

IV-6 Enter Isabella and Mariana. Enter Frier Peter. Exeunt.

V-1 Enter Duke, Varrius, Lords: () at one doore, Angelo, Escalus, Lucio, Citizens: () at another. Enter Frier Peter and Isabella. Exit Isabella guarded. Enter Mariana veiled. Exit the Duke. Enter the Duke disguised with Provost, Isabella. Exeunt Provost, Frier Peter, Angelo and Mariana. Enter the married Angelo and Mariana, Frier Peter, Provost. Exit Provost. Enter Provost with Barnadine, Claudio muffled, Julietta. Claudio is uncovered.

Finis.

Shakespeare *original* company

Presenter: PATRICK TUCKER
Book-Holder: CHRISTINE OZANNE

FRANCISCA:

Are not these large enough?

ISABELLA:

Yes truely; I speake not as desiring more,

But rather wishing a more strict restraint

Upon the Sisterhood, the Votarists of Saint *Clare*.

LUCIO WITHIN.

LUCIO:

Hoa? peace be in this place.

ISABELLA:

Who's that which cals?

FRANCISCA:

It is a mans voice: gentle *Isabella*

Turne you the key, and know his businesse of him;

You may; I may not: you are yet unsworne:

When you have vowd, you must not speake with men,

But in the presence of the *Prioresse*;

Then if you speake, you must not show your face;

Or if you show your face, you must not speake:

He cals againe: I pray you answere him.

ISABELLA:

Peace and prosperitie: who is't that cals?

ENTER LUCIO.

LUCIO:

Haile Virgin, (if you be) as those cheeke-Roses

Proclaime you are no lesse: can you so steed me,

As bring me to the sight of *Isabella*,

A Novice of this place, and the faire Sister

To her unhappie brother *Claudio*?

ISABELLA:

Why her unhappy Brother? Let me aske,

The rather for I now must make you know

I am that *Isabella*, and his Sister.

The novice nun *Isabella* is allowed to speak to men, but *Francisca* says that she herself can only speak in the presence of the Prioresse, or with her face obscured. Editors send her off when *Lucio* arrives, but this instruction to be mute adds wonderful drama to the scene, as she <u>wants</u> to speak out against *Lucio*'s bawdy language but <u>cannot</u> under the very rules she herself has just espoused. This is yet another example where the stage instructions in the original lead to a more interesting scene than those adjusted by others' hands.

The scenes with *Angelo* and *Isabella* played wonderfully each time we did them, always with different actors. One student felt that *Isabella* was being played far too knowingly for an innocent nun, but then her lines are:

ISABELLA:
    As much for my poore Brother, as my selfe;
    That is: were I under the tearmes of death,
    Th'impression of keene whips, I'ld weare as Rubies,
    And strip my selfe to death, as to a bed,
    That longing have bin sicke for, ere I'ld yeeld
    My body up to shame.

As the actress pointed out, she has to create the character who wants and needs to say those particular lines, not worry about what a supposed novice nun would feel or say.

Another student was amazed how well a scene between *Angelo* and *Isabella* had been staged, since she knew that there had been no rehearsal or direction and the actors did not know what the other character was going to say. "How did you know to make that big move away from her at that particular moment?" she asked Philip. "Ah, well," he said, "that was the moment when I changed from calling her *thee* to *you*, so I started the speech with *thee*, moved to *you*, went back to *thee*—and then kept getting closer to her each *thee* until I changed again, and then made a huge gap between us for the final *you*." She and the rest of the audience were duly impressed:

ANGELO:
    Who will beleeve thee *Isabell*?
    My unsoild name, th'austeerenesse of my life,
    My vouch against you, and my place i'th State,
    Will so your accusation over-weigh,
    That you shall stifle in your owne report,
    And smell of calumnie. I have begun,
    And now I give my sensuall race, the reine,
    Fit thy consent to my sharpe appetite,
    Lay by all nicetie, and prolixious blushes
    That banish what they sue for: Redeeme thy brother,
    By yeelding up thy bodie to my will,
    Or else he must not onelie die the death,
    But thy unkindnesse shall his death draw out
    To lingring sufferance: Answer me to morrow,
    Or by the affection that now guides me most,
    Ile prove a Tirant to him. As for you,
    Say what you can; my false, ore-weighs your true.

I dealt with the *Isabella/Claudio* scene in the *As He Liked It* performance notes, and I deal with the *Isabella/Angelo* meeting in the IAMBIC PENTAMETERS section. The students each time we have gone to Cambridge (and to the end of 2000 that is six visits) have always been rigorous in their questions, but found no difficulty in accepting the basic premises on which the work is built. One question that cropped up several times is "What happens at the end of the play? Does *Isabella* go off with the *Duke* or not?" The answer I give is always the same—look at the text, the original text:

DUKE:

    If he be like your brother, for his sake
    Is he pardon'd, and for your lovelie sake
    Give me your hand, and say you will be mine,
    He is my brother too: But fitter time for that:
    By this Lord *Angelo* perceives he's safe,
    Methinkes I see a quickning in his eye:
    Well *Angelo*, your evill quits you well.
    Looke that you love your wife: her worth, worth yours
    I finde an apt remission in my selfe:
    And yet heere's one in place I cannot pardon,
    You sirha, that knew me for a foole, a Coward,
    One all of Luxurie, an asse, a mad man:
    Wherein have I so deserv'd of you
    That you extoll me thus?

Now *Isabella* would have prepared her role from her Cue Script, which ends well <u>before</u> this speech, so she has no information as to what to do when the *Duke* offers her his hand. The end of her Cue Script looks like this:

CUE SCRIPT FOR ISABELLA

_____ at your service.

Oh give me pardon
That I, your vassaile, have imploid, and pain'd
Your unknowne Soveraigntie.

_____ is your Brother.

      ENTER ANGELO, MARIA, PETER, PROVOST.

I doe my Lord.

_____ for *Claudio*'s death.

Most bounteous Sir.
Looke if it please you, on this man condemn'd,
As if my Brother liv'd: I partly thinke,

A due sinceritie governed his deedes,
Till he did looke on me: Since it is so,
Let him not die: my Brother had but Justice,
In that he did the thing for which he dide.
For *Angelo*, his Act did not ore-take his bad intent,
And must be buried but as an intent
That perish'd by the way: thoughts are no subjects
Intents, but meerely thoughts.

_____ you all should know.
    FINIS.

So when she is propositioned, she literally does not know what to do. Could Shakespeare have made her reply unambiguous? (*I will, my Lord, consent to be thy bride*; or: *Why nay, my Lord, I must not marry you*), but he <u>did not</u>. Here is the last speech of the play, as printed in the Folio:

DUKE:
    Slandering a Prince deserves it.
    She *Claudio* that you wrong'd, looke you restore.
    Joy to you *Mariana*, love her *Angelo*:
    I have confes'd her, and I know her vertue.
    Thanks good friend, *Escalus*, for thy much goodnesse,
    There's more behinde that is more gratulate.
    Thanks *Provost* for thy care, and secrecie,
    We shall imploy thee in a worthier place.
    Forgive him *Angelo*, that brought you home
    The head of *Ragozine* for *Claudio's*,
    Th'offence pardons it selfe. Deere *Isabell*,
    I have a motion much imports your good,
    Whereto if you'll a willing eare incline;
    What's mine is yours, and what is yours is mine.
    So bring us to our Pallace, where wee'll show
    What's yet behinde, that meete you all should know.
    FINIS.

So *Isabella* is again propositioned by the *Duke*, again she has no information as to what to do, and is it a coincidence that there is <u>no</u> *EXEUNT* at the end? I believe that this is intentional, that the uncertainty is a deliberate choice by Shakespeare to leave the question unresolved, so that the audience is left with the moral dilemma of the play. *Isabella*, as an actress not knowing what to do, is exactly what is required, and Shakespeare does here what he does often elsewhere, putting the actor into the same situation as the character, so that the actor's natural reactions will also be the truthful ones for that character (the same happens to *Jessica* when no one will talk to her in *The Merchant of Venice*).

To "solve" a problem of a play, which we directors often think is our function, can ruin the very effect that was intended. Heady stuff indeed.

The Two Gentlemen of Verona (abridged), June 1995

It is an indictment of the English theatre scene that the next organization to pay for us to perform was again a German one: this time the Detmold Shakespeare Festival, in the depths of Germany. By now, I had started to receive pressure, from both my actors and from venues, to put presentations on for nothing. It is called profit share, but the result would be that the actors would receive very little or nothing at all. I felt that the stress on actors was bad enough, and that the stress of doing a Cue Script production, with all the necessary homework of learning and working on the lines by oneself, required remuneration. I had decided therefore that we would put on productions only when we could reward the actors—and Christine and myself—since the workload was spreading, and organizing the Company, running workshops to find new actors, planning a visit, and servicing a play were taking up a lot of unpaid time.

When we got to Detmold, we found that we were to put the play on in a park, and we assembled the stage underneath a canopy thoughtfully provided in case of rain. Our actors complained that they felt shut in, so we dragged the stage forward so that only the back part was under the cover, where they could act if it was raining, and that the downstage part was out in the open. This actors' instinct was part of the quarrel we were all to have with the academics who decreed that the whole of the new Shakespeare's Globe stage should be under the huge canopy that forced the use of downstage pillars there. I shall talk of this later.

The performance itself was a confirmation of our previous performance of the first part, since the comic pieces, even for a German audience, played well—even with the actors coming offstage still not knowing what it was they had done or why they had said what. They were getting useful information from the text, such as the exchange between *Julia* and her maid *Lucetta*:

JULIA:
    What thinkst thou of the faire sir *Eglamoure*?   She uses *thou* to her maidservant.

LUCETTA:
    As of a Knight, well-spoken, neat, and fine;
    But were I you, he never should be mine.   The reply is *you*.

JULIA:
    What think'st thou of the rich *Mercatio*?   She still uses *thou*.

LUCETTA:
    Well of his wealth; but of himselfe, so, so.

JULIA:

What think'st thou of the gentle *Protheus*?

LUCETTA:

Lord, Lord: to see what folly raignes in us.

JULIA:

How now? what meanes this passion at his name?

The Platt of The Two Gentlemen of Verona

Presented for the Detmold Shakespeare Festival
on Saturday, June 10th 1995 at 5:30 pm.

I-1: Enter Valentine and Protheus: (SCOTT AINSLIE; DUNCAN LAW). Exit Valentine. Enter Speed: (ANNE ATKINS), the clownish servant to Valentine. Protheus gives him money. Exeunt.

I-2: Enter Julia: (JULIETTE GRASSBY) and Lucetta: (SARAH FINCH), her waiting woman. Lucetta offers a letter to Julia. Exit Lucetta. Enter Lucetta, dropping and picking up the letter. Julia takes and tears the letter. Exit Lucetta. To Julia, Lucetta. Exeunt.

I-3: Enter Antonio father to Protheus: (LEWIS HANCOCK), and his servant Panthino: (EDMUND DEHN). Enter Protheus with a letter from Julia. Exeunt Antonio and Panthino. Re-enter Panthino. Exeunt.

II-1: Enter Valentine with a letter written for Silvia, and Speed with a glove. Enter Silvia: (NATASHA TAMAR), beloved of Valentine. Exit Silvia. Exeunt.

II-2: Enter Protheus, Julia and Panthino. Protheus and Julia exchange rings. Exeunt.

II-3: Enter Launce the clownish servant to Protheus: (PHILIP BIRD), with his dog, Crab. To him, Panthino. Exeunt.

II-4: Enter Valentine, Silvia, Thurio: (LEWIS HANCOCK) a foolish rival to Valentine, and Speed. Enter Duke: (EDMUND DEHN), father to Silvia. Exit Duke. Enter Protheus. Exeunt Silvia and Thurio. Exeunt Valentine and Speed. Exit Protheus.

II-5: Enter Speed and Launce, with his dog. Exeunt.

II-6: Enter Protheus solus. Exit.

II-7: Enter Julia and Lucetta. Exeunt.

III-1: *Enter Duke, Thurio, and Protheus. Exit Thurio. Exit Protheus. Enter Valentine. The Duke discovers a letter and cord ladder under Valentine's cloak. Exit Duke. Enter Protheus and Launce. Exeunt Protheus and Valentine. To Launce, Speed. Exit Speed running. Exit Launce.*

Interval

III-2: *Enter Duke and Thurio. Enter Protheus. Exeunt.*

IV-1: *Enter Valentine, Speed, and certaine Out-lawes: (   ). Exeunt.*

IV-2: *Enter Protheus. Enter Thurio and Musicians: (   ). Enter Host: (   ) where Julia lodges, and Julia disguised as a boy. Song: Who is Silvia? Exeunt Thurio and Musicians. Enter Silvia. Exeunt Protheus and Silvia. Exeunt Julia and Host.*

IV-3: *Enter Eglamoure: (   ), agent for Silvia in her escape. Enter Silvia. Exeunt.*

IV-4: *Enter Launce with his dog. Enter Protheus and Julia disguised as Sebastian. Exit Launce. Prothues gives Julia a ring, and a letter. Exit Protheus. Enter Silvia, and Ursula: (   ) carrying a Picture. Silvia gives the Picture to Julia. Julia gives first one, then another letter to Silvia, which she tears. Silvia gives Julia a purse, and exits with Ursula. Exit Julia.*

V-1: *Enter Eglamoure. Enter Silvia. Exeunt.*

V-2: *Enter Thurio, Protheus and Julia. Enter Duke. Exeunt.*

V-3: *Enter Silvia and Out-lawes. Exeunt.*

V-4: *Enter Valentine. Enter Protheus, Silvia and Julia. Julia faints, then gives Protheus' ring to Protheus, and shows the one he sent to Silvia. Julia reveals herself. Enter Out-lawes, with Duke and Thurio. Exeunt.*

Finis.

original
Shakespeare
company

Costumes	ELLIE COCKERILL
Book-Holder	CHRISTINE OZANNE
Presenter	PATRICK TUCKER

LUCETTA:

Pardon deare Madam, 'tis a passing shame,

That I (unworthy body as I am)

Should censure thus on lovely Gentlemen.

JULIA:

Why not on *Protheus*, as of all the rest?

The Platt of The Two Gentlemen of Verona
Presented for the Detmold Shakespeare Festival
on Saturday, June 10th 1995 at 8:30 pm.

I-1: Enter Valentine and Protheus: (SCOTT AINSLIE; DUNCAN LAW). Exit Valentine. Enter Speed: (ANNE ATKINS), the clownish servant to Valentine. Protheus gives him money. Exeunt.

I-2: Enter Julia: (JULIETTE GRASSBY) and Lucetta: (NATASHA TAMAR), her waiting woman. Lucetta offers a letter to Julia. Exit Lucetta. Enter Lucetta, dropping and picking up the letter. Julia takes and tears the letter. Exit Lucetta. To Julia, Lucetta. Exeunt.

I-3: Enter Antonio father to Protheus: (EDMUND DEHN), and his servant Panthino: (LEWIS HANCOCK). Enter Protheus with a letter from Julia. Exeunt Antonio and Panthino. Re-enter Panthino. Exeunt.

II-1: Enter Valentine with a letter written for Silvia, and Speed with a glove. Enter Silvia: (SARAH FINCH), beloved of Valentine. Exit Silvia. Exeunt.

II-2: Enter Protheus, Julia and Panthino. Protheus and Julia exchange rings. Exeunt.

II-3: Enter Launce the clownish servant to Protheus: (PHILIP BIRD), with his dog, Crab. To him, Panthino. Exeunt.

II-4: Enter Valentine, Silvia, Thurio: (EDMUND DEHN) a foolish rival to Valentine, and Speed. Enter Duke: (LEWIS HANCOCK), father to Silvia. Exit Duke. Enter Protheus. Exeunt Silvia and Thurio. Exeunt Valentine and Speed. Exit Protheus.

II-5: Enter Speed and Launce, with his dog. Exeunt.

II-6: Enter Protheus solus. Exit.

II-7: Enter Julia and Lucetta. Exeunt.

III-1: *Enter Duke, Thurio, and Protheus. Exit Thurio. Exit Protheus. Enter Valentine. The Duke discovers a letter and cord ladder under Valentine's cloak. Exit Duke. Enter Protheus and Launce. Exeunt Protheus and Valentine. To Launce, Speed. Exit Speed running. Exit Launce.*

Interval

III-2: *Enter Duke and Thurio. Enter Protheus. Exeunt.*

IV-1: *Enter Valentine, Speed, and certaine Outlawes: (   ). Exeunt.*

IV-2: *Enter Protheus. Enter Thurio and Musicians: (   ). Enter Host: (   ) where Julia lodges, and Julia disguised as a boy. Song: Who is Silvia? Exeunt Thurio and Musicians. Enter Silvia. Exeunt Protheus and Silvia. Exeunt Julia and Host.*

IV-3: *Enter Eglamoure: (   ), agent for Silvia in her escape. Enter Silvia. Exeunt.*

IV-4: *Enter Launce with his dog. Enter Protheus and Julia disguised as Sebastian. Exit Launce. Prothues gives Julia a ring, and a letter. Exit Protheus. Enter Silvia, and Ursula: (   ) carrying a Picture. Silvia gives the Picture to Julia. Julia gives first one, then another letter to Silvia, which she tears. Silvia gives Julia a purse, and exits with Ursula. Exit Julia.*

V-1: *Enter Eglamoure. Enter Silvia. Exeunt.*

V-2: *Enter Thurio, Protheus and Julia. Enter Duke. Exeunt.*

V-3: *Enter Silvia and Out-lawes. Exeunt.*

V-4: *Enter Valentine. Enter Protheus, Silvia and Julia. Julia faints, then gives Protheus' ring to Protheus, and shows the one he sent to Silvia. Julia reveals herself. Enter Out-lawes, with Duke and Thurio. Exeunt.*

Finis.

original
Shakespeare
company

Costumes	ELLIE COCKERILL
Book-Holder	CHRISTINE OZANNE
Presenter	PATRICK TUCKER

LUCETTA:

Then thus: of many good, I thinke him best.

JULIA:

Your reason?

Suddenly *Julia* changes to the
more formal *your*.

LUCETTA:

I have no other but a womans reason:

I thinke him so, because I thinke him so.

JULIA:

And would'st thou have me cast my love on him?   Now she is back to *thou*.

In a similar way, *Julia* had all the information she needed to know how to do the letter-tearing scene, where all the stage instructions are written in for her:

JULIA:

This babble shall not henceforth trouble me;

Here is a coile with protestation:

Goe, get you gone: and let the papers lye:

You would be fingring them, to anger me.

LUCETTA:

She makes it strange, but she would be best pleas'd

To be so angred with another Letter.

   EXIT LUCETTA.

JULIA:

Nay, would I were so angred with the same:

Oh hatefull hands, to teare such loving words;

Injurious Waspes, to feede on such sweet hony,

And kill the Bees that yeelde it, with your stings;

Ile kisse each severall paper, for amends:

Looke, here is writ, kinde *Julia*: unkinde *Julia*,

As in revenge of thy ingratitude,

I throw thy name against the bruzing-stones,

Trampling contemptuously on thy disdaine,

And here is writ, *Love wounded Protheus.*

Poore wounded name: my bosome, as a bed,

Shall lodge thee till thy wound be throughly heal'd;

And thus I search it with a soveraigne kisse.

But twice, or thrice, was *Protheus* written downe:

Be calme (good winde) blow not a word away,

Till I have found each letter, in the Letter,

Except mine own name: That, some whirle-winde beare

Unto a ragged, fearefull, hanging Rocke,

And throw it thence into the raging Sea.

Loe, here in one line is his name twice writ:
Poore forlorne Protheus, passionate Protheus:
To the sweet Julia: that ile teare away:
And yet I will not, sith so prettily
He couples it, to his complaining Names;
Thus will I fold them, one upon another;
Now kisse, embrace, contend, doe what you will.

The dreadful modern concept that good acting needs a total understanding of the whole situation and a detailed knowledge of all the interactions that can happen on a stage was completely disproved by the audience response and their understanding of what was going on. To know that the actors do not grasp all the inner workings only upsets certain strands of the theatrical profession, who take it almost as a religious belief that certain tenets must be followed.

I find that must is a small-minded response, since all sorts of actors through the ages have acted from different perspectives: some great actors understand everything, some great actors are bears of very little brain; some actors are amazingly understanding and analytical of their roles, and yet in front of the audience bore for the world. There seems to be no absolute link between internal processes and what is perceived and enjoyed by an audience, which leaves a lot of the fanatical Method devotees very upset. Once an American actress, in tears, accused me of undermining everything she had ever learned or believed about acting for twenty years. "But it works" was met with "That's not the point"; but actually that is the point, and the true philosophy I find for acting is "Whatever works."

The third Part of Henry the Sixt (scenes) and Macbeth (scenes), September 1995

The Globe was getting a lot of resistance to the stage, pillars, and canopy they had come up with, so it was decided to hold a series of presentations on a rough approximation of the stage and pillars. At long last the acting community could get a chance to try out this rather strange configuration and give the project the benefit of its input.

We presented the first part of *The third Part of Henry the Sixt* on a Friday, and on the Saturday the first part of *Macbeth*, using mostly the same actors.

The third Part of Henry the Sixt was a revelation in being very dramatic, fast paced, and funny. The staging all worked well, as my actors were now fully versed in one of the basic discoveries of nondirected productions: always cross over to the person you are speaking to, with the exception that a king is allowed to stay on his throne and make them come to him.

The debate between the two factions at the beginning was very clear for all to understand, and *Henry*'s response to his predicament was revealing:

FLOURISH. ENTER KING HENRY, CLIFFORD, NORTHUMBERLAND, WESTMERLAND,
EXETER, AND THE REST.

HENRY:

My Lords, looke where the sturdie Rebell sits,

Even in the Chayre of State: belike he meanes

Backt by the power of *Warwicke*, that false Peere,

To aspire unto the Crowne, and reigne as King.

Earle of Northumberland, he slew thy Father,

And thine, Lord *Clifford*, and you both have vow'd revenge

On him, his sonnes, his favorites, and his friends.

NORTHUMBERLAND:

If I be not, Heavens be reveng'd on me.

CLIFFORD:

The hope thereof, makes *Clifford* mourne in

Steele.

WESTMERLAND:

What, shall we suffer this: lets pluck him down,

The Platt of The third Part of Henry the Sixt
Presented for the Shakespeare's Globe Theatre Workshop Season
at 2:30 pm on Friday 8th September, 1995

I-1: Alarum. Enter Richard Plantagenet Duke of Yorke, his sons Edward and Richard: (NICHOLAS DAY; MARK R. BURGESS; SONIA RITTER), Norfolke, Mountague, Warwicke: (ROGER RINGROSE; SIMON PURSE; RICHARD CORDERY), and Yorke Souldiers: (S.AINSLIE; H.BARKER; L.DOHERTY; G.GRIZZARD; V.ORMISTON; S.WOODFIELD). Richard shows the severed head of Somerset. Plantagenet attended goes up to sit in the throne. Flourish. Enter King Henry, Clifford, Northumberland, Westmerland, Exeter: (GRAHAM POUNTNEY; CALLUM COATES; DUNCAN LAW; LEWIS HANCOCK; EDMUND DEHN), and the Lancaster Souldiers: (A.ATKINS; J.BURGESS; H.JACKSON; C.JONES; B.MUSTON; N.TAMAR). Warwicke stamps with his foot, and the Souldiers shew themselves. Exit Westmerland, then Northumberland, then Clifford. Senet. They come downe from the throne. Exeunt with their soldiers Yorke and his Sons, Warwicke, and Mountague. Enter the Queene and Prince: (JUDITH PARIS; SARAH FINCH). Exeunt Queene and Prince. Exeunt.

I-2: Flourish. Enter Richard, Edward, and Mountague. To them the Duke of Yorke. Enter Gabriel: (CAMILLA EVANS). Exit Mountague. Enter Mortimer and his Brother: (KATE BESWICK; GILLIAN McCUTCHEON). A March afarre off. Alarum. Exeunt.

I-3: Enter Rutland, and his Tutor: (JONATHAN ROBY; HUGH WALTERS). Enter Clifford and Lancaster Soldiers. Exit Tutor. Clifford kills Rutland. Exeunt.

I-4: Alarum. Enter Richard, Duke of Yorke. A short Alarum within. Enter the Queene, Clifford, Northumberland, the young Prince, and Lancaster Souldiers. They hold Yorke. The Queene puts a paper crown on his head. Clifford and the Queene kill him. Flourish. Exeunt.

II-1: A March. Enter Edward, Richard and their Yorke Souldiers. Enter one blowing: (SCOTT AINSLIE). March. ENDS.

Music	
Book-Holder	BARBARA MUSTON
Presenter	CHRISTINE OZANNE
	PATRICK TUCKER

My heart for anger burnes, I cannot brooke it.

HENRY:

Be patient, gentle Earle of Westmerland.

CLIFFORD:

Patience is for Poultroones, such as he:

He durst not sit there, had your Father liv'd.

My gracious Lord, here in the Parliament

Let us assayle the Family of *Yorke*.

NORTHUMBERLAND:

Well hast thou spoken, Cousin be it so.

HENRY:

Ah, know you not the Citie favours them,

And they have troupes of Souldiers at their beck?

WESTMERLAND:

But when the Duke is slaine, they'le quickly

flye.

The Platt of The third Part of Henry the Sixt

Presented for the Shakespeare's Globe Theatre Workshop Season at 4:00 pm on Sunday 8th October, 1995

I-1: Alarum. Enter Richard Plantagenet Duke of Yorke, his sons Edward and Richard: (NICHOLAS DAY; BARBARA MUSTON; SONIA RITTER), Norfolke, Mountague, Warwicke: (SIMON PURSE; DUNCAN LAW; ROGER RINGROSE), and Yorke Souldiers: (S.AINSLIE; D.ANGUS; H.BARKER; J.BURGESS; G.DEPOLNAY; N.HUTCHISON; S.WOODFIELD) Richard shows the severed head of Somerset. Plantagenet attended goes up to sit in the throne. Flourish. Enter King Henry, Clifford, Northumberland, Westmerland, Exeter: (GRAHAM POUNTNEY; CALLUM COATES; PHILIP BIRD; LEWIS HANCOCK; EDMUND DEHN), and the Lancaster Souldiers: (A.ATKINS; B.COLE; S.DENY JONES; D.HOPKINS; D.JARVIS; C.JONES; N.TAMAR). Warwicke stamps with his foot, and the Souldiers shew themselves. Exit Westmerland, then Northumberland, then Clifford. Senet. They come downe from the throne. Exeunt with their soldiers Yorke and his Sons, Warwicke, and Mountague. Enter the Queene and Prince: (JUDITH PARIS; SARAH FINCH). Exeunt Queene and Prince. Exeunt.

I-2: Flourish. Enter Richard, Edward, and Mountague. To them the Duke of Yorke. Enter Gabriel: (CAMILLA EVANS). Exit Mountague. Enter Mortimer and his Brother: (KATE BESWICK; GREGORY DE POLNAY). A March afarre off. Alarum. Exeunt.

I-3: Enter Rutland, and his Tutor: (JONATHAN ROBY; HUGH WALTERS). Enter Clifford and Lancaster Soldiers. Exit Tutor. Clifford kills Rutland. Exeunt.

I-4: Alarum. Enter Richard, Duke of Yorke. A short Alarum within. Enter the Queene, Clifford, Northumberland, the young Prince, and Lancaster Souldiers. They hold Yorke. The Queene puts a paper crown on his head. Clifford and the Queene kill him. Flourish. Exeunt.

II-1: A March. ENDS.

Music	BARBARA MUSTON
Book-Holder	CHRISTINE OZANNE
Presenter	PATRICK TUCKER

HENRY:

> Farre be the thought of this from *Henries* heart,
> To make a Shambles of the Parliament House.
> Cousin of Exeter, frownes, words, and threats,
> Shall be the Warre that *Henry* meanes to use.
> Thou factious Duke of Yorke descend my Throne,
> And kneele for grace and mercie at my feet,
> I am thy Soveraigne.

YORKE:

> I am thine.

After *Northumberland's* line *Well hast thou spoken, Cousin be it so.*, *Henry's* wonderful reply of *Ah* (<u>not</u> *Oh*) gave him his consistent weak character and ineffectiveness. Later on in the piece, when the young *Rutland* was murdered, there was an audible "Ahhh" from the audience, a first inkling that this wonderful acting space had a different actor/audience relationship built into it.

The great set piece of *Queene Margaret* and *Yorke* was quite splendid, with each having to react on the spot to what the other said, and it gave a tremendous vitality and immediacy to the struggle, and poignancy to *Yorke's* murder.

The *Henry the Sixt* plays deal with the Wars of the Roses, between the Houses of Lancaster and Yorke, and the relationships and arguments of the time can be a little confusing; I have therefore prepared a Genealogical Table for these History plays; see Appendix 2.

The first part of *Macbeth* was fascinating in being nondirected, and so the effects were those arising from the text, not from a concept.

At the beginning, the *Captaine* has a speech with several half-lines:

> *ALARUM WITHIN.*
> *ENTER KING, MALCOLME, DONALBAINE, LENOX, WITH*
> *ATTENDANTS, MEETING A BLEEDING CAPTAINE.*

KING:

> What bloody man is that? he can report,
> As seemeth by his plight, of the Revolt
> The newest state.

MALCOLME:

> This is the Serjeant,
> Who like a good and hardie Souldier fought
> 'Gainst my Captivitie: Haile brave friend;
> Say to the King, the knowledge of the Broyle,
> As thou didst leave it.

CAPTAINE:

> Doubtfull it stood,

As two spent Swimmers, that doe cling together,
And choake their Art: The mercilesse *Macdonwald*
(Worthie to be a Rebell, for to that
The multiplying Villanies of Nature
Doe swarme upon him) from the Westerne Isles
Of Kernes and Gallowgrosses is supply'd,
And Fortune on his damned Quarry smiling,
Shew'd like a Rebells Whore: but all's too weake:
For brave *Macbeth* (well hee deserves that Name)
Disdayning Fortune, with his brandisht Steele,
Which smoak'd with bloody execution
(Like Valours Minion) carv'd out his passage,
Till hee fac'd the Slave: A half-line.
Which nev'r shooke hands, nor bad farwell to him,
Till he unseam'd him from the Nave to th'Chops,
And fix'd his Head upon our Battlements.

The Platt of The Tragedie of Macbeth

Presented for the Shakespeare's Globe Theatre Workshop Season at 6:30 pm on Saturday 9th September, 1995

I-1: Thunder and Lightning. Enter three Witches: (CAROLYN JONES; JUDITH PARIS; GILLIAN MCCUTCHEON). Exeunt.

I-2: Alarum within. Enter King Duncan and his sons Malcolme, Donalbaine: (HUGH WALTERS; JONATHAN ROBY; GIGI GRIZZARD), Lenox: DUNCAN LAW), with attendants: (E.DEHN; S.FINCH; H.JACKSON; S.PURSE; R.RINGROSE; S.WOODFIELD), meeting a bleeding Captaine: (LEWIS HANCOCK). Enter Rosse and Angus: (PHILIP BIRD; SCOTT AINSLIE). Exeunt.

I-3: Thunder. Enter the three Witches. Drum within. Enter Macbeth and Banquo: (RICHARD CORDERY; CALLUM COATES). The Witches vanish. To Macbeth, Rosse and Angus. Exeunt.

I-4: Flourish. Enter King, Lenox, Malcolme, Donalbaine, and Attendants. Enter Macbeth, Banquo, Rosse, and Angus. Exit Macbeth. Flourish. Exeunt.

I-5: Enter Macbeth's Wife alone with a Letter: (SONIA RITTER). Enter a Messenger: (NATASHA TAMAR). Exit Messenger. Enter Macbeth. Exeunt.

I-6: Hoboyes, and Torches: (K.BESWICK; C.EVANS; J.HOPTON; V.ORMISTON). Enter King, Malcolme, Donalbaine, Banquo, Lenox, Macduff: (BARBARA MUSTON), Rosse, Angus, and Attendants. Enter Lady Macbeth, to welcome them to their Castle. Exeunt.

I-7: Hoboyes. Torches. Enter a Sewer, and divers Servants with Dishes and Service over the Stage: (H.BARKER; M.R.BURGESS; B.COLE). Then enter Macbeth. Enter Lady Macbeth. Exeunt.

II-1: Enter Banquo, and Fleance: (LOUISE DOHERTY), with a Torch before him: (J.HOPTON). Enter Macbeth, and a Servant with a Torch: (V.ORMISTON). Exit Banquo and Fleance. Exit Servant. A Bell rings. Exit Macbeth, to kill the King.

II-2: Enter Lady Macbeth. Enter Macbeth with the bloody daggers. Exit Lady Macbeth with the daggers. Knocke within. Enter Lady Macbeth with bloody hands. Knockes. Exeunt. ENDS.

Shakespeare *original* company

Music	BARBARA MUSTON
Book-Holder	CHRISTINE OZANNE
Presenter	PATRICK TUCKER

KING:

O valiant Cousin, worthy Gentleman.

CAPTAINE:

As whence the Sunne 'gins his reflection,
Shipwracking Stormes, and direfull Thunders:
So from that Spring, whence comfort seem'd to come,
Discomfort swells: Marke King of Scotland, marke,
No sooner Justice had, with Valour arm'd,
Compell'd these skipping Kernes to trust their heeles,
But the Norweyan Lord, surveying vantage,
With furbisht Armes, and new supplyes of men,
Began a fresh assault.

KING:

Dismay'd not this our Captaines, *Macbeth* and
Banquoh?

CAPTAINE:

Yes, as Sparrowes, Eagles;
Or the Hare, the Lyon:
If I say sooth, I must report they were
As Cannons over-charg'd with double Cracks,
So they doubly redoubled stroakes upon the Foe:
Except they meant to bathe in reeking Wounds,
Or memorize another *Golgotha*,
I cannot tell: but I am faint,
My Gashes cry for helpe.

> Starting a speech with <u>two</u> half-lines means there must be a pause somewhere.

> Another half-line.

KING:

So well thy words become thee, as thy wounds,
They smack of Honor both: Goe get him Surgeons.

Lewis Hancock, playing the *Captaine*, had the acting problem of justifying the half-lines: Was it that he was in awe of the King? Was he losing consciousness? Was he pausing for effect. In the end, he chose fainting from wounds, and it worked well—but was alarmingly funny.

Other parts of the play became much funnier than expected, even in some of the soliloquies. In particular, there is the stage instruction at the entrance of *Duncan* at *Macbeth*'s castle:

HOBOYES, AND TORCHES. ENTER KING, MALCOLME, DONALBAINE,
BANQUO, LENOX, MACDUFF, ROSSE, ANGUS, AND ATTENDANTS.

Then for the beginning of the next scene it is:

> *HO-BOYES. TORCHES.*
> *ENTER A SEWER, AND DIVERS SERVANTS WITH DISHES AND SERVICE*
> *OVER THE STAGE. THEN ENTER MACBETH.*

My musical director had suggested the *Hoboyes* meant that music should start play-ing when *Duncan* arrives, and should finish at the beginning of the next scene. I knew that a *Sewer* was a sort of Steward, but I had no idea why servants were needed here. The usual explanation that the author intended this to indicate passage of time, or that the audience needed to have a gap between *Duncan* arriving and the next scene, which is in the middle of a feast, holds no water, for Shakespeare does not need or use these devices. Not knowing why their entrances and exits were there, I provided the servants with baskets of apples and bread and told them to let whatever happens happen.

In performance all went well, and when *Duncan* arrived at the castle the accompa-nying tune to welcome him was a wonderful warning to the audience that he was enter-ing into danger (the sinister reedy sound of a traditional hautboy would have been even more effective). When the servants came on, one of them dropped a basket, the apples went all over the stage, and they all started to play with them, use them as juggling arti-cles, even stuffing them up their costumes in lewd byplay. I was aghast, thinking this was the worst moment I had ever seen, when the audience laughter made me realize that you need a cleansing of the mind, so to speak, just before a particular potent and tense speech, and this is what the servants did. A member of the audience came up to me afterward and confessed that now, for the first time, the role of the *Porter* in the play was understandable: he was one of many necessary laugh breaks that you need when playing in the open air in daylight, with no lights or set, to get the audience to concen-trate on the tragic action. Laughter acts rather like a glue, applied every now and again to keep the audience together during a tragedy. Very revealing and, alas, controversial for those who put plays into a tragedy box and want everything to be serious. As Chris-tine put it so succinctly, "The servants don't know they're in a tragedy."

The character of *Lady Macbeth* is much argued over, but I found that Shakespeare had quite carefully delineated who she was. First of all, we see her onstage asking three times for diabolical help (and who needs extra help, a strong or a weak person?), and then the very first person who meets and addresses her is the *Messenger*. Here is that lit-tle extract, with the comments derived from what the actors did:

LADY MACBETH:
> High thee hither,
> That I may powre my Spirits in thine Eare,
> And chastise with the valour of my Tongue
> All that impeides thee from the Golden Round,
> Which Fate and Metaphysicall ayde doth seeme
> To have thee crown'd withall.

ENTER MESSENGER.
What is your tidings?

MESSENGER:
The King comes here to Night.

LADY MACBETH:
Thou'rt mad to say it.
Is not thy Master with him? who, wer't so,
Would have inform'd for preparation.

MESSENGER:
So please you, it is true: our *Thane* is comming:
One of my fellowes had the speed of him;
Who almost dead for breath, had scarcely more
Then would make up his Message.

LADY MACBETH:
Give him tending,
He brings great newes.

EXIT MESSENGER.
The Raven himselfe is hoarse,
That croakes the fatall entrance of *Duncan*
Under my Battlements.

The *Messenger* enters, and says nothing: no instruction to kneel or bow (such as *Madam I bring news.*) *Lady Macbeth* has to ask him why he has come, and his reply is a very terse one, again with no respectful adornments.

And here the *Messenger* is almost cheeky, contradicting her, and using some rather obvious alliterations as well.

Her reply is not one of admonishment, but acceptance, and he goes off, again with no word of respect, or instruction to bow or in any way indicate that this is a powerful or dangerous lady.

And the scene ends with *Lady Macbeth* making a very feeble pun *Raven/hoarse* (horse) as well.

Now, is this the first appearance of a fatal Dragon Queen, a dominating harpy? Or is it a woman unable even to command the respect of her servants. With the character played this way, played from the text as written, it certainly made a lot more sense that she would finally kill herself at the end of the play.

After the workshops, the argument raged about the proposed pillars on the Globe stage, since they seemed to be in quite the worst position for actors, making it impossible to find a place on the stage where an actor could command the audience: a place where everyone in the theatre could see you. To try to take the debate further, we returned to the Globe to put on the first bit of our *The third Part of Henry the Sixt* with the temporary pillars being put in different places on the stage. I even tried putting the throne downstage with the King sitting on it with his back to the groundlings and facing the Lords up on their balcony.

A furious session followed, with actors all demanding that the pillars be placed upstage so they could use the stage the way they knew it must be, and the academic community arguing for pillars downstage. Actor after actor complained that their own experiences of playing vastly different spaces, and making them work, were being ignored in favor of relentless theory. They could not believe that a company of actors would construct a theatre with such problematical actor-audience transactions.

A small compromise was made to get the pillars not completely downstage, but a visit to the Globe—wonderful as it is—still raises the question of its stage arrangements.

A Midsommer Nights Dreame, February 1996

I had been invited to address a Shakespeare conference in Sydney, Australia, and as part of the package was to present three performances of *A Midsommer Nights Dreame*. Greta Scacchi had seen our work in London and was very interested in taking part, our lack of

---

The Platt of A Midsommer Nights Dreame

An OSC Presentation at the Fig Tree Theatre, Sydney
at 8:00 pm on Friday 16th February, 1996

I-1 Enter Theseus, Duke of Athens: (RICHARD MELLICK), his bride-to-be Hippolita Queene of the Amazons: (ELOISE EATON), Philostrate: (ANDRÉ LILLIS), with others: (HEIDI LAPAINE; SARAH KEARNEY; JULIE SHEARER; JEANETTE TAYLOR). To them, Egeus: (OWEN WEINGOTT), and his daughter Hermia: (SUSIE LINDEMAN), Lysander, and Demetrius: (ADAM GELIN; RHETT WALTON). Lysander and Demetrius stand forth. Exeunt all but Lysander and Hermia. To them Helena: (GRETA SCACCHI). Exit Hermia. Exit Lysander. Exit Helena.

I-2 Enter Quince the Carpenter, Snug the Joyner, Bottome the Weaver, Flute the bellowes-mender, Snout the Tinker, and Starveling the Taylor: (MICHAEL HORROCKS; RICHARD MORRIS; JAMES HUTCHINSON; PAUL WILLIAMSON; LAENI BAILLIE; CATHERINE ZEALAND). Quince gives out the scrolls. Exeunt.

II-1 Enter a Fairie at one doore: (KITTY BARKLEY), and Robin Goodfellow, known as Pucke, at another: (AMELIA LONGHURST). Enter the King of Fairies, Oberon: (IVAR KANTS) at one doore with his traine: (HEIDI LAPAINE; SARAH KEARNEY; JULIE SHEARER; JEANETTE TAYLOR), and the Queene of Fairies, Tytania: (ISOBEL KIRK) at another with hers: (REBECCA SLACK; BONNIE HILLMAN; CASSANDRA WEBB; SHERLY SULAIMAN). Exeunt the Queene with her traine. Exit Pucke. Enter Demetrius, Helena following him, the King being invisible. Exit Demetrius, Helena following. To the King, Pucke with the flower. Exeunt.

II-2 Enter the Queene of Fairies, with her traine. They sing her to sleep, and exit. To the Queene, Oberon. He puts a charm on her eyes. Exit Oberon. Enter Lysander and Hermia. They sleep. Enter Pucke, who puts a charm on Lysander mistaking him for Demetrius, and exits. Enter Demetrius and Helena running. Exit Demetrius. Lysander wakes. Exit Helena. Lysander rejects his old love Hermia and exits. Hermia wakes alone, and exits looking for Lysander.

III-1 Enter the Mechanicals: (MICHAEL HORROCKS; RICHARD MORRIS; JAMES HUTCHINSON; PAUL WILLIAMSON; LAENI BAILLIE; CATHERINE ZEALAND). Enter Robin. Exit Bottome, playing Pyramus in the Play. Pucke follows him to put on the Asse head. Enter Piramus with the Asse head, and Pucke. The Clownes all exit. Exit Pucke. To Bottome, Snout and Quince, who exit. Alone, Bottome sings. Tytania wakes. To the Queene her fairies Pease-blossome, Cobweb, Moth, Mustard-seede: (REBECCA SLACK; BONNIE HILLMAN; CASSANDRA WEBB; SHERLY SULAIMAN). Exeunt.

III-2 Enter the King of Pharies, Oberon, solus. To him Pucke. Enter Demetrius and Hermia. Exit Hermia. Demetrius lies down and sleeps. Exit Pucke. Oberon puts a charm on Demetrius' eye. To Oberon, Pucke. Enter Lysander and Helena. Demetrius wakes. To them Hermia. Exeunt Lysander and Demetrius. Exit Helena, chased off by Hermia. Exit Oberon. Enter Lysander led by Pucke. Enter Demetrius led by Pucke. Exeunt Demetrius and Pucke. Lysander shifts places, lies down and sleeps. Enter Pucke leading Demetrius, who lies down and sleeps. Enter Helena, who sleeps. Enter Hermia, who sleeps. Pucke removes the charm from Lysander with the magic herb. The lovers sleep all the Act. Exit Pucke.

IV-1 Enter Queene of Fairies and Clowne, and Fairies: (KITTY BARKLEY; REBECCA SLACK; BONNIE HILLMAN; CASSANDRA WEBB; SHERLY SULAIMAN), with Oberon hiding behind. Musicke. Tytania and Bottome sleep in each others arms. Enter Pucke. Oberon removes the charm from Tytania with the magic herb. Tytania awakes. Musick, and Pucke removes the Asse head from Bottome. Exeunt, the sleepers lying still.

IV-2 Winde horns. Enter Theseus, Egeus, Hippolita, and all his traine: (HEIDI LAPAINE; SARAH KEARNEY; JULIE SHEARER; JEANETTE TAYLOR). Hornes, and they wake. Shout within, they all start up. Exit the Duke and Lords. Exit the lovers. Bottome awakes, and exits.

IV-3 Enter Quince, Flute, Snout and Starveling. To them, Snug. To them Bottome, and all exeunt.

V-1 Enter Theseus, Hippolita, Philostrate, Egeus and his Lords: (HEIDI LAPAINE; SARAH KEARNEY; JULIE SHEARER; JEANETTE TAYLOR). To them the lovers, Lysander, Demetrius, Hermia and Helena. Egeus gives the entertainment briefe.

The Play: Flourish of trumpets. Enter the Prologue, Quince. Enter Piramus, Thisbie, Wall, Moone-shine, Lyon. Exit all but Wall. Enter Piramus, enter Thisbie. Exeunt Piramus and Thisbie, and exit Wall. Enter Lyon and Moone-shine carrying lanthorne, bush and with his dog. Enter Thisbie. Lyon roars and Thisbie exits, dropping her mantle. Lyon bites the mantle and exits. Enter Piramus, who sees the mantle, stabs himself and dies. Exit Moone-shine, enter Thisbie, who sees Piramus, stabs herself and dies.

Bottome and Flute dance a Burgomaske. Exeunt. Enter Pucke with his broome. Enter the King and Queene of Fairies, with their traines: (KITTY BARKLEY; REBECCA SLACK; BONNIE HILLMAN; CASSANDRA WEBB; SHERLY SULAIMAN; HEIDI LAPAINE; SARAH KEARNEY; JULIE SHEARER; JEANETTE TAYLOR). They sing and dance. Pucke speaks the Epilogue.

Finis.

Interval	
PRESENTER:	PATRICK TUCKER
BOOK-HOLDER:	CHRISTINE OZANNE

weeks of rehearsal and the limited performance commitment being for once a great attraction to such a busy actress.

I had talked to her as to what part she should perform, and she told me she supposed she would play *Tytania* but she had always had a yearning to play *Helena*. The solution was obvious: she would play *Helena* in the first and third performances, *Tytania*

The Platt of A Midsommer Nights Dreame

An OSC Presentation at the Fig Tree Theatre, Sydney
at 8:00 pm on Saturday 17th February, 1996

I-1 Enter Theseus, Duke of Athens: (RICHARD MELLICK), his bride-to-be Hippolita Queene of the Amazons: (LAENI BAILLIE), Philostrate: (ELOISE EATON), with others: (KITTY BARKLEY; DANIELLE CARTER; VIRGINIA GAY; VERONICA NEAVE). To them, Egeus: (OWEN WEINGOTT), and his daughter Hermia: (JULIE SHEARER), Lysander, and Demetrius: (LAWRENCE WOODWARD; RHETT WALTON). Lysander and Demetrius stand forth. Exeunt all but Lysander and Hermia. To them Helena: (JEANETTE TAYLOR). Exit Hermia. Exit Lysander. Exit Helena.

I-2 Enter Quince the Carpenter, Snug the Joyner, Bottome the Weaver, Flute the bellowes-mender, Snout the Tinker, and Starveling the Taylor: (MICHAEL HORROCKS; SERHAT CARADEE; JAMES HUTCHINSON; ADAM GELIN; ISOBEL KIRK; ANDRÉ LILLIS). Quince gives out the scrolls. Exeunt.

II-1 Enter a Fairie at one doore: (CASSANDRA WEBB), and Robin Goodfellow, known as Pucke, at another: (HEIDI LAPAINE). Enter the King of Fairies, Oberon: (IVAR KANTS) at one doore with his traine: (KITTY BARKLEY; DANIELLE CARTER; VIRGINIA GAY; VERONICA NEAVE), and the Queene of Fairies, Tytania: (GRETA SCACCHI) at another with hers: (REBECCA SLACK; BONNIE HILLMAN; SARAH KEARNEY; SHERLY SULAIMAN). Exeunt the Queene with her traine. Exit Pucke. Enter Demetrius, Helena following him, the King being invisible. Exit Demetrius, Helena following. To the King, Pucke with the flower. Exeunt.

II-2 Enter the Queene of Fairies, with her traine. They sing her to sleep, and exit. To the Queene, Oberon. He puts a charm on her eyes. Exit Oberon. Enter Lysander and Hermia. They sleep. Enter Pucke, who puts a charm on Lysander mistaking him for Demetrius, and exits. Enter Demetrius and Helena running. Exit Demetrius. Lysander wakes. Exit Helena. Lysander rejects his old love Hermia and exits. Hermia wakes alone, and exits looking for Lysander.

III-1 Enter the Mechanicals: (MICHAEL HORROCKS; SERHAT CARADEE; JAMES HUTCHINSON; ADAM GELIN; ISOBEL KIRK; ANDRÉ LILLIS). Enter Robin. Exit Bottome, playing Pyramus in the Play. Pucke follows him to put on the Asse head. Enter Piramus with the Asse head, and Pucke. The Clownes all exit. Exit Pucke. To Bottome, Snout and Quince, who exit. Alone, Bottome sings. Tytania wakes. To the Queene her fairies Pease-blossome, Cobweb, Moth, Mustardseede: (REBECCA SLACK; BONNIE HILLMAN; SARAH KEARNEY; SHERLY SULAIMAN). Exeunt.

Interval

III-2 Enter the King of Pharies, Oberon, solus. To him Pucke. Enter Demetrius and Hermia. Exit Hermia. Demetrius lies down and sleeps. Exit Pucke. Oberon puts a charm on Demetrius' eye. To Oberon, Pucke. Enter Lysander and Helena. Demetrius wakes. To them Hermia. Exeunt Lysander and Demetrius. Exit Helena, chased off by Hermia. Exit Oberon. Enter Lysander led by Pucke. Enter Demetrius led by Pucke. Exeunt Demetrius and Pucke. Lysander shifts places, lies down and sleeps. Enter Pucke leading Demetrius, who lies down and sleeps. Enter Helena, who sleeps. Enter Hermia, who sleeps. Pucke removes the charm from Lysander with the magic herb. The lovers sleep all the Act. Exit Pucke.

IV-1 Enter Queene of Fairies and Clowne, and Fairies: (CASSANDRA WEBB; REBECCA SLACK; BONNIE HILLMAN; SARAH KEARNEY; SHERLY SULAIMAN), with Oberon hiding behind. Musicke. Tytania and Bottome sleep in each others arms. Enter Pucke. Oberon removes the charm from Tytania with the magic herb. Tytania awakes. Musick, and Pucke removes the Asse head from Bottome. Exeunt, the sleepers lying still.

IV-2 Winde horns. Enter Theseus, Egeus, Hippolita, and all his traine: (KITTY BARKLEY; DANIELLE CARTER; VIRGINIA GAY; VERONICA NEAVE). Hornes, and they wake. Shout within, they all start up. Exit the Duke and Lords. Exit the lovers. Bottome awakes, and exits.

IV-3 Enter Quince, Flute, Snout and Starveling. To them, Snug. To them Bottome, and all exeunt.

V-1 Enter Theseus, Hippolita, Philostrate, Egeus and his Lords: (KITTY BARKLEY; DANIELLE CARTER; VIRGINIA GAY; VERONICA NEAVE). To them the lovers, Lysander, Demetrius, Hermia and Helena. Egeus gives the entertainment briefe.

The Play: Flourish of trumpets. Enter the Prologue, Quince. Enter Piramus, Thisbie, Wall, Moone-shine, Lyon. Exit all but Wall. Enter Piramus, enter Thisbie. Exeunt Piramus and Thisbie, and exit Wall. Enter Lyon and Moone-shine carrying lanthorne, bush and with his dog. Enter Thisbie. Lyon roars and Thisbie exits, dropping her mantle. Lyon bites the mantle and exits. Enter Piramus, with his sword, who sees the mantle, stabs himself and dies. Exit Moone-shine, enter Thisbie, who sees Piramus, stabs herself and dies.

Bottome and Flute dance a Burgomaske. Exeunt. Enter Pucke with his broome. Enter the King and Queene of Fairies, with their traines: (CASSANDRA WEBB; REBECCA SLACK; BONNIE HILLMAN; SARAH KEARNEY; SHERLY SULAIMAN; KITTY BARKLEY; DANIELLE CARTER; VIRGINIA GAY; VERONICA NEAVE) They sing and dance. Pucke speaks the Epilogue.

Finis.

PRESENTER: PATRICK TUCKER
BOOK-HOLDER: CHRISTINE OZANNE

in the second—and she was very happy to agree. I then decided that since, of the professional actors available and interested, there were far more actresses than actors, I would rotate the other parts also, and as you can see from the Platts, we had almost three different casts.

We had regular meetings with the full casts in the morning, giving them the tips and

---

The Platt of A Midsommer Nights Dreame

An OSC Presentation at the Fig Tree Theatre, Sydney
at 5:00 pm on Sunday 18th February, 1996

I-1 Enter Theseus, Duke of Athens: (RICHARD MELLICK), his bride-to-be Hippolita Queene of the Amazons: (CATHERINE ZEALAND), Philostrate: (SERHAT CARADEE), with others: (VIRGINIA GAY; SUSIE LINDEMAN;; AMELIA LONGHURST; CASSANDRA WEBB). To them, Egeus: (OWEN WEINGOTT), and his daughter Hermia: (VERONICA NEAVE), Lysander, and Demetrius: (PAUL WILLIAMSON; PAUL BISHOP). Lysander and Demetrius stand forth. Exeunt all but Lysander and Hermia. To them Helena: (GRETA SCACCHI). Exit Hermia. Exit Lysander. Exit Helena.

I-2 Enter Quince the Carpenter, Snug the Joyner, Bottome the Weaver, Flute the bellowes-mender, Snout the Tinker, and Starveling the Taylor: (MICHAEL HORROCKS; RHETT WALTON; JAMES MORRIS; ANDRÉ LILLIS). Quince gives out the scrolls. Exeunt.

II-1 Enter a Fairie at one doore: (SARAH KEARNEY), and Robin Goodfellow, known as Pucke, at another: (DANIELLE CARTER). Enter the King of Fairies, Oberon: (IVAR KANTS) at one doore with his traine: (VIRGINIA GAY; SUSIE LINDEMAN; AMELIA LONGHURST; CASSANDRA WEBB), and the Queene of Fairies, Tytania: (JULIE SHEARER) at another with hers: (REBECCA SLACK; BONNIE HILLMAN; KITTY BARKLEY; SHERLY SULAIMAN). Exeunt the Queene with her traine. Exit Pucke. Enter Demetrius, Helena following him, the King being invisible. Exit Demetrius, Helena following. To the King, Pucke with the flower. Exeunt.

II-2 Enter the Queene of Fairies, with her traine. They sing her to sleep, and exit. To the Queene, Oberon. He puts a charm on her eyes. Exit Oberon. Enter Lysander and Hermia. They sleep. Enter Pucke, who puts a charm on Lysander mistaking him for Demetrius, and exits. Enter Demetrius and Helena running. Exit Demetrius. Lysander wakes. Exit Helena. Lysander rejects his old love Hermia and exits. Hermia wakes alone, and exits looking for Lysander.

III-1 Enter the Mechanicals: (MICHAEL HORROCKS; RHETT WALTON; JAMES HUTCHINSON; LAWRENCE WOODWARD; RICHARD MORRIS; ANDRÉ LILLIS). Enter Robin. Exit Bottome, playing Pyramus in the Play. Pucke follows him to put on the Asse head. Enter Piramus with the Asse head, and Pucke. The Clownes all exit. Exit Pucke. To Bottome, Snout and Quince, who exit. Alone, Bottome sings. Tytania wakes. To the Queene her fairies Pease-blossome, Cobweb, Moth, Mustard-seede: (REBECCA SLACK; BONNIE HILLMAN; KITTY BARKLEY; SHERLY SULAIMAN). Exeunt.

III-2 Enter the King of Pharies, Oberon, solus. To him Pucke. Enter Demetrius and Hermia. Exit Hermia. Demetrius lies down and sleeps. Exit Pucke. Oberon puts a charm on Demetrius' eye. To Oberon, Pucke. Enter Lysander and Helena. Demetrius wakes. To them Hermia. Exeunt Lysander and Demetrius. Exit Helena, chased off by Hermia. Exit Oberon. Enter Lysander led by Pucke. Enter Demetrius led by Pucke. Exeunt Demetrius and Pucke. Lysander shifts places, lies down and sleeps. Enter Pucke leading Demetrius, who lies down and sleeps. Enter Helena, who sleeps. Enter Hermia, who sleeps. Pucke removes the charm from Lysander with the magic herb. The lovers sleep all the Act. Exit Pucke.

IV-1 Enter Queene of Fairies and Clowne, and Fairies: (SARAH KEARNEY; REBECCA SLACK; BONNIE HILLMAN; KITTY BARKLEY; SHERLY SULAIMAN), with Oberon hiding behind. Musicke. Tytania and Bottome sleep in each others arms. Enter Pucke. Oberon removes the charm from Tytania with the magic herb. Tytania awakes. Musick, and Pucke removes the Asse head from Bottome. Exeunt, the sleepers lying still.

IV-2 Winde horns. Enter Theseus, Egeus, Hippolita, and all his traine: (VIRGINIA GAY; SUSIE LINDEMAN; AMELIA LONGHURST; CASSANDRA WEBB). Hornes, and they wake. Shout within, they all start up. Exit the Duke and Lords. Exit the lovers. Bottome awakes, and exits.

IV-3 Enter Quince, Flute, Snout and Starveling. To them, Snug. To them Bottome, and all exeunt.

V-1 Enter Theseus, Hippolita, Philostrate, Egeus and his Lords: (VIRGINIA GAY; AMELIA LONGHURST; CASSANDRA WEBB). To them the lovers, Lysander, Demetrius, Hermia and Helena. Egeus gives the entertainment briefe.
The Play: Flourish of trumpets. Enter the Prologue, Quince. Enter a Tawyer with trumpet before them: (VIRGINIA GAY), enter Piramus, Thisbie, Wall, Mooneshine, Lyon. Exit all but Wall. Enter Piramus, enter Thisbie. Exeunt Piramus and Thisbie, and exit Wall. Enter Lyon and Moone-shine carrying lanthorne, bush and with his dog. Enter Thisbie. Lyon roars and Thisbie exits, dropping her mantle. Lyon bites the mantle and exits. Enter Piramus, with his sword, who sees the mantle, stabs himself and dies. Exit Mooneshine, enter Thisbie, who stabs herself and dies. Bottome and Flute dance a Burgomaske. Exeunt. Enter Pucke with his broome. Enter the King and Queene of Fairies, with their traines: (SARAH KEARNEY; REBECCA SLACK; BONNIE HILLMAN; KITTY BARKLEY; SHERLY SULAIMAN; VIRGINIA GAY; AMELIA LONGHURST; CASSANDRA WEBB). They sing and dance. Pucke speaks the Epilogue.

Interval

| PRESENTER: | PATRICK TUCKER |
| BOOK-HOLDER: | CHRISTINE OZANNE |

Finis.

tricks we had learned about Cue Script acting, and then had a really heavy series of verse nursing, sometimes even seeing three *Hermias* in a row to go over their lines and help them find the clues within the text. It was important to forget what you had told one actress, since what worked for one person could well not help another, and each person had to find her own character, not repeat what someone else had found.

One immediate clue concerned *Tytania's* lines when she woke up to the untuneful singing of *Bottome*. Her lines are usually given thus:

TYTANIA:
    I pray thee gentle mortall, sing againe,
    Mine eare is much enamored of thy note;
    So is mine eye enthralled to thy shape,
    And thy faire vertues force (perforce) doth move me
    On the first view to say, to sweare I love thee.

No problem there, except that in the Folio it is given:

TYTANIA:
    I pray thee gentle mortall, sing againe,
    Mine eare is much enamored of thy note;
    On the first view to say, to sweare I love thee.
    So is mine eye enthralled to thy shape.
    And thy faire vertues force (perforce) doth move me.

"Obviously" a misplacement, but when you get actors to play it, something rather wonderful happens. *Tytania* falls in love with the object she first espies, the tradesman *Bottome,* and then she is turned on by his "shape," and falls in lust with him. This is precisely what *Oberon* says he wants her to go through:

OBERON:
    Having once this juyce,
    Ile watch *Titania,* when she is asleepe,
    And drop the liquor of it in her eyes:
    The next thing when she waking lookes upon,
    (Be it on Lyon, Beare, or Wolfe, or Bull,
    On medling Monkey, or on busie Ape)
    Shee shall pursue it, with the soule of love.

Although hand on heart I cannot swear that the lines in the Folio are not in fact a misprint, I have to report that having now done seven different presentations of the play, it always performs well in a theatrical sense taking the Folio lineage.

The actors had different numbers of stage credits, and it was no secret that some of the *Mechanicals* were among the least experienced in the company. When it came to the "play-within-the-play" at the end, I was a little startled, and perhaps embarrassed, by some of the theatrical business and properties and costumes that ended up on stage; it was, however, all well meant. The scene got a very good audience reaction, and I was relieved that it had been so well appreciated. After the show, I was surrounded by theatre-goers and members of the academic community swearing that "that was the funniest *Piramus* and *Thisby* scene they had ever watched." So with no rehearsal, no directorial guidance, and frankly some quite limited artists, I got a better response than when I had directed the play with a full professional company.

Interestingly, when it came to this play of *Piramus* and *Thisby,* much against my expectations, the Folio showed that all the *Mechanicals* leave the stage when the play starts, so it does not have (as I myself had when directing the play in the traditional way) *Peter Quince* prompting and gesticulating when things go wrong, with the other actors all watching to see how each gets on. At the finale, there is just *Bottome* and *Flute* left on stage, and I have a feeling that by our concentrating on the principals in this way, and not showing a pretend ensemble, the audience was better able to follow the story, seeing the connections between how the lovers had gone into the woods and survived and *Piramus* and *Thisby* had gone into the woods and expired. The court was more prominent than usual here, and it made the playlet more relevant to the rest of the play, and certainly, in Sydney, made it the comic climax that the audience found it to be.

I wondered what I (and other directors) had been doing all these years.

The performances were sold out, and not wanting to send anyone away, I put extra seats on the stage itself at the sides, and found to my delight that the actors were very willing to incorporate the audience into the action. Indeed at one time a whole row of them were dragooned by the Fairies into playing musical instruments for *the tongs and the bones* music. This was the beginning of my seeing that audiences around the performance area worked very well, and led to our understanding better how to perform at Shakespeare's Globe itself when the time came.

It was at this presentation that we changed from the cue line's being a standard three words to its being a double iamb, as suggested by Professor David Carnegie of Victoria University. We found it so valuable, adding so much useful information, that we standardized on it from then on.

In the last performance, the actor playing *Lysander* had one of those theatrical nightmares, where all the lines go. During the quarrel scene, he had to be prompted on almost every speech, and, worse, he called out "Line!" every time. I was dying out front, fearing that all the good work the Company had been doing would be forgotten in the light of this obvious flaw. Afterward, the audience seemed almost not to have noticed, only admitting to hearing a few prompts, and all going on about how exciting and fresh the performance had been. This was where I understood that an audience, if you give them enough "golden moments," will forgive any <u>apparent</u> mistakes. Alas, some fellow professionals, less forgiving, focus on the flaws and not on the excitement.

It is rather like watching someone on the high wire in a circus. The circus may be a

minor one, and the wire may not be very high, but the reality remains that the performer could slip off, and the tension remains. Watching the same thing on television
has none of the same drama, for you know that if the performer had slipped off the very
high wire, it would have been reported, and the moment endlessly played on television
news. So although the skill and daring may be of a much higher level, the knowledge
that it will be performed successfully dulls the appreciation.

Cue Script acting is very like a circus, or a sports event. You know the format, but
you absolutely do not know the result. Going to see one of the blockbuster musicals
that litter world theatre, you know that the actors are going to be repeating moves and
stage business that were inspired some fifteen or so years ago by foreign actors in a
rehearsal room, and are now pumped out internationally in identical productions. They
can be very slick, very clever, and certainly very expensive, but, to me, they still lack that
essential danger that a live performance brings, and that Cue Script acting brings in
superabundance.

The Taming of the Shrew, April 1996

We were invited back to the World Stage Festival in Toronto, after being dubbed "the
surprise hit of the 1996 Festival." Again, we were to meet with a group of actors and
give them a general introduction to Cue Script acting, and then give out some scenes to
be done the next day. From this, all would gain experience of such a way of working,
and we would gain enough to be able to cast the show. Casting is always a problem in
such times, because the pressure is often to choose the "best" actors, rather than the
ones who might prove best in this particular way of working, which is not necessarily
suitable for all talents.

Our two leading players were precast by the festival organizer, and by the end of the
casting process we had assembled our company and started our group meetings. Several
of the *As you Like it* actors from two years before were in the group, so we felt we had
some allies on board. Explaining to the cast how it all works and bringing up examples
of theatrical outrageousness turned out to have a bad influence, since too many of them
set out to impress and show off rather than just do the roles as written.

A shining exception to this was our amazing actor David Ferry, whom we cast in
three different roles for the three performances that we were contracted to give: *Christopher Sly*, the foolish suitor *Gremio*, and the servant *Grumio*. Each was a marvel of theatrical invention and truth, and how he did all that work in the three weeks' preparation
I shall never know. As *Sly* he was panhandling outside the theatre with his shopping
trolley full of a vagrant's possessions before wheeling it down the aisle to start the play;
the next night as *Gremio* he played the part as a cross-dresser, complete with high heels
and makeup. Even I thought that he had gone too far when, in conversation with *Hortensio*, he opened his handbag and started applying nail varnish, then huffing on his
hand in the air to dry it:

GREMIO:

> You may go to the divels dam: your guifts are
> so good heere's none will holde you: Their love is not
> so great *Hortensio*, but we may blow our nails together,
> and fast it fairely out.

The audience collapsed, and I looked on with amazement as every comedic moment, every piece of business he did was strictly rooted in the text. His last night's perfor-

---

The Platt of The Taming of the Shrew

Presented for the World Stage Festival on Thursday, 25th April 1996, at 8:00 pm.

I-1: Enter Begger, Christophero Sly: (DAVID FERRY), and Hostes: (ELLEN-RAY HENNESSY). Exit Hostes. Sly falles asleepe. Winde hornes. Enter a Lord from hunting: (PAUL MILLER), with his traine: (MARK BURGESS; ROBERT DODDS; PAUL ESSIEMBRE; THOMAS HAUFF). Sly is carried off. Sound trumpets. Enter Servingman: (SALLY CAHILL). Enter Players: (TED ATHERTON; MICHAEL HANRAHAN; YANNA MCINTOSH; RICHARD MCMILLAN; LUCY PEACOCK; GERAINT WYN DAVIES; DAVID YOUNG) with the Players. Exit 2nd Huntsman with the Players. Exit 1st Serv. Exeunt.

I-2 Enter aloft the drunkard, Sly, with Servingmen: (SALLY CAHILL; SARAH EVANS; LAUREN PIECH), some with apparel, Bason, and Ewer, and other appurtenances, and Lord. Sly drinks. Musick. Enter the Page dressed as a Lady: (TORRI HIGGINSON), with Attendants: (ELLEN-RAY HENNESSY; JOHN RALSTON). Enter a Messenger: (THOMAS HAUFF). Exeunt above, Manet Sly, 1st Servingman and Lady.

I-3 Flourish. Enter Lucentio, and his man Tranio: (YANNA MCINTOSH; RICHARD MCMILLAN). Enter Baptista: (MICHAEL HANRAHAN) with his two daughters, Katerina and Bianca: (LUCY PEACOCK; SARAH EVANS), Gremio a Pantelowne, Hortensio suitor to Bianca: (DAVID YOUNG; TED ATHERTON). Lucentio and Tranio stand by. Exit Bianca. Exit Baptista. Exit Katerina. Exeunt Gremio and Hortensio, Manet Tranio and Lucentio. They exchange clothes. Enter Biondello, boy to Lucentio: (LAUREN PIECH). Exeunt. The Presenters above speakes. They sit and marke.

I-4 Enter Petruchio, and his man Grumio: (GERAINT WYN DAVIES; MARK BURGESS). Petruchio rings him by the eares. Enter Hortensio. Enter Gremio with a list, and Lucentio disguised as a schoolmaster. Petruchio and Grumio stand aside. Enter Tranio brave, disguised as Lucentio, and Biondello. Exeunt.

II-1 Enter Katherina and Bianca, with her hands bound. Katherina strikes her. To them, Baptista. Katherina flies after Bianca. Exit Bianca. Exit Katherina. Enter Gremio, Lucentio, disguised as Cambio, in the habit of a mean man, Petruchio with Hortensio disguised as Litio a musician, and Tranio, dressed as Lucentio, with his boy Biondello bearing a Lute and Bookes. Enter a Servant: (SALLY CAHILL). Exeunt Servant with Hortensio, Lucentio and Biondello. Enter Hortensio with his head broke. Exeunt, Manet Petruchio. Enter Katerina. She strikes him. Enter Baptista, Gremio, Tranio. Exit Petruchio and Katherine. Tranio and Gremio bid for Bianca's hand. Exit Baptista. Exit Gremio. Exit Tranio.

III-1 Enter Lucentio as Cambio with his books, Hortensio as Litio with his lute and gamouth, and Bianca. To them, a Messenger, Nicke: (THOMAS HAUFF). Exeunt, Manet Hortensio. Exit Hortensio.

III-2 Enter Baptista, Gremio, Tranio, Lucentio, Katherine, Bianca, and others, attendants: (SALLY CAHILL; ROBERT DODDS; PAUL ESSIEMBRE; ELLEN-RAY HENNESSY; JOHN RALSTON), ready for the wedding of Katherine. To them, Biondello. Enter Petruchio and Grumio, both madly dressed. Exit Petruchio and Grumio. Exeunt, Manet Lucentio and Tranio. Enter Gremio. Musicke plays. Enter Petruchio, Kate, Bianca, Hortensio, Baptista, with Grumio, attendants: (SALLY CAHILL; ROBERT DODDS; PAUL ESSIEMBRE; ELLEN-RAY HENNESSY; JOHN RALSTON). Exeunt Petruchio, Kate, and Grumio. Exeunt.

Interval

mance of *Grumio* had him playing the servant with a tuxedo and a Chico Marx accent.

The lead actor was Geraint Wyn Davies, star of the cult television series *Forever Knight*, and so had many followers coming to see the production. In fact, about 120 of them saw all three performances, which were as different as could be, and yet each valid in its own way. By the third performance, the audience was getting hysterical in their response to yet more original theatrical moments when, in the second act, a genuine pizza deliveryman slowly walked down the aisle and onto the stage. In the interval that night, the actor playing *Christopher Sly* (yes, it was Mark Burgess again) had ordered a pizza,

---

The Platt of The Taming of the Shrew

Presented for the World Stage Festival on Friday, 26th April 1996, at 8:00 pm.

I-1: Enter Begger, Christophero Sly: (RICHARD MCMILLAN), and Hostes: (ELLEN-RAY HENNESSY). Exit Hostes. Sly falles asleepe. Winde hornes. Enter a Lord from hunting: (MICHAEL HANRAHAN), with his traine: (MARK BURGESS; PAUL ESSIEMBRE; THOMAS HAUFF; LAUREN PIECH). Sly is carried off. Sound trumpets. Enter Servingman: (PAUL MILLER). Enter Players: (TED ATHERTON; ROBERT DODDS; DAVID FERRY; LUCY PEACOCK; JOHN RALSTON; GERAINT WYN DAVIES; DAVID YOUNG). Exit 2nd Huntsman with the Players. Exit 1st Servingman. Exeunt.

I-2 Enter aloft the drunkard, Sly, with Servingmen: (SARAH EVANS; TORRI HIGGINSON; PAUL MILLER), some with apparel, Bason, and Ewer, and other appurtenances, and Lord. Sly drinks. Musick. Enter the Page dressed as a Lady: (SALLY CAHILL), with Attendants: (ELLEN-RAY HENNESSY; YANNA MCINTOSH). Enter a Messenger: (DAVID YOUNG). Exeunt above, Manet Sly, 1st Servingman and Lady.

I-3 Flourish. Enter Lucentio, and his man Tranio: (TED ATHERTON; JOHN RALSTON). Enter Baptista: (THOMAS HAUFF) with his two daughters, Katerina and Bianca: (LUCY PEACOCK; TORRI HIGGINSON), Gremio a Pantelowne, Hortensio suitor to Bianca: (DAVID FERRY; ROBERT DODDS). Lucentio and Tranio stand by. Exit Bianca. Exit Baptista. Exit Katerina. Exeunt Gremio and Hortensio, Manet Tranio and Lucentio. They exchange clothes. Enter Biondello, boy to Lucentio: (PAUL ESSIEMBRE) Exeunt. The Presenters above speakes. They sit and marke.

I-4 Enter Petruchio, and his man Grumio: (GERAINT WYN DAVIES; ELLEN-RAY HENNESSY). Petruchio rings him by the eares. Enter Hortensio. Enter Gremio with a list, and Lucentio disguised as a schoolmaster. Petruchio and Grumio stand aside. Enter Tranio brave, disguised as Lucentio, and Biondello. Exeunt.

II-1 Enter Katherina and Bianca, with her hands bound. Katherina strikes her. To them, Baptista. Katherina flies after Bianca. Exit Bianca. Exit Katherina. Enter Gremio, Lucentio, disguised as Cambio, in the habit of a mean man, Petruchio with Hortensio disguised as Litio a musician, with Tranio, dressed as Lucentio, with his boy Biondello bearing a Lute and Bookes. Enter a Servant: (SARAH EVANS). Exeunt Servant with Hortensio, Lucentio and Biondello. Enter Hortensio with his head broke. Exeunt, Manet Petruchio. Enter Katerina. She strikes him. Enter Baptista, Gremio, Tranio. Exit Petruchio and Katherine. Tranio and Gremio bid for Bianca's hand. Exit Baptista. Exit Gremio. Exit Tranio.

III-1 Enter Lucentio as Cambio with his books, Hortensio as Litio with his lute and gamouth, and Bianca. To them, a Messenger, Nicke: (DAVID YOUNG). Exeunt, Manet Hortensio. Exit Hortensio.

III-2 Enter Baptista, Gremio, Tranio, Lucentio, Katherine, Bianca, and others, attendants: (MARK BURGESS; SARAH EVANS; YANNA MCINTOSH; LAUREN PIECH), ready for the wedding of Katherine. Exit Katherine weeping. To them, Biondello. Enter Petruchio and Grumio, both madly dressed. Exit Petruchio and Grumio. Exeunt, Manet Lucentio and Tranio. Enter Gremio. Musicke playes. Enter Petruchio, Kate, Bianca, Hortensio, Baptista, with Grumio, attendants: (MARK BURGESS; SARAH EVANS; YANNA MCINTOSH; LAUREN PIECH). Exeunt Petruchio, Kate, and Grumio. Exeunt.

Interval

---

and there and then paid off the startled deliveryman, shared out the food among those on stage—including the Book-Holder—and looked on bemused as the audience stood and cheered. The work of the OSC has, in different places and at different times, brought out some of the most extraordinary theatrical moments I have ever experienced, and here was another classic. Asked about it afterward, he justified it by saying that "as an observer, *Sly* would have wanted to be fed—and after all, it was the man from Pisa!"

In preparing the show, our costume lady went over to the Stratford Theatre to pick up some costumes and properties that we needed, especially the food and platters for

---

The Platt of The Taming of the Shrew

*Presented for the World Stage Festival
on Saturday, 27th April 1996, at 8:00 pm.*

I-1: Enter Begger, Christophero Sly: (MARK BURGESS), and Hostes: (ELLEN-RAY HENNESSY). Exit Hostes. Sly falles asleepe. Winde hornes. Enter a Lord from hunting: (PAUL MILLER), with his traine: (ROBERT DODDS; PAUL ESSIEMBRE; THOMAS HAUFF; JOHN RALSTON). Sly is carried off. Sound trumpets. Enter Servingman: (SALLY CAHILL). Enter Players: (TED ATHERTON; DAVID FERRY; MICHAEL HANRAHAN; RICHARD MCMILLAN; LUCY PEACOCK; GERAINT WYN DAVIES; DAVID YOUNG). Exit 2nd Huntsman with the Players. Exit 1st Servingman. Exeunt.

I-2 Enter aloft the drunkard, Sly, with Servingmen: (SALLY CAHILL; SARAH EVANS; TORRI HIGGINSON), some with apparel, Bason, and Ewer, and other appurtenances, and Lord. Sly drinks. Musick. Enter the Page dressed as a Lady: (LAUREN PIECH), with Attendants: (ELLEN-RAY HENNESSY; YANNA MCINTOSH). Enter a Messenger: (THOMAS HAUFF). Exeunt above, Manet Sly and Lady.

I-3 Flourish. Enter Lucentio, and his man Tranio: (PAUL ESSIEMBRE; RICHARD MCMILLAN). Enter Baptista: (MICHAEL HANRAHAN) with his two daughters, Katerina and Bianca: (LUCY PEACOCK; SALLY CAHILL), Gremio a Pantelowne, Hortensio suitor to Bianca: (DAVID YOUNG; TED ATHERTON). Lucentio and Tranio stand by. Exit Bianca. Exit Baptista. Exeunt Katerina. Exeunt Gremio and Hortensio, Manet Tranio and Lucentio. They exchange clothes. Enter Biondello, boy to Lucentio: (YANNA MCINTOSH). Exeunt. The Presenters above speakes. They sit and marke.

I-4 Enter Petruchio, and his man Grumio: (GERAINT WYN DAVIES; DAVID FERRY). Petruchio rings him by the eares. Enter Hortensio. Enter Gremio with a list, and Lucentio disguised as a schoolmaster. Petruchio and Grumio stand aside. Enter Tranio brave, disguised as Lucentio, and Biondello. Exeunt.

II-1 Enter Katherina and Bianca, with her hands bound. Katherina strikes her. To them, Baptista. Katherina flies after Bianca. Exit Bianca. Exit Katherina. Enter Gremio, Lucentio, disguised as Cambio, in the habit of a mean man, Petruchio with Hortensio disguised as Litio a musician, with Tranio, dressed as Lucentio, with his boy Biondello bearing a Lute and Bookes. Enter a Servant: (TORRI HIGGINSON). Exeunt Servant with Hortensio, Lucentio and Biondello. Enter Hortensio with his head broke. Exeunt, Manet Petruchio. Enter Katerina. She strikes him. Enter Baptista, Gremio, Tranio. Exit Petruchio and Katherine. Tranio and Gremio bid for Bianca's hand. Exit Baptista. Exit Gremio. Exit Tranio.

III-1 Enter Lucentio as Cambio with his books, Hortensio as Litio with his lute and gamouth, and Bianca. To them, a Messenger, Nicke: (THOMAS HAUFF). Exeunt, Manet Hortensio. Exit Hortensio.

III-2 Enter Baptista, Gremio, Tranio, Lucentio, Katherine, Bianca, and others, attendants: (ROBERT DODDS; SARAH EVANS; ELLEN-RAY HENNESSY; TORRI HIGGINSON; JOHN RALSTON), ready for the wedding of Katherine. Exit Katherine weeping. To them, Biondello. Enter Petruchio and Grumio, both madly dressed. Exit Petruchio and Grumio. Exeunt, Manet Lucentio and Tranio. Enter Gremio. Musicke playes. Enter Petruchio, Kate, Bianca, Hortensio, Baptista, with Grumio, attendants: (ROBERT DODDS; SARAH EVANS; ELLEN-RAY HENNESSY; TORRI HIGGINSON; JOHN RALSTON). Exeunt Petruchio, Kate, and Grumio. Exeunt.

Interval

the final scene. She came back triumphantly, waving a lute with a head-sized hole in it. She had got *The Taming of the Shrew* lute, she explained, the one that *Hortensio* wears when he returns on stage having failed to teach *Kate* the lute.

I pointed out that this was not in the script. "But everyone wears it who plays *Hortensio*," she replied. I was tempted—after all, it would look funny, but since it was not there in the lines, *Hortensio* had to go onstage without it.

Inadvertently, I was to be taught a lesson in comedy. Here are the lines he has to say, with what he actually did in performance:

ENTER HORTENSIO WITH HIS HEAD BROKE.

BAPTISTA:

   How now my friend, why dost thou looke so pale?

He was holding a bloody cloth to his head. The audience did not know what had happened, so there was no laugh on his entrance (as there would have been if he came on with the "comic" lute round his neck).

HORTENSIO:

   For feare I promise you, if I looke pale.

BAPTISTA:

   What, will my daughter prove a good Musitian?

HORTENSIO:

   I thinke she'l sooner prove a souldier,

   Iron may hold with her, but never Lutes.

BAPTISTA:

   Why then thou canst not break her to the Lute?

HORTENSIO:

   Why no, for she hath broke the Lute to me:

The audience, now knowing why he had the injury, laughs.

   I did but tell her she mistooke her frets,

   And bow'd her hand to teach her fingering,

   When (with a most impatient divellish spirit)

   Frets call you these? (quoth she) Ile fume with them:

   And with that word she stroke me on the head,

   And through the instrument my pate made way,

   And there I stood amazed for a while,

   As on a Pillorie, looking through the Lute,

   While she did call me Rascall, Fidler,

   And twangling Jacke, with twentie such vilde tearmes,

   As had she studied to misuse me so.

The <u>imagery</u> of a head going through a lute is funnier than the reality—the audience laughed louder; *looking through the Lute* is such a bizarre image, the audience laughed loudest. Shakespeare has done the classic comic build, of getting three laughs, each bigger than the one before.

In retrospect it was quite obvious to me why we had the delight of getting three laughs instead of just one. If *Hortensio* had come on with the prop lute, there would have been an instant laugh, and then the subsequent speeches would merely be illustrating what we already know. By doing it from the lines, you get a delightful build; and on the second night, when a different *Hortensio* had the same piece to do, although he acted it differently, he still got the same three building laughs. The prop lute was a property that secretly every member of the audience would know was made in the workshop, and not a realistic presentation of what would happen if you actually did break a lute over some else's head. So it was an artificial piece of comedy business, rather than the classic build that Shakespeare wrote—and yet I <u>was</u> tempted to give it to the actor, rather than trust the lines as written.

The part of *Kate* has worried many in these politically correct days, yet too much is given to the situation and not the text. On one performance my *Kate* appeared with a bullwhip, which she cracked. Why? Her first lines are:

KATE:

I pray you sir, is it your will
To make a stale of me amongst these mates?

No ball-breaking tyrant here, but a genuine question that would be asked by any elder daughter, worried that her father may be marrying off the younger before she herself has been taken to the marriage market. She could not justify the bullwhip from her text, and so it got left in the dressing room for the next performance.

Kate's relationship with *Petruchio* is often widely mistaken by filling their first scene with all sorts of comic stage "business," with pratfalls and physicality, when the scene itself is rather more interesting:

ENTER KATERINA.

PETRUCHIO:

Good morrow *Kate*, for thats your name I heare.

> He had been told her name was *Kate*, and naturally calls her by this name.

KATE:

Well have you heard, but something hard of hearing:
They call me *Katerine*, that do talke of me.

> She contradicts him. The scene—and in fact the rest of the play—will come down to what things are <u>named</u> (not what they <u>are</u>).

PETRUCHIO:

You lye infaith, for you are call'd plaine *Kate*,
And bony *Kate*, and sometimes *Kate* the curst:
But *Kate*, the prettiest *Kate* in Christendome,
Kate of *Kate*-hall, my super-daintie *Kate*,
For dainties are all *Kates*, and therefore *Kate*

> He then makes wordplay on her name.

Take this of me, *Kate* of my consolation,
Hearing thy mildnesse prais'd in every Towne,
Thy vertues spoke of, and thy beautie sounded,

> As he turns to flattery, so he changes from *you* to *thy*.

Yet not so deeply as to thee belongs,
My selfe am moov'd to woo thee for my wife.

KATE:

Mov'd, in good time, let him that mov'd you hether
Remove you hence: I knew you at the first

> She replies with wordplay of her own. The battle is one of words,

You were a movable.

PETRUCHIO:

Why, what's a movable?

KATE:

A joyn'd stoole.

PETRUCHIO:

Thou hast hit it: come sit on me.

KATE:

Asses are made to beare, and so are you.

PETRUCHIO:

Women are made to beare, and so are you.

KATE:

No such Jade as you, if me you meane.

PETRUCHIO:

Alas good *Kate*, I will not burthen thee,

For knowing thee to be but yong and light.

KATE:

Too light for such a swaine as you to catch,

And yet as heavie as my waight should be.

PETRUCHIO:

Shold be, should: buzze.

KATE:

Well tane, and like a buzzard.

PETRUCHIO:

Oh slow-wing'd Turtle, shal a buzard take thee?

KATE:

I for a Turtle, as he takes a buzard.

PETRUCHIO:

Come, come you Waspe, y'faith you are too

angrie.

KATE:

If I be waspish, best beware my sting.

PETRUCHIO:

My remedy is then to plucke it out.

KATE:

I, if the foole could finde it where it lies.

PETRUCHIO:

Who knowes not where a Waspe does weare

his sting? In his taile.

KATE:

In his tongue?

of intellect, not of cheap theatrical falls and stumbles.

And a stool is not the only thing that has three legs; Shakespeare as usual finding the bawdy meanings for *Petruchio* to speak of; *Kate* is well able to reply in kind.

Petruchio is stung to reply with a *you*.

But changes back to the more soft *thee*.

PETRUCHIO:

Whose tongue.

KATE:

Yours if you talke of tales, and so farewell.

PETRUCHIO:

What with my tongue in your taile.

Nay, come again, good *Kate*, I am a Gentleman,

KATE:

That Ile trie.

SHE STRIKES HIM.

PETRUCHIO:

I sweare Ile cuffe you, if you strike againe.

KATE:

So may you loose your armes,

If you strike me, you are no Gentleman,

And if no Gentleman, why then no armes.

PETRUCHIO:

A Herald *Kate*? Oh put me in thy bookes.

KATE:

What is your Crest, a Coxcombe?

PETRUCHIO:

A comblesse Cocke, so *Kate* will be my Hen.

KATE:

No Cocke of mine, you crow too like a craven.

PETRUCHIO:

Nay come *Kate*, come: you must not looke so sowre.

KATE:

It is my fashion when I see a Crab.

PETRUCHIO:

Why heere's no crab, and therefore looke not sowre.

KATE:

There is, there is.

PETRUCHIO:

Then shew it me.

KATE:

Had I a glasse, I would.

PETRUCHIO:

What, you meane my face.

KATE:

Well aym'd of such a yong one.

PETRUCHIO:

Now by Saint George I am too yong for you.

The wordplay is well matched, point for point, but when he gets really bawdy, *Kate* makes a final reply, and goes to exit, but being forced <u>for the first time</u> to use physical force, might be said to have lost the first round; and he is stung into a *you*.

But he quickly reverts to his wooing *thy*.

References to his own attractiveness puts *Petruchio* into the *you* mode.

KATE:

Yet you are wither'd.

PETRUCHIO:

'Tis with cares.

KATE:

I care not.

PETRUCHIO:

Nay heare you *Kate*. Insooth you scape not so.

KATE:

I chafe you if I tarrie. Let me go.

PETRUCHIO:

No, not a whit, I finde you passing gentle:

'Twas told me you were rough, and coy, and sullen,

And now I finde report a very liar:

For thou art pleasant, gamesome, passing courteous,

But slow in speech: yet sweet as spring-time flowers.

Thou canst not frowne, thou canst not looke a sconce,

Nor bite the lip, as angry wenches will,

Nor hast thou pleasure to be crosse in talke:

But thou with mildnesse entertain'st thy wooers,

With gentle conference, soft, and affable.

Why does the world report that *Kate* doth limpe?

Oh sland'rous world: *Kate* like the hazle twig

Is straight, and slender, and as browne in hue

As hazle nuts, and sweeter then the kernels:

Oh let me see thee walke: thou dost not halt.

KATE:

Go foole, and whom thou keep'st command.

PETRUCHIO:

Did ever *Dian* so become a Grove

As *Kate* this chamber with her princely gate:

O be thou *Dian*, and let her be *Kate*,

And then let *Kate* be chaste, and *Dian* sportfull.

KATE:

Where did you study all this goodly speech?

PETRUCHIO:

It is *extempore*, from my mother wit.

KATE:

A witty mother, witlesse else her sonne.

And now *Petruchio*, being forced into a physical action, can be said to have lost the second round. The physicality of the scene is carefully plotted into the language, and extraneous stuff will only blur the fascinating battle of wits and words that is going on.

Here, where for the first time, *Petruchio* is using flattering soft words, *Kate* has no quick response. The actress will only find this out in performance, that she <u>wants</u> to listen to this more traditional wooing.

The proof that this has worked (and the clue for the actress that a change is about to happen to her) is that <u>here</u> *Kate* uses *thou* for the first time in the scene—so Shakespeare had carefully indicated to her <u>where</u> her gear change was, and in performance she discovers <u>why</u>.

She quickly reverts back to *you*.

PETRUCHIO:

Am I not wise?

KATE:

Yes, keepe you warme.

PETRUCHIO:

Marry so I meane sweet *Katherine* in thy bed:
And therefore setting all this chat aside,
Thus in plaine termes: your father hath consented
That you shall be my wife; your dowry greed on,
And will you, nill you, I will marry you.
Now *Kate*, I am a husband for your turne,
For by this light, whereby I see thy beauty,
Thy beauty that doth make me like thee well,
Thou must be married to no man but me,

ENTER BAPTISTA, GREMIO, TRANIO.

For I am he am borne to tame you *Kate*,
And bring you from a wilde *Kate* to a *Kate*
Conformable as other houshold *Kates*:
Heere comes your father, never make deniall,
I must, and will have *Katherine* to my wife.

Bed talk gets *Petruchio* into his next *thy* mode, quickly followed by *your* when it comes to giving her the details of their upcoming nuptials.

Back to *thy* for the flattery.

But at the entrance of the family—and so they can overhear—he reverts to the public *you*, and makes a declaration of what he will be doing. Editors who change the position of this stage instruction to just before *Here comes your father*, do so at the peril of changing the meaning of the scene; it is clear that when he changes to *you* is the moment he <u>expects</u> to be overheard.

So the battle between *Petruchio* and *Kate* was as much about what things are <u>named</u>, which is shown again by the *Moon/Sun* argument on the way back to her father's after the marriage. By the end of the play, *Kate* seems to have learned that she does not have to <u>believe</u> what *Petruchio* says, she just has to <u>say</u> or <u>do</u> it. The result of this is the wager that *Petruchio* wins by having *Kate* do as he says, and this can be extended to her famous "difficult" last speech, where when my actress played it as saying what he asked her to say, not having to believe it, it came over as a wonderful <u>partnership</u> between them, not a submissive wife at all. This interpretation came from seeing how that first scene went, seeing how the arguments in the house are again about what *Petruchio* says *I tell thee Kate, 'twas burnt and dried away*, and so to the turning point of the play, an argument about what the sun should be called, and when she realizes she has to agree with (not believe) what he says, she asks to be called *Katherine*:

ENTER PETRUCHIO, KATE, HORTENTIO.

PETRUCHIO:

Come on a Gods name, once more toward our fathers:
Good Lord how bright and goodly shines the Moone.

KATE:

The Moone, the Sunne: it is not Moonelight now.

PETRUCHIO:

I say it is the Moone that shines so bright.

KATE:

I know it is the Sunne that shines so bright.

PETRUCHIO:

Now by my mothers sonne, and that's my selfe,
It shall be moone, or starre, or what I list,
Or ere I journey to your Fathers house:
Goe on, and fetch our horses backe againe,
Evermore crost and crost, nothing but crost.

HORTENTIO:

Say as he saies, or we shall never goe.

KATE:

Forward I pray, since we have come so farre,
And be it moone, or sunne, or what you please:
And if you please to call it a rush Candle,
Henceforth I vowe it shall be so for me.

PETRUCHIO:

I say it is the Moone.

KATE:

I know it is the Moone.

PETRUCHIO:

Nay then you lye: it is the blessed Sunne.

KATE:

Then God be blest, it is the blessed sun,
But sunne it is not, when you say it is not.
And the Moone changes even as your minde:
What you will have it nam'd, even that it is,
And so it shall be so for *Katherine*.

The rules established, they now understand each other, and go on to be the only really happy partnership at the end of the play. And the last speech by *Katherine*? This can be seen to be what she says to *Petruchio*'s request, and just as she has said that the sun is the moon, so she will say the last speech—but it does not have to be what she believes:

KATE:

Fie, fie, unknit that thretaning unkinde brow,
And dart not scornefull glances from those eies,
To wound thy Lord, thy King, thy Governour.

It blots thy beautie, as frosts doe bite the Meads,
Confounds thy fame, as whirlewinds shake faire budds,
And in no sence is meete or amiable.
A woman mov'd, is like a fountaine troubled,
Muddie, ill seeming, thicke, bereft of beautie,
And while it is so, none so dry or thirstie
Will daigne to sip, or touch one drop of it.
Thy husband is thy Lord, thy life, thy keeper,
Thy head, thy soveraigne: One that cares for thee,
And for thy maintenance. Commits his body
To painfull labour, both by sea and land:
To watch the night in stormes, the day in cold,
Whil'st thou ly'st warme at home, secure and safe,
And craves no other tribute at thy hands,
But love, faire lookes, and true obedience;
Too little payment for so great a debt.
Such dutie as the subject owes the Prince,
Even such a woman oweth to her husband:
And when she is froward, peevish, sullen, sowre,
And not obedient to his honest will,
What is she but a foule contending Rebell,
And gracelesse Traitor to her loving Lord?
I am asham'd that women are so simple,
To offer warre, where they should kneele for peace:
Or seeke for rule, supremacie, and sway,
When they are bound to serve, love, and obay.
Why are our bodies soft, and weake, and smooth,
Unapt to toyle and trouble in the world,
But that our soft conditions, and our harts,
Should well agree with our externall parts?
Come, come, you froward and unable wormes,
My minde hath bin as bigge as one of yours,
My heart as great, my reason haplie more,
To bandie word for word, and frowne for frowne;
But now I see our Launces are but strawes:
Our strength as weake, our weakenesse past compare,
That seeming to be most, which we indeed least are.
Then vale your stomackes, for it is no boote,
And place your hands below your husbands foote:
In token of which dutie, if he please,
My hand is readie, may it do him ease.

Margaret of Anjou, October 1996

We were asked to put on a showcase presentation at Hampton Court, with the idea that we might put on full-length plays there in the Great Hall. This place had a special excitement for us, for we know from historical records that Shakespeare and his company performed here for King James, and that those walls that echoed back our words would have heard Shakespeare's own voice four hundred years ago.

I decided to put on an hour long adaptation of some of the *Queene Margaret* scenes from the *Henry the Sixt* plays and from *Richard the Third*, and since it was all based around her and her conflicts, to call it *Margaret of Anjou*. The Cue Scripts were assembled and sent out to the actors, and the verse nursing done.

The Great Hall is long and narrow, and has a balcony with two entrances beneath. We decided to play with rows of audience on either side, and at the end opposite the entrances a special chair and seats for where King James would have sat. The staging worked very well—in fact, traverse staging has turned out to be my favorite—but the long hall made entrances a very long way from the "King," and I wondered if this was how it was done. The various theatre companies would have played in many different spaces and halls, and could not always guarantee that, for example, the balcony would be available and visible for a *Romeo and Juliet*, or that there would be a balcony at all. Looking up the records, I realized that often the actors would be surrounded on all four sides by the audience. A thought process started that ended up with a theatrical solution learned from practical experience about how to deal with the balcony in *Romeo and Juliet*—or, indeed, any pieces of scenery that were at a different level to stage height. Much more of this later.

The different scenes all had a consistency that surprised me, since I know that Shakespeare had written the plays at different times. The compilation played well for the invited audience. Shakespeare's writing style may have changed, but his input of theatrical messages to the actors was consistent, and each actor felt guided, even without any access to the rest of the portion of the play being done.

The staging as I said worked well, none better than when *Prince Edward* comes on, tries to assert his authority, and is killed by the brothers:

ENTER THE PRINCE.
KING EDWARD:
    Bring forth the Gallant, let us heare him speake.
    What? can so young a Thorne begin to prick?
    Edward, what satisfaction canst thou make,   The *King* addressed him without
    For bearing Armes, for stirring up my Subjects,   his title, but did use *thou*.
    And all the trouble thou hast turn'd me to?
PRINCE EDWARD:
                                      The *Prince* replied in kind, and
    Speake like a Subject, prowd ambitious *Yorke*.   since the brothers did not know
    Suppose that I am now my Fathers Mouth,   what he was to say, their sponta-

HAMPTON COURT   *Original Shakespeare Company*
THE GREAT HALL   Monday 7th October, 1996

The Platt for Part of Margaret of Anjou

Flourish. Enter King Edward in triumph: (GRAHAM POUNTNEY), *with his brothers Richard, Clarence:* (PHILIP BIRD; DUNCAN LAW), *and the rest:* (TESS DIGNAN; HANNAH JACKSON; DANIEL HOPKINS; BARBARA MUSTON; SIMON PURSE). *Exeunt. Flourish. March. Enter the Queene Margaret, young Edward:* (SONIA RITTER; DREW ASHTON), *Somerset, Oxford:* (DOROTHY LAWRENCE; DAVID ANGUS), *and Souldiers:* (DAVID DELVE; SARA NEIGHBOUR; TUCKER STEVENS; NATASHA TAMAR). *The Queene rallies her troops. To them, a Messenger:* (PHILIPPE SPALL). *Flourish, and march. Enter King Edward, Richard, Clarence, and Souldiers. Alarum, Retreat, Excursions. Exeunt. Flourish. Enter King Edward, Richard, Queene Margaret, Clarence, Oxford, Somerset and Soldiers:* (DAVID DELVE; TESS DIGNAN; SARA NEIGHBOUR; PHILIPPE SPALL; TUCKER STEVENS; NATASHA TAMAR). *Exeunt Somerset and Oxford guarded:* (SARA NEIGHBOUR; TUCKER STEVENS), *to their deaths. Enter the Prince. King Edward, Richard and Clarence stab the Prince to death. Richard offers to kill Queene Margaret. She swounds. Exit Richard to the Tower. Exit Queene Margaret. Exeunt.*

Enter the Queene Mother Elizabeth: (JENNIFER BURGESS), *Lords Rivers, Dorset and Lord Gray:* (DANIEL HOPKINS; BARBARA MUSTON; HANNAH JACKSON). *Enter Buckingham and Derby:* (GREGORY DE POLNAY; SIMON PURSE). *Enter Richard and Hastings:* (SARA NEIGHBOUR) *They all quarrel. Enter old Queene Margaret behind. Queene Margaret comes forward to blame them. She invokes a charm against Richard. Exit Queene Margaret. Richard speakes to himselfe. To them, Catesby:* (TUCKER STEVENS). *Exeunt.*

Enter the old Dutchesse of Yorke: (HEATHER TRACY), *with Boy Edward and Daughter Margaret:* (SARAH FINCH; SALLY WOODFIELD), *the two children of her dead son Clarence. Enter the Queene Elizabeth with her haire about her ears, Rivers and Dorset after her. Enter Richard, Buckingham, Derby, Hastings, and Ratcliffe:* (PHILIPPE SPALL). *Exeunt. Manet Buckingham and Richard. Exeunt.*

Enter Queene Elizabeth and the old Dutchesse of Yorke and Dorset at one door, Anne Duchesse of Glouster: (CAMILLA EVANS) *and Margaret Plantagenet daughter of Clarence at another door. Enter the Lieutenant:* (NATASHA TAMAR). *Exit Lieutenant. Enter Stanley:* (DAVID DELVE). *Exeunt.*

Enter old Queene Margaret.
Ends

PRESENTER: Patrick Tucker   **BOOK-HOLDER: Christine Ozanne**

Musical Director	Barbara Muston
Singers/Musicians	Hannah Jackson; Drew Ashton; Jennifer Burgess; Duncan Law; Barbara Muston; Sara Neighbour; Christine Ozanne; Simon Purse; Tucker Stevens; Sally Woodfield
Costumes	Ellie Cockerill
Assistant	Gillian King

Resigne thy Chayre, and where I stand, kneele thou,
Whil'st I propose the selfe-same words to thee,
Which (Traytor) thou would'st have me answer to.

QUEENE MARGARET:
Ah, that thy Father had beene so resolv'd.

RICHARD:
That you might still have worne the Petticoat,
And ne're have stolne the Breech from *Lancaster*.

PRINCE EDWARD:
Let *Æsop* fable in a Winters Night,
His Currish Riddles sorts not with this place.

RICHARD:
By Heaven, Brat, Ile plague ye for that word.

QUEENE MARGARET:
I, thou wast borne to be a plague to men.

RICHARD:
For Gods sake, take away this Captive Scold.

PRINCE EDWARD:
Nay, take away this scolding Crooke-backe, rather.

KING EDWARD:
Peace wilfull boy, or I will charme your tongue.

CLARENCE:
Untutor'd Lad, thou art too malapert.

PRINCE EDWARD:
I know my dutie, you are all undutifull:
Lascivious *Edward*, and thou perjur'd *George*,
And thou mis-shapen *Dicke*, I tell ye all,
I am your better, Traytors as ye are,
And thou usurp'st my Fathers right and mine.

KING EDWARD:
Take that, the likenesse of this Rayler here.
STABS HIM.

RICHARD:
Sprawl'st thou? take that, to end thy agonie.
RICHARD STABS HIM.

CLARENCE:
And ther's for twitting me with perjurie.
CLARENCE STABS HIM.

QUEENE MARGARET:
Oh, kill me too.

RICHARD:
Marry, and shall.

---

neous indignation at this speech was marvelous.

The *Queene*'s *Ah* was so much more effective than an *Oh*.

Richard had a continuous word battle with *Margaret*, and only called her *you*.

He called *Edward* by the interesting declamatory *ye*.

Now the *King* changed to the more formal *your*.

Edward addressed them all as *you*, then individualized them with *thou*, finding a particularly bawdy term for *Richard*. He changed to the oratorical *ye* toward the end, but his final *thou* had to be to a single person—and so he was guided to speak to the *King* for his last statement.

He got killed for his pains, with each brother joining in. They went up to him in turn, and the final staging was quite beautiful: the dead body of the young *Prince* on the floor, the assassins standing round, with the ancient tapestries of the Great Hall glowing in the background, and *Margaret* coming up, expecting to die too.

This comment by *Richard* got a big laugh, and it was entirely appro-

OFFERS TO KILL HER.

KING EDWARD:

Hold, *Richard*, hold, for we have done too much.

RICHARD:

Why should shee live, to fill the World with words.

KING EDWARD:

What? doth shee swowne? use meanes for her recoverie.

RICHARD:

Clarence excuse me to the King my Brother:

Ile hence to London on a serious matter,

Ere ye come there, be sure to heare some newes.

CLARENCE:

What? what?

RICHARD:

Tower, the Tower.

EXIT RICHARD.

priate: it released the tension caused by the young boy's death.

Margaret was told during the Burbadge time that here she was required to faint.

The timing of these two lines set up *Richard* as a lovable rogue—very much the character we see later in *Richard the Third*.

The Hampton Court personnel loved the evening. The stumbling block was the fact that we could not perform with fewer than twenty actors, and since no more than about 150 seats could be put into the Great Hall, this made any commercial undertaking of putting on plays completely impossible without massive subsidy. So that turned out to be our only performance there (to date).

See Appendix 2 for the Genealogical Table covering these plays.

A Midsommer Nights Dreame, July 1997

We were invited to present two performances at the Jerash Festival in Jordan at the height of the nontourist season (and the height of their summer heat), and I felt that this would be a good time to "double cast" my English actors the way I had with the Canadian and Australian ones. Most of the cast therefore played two very different roles, with consequent increase in work for the costume and verse departments. Christine for the first time took a role, and so I brought in Simon Purse to be the Book-Holder and fellow Verse Nurse.

I did decide on a particular double, that of *Theseus* and *Oberon*, that I wish I had not. Back in the Platt for *The Second parte of the Seven Deadlie Sinnes* it could be seen that the actors did double up, but there was mostly quite a gap between playing one part and another—and this is what is not possible for the *Theseus/Oberon* double. Both my actors doing this had problems, and I realized that it was because in doing a Cue Script, the actor needs a little time to come out of one character and get into another, and this is not possible for two characters who have to change over very rapidly. With rehearsal, such doubling is no problem, but with our type of preparation, a reasonable breathing space is needed to get the actor from one state to the other.

By now, our "regular" actors were very used to devising and preparing their own parts and costumes, and we had some wonderful artistic contributions. *Lysander* in the first performance became *Snout* in the second, and back in England he had built himself a wall costume that included a flower pot complete with trailing vine that was hidden from all and sundry until the actual moment he walked on stage—the sort of

The Platt of A Midsommer Nights Dreame

An OSC Presentation on the Artimes Steps at the Jerash Festival, Jordan at 8:30 pm on Thursday 24th July, 1997

I-1 Enter Theseus, Duke of Athens: (CALLUM COATES), with his bride-to-be Hippolita Queene of the Amazons: (SARAH FINCH). To them, Egeus: (HUGH WALTERS), and his daughter Hermia: (KERRY OWEN), and Lysander, and Demetrius: (JONATHAN ROBY; DAVID JARVIS). Lysander and Demetrius stand forth. Exeunt all but Lysander and Hermia. To them Helena: (TESS DIGNAN). Exit Hermia. Exit Lysander. Exit Helena.

I-2 Enter Quince the Carpenter, Snug the Joyner, Bottome the Weaver, Flute the bellowes-mender, Snout the Tinker, and Starveling the Taylor: (HUGH WALTERS; DAVID HALL; DAVID DELVE; SCOTT AINSLIE; GRAHAM POUNTNEY; CHRISTINE OZANNE) Quince gives out the scrolls. Exit Starveling. Exeunt.

II-1 Enter a Fairie at one doore: (CHRISTINE OZANNE), and Robin Goodfellow, known as Pucke, at another: (SONIA RITTER). Enter the King of Fairies, Oberon: (CALLUM COATES) at one door, and the Queen of Fairies, Tytania: (SARAH FINCH) at another with her traine: (SCOTT AINSLIE; DAVID HALL; GRAHAM POUNTNEY). They argue. Exeunt the Queen with her traine. Exit Pucke. Enter Demetrius, Helena following him, the King being invisible. Exit Demetrius, Helena following. To the King, Pucke with the flower. Exeunt.

II-2 Enter the Queen of Fairies, with her traine. They sing her to sleep, and exit. First Fairy exits. To the Queene, Oberon. He puts a charm on her eyes. Exit Oberon. Enter Lysander and Hermia. They sleep. Enter Pucke, who puts a charm on Lysander mistaking him for Demetrius, and exits. Enter Demetrius and Helena running. Exit Demetrius. Lysander wakes, loving Helena. Exit Helena. Lysander rejects his old love Hermia and exits. Hermia wakes alone, and exits looking for Lysander.

III-1 Enter the Mechanicals: (HUGH WALTERS; DAVID HALL; DAVID DELVE; SCOTT AINSLIE; GRAHAM POUNTNEY; CHRISTINE OZANNE). Enter Robin. Exit Bottome, playing Pyramus in the Play. Pucke follows him to put on the Asse head. Enter Piramus with the Asse head, and Pucke. The Clownes all exit. Exit Pucke. To Bottome, Snout and Quince, who exit. Alone, Bottome sings. Tytania wakes, loving Bottome. To the Queene her fairies Peasblossome, Cobweb, Moth, Mustard-seede: (CHRISTINE OZANNE; DAVID HALL; SCOTT AINSLIE; GRAHAM POUNTNEY). Exeunt.

III-2 Enter the King of Pharies, Oberon, solus. To him Pucke. Enter Demetrius and Hermia. They quarrel. Exit Hermia. Demetrius lies down and sleeps. Exit Pucke. Oberon puts a charm on Demetrius' eye. To Oberon, Pucke. Enter Lysander and Helena. Demetrius wakes, loving Helena. To them Hermia. Lysander and Hermia quarrel. Exeunt Lysander and Demetrius. Exit Helena, chased off by Hermia. Exit Oberon. Enter Lysander led by Pucke. Enter Demetrius led by Pucke. Exeunt Demetrius and Pucke. Lysander shifts places, lies down and sleeps. Enter Pucke leading Demetrius, who lies down and sleeps. Enter Helena, who sleeps. Enter Hermia, who sleeps. Pucke removes the charm from Lysander with the magic herb. The lovers sleep all the Act. Exit Pucke.

IV-1 Enter Queene of Fairies and Clowne and fairies, with Oberon hiding behind. Musicke. Tytania and Bottome sleep in each others arms. Enter Pucke. Oberon removes the charm from Tytania with the magic herb. Tytania awakes. Musick, and Pucke removes the Asse head from Bottome. Exeunt Oberon, Pucke and Tytania, the sleepers lying still. The Fairies sing song, and exeunt. Winde horns. Enter Theseus, Egeus, Hippolita, for a hunt. Hornes, and they wake. Shout within, they all start up. Exit the Duke and Lords. Exit the lovers. Bottome awakes, and exits.

IV-2 Enter Quince, Flute, Snout and Starveling. To them, Snug. To them Bottome, and all exeunt.

V-1 Enter Theseus, Hippolita and Philostrate (SIMON PURSE). To them the lovers, Lysander, Demetrius, Hermia and Helena. Philostrate gives the entertainment briefe.
The Play: Flourish of trumpets. Enter the Prologue, Quince. Enter Piramus, Thisbie, Wall, Moone-shine, Lyon: (DAVID DELVE; SCOTT AINSLIE; GRAHAM POUNTNEY; CHRISTINE OZANNE; DAVID HALL). Exit all but Wall. Enter Piramus, enter Thisbie. Exeunt Piramus and Thisbie, and exit Wall. Enter Lyon and Moone-shine carrying lanthorne, bush and with his dog. Enter Thisbie. Lyon roars and Thisbie exits, dropping her mantle. Lyon bites the mantle and exits. Enter Piramus, with his sword, who sees the mantle, stabs himself and dies. Exit Moone-shine, enter Thisbie, who sees Piramus, stabs herself and dies. Bottome and Flute dance a Burgomaske. Exeunt. Enter Pucke with his broome. Enter the King and Queene of Fairies, with their traines. They sing and dance. Pucke speaks the Epilogue.

Interval	Finis.

Costumes	ELLIE COCKERILL
Book-Holder	SIMON PURSE
Presenter	PATRICK TUCKER

surprise I am sure would have happened in Elizabethan days. Our two *Puckes* were also very different: one a dark, brooding character with tatty feathered wings, the other a green-faced and costumed sprite; yet despite the differences, the two performances were as fresh and as inspirational as each other.

When *Lysander* is first left with his *Hermia*, he says:

The Platt of A Midsommer Nights Dreame

An OSC Presentation on the Artimes Steps at the Jerash Festival, Jordan at 8:30 pm on Friday 25th July, 1997

I-1 Enter Theseus, Duke of Athens: (GRAHAM POUNTNEY), with his bride-to-be Hippolita Queene of the Amazons: (KERRY OWEN). To them, Egeus: (HUGH WALTERS), and his daughter Hermia: (SONIA RITTER), and Lysander, and Demetrius: (DAVID HALL; SCOTT AINSLIE). Lysander and Demetrius stand forth. Exeunt all but Lysander and Hermia. To them Helena: (SARAH FINCH). Exit Hermia. Exit Lysander. Exit Helena.

I-2 Enter Quince the Carpenter, Snug the Joyner, Bottome the Weaver, Flute the bellowes-mender, Snout the Tinker, and Starveling the Taylor: (HUGH WALTERS; CALLUM COATES; DAVID DELVE; JONATHAN ROBY; DAVID JARVIS; CHRISTINE OZANNE) Quince gives out the scrolls. Exit Starveling. Exeunt.

II-1 Enter a Fairie at one doore: (CHRISTINE OZANNE), and Robin Goodfellow, known as Pucke, at another: (TESS DIGNAN). Enter the King of Fairies, Oberon: (GRAHAM POUNTNEY) at one door, and the Queen of Fairies, Tytania: (KERRY OWEN) at another with her traine: (DAVID JARVIS; JONATHAN ROBY; CALLUM COATES). They argue. Exeunt the Queen with her traine. Enter Pucke. Enter Demetrius, Helena following him, the King being invisible. Exit Demetrius, Helena following. To the King, Pucke with the flower. Exeunt.

II-2 Enter the Queen of Fairies, with her traine. They sing her to sleep, and exit. First Fairy exits. To the Queene, Oberon. He puts a charm on her eyes. Exit Oberon. Enter Lysander and Hermia. They sleep. Enter Pucke, who puts a charm on Lysander mistaking him for Demetrius, and exits. Enter Demetrius and Helena running. Exit Demetrius. Lysander wakes, loving Helena. Exit Helena. Lysander rejects his old love Hermia and exits. Hermia wakes alone, and exits looking for Lysander.

III-1 Enter the Mechanicals: (HUGH WALTERS; CALLUM COATES; DAVID DELVE; JONATHAN ROBY; DAVID JARVIS; CHRISTINE OZANNE). Enter Robin. Exit Bottome, playing Pyramus in the Play. Pucke follows him to put on the Asse head. Enter Piramus with the Asse head, and Pucke. The Clownes all exit. Exit Pucke. To Bottome, Snout and Quince, who exit. Alone, Bottome sings. Tytania wakes, loving Bottome. To the Queene her fairies Peasblossome, Cobweb, Moth, Mustard-seede: (CHRISTINE OZANNE; JONATHAN ROBY; DAVID JARVIS; CALLUM COATES). Exeunt.

III-2 Enter the King of Pharies, Oberon, solus. To him Pucke. Enter Demetrius and Hermia. They quarrel. Exit Hermia. Demetrius lies down and sleeps. Exit Pucke. Oberon puts a charm on Demetrius' eye. To Oberon, Pucke. Enter Lysander and Helena. Demetrius wakes, loving Helena. To them Hermia. Lysander and Hermia quarrel. Exeunt Lysander and Demetrius. Exit Helena, chased off by Hermia. Exit Oberon. Enter Lysander led by Pucke. Enter Demetrius led by Pucke. Exeunt Demetrius and Pucke. Lysander shifts places, lies down and sleeps. Enter Pucke leading Demetrius, who lies down and sleeps. Enter Helena, who sleeps. Enter Hermia, who sleeps. Pucke removes the charm from Lysander with the magic herb. The lovers sleep all the Act. Exit Pucke.

IV-1 Enter Queene of Fairies and Clowne and fairies, with Oberon hiding behind. Musicke. Tytania and Bottome sleep in each others arms. Enter Pucke. Oberon removes the charm from Tytania with the magic herb. Tytania awakes. Musick, and Pucke removes the Asse head from Bottome. Exeunt Oberon, Pucke and Tytania, the sleepers lying still. The Fairies sing the song, and exeunt. Winde horns. Enter Theseus, Egeus, Hippolita, for a hunt. Hornes, and they wake. Shout within, they all start up. Exit the Duke and Lords. Exit the lovers. Bottome awakes, and exits.

IV-2 Enter Quince, Flute, Snout and Starveling. To them, Snug. To them Bottome, and all exeunt.

V-1 Enter Theseus, Hippolita, and Philostrate (SIMON PURSE). To them the lovers, Lysander, Demetrius, Hermia and Helena. Philostrate gives the entertainment briefe.
The Play: Flourish of trumpets. Enter the Prologue, Quince. Enter Piramus, Thisbie, Wall, Moone-shine, Lyon: (DAVID DELVE; JONATHAN ROBY; DAVID JARVIS; CHRISTINE OZANNE; CALLUM COATES). Exit all but Wall. Enter Piramus, enter Thisbie. Exeunt Piramus and Thisbie, and exit Wall. Enter Lyon and Moone-shine carrying lanthorne, bush and with his dog. Enter Thisbie. Lyon roars and Thisbie exits, dropping her mantle. Lyon bites the mantle and exits. Enter Piramus, with his sword, who sees the mantle, stabs himself and dies. Exit Moone-shine, enter Thisbie, who sees Piramus, stabs herself and dies. Bottome and Flute dance a Burgomaske. Exeunt. Enter Pucke with his broome. Enter the King and Queene of Fairies, with their traines. They sing and dance. Pucke speaks the Epilogue.

| Interval | Finis. |

Costumes   ELLIE COCKERILL
Book-Holder   SIMON PURSE
Presenter   PATRICK TUCKER

LYSANDER:

> How now my love? Why is your cheek so pale?
> How chance the Roses there do fade so fast?

This is a classic case of the language's changing from simple at first to the complex language containing a metaphor. Both *Lysanders* used this to make a theatrical gear change, one deciding that this meant they were becoming overwhelmed with emotion, the other that they were putting on a brave face at their impending separation. Both were valid, and both worked well with the audience.

In the verse nurse sessions, I had a bit of a tussle with both the *Helenas*, who wanted to play her as if she were trying to gain credit with *Demetrius* when she tells him of *Lysander* and *Hermia's* flight into the woods. But that is not what the words say (although it is the way it is usually played, and I often have to fight embedded ideas from previously seen or been-in productions):

HELENA:

> How happy some, ore othersome can be?
> Through *Athens* I am thought as faire as she.
> But what of that? *Demetrius* thinkes not so:
> He will not know, what all, but he doth know,
> And as hee erres, doting on *Hermias* eyes;
> So I, admiring of his qualities:
> Things base and vilde, holding no quantity,
> Love can transpose to forme and dignity,
> Love lookes not with the eyes, but with the minde,
> And therefore is wing'd *Cupid* painted blinde.
> Nor hath loves minde of any judgement taste:
> Wings and no eyes, figure, unheedy haste.
> And therefore is Love said to be a childe,
> Because in choise he is often beguil'd,
> As waggish boyes in game themselves forsweare;
> So the boy Love is perjur'd every where.
> For ere *Demetrius* lookt on *Hermias* eyne,
> He hail'd downe oathes that he was onely mine.
> And when this Haile some heat from *Hermia* felt,
> So he dissolv'd, and showres of oathes did melt,
> I will goe tell him of faire *Hermias* flight:
> Then to the wood will he, to morrow night
> Pursue her; and for his intelligence,
> If I have thankes, it is a deere expence:
> But heerein meane I to enrich my paine,
> To have his sight thither, and backe againe.

The comma at the end of *showres of oathes did melt,* means that the idea of *Hermia* leads her to her next decision, that she will enrich her pain by telling *Demetrius.* The result of this can only be that instead of a lonely *Demetrius* being left in Athens, and perhaps turning back to his old love *Helena,* he will pursue the fleeing lovers, *and backe againe* with *Hermia,* and the sad *Helena* will definitely be a witness to their subsequent marriage; enrich her pain indeed, helping her old lover to marry someone else!

The famous lovers' quarrel scene on both nights played extremely well, funny and full of indignation, as the actors did not have to act their surprise at the changing arguments that occurred. I have often been told that Cue Script acting must rely on the actors already knowing the play, but when I was working on the verse for the individuals, it was apparent that although they all knew the play, and many had been in it, when confronted with a Cue Script speech, they often had no idea who else was onstage with them, or to whom they were speaking, or indeed which of the various characters onstage might be giving them their cue to speak. Often the guess they had made as to who was speaking to them was completely wrong, and all this added to the intense, exciting, and entertaining lovers' quarrel scene on both nights.

The dialogue by *Lysander* to *Hermia*:

LYSANDER:
Hang off thou cat, thou bur; vile thing let loose,
Or I will shake thee from me like a serpent.

presents a problem of staging, since the receiving actor (*Hermia* in this case) needs to know to hang on, and I have found that in the preperformance Burbadge, there are usually one or two moments (this being one) that the actors need to talk to each other about. We also found it useful for all the actors to stand for a brief time in their family groups, to be reminded who they were related to for this performance. Interestingly, in the existing Cue Script for *Orlando* at Dulwich College, there are more stage instructions in the Cue Script than in the full text.

For the two nights, the interpretations were all varied, yet the play worked so well each night it was impossible to say any was "better" on one night or the other. What happened was that each night was a happening, and they were equally exciting and a grand exploration of the play. I know that it is often felt that Shakespeare wrote for particular actors, but my experiences are that with such skillful writing we do not need to know for whom they were originally planned. Anyway, over a period of time many parts, especially the boys' parts, would have been tackled by many different actors in turn as their voices broke, which again reinforces the thought that Shakespeare made his parts actor proof, whoever was playing them.

The Comedie of Errors, August 1997

We were invited to put on a play at the International Festival in Ross-on-Wye, and (perhaps foolishly) we decided to do a different play from the one we would have just done three weeks before in Jordan, or the one we were about to do two weeks later at the Globe.

Those actors in all three productions had a mammoth learning job to do, and a vivid memory, during the Jordan trip, is of an actor floating in the Dead Sea while trying to learn the part of *Antipholus*. So we all went down to the venue by coach, performed in the large marquee they had erected there, and returned to London, all in one day.

There was a very noisy generator immediately behind the back masking curtains, which made it very difficult to hear cues offstage, and I saw to my horror that actors were staying in the wings for a very long time, frantically trying to hear their cue line for entering, and I decided that the original actors could not have done this.

From then on, we always had a script backstage, which allowed the actors to look at it—not to learn more about their part but to reassure them that they had time for a rest, and not spend their precious energies on waiting for a three-word cue. We then felt that to have a person backstage doing this would be of use, getting actors ready for their entrances and making sure that all properties and furniture were ready, and we named the person the Book-Keeper. It was only much later that I discovered that there is in fact historical evidence for such a person, and that there <u>was</u> more than one copy of a script available to "run" the show. Having more than one script, one for the Book-Holder, or prompter, who well might update the script with what the actors were actually saying, and one script that was essentially for the stage management team.

This way of working throws up so many events from the practical necessity of putting on a play, events that then turn out to be of significance, and have historical relevance.

At the beginning of the play, the Merchant *Egeon* has a very long speech:

EGEON:
    A heavier taske could not have beene impos'd,
    Then I to speake my griefes unspeakeable:
    Yet that the world may witnesse that my end
    Was wrought by nature, not by vile offence,
    Ile utter what my sorrow gives me leave.   End of the first thought.
    In *Syracusa* was I borne, and wedde
    Unto a woman, happy but for me,
    And by me; had not our hap beene bad:
    With her I liv'd in joy, our wealth increast
    By prosperous voyages I often made
    To *Epidamium*, till my factors death,
    And the great care of goods at randone left,
    Drew me from kinde embracements of my spouse;

From whom my absence was not six moneths olde,

Before her selfe (almost at fainting under

The pleasing punishment that women beare)

Had made provision for her following me,

And soone, and safe, arrived where I was:

The Platt of The Comedie of Errors

An OSC Presentation for the Ross-on-Wye International Festival at 2:00 pm on Saturday 16th August, 1997

I-1 Enter the Duke of Ephesus, with Egeon, the Merchant of Siracusia: (CRISPIN HARRIS; MICHAEL ELLIOTT), Jaylor, and other attendants: (ADRIAN O'DONNELL; GREGORY DE POLNAY; TESS DIGNAN; SONIA RITTER; SALLY WOODFIELD). Exeunt, Egeon being taken to prison.

I-2 Enter Antipholus of Siracusia, his servant Dromio of Siracusia and the First Marchant: (DAVID JARVIS; JONATHAN ROBY; CALLUM COATES), who gives S.Antipholus a bag of money. Exit S.Dromio with the bag of money. Exit the Marchant. Enter Dromio of Ephesus: (DANIEL HOPKINS). He gets beaten. Exit E.Dromio. Exit S.Antipholus.

II-1 Enter the wife to Antipholus of Ephesus, Adriana with her sister Luciana: (JULIETTE GRASSBY; KERRY OWEN). Enter Dromio of Ephesus. Exit E.Dromio. Exeunt.

II-2 Enter Antipholus of Siracusia. Enter Dromio of Siracusia. S.Antipholus beats S.Dromio. To them, Adriana and Luciana. Exeunt.

III-1 Enter Antipholus of Ephesus: (DAVID HALL), his man Dromio, Angelo the Goldsmith, and Balthaser the Merchant: (PHILIP BIRD; GRAHAM POUNTNEY). The Officers hold the Rope: (JENNIFER BURGESS; HANNAH JACKSON; DUNCAN LAW; BARBARA MUSTON). Enter Dromio of Siracusia within, who bars entrance to E.Antipholus. To S.Dromio, Luce: (TESS DIGNAN). To S.Dromio, Adriana. Exit Adriana with Luce. Exit S.Dromio. Exeunt.

III-2 Enter Luciana, with Antipholus of Siracusia. Exit Luciana. Enter Dromio of Siracusia. Exit S.Dromio. Enter Angelo the Goldsmith with the Chaine, which he gives to Antipholus. Exit Angelo. Exit S.Antipholus.

Interval

IV-1 Enter the Second Merchant: (GREGORY DE POLNAY), Angelo the Goldsmith, and an Officer: (ADRIAN O'DONNELL). Enter Antipholus and Dromio of Ephesus. Exit E.Dromio. Enter Dromio of Siracusia. E.Antipholus is taken in custody to prison by the Officer, Goldsmith and Second Merchant. Exit S.Dromio.

IV-2 Enter Adriana and Luciana. To them, Dromio of Siracusia. Exit Luciana. Enter Luciana with the purse. Exeunt, S.Dromio with the purse.

IV-3 Enter Antipholus of Siracusia, wearing the Chaine. To him, Dromio of Siracusia with the money. To them, the Courtezan: (SALLY WOODFIELD). Exeunt S.Antipholus and S.Dromio. Exit the Courtezan.

IV-4 Enter Antipholus of Ephesus in the custody of the Jailor. Enter Dromio of Ephesus with the rope's end. Enter Adriana, Luciana, the Courtezan, and a Schoole-master called Pinch: (CALLUM COATES). Enter three or foure: (JENNIFER BURGESS; HANNAH JACKSON; DUNCAN LAW; BARBARA MUSTON), and offer to bind E.Antipholus - he strives. Pinch and the others bind and take off E.Antipholus and E.Dromio. Manet Officer, Adriana, Luciana and the Courtezan. Enter Antipholus of Siracusia with his Rapier drawn, and Dromio of Siracusia. They all runne about. Exeunt omnes, as fast as may be, frightened. Manet S.Antipholus and S.Dromio. Exeunt.

V-1 Enter the Second Merchant and the Goldsmith. Enter Antipholus and Dromio of Siracusia againe. The Merchant and S.Antipholus draw on each other. Enter Adriana, Luciana, the Courtezan, and others: (TESS DIGNAN). Exeunt S.Antipholus and S.Dromio to the Priorie for sanctuary. Enter the Lady Abbesse: (SONIA RITTER). Exit the Abbesse. Enter the Duke of Ephesus, and Egeon the Merchant of Siracusia, with the headsman, and other officers: (ADRIAN O'DONNELL; JENNIFER BURGESS; HANNAH JACKSON; DUNCAN LAW; BARBARA MUSTON). To Adriana, a Messenger: (GRAHAM POUNTNEY). E.Antipholus cries within. Enter Antipholus and Dromio of Ephesus. Exit the Messenger to the Abbesse. Enter the Abbesse with Antipholus and Dromio of Siracusia. All gather to see them. E.Antipholus gives the diamond ring to the Courtezan. Exeunt omnes. Manet the two Dromio's and the two brothers Antipholus. Exit S.Antipholus with E.Antipholus. Exeunt S.Dromio with E.Dromio.

Finis

Singers: PHILIP BIRD; JENNIFER BURGESS; ROSALIND CRESSY; DANIEL HOPKINS; DUNCAN LAW; BARBARA MUSTON; ADRIAN O'DONNELL; CHRISTINE OZANNE; SIMON PURSE; SALLY WOODFIELD

Music: HANNAH JACKSON
Costumes: ELLIE COCKERILL

Shakespeare
original
company

Book-Holder: CHRISTINE OZANNE
Presenter: PATRICK TUCKER

There had she not beene long, but she became
A joyfull mother of two goodly sonnes:
And, which was strange, the one so like the other,
As could not be distinguish'd but by names.   End of the second.
That very howre, and in the selfe-same Inne,
A meane woman was delivered
Of such a burthen Male, twins both alike:
Those, for their parents were exceeding poore,
I bought, and brought up to attend my sonnes.   End of the third.
My wife, not meanely prowd of two such boyes,
Made daily motions for our home returne:
Unwilling I agreed, alas, too soone wee came aboord. End of the fourth.
A league from *Epidamium* had we saild
Before the alwaies winde-obeying deepe
Gave any Tragicke Instance of our harme:
But longer did we not retaine much hope;
For what obscured light the heavens did grant,
Did but convay unto our fearefull mindes
A doubtfull warrant of immediate death,
Which though my selfe would gladly have imbrac'd,
Yet the incessant weepings of my wife,
Weeping before for what she saw must come,
And pitteous playnings of the prettie babes
That mourn'd for fashion, ignorant what to feare,
Forst me to seeke delayes for them and me,
And this it was: (for other meanes was none)
The Sailors sought for safety by our boate,
And left the ship then sinking ripe to us.   End of the fifth.
My wife, more carefull for the latter borne,
Had fastned him unto a small spare Mast,
Such as sea-faring men provide for stormes:
To him one of the other twins was bound,
Whil'st I had beene like heedfull of the other. End of the sixth.
The children thus dispos'd, my wife and I,
Fixing our eyes on whom our care was fixt,
Fastned our selves at eyther end the mast,
And floating straight, obedient to the streame,
Was carried towards *Corinth*, as we thought. End of the seventh.
At length the sonne gazing upon the earth,
Disperst those vapours that offended us,
And by the benefit of his wished light
The seas waxt calme, and we discovered

Two shippes from farre, making amaine to us:
Of *Corinth* that, of *Epidarus* this,
But ere they came, oh let me say no more,
Gather the sequell by that went before.   End of the eighth.

In the modern edited texts, this speech can be divided into as many as <u>eighteen</u> different thoughts, but by sticking with the Folio punctuation and making the actor really drive each thought to where the full stop occurred, it changed into a comedy routine, with everyone thinking the old man had finished, only to have him launch into another section of his laborious tale. The punctuation played really well, and although I was and am well aware of the Folio's reputation for much randomness in its punctuation, I continue to be surprised at just how well it comes off as a theatrical event.

When *Antipholus* is confronted by a *Dromio* who seems to have forgotten that he recently took a bag of gold from him, he is often played as in a white heat of anger, but the gear change in his own language between *you* and *thee* is quite revealing:

S.ANTIPHOLUS:
    Stop in your winde sir, tell me this I pray?   *Antipholus* uses the usual *your*
    Where have you left the mony that I gave you.   and *you*.
E.DROMIO:
    Oh six pence that I had a wensday last,   *Dromio* replies with a *you*, which
    To pay the Sadler for my Mistris crupper: he stays with for the whole
    The Sadler had it Sir, I kept it not.   scene.
S.ANTIPHOLUS:
    I am not in a sportive humor now:
    Tell me, and dally not, where is the monie?
    We being strangers here, how dar'st thou trust   Once he asks about the money,
    So great a charge from thine owne custodie.   he switches to *thou* and *thine*.
E.DROMIO:
    I pray you jest sir as you sit at dinner:
    I from my Mistris come to you in post:
    If I returne I shall be post indeede.
    For she will scoure your fault upon my pate:
    Me thinkes your maw, like mine, should be your cooke,
    And strike you home without a messenger.
S.ANTIPHOLUS:
    Come *Dromio*, come, these jests are out of season,
    Reserve them till a merrier houre then this:
    Where is the gold I gave in charge to thee?   Again, he uses *thee* to talk
E.DROMIO: about the money.
    To me sir? why you gave no gold to me?

S.ANTIPHOLUS:
    Come on sir knave, have done your foolishnes,
    And tell me how thou hast dispos'd thy charge.
E.DROMIO:
    My charge was but to fetch you from the Mart
    Home to your house, the *Phœnix* sir, to dinner;
    My Mistris and her sister staies for you.
S.ANTIPHOLUS:
    Now as I am a Christian answer me,
    In what safe place you have bestow'd my monie;
    Or I shall breake that merrie sconce of yours
    That stands on tricks, when I am undispos'd:
    Where is the thousand Markes thou hadst of me?
E.DROMIO:
    I have some markes of yours upon my pate:
    Some of my Mistris markes upon my shoulders:
    But not a thousand markes betweene you both.
    If I should pay your worship those againe,
    Perchance you will not beare them patiently.
S.ANTIPHOLUS:
    Thy Mistris markes? what Mistris slave hast thou?
E.DROMIO:
    Your worships wife, my Mistris at the *Phœnix*;
    She that doth fast till you come home to dinner:
    And praies that you will hie you home to dinner.

S.ANTIPHOLUS:
    What wilt thou flout me thus unto my face
    Being forbid? There take you that sir knave.
E.DROMIO:
    What meane you sir, for God sake hold your hands:
    Nay, and you will not sir, Ile take my heeles.
    EXIT E.DROMIO.

He switches to *your* when criticizing him, but quickly changes to *thy* on asking for the money.

Back to *you* and *yours* for the angry bit, and back to *thou* for the last question.

Staying with *thy* and *thou* to ask about this supposed mistress.

There is a repeated cue line here, and so *Antipholus* will start to speak, and then stop until *Dromio* has said his final line. When these repeated cue lines appear, I am sure they are intentional and are used often for comic effect or to get actors to speak simultaneously.

A quiet *thou* is followed by the violent *you* when he actually strikes *Dromio*.

This switching from *you* to *thee* shows that *Antipholus*, however angry he may be, always changes to a more gentle mode of address whenever he asks about the money; it is as if he stops being loud and formal, and tries to be more calm, more intimate; it is almost as if he dare not shout and scream when so much money is involved. It is a delightful variation on just being continuously angry, and a great acting note from Shakespeare.

It was fascinating that Jon Roby, playing *Dromio*, although a very different actor from Richard Cordery, who first played the part six years before, got just the same riotous response to his description of the fat kitchen maid.

I had some of the actors asking if the part of *Luce* should in fact be the *Nell* that *Dromio* talks of, as it often is in more conventional productions, but as usual I said we would do the play as written, and then see what we felt. What happened was another revelation, that the actress playing *Luce* could never match the visual description of this enormously fat kitchen wench that *Dromio* talks of, and to have her appear with the same name as the kitchen wench would dull the audience's imagining of a truly gargantuan woman trying to ensnare the desperate *Dromio*. To have her depicted on stage would be to reduce the horror to one of "Well, she is not really <u>that</u> bad," and that is obviously (to me) what Shakespeare intended: to leave her to the audience's fantasy.

As you Like it, September 1997

For the first full-length season at the newly opened Shakespeare's Globe, we decided to present *As you Like it*. Our English company was at full strength, with Sonia Ritter as *Rosalind* and Philip Bird as *Orlando*, and we had to be careful not to guide them toward what our Canadian company had done, but to discover the play for themselves, to find their own specific moments.

We had no preconceived idea as to how to use the Globe stage, except to insist that there be people sitting in the Lords room, to give a complete "in the round" audience, which we knew to be the original way. The other productions that season (and subsequent ones) had given over the central balcony area to the musicians, or to an acting area, but the Lords who would have seated themselves up there would certainly not have given over the prime viewing place to mere musicians or actors. Seeing a play from that angle was one of the most revelatory experiences during that first season. You feel as if you are <u>inside</u> the play, and only require the occasional glance from the actors to keep you involved in the production. Just as being a groundling, and standing, was considered inappropriate for a modern audience, but it has turned out to be one of the most attractive features of the new building, so watching a play from the position of the Lords has turned out to be a favorite viewing platform, not just a place where you can be seen or from which you get a rotten view.

We planned some entrances through the audience, and found that they did not work at all. Some of the audience could see them, others could not, so the play had to wait until the actors had finally pushed their way onto the stage—we played to more than 100 percent capacity, and the place was packed. Lesson number one: keep to the stage, and leave the auditorium to the audience.

Just as we had done in Toronto, we "rehearsed" the fight between *Charles* and *Orlando* for twenty minutes, and the result was as good as one prepared over a much

The Platt of As you Like it
An OSC Presentation for Shakespeare's Globe, London
at 7:30 pm on Monday 1st September, 1997

I-1: Enter Orlando and Adam: (PHILIP BIRD; DUNCAN LAW). Enter Oliver, elder brother to Orlando: (DAVID JARVIS). Oliver strikes Orlando. Exit Orlando and Adam. To Oliver, Dennis his servant: (JONATHAN ROBY). To Oliver, Charles the wrestler: (DAVID HALL). Exit Dennis. Exit Charles. Exit Oliver.

I-2: Enter Rosalind, daughter of the banished Duke, and Celia, daughter of Duke Frederick: (SONIA RITTER; TESS DIGNAN). Enter the Clowne, Touchstone: (CALLUM COATES). Enter le Beau: (SARAH FINCH). Flourish. Enter Duke Frederick: (GRAHAM POUNTNEY), Lords: (SCOTT AINSLIE; KERRY OWEN), Orlando, Charles, and Attendants with the Mat: (ADRIAN O'DONNELL; SALLY WOODFIELD). Charles and Orlando wrestle. Charles is thrown and defeated. Shout. Exeunt all but Celia, Rosalind and Orlando, Charles being carried out. Rosalind gives Orlando a chain from around her neck. Exit Rosalind and Celia. Enter Le Beau. Exit Orlando and Le Beau.

I-3: Enter Celia and Rosalind. Enter Duke Frederick with Lords: (SCOTT AINSLIE; SARAH FINCH; ADRIAN O'DONNELL; KERRY OWEN; SALLY WOODFIELD). The Duke banishes Rosalind. Exit the Duke and Lords. Exeunt Rosalind and Celia.

Short break

II-1: Enter Duke Senior, Amyens: (DAVID DELVE; DANIEL HOPKINS), and two or three Lords like Forresters: (DAVID HALL; DAVID JARVIS). Exeunt.

II-2: Enter Duke Frederick, with Lords. Exeunt.

II-3: Enter Orlando and Adam. Adam offers Orlando a bag of gold. Exeunt.

II-4: Enter Rosaline dressed as the page Ganimed, Celia dressed as Aliena, and the Clowne Touchstone. Enter Corin and Silvius, two shepherds: (MICHAEL ELLIOTT; JONATHAN ROBY). Exit Silvius. Touchstone calls out to Corin. Exeunt.

II-5: Enter Amyens, Jaques: (GREGORY DE POLNAY) and others: (DAVID HALL; DAVID JARVIS; ADRIAN O'DONNELL; SALLY WOODFIELD). Amyens sings a Song. They all sing the Song. Jaques does a parody of the Song. Exeunt.

II-6: Enter Orlando, and Adam. Exeunt, Orlando carrying Adam.

II-7: Enter Duke Senior, Amyens, Lords, like Out-lawes. A meal is set out. Enter Jaques. To them Orlando, with his sword drawn. Exit Orlando. Enter Orlando with Adam. Amyens sings a Song as they eat. Exeunt.

Interval – 15 minutes

III-1: Enter Duke Frederick, Lords, and Oliver. Exeunt, pushing out Oliver.

III-2: Enter Orlando, who fastens a poem to a tree. Exit Orlando. Enter Corin and Clowne. Enter Rosalind, reading a poem. Enter Celia with a writing, which she reads. Exit Clowne with Corin. Enter Orlando and Jaques, Rosalind and Celia hiding behind. Rosalind comes forward. Exit Jaques. Exeunt.

III-3: Enter Clowne, Audrey: (KERRY OWEN), and Jaques observing from behind. Enter Sir Oliver Martext, a vicar: (DUNCAN LAW). Jaques comes forward. Exeunt.

III-4: Enter Rosalind and Celia. To them, Corin. Exeunt.

III-5: Enter Silvius and Phebe: (SARAH FINCH). Enter behind, Rosalind, Celia and Corin. Rosalind comes forward. Exit Rosalind, Celia, and Corin. Exeunt Silvius and Phebe.

Interval – 10 minutes

IV-1: Enter Rosalind, and Celia, and Jaques. Enter Orlando. Exit Jaques. Orlando woos Ganimed as Rosalind. Exit Orlando. Exeunt.

IV-2: Enter Jaques and Lords like Forresters: (DAVID HALL; DANIEL HOPKINS; DUNCAN LAW; ADRIAN O'DONNELL; SALLY WOODFIELD). They sing a Song. Exeunt.

IV-3: Enter Rosalind and Celia. Enter Silvius with a letter. Exit Silvius. Enter Oliver with a bloody napkin. Rosalind faints. Exeunt.

V-1: Enter Clowne and Awdrie. Enter William, a former follower of Awdrie: (GRAHAM POUNTNEY). Exit William. To them, Corin. Exeunt.

V-2: Enter Orlando with his arm in a scarf, and Oliver. Enter Rosalind. Exit Oliver. Enter Silvius and Phebe. Rosalind gives them commands. Exeunt.

V-3: Enter Clowne and Audrey. Enter two Pages: (SALLY WOODFIELD; ADRIAN O'DONNELL). They sing a Song. Exeunt.

V-4: Enter Duke Senior, First Forrester, Jaques, Orlando, Oliver, Celia. Enter Rosalinde, Silvius, and Phebe. Exit Rosalinde and Celia. Enter Clowne and Audrey. Enter Hymen: (DANIEL HOPKINS), with Rosalind and Celia dressed as themselves. Still Musicke. They all sing the Wedding Song. To them, the Second Brother of Orlando: (MICHAEL MALONEY). Exit Jaques. A Dance. Exit all but Rosalind. Rosalind delivers the Epilogue. Exit Rosalind.

Finis.

Singers: PHILIP BIRD; JENNIFER BURGESS; ROSALIND CRESSY; DANIEL HOPKINS; HANNAH JACKSON; DUNCAN LAW; BARBARA MUSTON; ADRIAN O'DONNELL; CHRISTINE OZANNE; SIMON PURSE; SALLY WOODFIELD
Musicians: PATRICK CRUMLEY; MARTIN ETHERIDGE; MARTIN POPE

Costumes: ELLIE COCKERILL   Musical director: HANNAH JACKSON

Book-Holder: CHRISTINE OZANNE   Presenter: PATRICK TUCKER

longer period. The audience joined in the production from the earliest moment, and gave in glowing reports on the show afterward. *Orlando* had felt that he wanted to proclaim his love for *Rosalind* all around the stage, so he put up a rolled banner, which when he unfurled, read "O ♥ R."

There is a scene that seems to be very difficult in Cue Script form, since the cues are similar for several of the actors:

ROSALIND:

> Therefore put you in your best aray,
> bid your friends, for if you will be married to morrow,
> you shall: and to *Rosalind* if you will.
>> *ENTER SILVIUS AND PHEBE.*
> Looke, here comes a Lover of mine, and a lover of hers.

Rosalind, disguised as the boy Ganimed, is talking to Orlando (the one she loves).

Phebe has fallen in love with Ganimed, and Silvius is in love with Phebe.

PHEBE:

> Youth, you have done me much ungentlenesse,
> To shew the letter that I writ to you.

ROSALIND:

> I care not if I have: it is my studie
> To seeme despightfull and ungentle to you:
> You are there followed by a faithful shepheard,
> Looke upon him, love him: he worships you.

PHEBE:

> Good shepheard, tell this youth what 'tis to love.

SILVIUS:

> It is to be all made of sighes and teares,
> And so am I for *Phebe*.

PHEBE:

> And I for *Ganimed*.

If each actor crosses over to the person they are talking to, then a wonderful pattern of movements occurs, with each actor trying to get close to a different one.

ORLANDO:

> And I for *Rosalind*.

ROSALIND:

> And I for no woman.

SILVIUS:

> It is to be all made of faith and service,
> And so am I for *Phebe*.

PHEBE:

> And I for *Ganimed*.

Here the cue is the same as before, and the actors know they have had two similar cues for two different speeches.

ORLANDO:

> And I for *Rosalind*.

ROSALIND:

> And I for no woman.

SILVIUS:

It is to be all made of fantasie,
All made of passion, and all made of wishes,
All adoration, dutie, and observance,
All humblenesse, all patience, and impatience,
All puritie, all triall, all observance:
And so am I for *Phebe*.

PHEBE:

And so am I for *Ganimed*.

ORLANDO:

And so am I for *Rosalind*.

ROSALIND:

And so am I for no woman.

PHEBE:

If this be so, why blame you me to love you?

SILVIUS:

If this be so, why blame you me to love you?

ORLANDO:

If this be so, why blame you me to love you?

ROSALIND:

Why do you speake too, Why blame you mee
to love you.

ORLANDO:

To her, that is not heere, nor doth not heare.

ROSALIND:

Pray you no more of this, 'tis like the howling
of Irish Wolves against the Moone: I will helpe you
if I can: I would love you if I could: To morrow meet
me altogether: I wil marrie you, if ever I marrie Woman, and Ile be married to morrow: I will satisfie you,
if ever I satisfi'd man, and you shall bee married to morrow. I wil content you, if what pleases you contents
you, and you shal be married to morrow: As you love
Rosalind meet, as you love *Phebe* meet, and as I love no
woman, Ile meet: so fare you wel: I have left you commands.

SILVIUS:

Ile not faile, if I live.

PHEBE:

Nor I.

ORLANDO:

Nor I.

EXEUNT.

The repetition of the word *All* allows a wonderful build to the speech, far more than most actors will allow, and yet fully justified by the amazing number of *alls* in the speech.

The cue words *me to love you* are the same for their next speech by *Silvius* <u>and</u> for *Orlando*. Two things can happen: either they speak simultaneously or start to speak, stop when the other has the lines, and then speak. Whatever happens, it leads to confusion.

And here *Rosalind* herself acknowledges that confusion: *'tis like the howling of Irish Wolves against the Moone*, with either simultaneous speaking or interruptions going on. This scene <u>must</u> have had the same effect in Shakespeare's time, and so this must be what was intended; it is a glorious example of the actors' attitude matching that of their characters.

At the end of the performance—which indeed went on for too long—I saw that our actors were carefully explaining everything in Act Five, even though the audience already knew all the information given there, and that it is only seeing the actors on stage reacting to our already known information that is of interest. We discovered a new disease called "Act Fivitis," and swore we would never suffer from it again. It has taken us quite a while to get this particular bug out of our system. Speeding up Act Five is one of our most useful (and highly recommended) guidelines.

The audience response to the production included "that's the clearest *As you Like it* I have seen," and even "the funniest," a worrying rebuke to those of us who insist that weeks of rehearsal are necessary to realize a Shakespeare text.

I am not advocating that this is the only way to approach Shakespeare, or even that this is a superior way; only that this way unlocks certain attitudes and theatricalities that perhaps get lost in a more conventional approach. Perhaps the best parallel is that of music played in original arrangements on original musical instruments. It would never be claimed that this was a superior method of doing it, but it does bring to our attention perhaps some of the original intent that has become hidden under our modern orchestras and instruments. We think Shakespeare should be regarded in the same way, that an original approach is simply to release and bring out additional points of view, not supplant the whole of the Shakespeare industry.

Twelfe Night, July 1998

For our second visit to Jordan, I decided that the Company should learn how to cope without my presence, as I had a fear that this way of working was getting too closely connected with my own certainties, and if it was to flourish and prove its point, it must be able to do so in other circumstances. I appointed Simon Purse, who had been our Book-Holder in Jordan the year before, to be the complete Presenter, and to continue to share the verse work with me.

We therefore prepared the production, with all its connected problems of arrangements, costumes, and properties, but did not go to Jordan ourselves. On a personal level, this was a mistake, since Christine and I had all the angst of the preparation and none of the payback, but as a production it worked well.

Our problem was to get a suitable *Sir Toby Belch,* and we settled on two as well as two *Olivias,* two *Festes* and two *Fabians.* This led to a lot of verse work, and it was fascinating to see the two *Olivias* work out how to justify the change from prose to poetry in their first scene with *Viola*:

OLIVIA: *Olivia* speaks in prose.
　　Now sir, what is your text?
VIOLA: *Viola* also speaks in prose.
　　Most sweet Ladie.

OLIVIA:

A comfortable doctrine, and much may bee saide
of it. Where lies your Text?

VIOLA:

In *Orsinoes* bosome.

The Platt of Twelfe Night, Or what you will

*An OSC Presentation on the Artimes Steps at the Jerash Festival, Jordan
at 8:30 pm on Thursday 23rd July, 1998*

I-1 Enter Orsino (Duke of Illyria), Curio: (RICHARD BURNIP; STEVE BLACK), Music playing. To the Duke, Valentine: (RAY ARMSTRONG). Exeunt.

I-2 Enter Viola: (SARAH FINCH), a Captaine: (RICHARD LANCASTER), and Saylors: (PHILIPPE SPALL; DUNCAN LAW). Viola gives him gold. Exeunt.

I-3 Enter Sir Toby (Uncle to Olivia): (DAVID HALL), and Maria: (CAROLYN JONES). To them, Sir Andrew: (JONATHAN ROBY), a foolish knight. Exit Maria. Exeunt, Sir Andrew dancing.

I-4 Enter Valentine and Viola as Cesario, in man's attire. Enter Orsino, Curio. Exeunt.

I-5 Enter Maria, and Feste the Clowne: (DANIEL HOPKINS). Exit Maria, and enter Lady Olivia: (HANNAH JACKSON), with Malvolio: (CALLUM COATES) her Steward. To Olivia, Maria. Enter Sir Toby and Malvolio. Enter Sir Toby, drunk and belching. Exit Sir Toby. Exit Feste, and enter Malvolio. Malvolio calls in Maria, and exits. Olivia is veiled. Enter Viola as Cesario. Exeunt, manet Viola and Olivia. Viola refuses money from Olivia, and exits. To Olivia, Malvolio. She gives him a ring. Exit Malvolio. Exit Olivia.

II-1 Enter Antonio a Captain and Sebastian: (RICHARD LANCASTER; HEATHER TRACY) (twin to Viola). Exit Sebastian. Exit Antonio.

II-2 Enter Viola at one door, Malvolio at another. Malvolio leaves the ring, and exits. Exit Viola.

II-3 Enter Sir Toby, and Sir Andrew. To them, Feste the Clowne. The Clowne sings. They all sing a Catch. To them, Maria. To them, Malvolio angry at the noise. They all sing again. Exit Malvolio. Exit Maria. Exeunt.

II-4 Enter Orsino the Duke, Viola, Curio and Valentine. Musicke playes, and Curio exits. Enter Curio and Feste the Clowne. Musicke and Feste sings the Song. Orsino pays him. Exit Feste. Exeunt, manet Orsino and Viola. Orsino gives her a jewell, and exeunt.

II-5 Enter Sir Toby, Sir Andrew and Fabian: (DUNCAN LAW). To them, Maria with her letter. Sir Toby, Sir Andrew and Fabian hide in the box tree. Maria drops her letter and exits. Enter Malvolio musing. He picks up and reads the letter. Exit Malvolio. Enter Maria. Exeunt.

Interval.

Book-Holder/Presenter: SIMON PURSE
Tour Manager: CAROLYN JONES
Costumes: ELLIE COCKERILL
Musical director: HANNAH JACKSON

III-1 Enter Viola and Feste the Clowne, playing the tabor. Feste is paid by Viola, and exits. Enter Sir Toby and Sir Andrew. Enter Olivia, and Maria. Exeunt, manet Olivia and Viola. The clocke strikes. Exeunt.

III-2 Enter Sir Toby, Sir Andrew, and Fabian. Exit Sir Andrew to write a challenge. To them, Maria. Exeunt Omnes.

III-3 Enter Sebastian and Anthonio. Anthonio gives him his purse. Exeunt.

III-4 Enter Olivia and Maria. To Olivia, Malvolio with yellow stockings cross gartered. To Olivia, a Servant: (STEVE BLACK). Exeunt, manet Malvolio. Enter Sir Toby, Fabian and Maria. Exit Malvolio. To them, Sir Andrew with his Challenge, which Sir Toby reads. Exit Sir Andrew. Enter Olivia and Viola. Exeunt Sir Toby, Fabian and Maria. Olivia gives Viola a picture jewell. Exit Olivia at one door, and enter Sir Toby and Fabian at another. Sir Toby tells her she must duel with Sir Andrew. Exit Sir Toby. Exeunt Viola and Fabian. Enter Sir Toby and Sir Andrew, who is told he must duel with Viola. Enter Fabian dragging on Viola. They prepare to fight. To them, Antonio to stop the fight. Enter Officers: (PHILIPPE SPALL; LOUISE DOHERTY) to arrest Antonio. Viola offers half her purse to him. Exeunt Antonio and Officers. Exit Viola. Exeunt.

IV-1 Enter Sebastian and Feste the Clowne. To them, Sir Andrew, Sir Toby, and Fabian. Sir Andrew slaps Sebastian, and gets slapped back. Sir Toby holds Sebastian. Exit Feste. Sebastian prepares to fight Sir Toby. Enter Olivia to stop the fight. Exeunt.

IV-2 Enter Maria with beard and gown, and Feste the Clowne, Malvolio being within the prison cell. Feste dresses as Sir Topas the Curate. Enter Sir Toby. Feste talks to Malvolio within as Sir Topas. Exeunt Sir Toby and Maria. Feste comes to Malvolio in his own voice, then as Sir Topas. Exit Feste.

IV-3 Enter Sebastian, with a pearle. To him, Olivia, and the Priest: (RAY ARMSTRONG). Exeunt.

V-1 Enter Feste with Malvolio's letter, and Fabian. Enter Orsino, Viola, Curio. Orsino pays Feste. Exit Feste and Fabian at one door, and enter Anthonio and Officers at another. Enter Olivia. To her, the Priest. Enter Sir Andrew with a bloody head. Enter Sir Toby with a bloody head, and Feste. Exeunt Feste, Sir Toby and Sir Andrew, and enter Sebastian. All marvel at the identical twins. Enter Feste with Malvolio's letter, and Fabian. Feste reads the letter; Olivia gives it to Fabian to finish reading. Exit Fabian. Enter Fabian with Malvolio. Malvolio shows Maria's letter to Olivia. Exit Malvolio. Exeunt, manet Feste, who sings.

Finis.

OLIVIA:

In his bosome? In what chapter of his bosome?

VIOLA:

To answer by the method, in the first of his hart.

The Platt of Twelfe Night, Or what you will

An OSC Presentation on the Artimes Steps at the Jerash Festival, Jordan at 8:30 pm on Friday 24th July, 1998

I-1 Enter Orsino (Duke of Illyria), Curio: (RICHARD BURNIP; DUNCAN LAW), Music playing. To the Duke, Valentine: (DAVID HALL). Exeunt.

I-2 Enter Viola: (SARAH FINCH), a Captaine: (RICHARD LANCASTER), and Saylors: (STEVE BLACK; DANIEL HOPKINS). Viola gives him gold. Exeunt.

I-3 Enter Sir Toby (Uncle to Olivia): (RAY ARMSTRONG), and Maria: (CAROLYN JONES). To them, Sir Andrew: (JONATHAN ROBY), a foolish knight. Exit Maria. Exeunt, Sir Andrew dancing.

I-4 Enter Valentine and Viola as Cesario, in man's attire. Enter Orsino, Curio. Exeunt.

I-5 Enter Maria, and Feste the Clowne: (PHILIPPE SPALL). Exit Maria, and enter Lady Olivia: (LOUISE DOHERTY), with Malvolio: (CALLUM COATES) her Steward. To Olivia, Maria. Exit Maria and Malvolio. Enter Sir Toby, drunk and belching. Exit Sir Toby. Exit Feste, and enter Malvolio. Malvolio calls in Maria, and exits. Olivia is veiled. Enter Viola as Cesario. Exeunt, manet Viola and Olivia. Viola refuses money from Olivia, and exits. To Olivia, Malvolio. She gives him a ring. Exit Malvolio. Exit Olivia.

II-1 Enter Antonio a Captain and Sebastian: (RICHARD LANCASTER; HEATHER TRACY) (twin to Viola). Exit Sebastian. Exit Antonio.

II-2 Enter Viola at one door, Malvolio at another. Malvolio leaves the ring, and exits. Exit Viola.

II-3 Enter Sir Toby, and Sir Andrew. To them, Feste the Clowne. The Clowne sings. They all sing a Catch. To them, Maria. To them, Malvolio angry at the noise. They all sing again. Exit Malvolio. Exit Maria. Exeunt.

II-4 Enter Orsino the Duke, Viola, Curio and Valentine. Musicke playes, and Curio exits. Enter Curio and Feste the Clowne. Musicke and Feste sings the Song. Orsino pays him. Exit Feste. Exeunt, manet Orsino and Viola. Orsino gives her a jewell, and exeunt.

II-5 Enter Sir Toby, Sir Andrew and Fabian: (STEVE BLACK). To them, Maria with her letter. Sir Toby, Sir Andrew and Fabian hide in the box tree. Maria drops her letter and exits. Enter Malvolio musing. He picks up and reads the letter. Exit Malvolio. Enter Maria. Exeunt.

Interval.

III-1 Enter Viola and Feste the Clowne, playing the tabor. Feste is paid by Viola, and exits. Enter Sir Toby and Sir Andrew. Enter Olivia, and Maria. Exeunt, manet Olivia and Viola. The clocke strikes. Exeunt.

III-2 Enter Sir Toby, Sir Andrew, and Fabian. Exit Sir Andrew to write a challenge. To them, Maria. Exeunt Omnes.

III-3 Enter Sebastian and Anthonio. Anthonio gives him his purse. Exeunt.

III-4 Enter Olivia and Maria. To Olivia, Malvolio with yellow stockings cross gartered. To Olivia, a Servant: (DUNCAN LAW). Exeunt, manet Malvolio. Enter Sir Toby, Fabian and Maria. Exit Malvolio. To them, Sir Andrew with his Challenge, which Sir Toby reads. Exit Sir Andrew. Enter Olivia and Viola. Exeunt Sir Toby, Fabian and Maria. Olivia gives Viola a picture jewell. Exit Olivia at one door, and enter Sir Toby and Fabian at another. Sir Toby tells her she must duel with Sir Andrew. Exit Sir Toby. Exeunt Viola and Fabian. Enter Sir Toby and Sir Andrew, who is told he must duel with Viola. Enter Fabian dragging on Viola. They prepare to fight. To them, Antonio to stop the fight. Enter Officers: (DANIEL HOPKINS; HANNAH JACKSON) to arrest Antonio. Viola offers half her purse to him. Exeunt Antonio and Officers. Exit Viola. Exeunt.

IV-1 Enter Sebastian and Feste the Clowne. To them, Sir Andrew, Sir Toby, and Fabian. Sir Andrew slaps Sebastian, and gets slapped back. Sir Toby holds Sebastian. Exit Feste. Sebastian prepares to fight Sir Toby. Enter Olivia to stop the fight. Exeunt.

IV-2 Enter Maria with beard and gown, and Feste the Clowne, Malvolio being within the prison cell. Feste dresses as Sir Topas the Curate. Enter Sir Toby. Feste talks to Malvolio within as Sir Topas. Exeunt Sir Toby and Maria. Feste comes to Malvolio in his own voice, then as Sir Topas. Exit Feste.

IV-3 Enter Sebastian, with a pearle. To him, Olivia, and the Priest: (DAVID HALL). Exeunt.

V-1 Enter Feste with Malvolio's letter, and Fabian. Enter Orsino, Viola, Curio. Orsino pays Feste. Exit Feste and Fabian at one door, and enter Anthonio and Officers at another. Enter Olivia. To her, the Priest. Enter Sir Andrew with a bloody head. Enter Sir Toby with a bloody head, and Feste. Exeunt Feste, Sir Toby and Sir Andrew, and enter Sebastian. All marvel at the identical twins. Enter Feste with Malvolio's letter, and Fabian. Feste reads the letter; Olivia gives it to Fabian to finish reading. Exit Fabian. Enter Fabian with Malvolio. Malvolio shows Maria's letter to Olivia. Exit Malvolio. Exeunt, manet Feste, who sings.

Finis.

Book-Holder/Presenter: SIMON PURSE
Tour Manager: CAROLYN JONES
Costumes: ELLIE COCKERILL
Musical director: HANNAH JACKSON

OLIVIA:

O, I have read it: it is heresie. Have you no more
to say?

VIOLA:

Good Madam, let me see your face.

OLIVIA:

Have you any Commission from your Lord, to
negotiate with my face: you are now out of your Text:
but we will draw the Curtain, and shew you the picture.
Looke you sir, such a one I was this present: Ist not well
done?

VIOLA:

Excellently done, if God did all.

OLIVIA:

'Tis in graine sir, 'twill endure winde and weather.

VIOLA:

'Tis beauty truly blent, whose red and white,   *Viola* changes to speaking in
Natures owne sweet, and cunning hand laid on: poetry.
Lady, you are the cruell'st shee alive,
If you will leade these graces to the grave,
And leave the world no copie.

OLIVIA:

O sir, I will not be so hard-hearted: I will give   *Olivia* is still speaking in prose.
out divers scedules of my beautie. It shal be Inventoried
and every particle and utensile labell'd to my will: As,
Item two lippes indifferent redde, Item two grey eyes,
with lids to them: Item, one necke, one chin, and so forth.
Were you sent hither to praise me?

VIOLA:

I see you what you are, you are too proud: *Viola* speaks in poetry.
But if you were the divell, you are faire:
My Lord, and master loves you: O such love
Could be but recompenc'd, though you were crown'd
The non-pareil of beautie.

OLIVIA:

How does he love me?   *Olivia* speaks in prose.

VIOLA:

With adorations, fertill teares,   *Viola* speaks poetry.
With groanes that thunder love, with sighes of fire.

OLIVIA:

Your Lord does know my mind, I cannot love him   *Olivia* now changes to speaking
Yet I suppose him vertuous, know him noble,   in poetry. This is the main gear

Of great estate, of fresh and stainlesse youth;
In voyces well divulg'd, free, learn'd, and valiant,
And in dimension, and the shape of nature,
A gracious person; But yet I cannot love him:
He might have tooke his answer long ago.

change in the scene, in her very characterization; looking at her part in Cue Script form, you can see that from the first moment she walked onstage, she was speaking in prose—and it is here that she changes.

The gear change can be seen as where she notices *Viola/Cesario* for the first time (one of our *Olivias*), or when she falls in love with her (the other of our *Olivias*); both interpretations worked well for the play, with each being specific to that particular choice, and unique to that actress. This means that *Olivia* needs to prepare for the gear change when working on the part, without knowing why it is there.

I have dealt with *Viola* and the *Captaine* earlier.

King John, September 1998

For our second presentation at the Globe, I felt that the criticism that we only did plays that the actors and audience already knew, and so would bring past knowledge into the production, had to be addressed. It was not true, of course, since even the most well known scene can seem much less straightforward and familiar when seen in Cue Script form.

King John was chosen because it is truly a play that none of my actors—nor I suspect my audience—have an internal map for. The play would have to stand on its own merits, since there would be no template either to guide the actors' decisions or the audience's perception of it. For the Genealogical Table covering the period of this play, see Appendix 1.

Having performed it, I can say it is a great play, and performs in quite unexpected ways. From the opening season, the resident company at the Globe had found that the audience would boo the French, however the actors tried to stop this (strange to say, this quite natural reaction was much resisted at first, and all sorts of techniques were tried to stop what turned out to be a guaranteed reaction from each audience during the run of *Henry V*). In this *King John* the audience started booing the French, but a strange thing happened when the French joined together with the English, and the alliance thus formed was broken up by the legate from the Pope, *Pandulphe*. The audience spent the rest of the evening booing the Pope's representative, and allowed the French to be their friends.

The actor playing *Hubert* had assumed he was a villain, since he knew from his lines that he would attempt to put out young *Arthur*'s eyes. What confounded him was his first scene, when it became plain to him from the audience laughter that he was an amusing character, so all his plans went out of the window as he adjusted to the new situation. It also made the *Arthur* scene even more moving, since we had laughed at this character, and now we saw him in a very different light.

The Platt of The life and death of King John

An OSC Presentation for Shakespeare's Globe, London
at 7:30 pm on Monday 7th September, 1998

I-1: Enter King John to his throne: (PHILIP BIRD), Queene Elinor: (JUDITH PARIS), Pembroke, Essex, and Salisbury, carrying the sword: (RICHARD BURNIP; PHILIP ROSCH; RAY ARMSTRONG), with the Chattylion of France: (GRAHAM POUNTNEY), who delivers an ultimatum. Exit Chattilion, and Pembroke. Enter a Sheriffe: (SARAH HOWE). Enter Robert Faulconbridge: (PHILIPPE SPALL), and his elder bastard brother Philip: (DAVID HALL), to ask the King to arbitrate on their inheritance. The King knights the Bastard. Exeunt all but Bastard. Enter his mother Lady Faulconbridge: (CAROLYN JONES) and James Gurney: (SIMON PURSE). Exit James. Exeunt. Strike the throne. Close the gates.

II-1: Enter before Angiers on one side, Philip King of France, Lewis the Daulphin: (NICHOLAS DAY; JONATHAN ROBY), Constance, Arthur: (SONIA RITTER; LOUISE DOHERTY) and forces: (DUNCAN LAW; SIMON PURSE); on the other side Austria: (STEVE BLACK) and forces: (SARAH FINCH; PHILIPPE SPALL). They pledge to support Arthur's claim to the English throne. Enter Chattilion, with news that the English have landed in France. Drum beats. Enter King of England, Bastard, Queene Elianor, Blanch: (JULIETTE GRASSBY), Pembroke, and Soldiers: (MICHAEL ELLIOTT; SARAH HOWE; PHILIP ROSCH). The two sides decide to ask the people of Angiers which monarch they accept. Trumpet sounds. Enter a Citizen (Hubert): (DANIEL HOPKINS) upon the walles of Angiers, who asks for proof of kingship. Exeunt. Heere after excursions, enter the Herald of France: (DUNCAN LAW) with Trumpets to the gates. Enter English Herald: (MICHAEL ELLIOTT) with Trumpet. The Citizen will not decide. Enter at one door King John, Queene Elianor, Blanche, Bastard, Pembroke, with their power, at the other door King Philip, Lewis, Austria with their power. The Bastard persuades them to join in defeating the town, but Hubert proposes a peace by marriage. The Dolphin whispers with Blanch, and the agreement is made. Exeunt, manet Bastard. Exit.

III-1: Open the gates and enter Constance, Arthur, and Salisbury. Enter King John, King Philip, Dolphin, Blanch, Queen Elianor, Philip, Austria. Enter Pandulph: (CALLUM COATES), the Legat of the Pope. He excommunicates King John, whose hand is held by King Philip. He threatens King Philip, who finally lets go his connection with England. Exeunt, planning war.

III-2: Allarums, Excursions: Enter Bastard with Austria's head. Enter King John, Arthur, and Hubert, Arthur having been captured. Exeunt. Alarums, excursions, Retreat. Enter King John, Queen Elianor, Arthur, Bastard, Hubert, Pembroke, Salisbury, Soldiers: (MICHAEL ELLIOTT; SARAH HOWE; SIMON PURSE; PHILIP ROSCH. Exit Bastard for England. King John speaks to Hubert aside. Exeunt.

Interval.

III-3: Enter King Philip, Dolphin, Pandulph, Attendants: (DUNCAN LAW; GRAHAM POUNTNEY; SIMON PURSE; PHILIPPE SPALL). Enter Constance, who tears her hair. Exit Constance. Exit King Philip, following her. Exeunt.

IV-1: Enter Hubert and Executioners: (PHILIP ROSCH; STEVE BLACK), with the warrant, ropes, irons and brazier. The Executioners withdraw. Enter Arthur. Hubert shows him the warrant. Hubert calls, and the Executioners come forward. Exeunt Executioners. Exeunt, Hubert taking brazier and irons.

IV-2: Enter King John to sit on his throne, Pembroke, Salisbury, Bigot: (MICHAEL ELLIOTT), and Attendants: (JULIETTE GRASSBY; CAROLYN JONES; JUDITH PARIS; PHILIP ROSCH). Enter Hubert, to tell the King privately that Arthur is dead. Exeunt Lords. Enter Messenger: (SARAH HOWE) with news of invasion, and the deaths of Elianor and Constance. Enter Bastard and Peter of Pomfret: (SIMON PURSE), a prophet. Exeunt Hubert and Peter. Exit Bastard, to speak to the Peers. Exit Messenger, following. Enter Hubert, with the warrant. He tells King John that Arthur is alive. Exeunt.

IV-3: Enter Arthur, disguised, on the walles: (STEVE BLACK; DUNCAN LAW; GRAHAM POUNTNEY; PHILIPPE SPALL). He leaps down, and dies. Enter Pembroke, Salisbury with a Letter, and Bigot. Enter Bastard. They discover Arthur's body. Enter Hubert. They all draw their swords. Exeunt Lords, to join the French. Exit, Hubert carrying Arthur.

V-1: Enter King John and Pandolph, attendants: (SARAH HOWE; CAROLYN JONES; JUDITH PARIS; PHILIP ROSCH). The King gives his crown to Pandolph, who crowns him again. Exit Pandolph, to pacify the French. Enter Bastard. Exeunt. Strike the throne.

V-2: Enter (in Armes) Dolphin, Salisbury, Meloone: (DUNCAN LAW), Pembroke, Bigot, Souldiers: (JULIETTE GRASSBY; GRAHAM POUNTNEY; SIMON PURSE; PHILIPPE SPALL). Dolphin gives a paper to Meloone. Enter Pandulphe, with news of King John's reconciliation with Rome. Trumpet sounds. Enter Bastard. The Dolphin rejects all arguments. Exeunt, getting ready for war.

V-3: Alarums. Enter King John sick, and Hubert. Enter a Messenger: (SARAH HOWE). Exeunt.

V-4: Enter Salisbury, Pembroke, and Bigot. Enter Meloon wounded, with news of danger for the rebels. They exeunt, to return to England's side.

V-5: Enter Dolphin, and his Traine: (STEVE BLACK; JULIETTE GRASSBY; GRAHAM POUNTNEY; SIMON PURSE). Enter a Messenger: (PHILIPPE SPALL). Exeunt.

V-6: Enter Bastard and Hubert severally, Hubert with a weapon. Exeunt.

V-7: Enter Prince Henry: (SARAH FINCH), Salisburie, Bigot, and Soldiers: (SARAH HOWE; CAROLYN JONES; SIMON PURSE; PHILIP ROSCH). Enter Pembroke. King John is brought in on a litter: (STEVE BLACK; DUNCAN LAW; GRAHAM POUNTNEY; PHILIPPE SPALL). Enter Bastard. The King dies. They give their allegiance to Prince Henry. Exeunt.

Finis.

original Shakespeare company

Book-Holder: CHRISTINE OZANNE;   Presenter: PATRICK TUCKER

Singers: JENNIFER BURGESS; ROSALIND CRESSY; DANIEL HOPKINS; HANNAH JACKSON; DUNCAN LAW; BARBARA MUSTON; SIMON PURSE; PHILIPPE SPALL; SALLY WOODFIELD

Musical director: HANNAH JACKSON; Musicians: DAVID CLEWLOW; PATRICK CRUMLEY; MARTIN ETHERIDGE

Costumes: ELLIE COCKERILL;   Book-Keeper: HEATHER TRACY

The *Bastard* knows he is a bastard, but our actor did not know who his father was until he was in front of the audience:

BASTARD:
    Knight, knight, good mother, Basilisco-like:
    What, I am dub'd, I have it on my shoulder:
    But mother, I am not Sir *Roberts* sonne,
    I have disclaim'd Sir *Robert* and my land,
    Legitimation, name, and all is gone;
    Then good my mother, let me know my father,
    Some proper man I hope, who was it mother?
LADY FAULCONBRIDGE:
    Hast thou denied thy selfe a *Faulconbridge*?
BASTARD:
    As faithfully as I denie the devill.
LADY FAULCONBRIDGE:
    King Richard Cordelion was thy father,
    By long and vehement suit I was seduc'd
    To make roome for him in my husbands bed:
    Heaven lay not my transgression to my charge,
    That art the issue of my deere offence
    Which was so strongly urg'd past my defence.

The joy of discovery on his face was wonderful to behold, and the audience responded as well to this totally truthful revelation. Now, I know that for a second performance of a Cue Script production, the actor would not be so ignorant, as it was only in this first performance that certain discoveries are made. This leads me to an interesting thought: we know that in those days a first performance was twice the entrance fee of a normal one. Might the knowledge that the audience was in on a whole series of discoveries, finding out about the play just as the actors were, be a good reason for charging more for this certainly roughly staged but insightful performance? As a play was performed more often, it would undoubtedly get more slick as the actors got more comfortable with their roles, but it might also lose some of the spontaneity that I found was such a plus for our audiences.

Nick Day had a problem with the *King of France*, since he had an instruction to hold *King John*'s hand, but could not tell how long he had to hold on. He went to the script on the day of performance (as the actors in those days would have been able to) and found that he would have to hold hands for an inordinately long period. He asked me if it would be all right to let go the hand for a chunk of time, and then grab hold again when *Pandulphe* speaks of it:

PANDULPHE:

> *Philip* of *France*, on perill of a curse,
> Let goe the hand of that Arch-heretique,
> And raise the power of *France* upon his head,
> Unlesse he doe submit himselfe to *Rome*.

ELEANOR:

> Look'st thou pale *France*? do not let go thy hand.

And then very much later:

FRANCE:

> Thou shalt not need. *England*, I will fall from thee.

I simply told Nick that if it had been intended to hold, let go, then hold on again, that would have been made obvious to the actor in his Cue Script. He then said he would just do as it said, with the result that the whole scene became a battle of trying to loosen the hands of *France* and *King John*—*Pandulphe* tugging on one arm of the hapless King, and *King John* on the other. In <u>performance</u> this stage business worked fine. It is just that we are so used to "solving" stage problems from a text, we forget that the plays of Shakespeare as published were originally written as actors' texts, and if there were any major problems in them when first put down, then by the time they got to a Quarto or to a scribal copy and then to the Folio, they would have been acted out, and so to a great extent be "actor proved," with the solutions neatly stitched inside them.

Sute the Action to the Word, the Word to the Action can go badly wrong, if it is not in your own lines. When *Constance* is berating the Lords, she says:

CONSTANCE:

> Gone to be married? Gone to sweare a peace?
> False blood to false blood joyn'd. Gone to be freinds?
> Shall *Lewis* have *Blaunch*, and *Blaunch* those Provinces?
> It is not so, thou hast mispoke, misheard,
> Be well advis'd, tell ore thy tale againe.
> It cannot be, thou do'st but say 'tis so.
> I trust I may not trust thee, for thy word
> Is but the vaine breath of a common man:
> Beleeve me, I doe not beleeve thee man,
> I have a Kings oath to the contrarie.
> Thou shalt be punish'd for thus frighting me,
> For I am sicke, and capeable of feares,
> Opprest with wrongs, and therefore full of feares,
> A widdow, husbandles, subject to feares,

A woman naturally borne to feares;
And though thou now confesse thou didst but jest
With my vext spirits, I cannot take a Truce,
But they will quake and tremble all this day.
What dost thou meane by shaking of thy head?
Why dost thou looke so sadly on my sonne?
What meanes that hand upon that breast of thine?
Why holdes thine eie that lamentable rhewme,
Like a proud river peering ore his bounds?
Be these sad signes confirmers of thy words?
Then speake againe, not all thy former tale,
But this one word, whether thy tale be true.

So when she said *by shaking of thy head?* that is what the Lord did, as well as *What meanes that hand upon that breast of thine?* which he then did, and got an unfortunate laugh from the audience. I realized afterward that if he had done nothing, we could have put all this bombast down to *Constance's* state of mind, and it would not matter whether she was following what they were doing or she was assuming that this is what they were doing. Doing afterward what she had just said came over as amateur, and unfortunately started to undermine the trust the Globe artistic personnel had in us.

Young *Arthur* has to throw himself to his death, and we knew that the balcony at the Globe was too high and dangerous for this, and we had not yet come up with our portable balcony, so we had him dive from the shoulders of a living "wall." When the Lords come on, it was very poignant having him lie there and them not "see" him for quite a while.

Twelfe Night, November 1998

I had not, of course, seen the *Twelfe Night* that Simon Purse had put on in Jordan, so the opportunity of presenting it at the Riverhouse Barn in Walton-on-Thames was gratefully taken up. This was a long narrow building, and so we decided to present the play in the traverse mode—with the audience on three sides. Due to so many actors wanting to be involved, and also our wanting to see their talents and abilities, this led us to put the play on three times, with three changes of cast (well, three *Olivias*, *Marias*, and *Sebastians*; and two *Violas*, *Orsinos*, *Sir Tobys*, *Sir Andrews*, *Malvolios*, and *Fabians*.) Our second *Feste* was not available, and so Danny played all three *Festes*—but fascinatingly: he played them all with different costumes, and with different interpretations. None of us could say which was better or more appropriate; they all seemed just right for that night's performance.

The plays starts with a very famous line, but one that does <u>not</u> end with a full stop:

ORSINO:
If Musicke be the food of Love, play on,

Give me excesse of it: that surfetting,

The appetite may sicken, and so dye.

That straine agen, it had a dying fall:

O, it came ore my eare, like the sweet sound

That breathes upon a banke of Violets;

The Platt of Twelfe Night, Or what you will

An OSC Presentation at the Riverhouse Barn
7:30 pm on Friday 13th November, 1998

I-1 Enter Orsino (Duke of Illyria), Curio: (**PHILIP BIRD; ALISON SEDDON**), Music playing. To the Duke, Valentine: (**MICHAEL PALMER**). Exeunt.

I-2 Enter Viola: (**JULIETTE GRASSBY**), a Captaine: (**GRAHAM POUNTNEY**), and Saylors: (**LEWIS HANCOCK; LOUISA SPICER**). Viola gives him gold. Exeunt.

I-3 Enter Sir Toby (Uncle to Olivia): (**DAVID HALL**), and Maria: (**CAROLYN JONES**). To them, Sir Andrew: (**JONATHAN ROBY**), a foolish knight. Exit Maria. Exeunt, Sir Andrew dancing.

I-4 Enter Valentine and Viola as Cesario, in man's attire. Enter Orsino, Curio. Exeunt.

I-5 Enter Maria, and Feste the Clowne: (**DANIEL HOPKINS**). Exit Maria, and enter Lady Olivia: (**ROSALIND CRESSY**), with Malvolio: (**NICHOLAS DAY**) her Steward. To Olivia, Maria. Exit Maria and Malvolio. Enter Sir Toby, drunk and belching. Exit Sir Toby. Exit Feste, and enter Malvolio. Malvolio calls in Maria, and exits. Olivia is veiled. Enter Viola as Cesario. Exeunt, manet Viola and Olivia. Viola refuses money from Olivia, and exits. To Olivia, Malvolio. She gives him a ring. Exit Malvolio. Exit Olivia.

II-1 Enter Antonio a Captain and Sebastian: (**GRAHAM POUNTNEY; SARAH HOWE**) (twin to Viola). Exit Sebastian. Exit Antonio.

II-2 Enter Viola at one door, Malvolio at another. Malvolio leaves the ring, and exits. Exit Viola.

II-3 Enter Sir Toby, and Sir Andrew. To them, Feste the Clowne. The Clowne sings. They all sing a Catch. To them, Maria. To them, Malvolio angry at the noise. They all sing again. Exit Malvolio. Exit Maria. Exeunt.

II-4 Enter Orsino the Duke, Viola, Curio and Valentine. Musicke playes, and Curio exits. Enter Curio and Feste the Clowne. Musicke and Feste sings the Song. Orsino pays him. Exit Feste. Exeunt, manet Orsino and Viola. Orsino gives her a jewell, and exeunt.

II-5 Enter Sir Toby, Sir Andrew and Fabian: (**LEWIS HANCOCK**). To them, Maria with her letter. Sir Toby, Sir Andrew and Fabian hide in the box tree. Maria drops her letter and exits. Enter Malvolio musing. He picks up and reads the letter. Exit Malvolio. Enter Maria. Exeunt.

Interval.

Book-Holder: CHRISTINE OZANNE
Book-Keeper: **RICHARD BURNIP**
Musical director: **HANNAH JACKSON**
Costumes: **ELLIE COCKERILL**

III-1 Enter Viola and Feste the Clowne, playing the tabor. Feste is paid by Viola, and exits. Enter Sir Toby and Sir Andrew. Enter Olivia, and Maria. Exeunt, manet Olivia and Viola. The clocke strikes. Exeunt.

III-2 Enter Sir Toby, Sir Andrew, and Fabian. Exit Sir Andrew to write a challenge. To them, Maria. Exeunt Omnes.

III-3 Enter Sebastian and Anthonio. Anthonio gives him his purse. Exeunt.

III-4 Enter Olivia and Maria. To Olivia, Malvolio with yellow stockings cross gartered. To Olivia, a Servant: (**ALISON SEDDON**). Exeunt, manet Malvolio. Enter Sir Toby, Fabian and Maria. Exit Malvolio. To them, Sir Andrew with his Challenge, which Sir Toby reads. Exit Sir Andrew. Enter Olivia and Viola. Exeunt Sir Toby, Fabian and Maria. Olivia gives Viola a picture jewell. Exit Olivia at one door, and enter Sir Toby and Fabian at another. Sir Toby tells her she must duel with Sir Andrew. Exit Sir Toby. Exeunt Viola and Fabian. Enter Sir Toby and Sir Andrew, who is told he must duel with Viola. Enter Fabian dragging on Viola. They prepare to fight. To them, Antonio to stop the fight. Enter Officers: (**LOUISA SPICER; HANNAH JACKSON**) to arrest Antonio. Viola offers half her purse to him. Exeunt Antonio and Officers. Exit Viola. Exeunt.

IV-1 Enter Sebastian and Feste the Clowne. To them, Sir Andrew, Sir Toby, and Fabian. Sir Andrew slaps Sebastian, and gets slapped back. Sir Toby holds Sebastian. Exit Feste. Sebastian prepares to fight Sir Toby. Enter Olivia to stop the fight. Exeunt.

IV-2 Enter Maria with beard and gown, and Feste the Clowne, Malvolio being within the prison cell. Feste dresses as Sir Topas the Curate. Enter Sir Toby. Feste talks to Malvolio within as Sir Topas. To them Sir Toby and Maria. Feste comes to Malvolio in his own voice, then as Sir Topas. Exit Feste.

IV-3 Enter Sebastian, with a pearle. To him, Olivia, and the Priest: (**MICHAEL PALMER**). Exeunt.

V-1 Enter Feste with Malvolio's letter, and Fabian. Enter Orsino, Viola, Curio. Orsino pays Feste. Exit Feste and Fabian at one door, and enter Anthonio and Officers at another. Enter Olivia. To her, the Priest. Enter Sir Andrew with a bloody head. Enter Sir Toby with a bloody head, and Feste. Exeunt Feste, Sir Toby and Sir Andrew, and enter Sebastian. All marvel at the identical twins. Enter Feste with Malvolio's letter, and Fabian. Feste reads the letter; Olivia gives it to Fabian to finish reading. Exit Fabian. Enter Fabian with Malvolio. Malvolio shows Maria's letter to Olivia. Exit Malvolio. Exeunt, manet Feste, who sings.

Finis.

Stealing, and giving Odour. Enough, no more,

'Tis not so sweet now, as it was before.

O spirit of Love, how quicke and fresh art thou,

That notwithstanding thy capacitie,

Receiveth as the Sea. Nought enters there,

The Platt of Twelfe Night, Or what you will

An OSC Presentation at the Riverhouse Barn
2:30 pm on Saturday 14th November, 1998

I-1 Enter Orsino (Duke of Illyria), Curio: (PHILIP BIRD; FRED WEIR), Music playing. To the Duke, Valentine: (MARK SUMNER). Exeunt.

I-2 Enter Viola: (SARAH FINCH), a Captaine: (RICHARD LANCASTER), and Saylors: (STEVE BLACK; DOROTHY LAWRENCE). Viola gives him gold. Exeunt.

I-3 Enter Sir Toby (Uncle to Olivia): (RAY ARMSTRONG), and Maria: (SONIA RITTER). To them, Sir Andrew: (DUNCAN LAW), a foolish knight. Exit Maria. Exeunt, Sir Andrew dancing.

I-4 Enter Valentine and Viola as Cesario, in man's attire. Enter Orsino, Curio. Exeunt.

I-5 Enter Maria, and Feste the Clowne: (DANIEL HOPKINS). Exit Maria, and enter Lady Olivia: (HANNAH JACKSON), with Malvolio: (NICHOLAS DAY) her Steward. To Olivia, Maria. Exit Maria and Malvolio. Enter Sir Toby, drunk and belching. Exit Toby. Exit Feste, and enter Malvolio. Malvolio calls in Maria, and exits. Olivia is veiled. Enter Viola as Cesario. Exeunt, manet Viola and Olivia. Viola refuses money from Olivia, and exits. To Olivia, Malvolio. She gives him a ring. Exit Malvolio. Exit Olivia.

II-1 Enter Antonio a Captain and Sebastian: (RICHARD LANCASTER; ANDREA NEWLAND) (twin to Viola). Exit Sebastian. Exit Antonio.

II-2 Enter Viola at one door, Malvolio at another. Malvolio leaves the ring, and exits. Exit Viola.

II-3 Enter Sir Toby, and Sir Andrew. To them, Feste the Clowne. The Clowne sings. They all sing a Catch. To them, Maria. To them, Malvolio angry at the noise. They all sing again. Exit Malvolio. Exit Maria. Exeunt.

II-4 Enter Orsino the Duke, Viola, Curio and Valentine. Musicke plays, and Curio exits. Enter Curio and Feste the Clowne. Musicke and Feste sings the Song. Orsino pays him. Exit Feste. Exeunt, manet Orsino and Viola. Orsino gives her a jewell, and exeunt.

II-5 Enter Sir Toby, Sir Andrew and Fabian: (STEVE BLACK). To them, Maria with her letter. Sir Toby, Sir Andrew and Fabian hide in the box tree. Maria drops her letter and exits. Enter Malvolio musing. He picks up and reads the letter. Exit Malvolio. Enter Maria. Exeunt.

Interval.

Book-Holder: SIMON PURSE
Book-Keeper: SARAH HOWE
Musical director: HANNAH JACKSON
Costumes: ELLIE COCKERILL

III-1 Enter Viola and Feste the Clowne, playing the tabor. Feste is paid by Viola, and exits. Enter Sir Toby and Sir Andrew. Enter Olivia, and Maria. Exeunt, manet Olivia and Viola. The clocke strikes. Exeunt.

III-2 Enter Sir Toby, Sir Andrew, and Fabian. Exit Sir Andrew to write a challenge. To them, Maria. Exeunt Omnes.

III-3 Enter Sebastian and Anthonio. Anthonio gives him his purse. Exeunt.

III-4 Enter Olivia and Maria. To Olivia, Malvolio with yellow stockings cross gartered. To Olivia, a Servant: (FRED WEIR). Exeunt, manet Malvolio. Enter Sir Toby, Fabian and Maria. Exit Malvolio. To them, Sir Andrew with his Challenge, which Sir Toby reads. Exit Sir Andrew. Enter Olivia and Viola. Exeunt Sir Toby, Fabian and Maria. Olivia gives Viola a picture jewell. Exit Olivia at one door, and enter Sir Toby and Fabian at another. Sir Toby tells her she must duel with Sir Andrew. Exit Sir Toby. Exeunt Viola and Fabian. Enter Sir Toby and Sir Andrew, who is told he must duel with Viola. Enter Fabian dragging on Viola. They prepare to fight. To them, Antonio to stop the fight. Enter Officers: (DOROTHY LAWRENCE; LOUISE DOHERTY) to arrest Antonio. Viola offers half her purse to him. Exeunt Antonio and Officers. Exit Viola. Exeunt.

IV-1 Enter Sebastian and Feste the Clowne. To them, Sir Andrew, Sir Toby, and Fabian. Sir Andrew slaps Sebastian, and gets slapped back. Sir Toby holds Sebastian. Exit Feste. Sebastian prepares to fight Sir Toby. Enter Olivia to stop the fight. Exeunt.

IV-2 Enter Maria with beard and gown, and Feste the Clowne, Malvolio being within the prison cell. Feste dresses as Sir Topas the Curate. Enter Sir Toby. Feste talks to Malvolio within as Sir Topas. Exeunt Sir Toby and Maria. Feste comes to Malvolio in his own voice, then as Sir Topas. Exit Feste.

IV-3 Enter Sebastian, with a pearle. To him, Olivia, and the Priest: (MARK SUMNER). Exeunt.

V-1 Enter Feste with Malvolio's letter, and Fabian. Enter Orsino, Viola, Curio. Orsino pays Feste. Exit Feste and Fabian at one door, and enter Anthonio and Officers at another. Enter Olivia. To her, the Priest. Enter Sir Andrew with a bloody head. Enter Sir Toby with a bloody head, and Feste. Exeunt Feste, Sir Toby and Sir Andrew, and enter Sebastian. All marvel at the identical twins. Enter Feste with Malvolio's letter, and Fabian. Feste reads the letter; Olivia gives it to Fabian to finish reading. Exit Fabian. Enter Fabian with Malvolio. Malvolio shows Maria's letter to Olivia. Exit Malvolio. Exeunt, manet Feste, who sings.

Finis.

Of what validity, and pitch so ere,
But falles into abatement, and low price
Even in a minute; so full of shapes is fancie,
That it alone, is high fantasticall.

The Platt of Twelfe Night, Or what you will

An OSC Presentation at the Riverhouse Barn
8:00 pm on Saturday 14th November, 1998

I-1 Enter Orsino (Duke of Illyria), Curio: (RICHARD BURNIP; MARK SUMNER), Music playing. To the Duke, Valentine: (WILLIAM WHYMPER). Exeunt.

I-2 Enter Viola: (JULIETTE GRASSBY), a Captaine: (GRAHAM POUNTNEY), and Saylors: (LEWIS HANCOCK; ROSA BLACKER). Viola gives him gold. Exeunt.

I-3 Enter Sir Toby (Uncle to Olivia): (DAVID HALL), and Maria: (DANIELLE ALLAN). To them, Sir Andrew: (JONATHAN ROBY), a foolish knight. Exit Maria. Exeunt, Sir Andrew dancing.

I-4 Enter Valentine and Viola as Cesario, in man's attire. Enter Orsino, Curio. Exeunt.

I-5 Enter Maria, and Feste the Clowne: (DANIEL HOPKINS). Exit Maria, and enter Lady Olivia: (LOUISE DOHERTY), with Malvolio: (CALLUM COATES) her Steward. To Olivia, Maria. Exit Maria and Malvolio. Enter Sir Toby, drunk and belching. Exit Sir Toby. Exit Feste, and enter Malvolio. Malvolio calls in Maria, and exits. Olivia is veiled. Enter Viola as Cesario. Exeunt, manet Viola and Olivia. Viola refuses money from Olivia, and exits. To Olivia, Malvolio. She gives him a ring. Exit Malvolio. Exit Olivia.

II-1 Enter Antonio a Captain and Sebastian: (GRAHAM POUNTNEY; HEATHER TRACY) (twin to Viola). Exit Sebastian. Exit Antonio.

II-2 Enter Viola at one door, Malvolio at another. Malvolio leaves the ring, and exits. Exit Viola.

II-3 Enter Sir Toby, and Sir Andrew. To them, Feste the Clowne. The Clowne sings. They all sing a Catch. To them, Maria. To them, Malvolio angry at the noise. They all sing again. Exit Malvolio. Exit Maria. Exeunt.

II-4 Enter Orsino the Duke, Viola, Curio and Valentine. Musicke playes, and Curio exits. Enter Curio and Feste the Clowne. Musicke and Feste sings the Song. Orsino pays him. Exit Feste. Exeunt, manet Orsino and Viola. Orsino gives her a jewell, and exeunt.

II-5 Enter Sir Toby, Sir Andrew and Fabian: (LEWIS HANCOCK). To them, Maria with her letter. Sir Toby, Sir Andrew and Fabian hide in the box tree. Maria drops her letter and exits. Enter Malvolio musing. He picks up and reads the letter. Exit Malvolio. Enter Maria. Exeunt.

Interval.

III-1 Enter Viola and Feste the Clowne, playing the tabor. Feste is paid by Viola, and exits. Enter Sir Toby and Sir Andrew. Enter Olivia, and Maria. Exeunt, manet Olivia and Viola. The clocke strikes. Exeunt.

III-2 Enter Sir Toby, Sir Andrew, and Fabian. Exit Sir Andrew to write a challenge. To them, Maria. Exeunt Omnes.

III-3 Enter Sebastian and Anthonio. Anthonio gives him his purse. Exeunt.

III-4 Enter Olivia and Maria. To Olivia, Malvolio with yellow stockings cross gartered. To Olivia, a Servant: (MARK SUMNER). Exeunt, manet Malvolio. Enter Sir Toby, Fabian and Maria. Exit Malvolio. To them, Sir Andrew with his Challenge, which Sir Toby reads. Exit Sir Andrew. Enter Olivia and Viola. Exeunt Sir Toby, Fabian and Maria. Olivia gives Viola a picture jewell. Exit Olivia at one door, and enter Sir Toby and Fabian at another. Sir Toby tells her she must duel with Sir Andrew. Exit Sir Toby. Exeunt Viola and Fabian. Enter Sir Toby and Sir Andrew, who is told he must duel with Viola. Enter Fabian dragging on Viola. They prepare to fight. To them, Antonio to stop the fight. Enter Officers: (ROSA BLACKER; HANNAH JACKSON) to arrest Antonio. Viola offers half her purse to him. Exeunt Antonio and Officers. Exit Viola. Exeunt.

IV-1 Enter Sebastian and Feste the Clowne. To them, Sir Andrew, Sir Toby, and Fabian. Sir Andrew slaps Sebastian, and gets slapped back. Sir Toby holds Sebastian. Exit Feste. Sebastian prepares to fight Sir Toby. Enter Olivia to stop the fight. Exeunt.

IV-2 Enter Maria with beard and gown, and Feste the Clowne, Malvolio being within the prison cell. Feste dresses as Sir Topas the Curate. Enter Sir Toby. Feste talks to Malvolio within as Sir Topas. Exeunt Sir Toby and Maria. Feste comes to Malvolio in his own voice, then as Sir Topas. Exit Feste.

IV-3 Enter Sebastian, with a pearle. To him, Olivia, and the Priest: (WILLIAM WHYMPER). Exeunt.

V-1 Enter Feste with Malvolio's letter, and Fabian. Enter Orsino, Viola, Curio. Orsino pays Feste. Exit Feste and Fabian at one door, and enter Anthonio and Officers at another. Enter Olivia. To her, the Priest. Enter Sir Andrew with a bloody head. Enter Sir Toby with a bloody head, and Feste. Exeunt Feste, Sir Toby and Sir Andrew, and enter Sebastian. All marvel at the identical twins. Enter Feste with Malvolio's letter, and Fabian. Feste reads the letter; Olivia gives it to Fabian to finish reading. Exit Fabian. Enter Fabian with Malvolio. Malvolio shows Maria's letter to Olivia. Exit Malvolio. Exeunt, manet Feste, who sings.

Finis.

Book-Holder: CHRISTINE OZANNE
Book-Keeper: DOROTHY LAWRENCE
Musical director: HANNAH JACKSON
Costumes: ELLIE COCKERILL

Playing it so that the punctuation—yes, the Folio punctuation—is strictly adhered to gives a wonderful drive, and prevents it being a bald statement of fact; it becomes the beginning of an argument that *Orsino* then takes the audience through with him. The two actors playing him were both rigorously verse nursed to do this, and it started the evening off very well.

I asked as many of the actors as possible to see one another's performances, because our regular performers have rarely been exposed to Cue Script acting, and I hoped they could learn from what they saw. This side of the productions worked very well indeed. In fact, the actors sat on the fourth side of the theatre, leaving us effectively playing in the round. This was so acceptable I finally came back to the thought that the original productions would well work in this format. Plays at the Globe, we had discovered, worked well playing in the round, and now a small theatre, rather like a small lord's mansion that a touring company could have played at, also worked in the round.

One of the major questions about the Elizabethan actors, how they adjusted their performances to the many different venues they would play at, was being answered: they could have performed in a similar manner whatever the size and layout of the playing area.

In all the performances, the part of *Sebastian* was played by an actress. I was partly moved by the plight of the modern actress, with fewer opportunities to play a role especially in Shakespeare, but I was also interested in the light voice and physicality that the original boy players would have had. As boys, the actresses were completely convincing, but more important, it was more believable that the others in the play could have mistaken *Sebastian* for *Viola*. These thoughts eventually culminated in our Boys' Company presentation in 2000.

The Two Gentlemen of Verona, July 1999

Jordan had asked us to return for a third visit, and I felt it was time to try out a less well known play: *The Two Gentlemen of Verona*. It was so unknown to them, I had to reassure them that it was, in fact, written by William Shakespeare.

The part of the "foolish suitor" *Thurio* was made much easier by our text having no "asides" printed in it, so the obvious rude remarks about him by *Julia* were not made behind his back as is usual, but straight to his face, making him appear even more foolish, since he knew he was being bad-mouthed but had no lines to reply to the insults:

THURIO:

How likes she my discourse?

PROTHEUS:

Ill, when you talke of war.

THURIO:

But well, when I discourse of love and peace.

JULIA:

But better indeede, when you hold your peace.

THURIO:

What sayes she to my valour?

PROTHEUS:

Oh Sir, she makes no doubt of that.

The Platt of The Two Gentlemen of Verona
by William Shakespeare
An OSC Presentation on the Artimes Steps at the Jerash Festival, Jordan on Thursday 22nd July, 1999

I-1: Enter Valentine and Protheus: (SCOTT AINSLIE; ADRIAN O'DONNELL), the two Gentlemen. Exit Valentine. To Protheus, Speed: (SARAH HOWE), the clownish servant to Valentine. Protheus gives him money. Exeunt.

I-2: Enter Julia: (EMMA BOWN) beloved of Protheus, and Lucetta: (JUDITH PARIS), her waighting-woman. Lucetta offers a letter to Julia. Exit Lucetta. Enter Lucetta, dropping and picking up the letter. Julia takes and tears the letter. Exit Lucetta. To Julia, Lucetta. Exeunt, Lucetta taking up the torn papers.

I-3: Enter Antonio father to Protheus, and Panthino his servant: (LEWIS HANCOCK; BRENDAN FLEMING). Enter Protheus reading a letter. Exeunt Antonio and Panthino. To Protheus, Panthino. Exeunt.

II-1: Enter Valentine, and Speed with a glove. Enter Silvia: (ROSALIND CRESSY) beloved of Valentine. Valentine offers his letter to Sylvia. Exit Silvia. Exeunt.

II-2: Enter Protheus, Julia and Panthino. Protheus and Julia exchange rings. Exeunt.

II-3: Enter Launce the clownish servant to Protheus: (JONATHAN ROBY), with his dog, Crab, and a stick. To him, Panthino. Exeunt.

II-4: Enter Valentine, Silvia, Thurio: (MICHAEL PALMER) a foolish rival to Valentine, and Speed. Enter Duke: (BRYAN TORFEH), father to Silvia. Exit Duke. Enter Protheus. Exeunt Silvia and Thurio. Exit Valentine and Speed. Exit Protheus.

II-5: Enter Speed and Launce, with his dog. Exeunt.

II-6: Enter Protheus solus. Exit.

II-7: Enter Julia and Lucetta. Exeunt.

Interval.

III-1: Enter Duke, Thurio, and Protheus. Exit Thurio. Exit Protheus. Enter Valentine in a hurry. The Duke discovers a letter and cord ladder under his cloak, and reads the letter. Exit Duke. Enter Protheus and Launce. Exeunt Protheus and Valentine, with the cords. Launce reads his Catelog. To him, Speed, who also reads it. Exit Speed running. Exit Launce.

III-2: Enter Duke and Thurio. Enter Protheus. Exeunt.

IV-1: Enter Valentine, Speed, and certaine Outlawes: (LEWIS HANCOCK; RICHARD JACOBS; ANDREA NEWLAND). Exeunt.

IV-2: Enter Protheus. Enter Thurio and Musicians: (CHRISTINE OZANNE; JUDITH PARIS; BRYAN TORFEH). They tune up. Enter Host: (BRENDAN FLEMING) where she lodges, and Julia disguised as a boy. Song: Who is Silvia? Exeunt Thurio and Musicians and enter Silvia. Exeunt Protheus and Silvia. Exeunt Julia and Host.

IV-3: Enter Eglamoure: (LEWIS HANCOCK) agent for Silvia in her escape. To him, Silvia. Exeunt.

IV-4: Enter Launce with his dog. Enter Protheus, and Julia disguised as Sebastian. Exit Launce. Protheus gives Julia his ring, and a letter. Exit Protheus. Enter Silvia, and Ursula: (JUDITH PARIS) carrying a Picture. Silvia gives the Picture to Julia. Julia gives first one, then another letter to Silvia, which she tears. Silvia gives Julia a purse, and exits with Ursula. Exit Julia.

V-1: Enter Eglamoure. To him, Silvia. Exeunt.

V-2: Enter Thurio, Protheus and Julia. To them, the Duke. Exit Duke. Exit Thurio. Exit Protheus. Exit Julia.

V-3: Enter Silvia and Out-lawes: (LEWIS HANCOCK; RICHARD JACOBS; ANDREA NEWLAND; BRENDAN FLEMING; SARAH HOWE; JONATHAN ROBY). Exeunt.

V-4: Enter Valentine, who conceals himself. Enter Protheus, Silvia and Julia. Valentine comes forth. Julia faints, gives Protheus' ring back to him, shows the one he sent to Silvia. Julia reveals herself. Enter Out-lawes, with Duke and Thurio. Exeunt.

Finis.

Verse Nurses: CHRISTINE OZANNE; PATRICK TUCKER	Book-Keeper:	ANDREA NEWLAND
Tour Managers: SARAH HOWE; JONATHAN ROBY	Book-Holder:	CHRISTINE OZANNE
Costumes: ELLIE COCKERILL	Presenter:	PATRICK TUCKER

JULIA:

She needes not, when she knowes it cowardize.

THURIO:

What saies she to my birth?

The Platt of The Two Gentlemen of Verona

by William Shakespeare

An OSC Presentation on the Artimes Steps at the Jerash Festival, Jordan on Friday 23rd July, 1999

I-1: Enter Valentine and Protheus: (RICHARD JACOBS; ADRIAN O'DONNELL), the two Gentlemen. Exit Valentine. To Protheus, Speed: (SARAH HOWE), the clownish servant to Valentine. Protheus gives him money. Exeunt.

I-2: Enter Julia: (ANDREA NEWLAND) beloved of Protheus, and Lucetta: (JUDITH PARIS), her waighting-woman. Lucetta offers a letter to Julia. Exit Lucetta. Enter Lucetta, dropping and picking up the letter. Julia takes and tears the letter. Exit Lucetta. To Julia, Lucetta. Exeunt, Lucetta taking up the torn papers.

I-3: Enter Antonio father to Protheus, and Panthino his servant: (LEWIS HANCOCK; BRENDAN FLEMING). Enter Protheus reading a letter. Exeunt Antonio and Panthino. To Protheus, Panthino. Exeunt.

II-1: Enter Valentine, and Speed with a glove. Enter Silvia: (ROSALIND CRESSY) beloved of Valentine. Valentine offers his letter to Sylvia. Exit Silvia. Exeunt.

II-2: Enter Protheus, Julia and Panthino. Protheus and Julia exchange rings. Exeunt.

II-3: Enter Launce the clownish servant to Protheus: (JONATHAN ROBY), with his dog, Crab, and a stick. To him, Panthino. Exeunt.

II-4: Enter Valentine, Silvia, Thurio: (MICHAEL PALMER) a foolish rival to Valentine, and Speed. Enter Duke: (BRYAN TORFEH), father to Silvia. Exit Duke. Enter Protheus. Exeunt Silvia and Thurio. Exit Valentine and Speed. Exit Protheus.

II-5: Enter Speed and Launce, with his dog. Exeunt.

II-6: Enter Protheus solus. Exit.

II-7: Enter Julia and Lucetta. Exeunt.

Interval.

III-1: Enter Duke, Thurio, and Protheus. Exit Thurio. Exit Protheus. Enter Valentine in a hurry. The Duke discovers a letter and cord ladder under his cloak, and reads the letter. Exit Duke. Enter Protheus and Launce. Exeunt Protheus and Valentine, with the cords. Launce reads his Catelog. To him, Speed, who also reads it. Exit Speed running. Exit Launce.

III-2: Enter Duke and Thurio. Enter Protheus. Exeunt.

IV-1: Enter Valentine, Speed, and certaine Outlawes: (LEWIS HANCOCK; SCOTT AINSLIE; EMMA BOWN). Exeunt.

IV-2: Enter Protheus. Enter Thurio and Musicians: (CHRISTINE OZANNE; JUDITH PARIS; BRYAN TORFEH). They tune up. Enter Host: (BRENDAN FLEMING) where she lodges, and Julia disguised as a boy. Song: Who is Silvia? Exeunt Thurio and Musicians and enter Silvia. Exeunt Protheus and Silvia. Exeunt Julia and Host.

IV-3: Enter Eglamoure: (LEWIS HANCOCK) agent for Silvia in her escape. To him, Silvia. Exeunt.

IV-4: Enter Launce with his dog. Enter Protheus, and Julia disguised as Sebastian. Exit Launce. Protheus gives Julia his ring, and a letter. Exit Protheus. Enter Silvia, and Ursula: (JUDITH PARIS) carrying a Picture. Silvia gives the Picture to Julia. Julia gives first one, then another letter to Silvia, which she tears. Silvia gives Julia a purse, and exits with Ursula. Exit Julia.

V-1: Enter Eglamoure. To him, Silvia. Exeunt.

V-2: Enter Thurio, Protheus and Julia. To them, the Duke. Exit Duke. Exit Thurio. Exit Protheus. Exit Julia.

V-3: Enter Silvia and Out-lawes: (LEWIS HANCOCK; SCOTT AINSLIE; EMMA BOWN; BRENDAN FLEMING; SARAH HOWE; JONATHAN ROBY). Exeunt.

V-4: Enter Valentine, who conceals himself. Enter Protheus, Silvia and Julia. Valentine comes forth. Julia faints, gives Protheus' ring back to him, shows the one he sent to Silvia. Julia reveals herself. Enter Out-lawes, with Duke and Thurio. Exeunt.

Finis.

original
Shakespeare
company

Verse Nurses:	CHRISTINE OZANNE; PATRICK TUCKER	Book-Keeper:	SCOTT AINSLIE
Tour Managers:	SARAH HOWE; JONATHAN ROBY	Book-Holder:	CHRISTINE OZANNE
Costumes:	ELLIE COCKERILL	Presenter:	PATRICK TUCKER

PROTHEUS:
That you are well deriv'd.
JULIA:
True: from a Gentleman, to a foole.

The *First Out-lawe* played his role like a gentleman, posh accent and all. When I gently asked him why, he pointed out that his language was truly heightened, and so he had imagined that he was well born but driven to be a thief, and his background would make him an automatic leader. Here is his first scene, as it would be seen from a Cue Script, from which this idea came:

CUE SCRIPT FOR FIRST OUT-LAWE

Enter Valentine, Speed, and certaine Out-lawes.
Fellowes, stand fast: I see a passenger.
_____ My friends.
That's not so, sir: we are your enemies.
_____ To *Verona*.
Whence came you?
_____ not thwarted me.
What, were you banish'd thence?
_____ base treachery.
Why nere repent it, if it were done so;
But were you banisht for so small a fault?
_____ our wilde faction.
We'll have him: Sirs, a word.
_____ unto the heart.
And I, for such like petty crimes as these.
But to the purpose: for we cite our faults,
That they may hold excus'd our lawlesse lives;
And partly seeing you are beautifide
With goodly shape; and by your owne report,
A Linguist, and a man of such perfection,
As we doe in our quality much want.
_____ Commander, and our King.
But if thou scorne our curtesie, thou dyest.
_____ at thy dispose.
Exeunt.

I had noticed in all our productions that the last act tended to slow down and get ponderous, as the actors felt it necessary to explain carefully to the audience all that had happened. I perceived that for the most part, the audience already knew everything, and so the revelations at the end of the play were for the audience to enjoy the reactions, not to have to understand everything from scratch. The actors were therefore under strict instructions to act faster than they ever had before in Act Five, and I must say it paid great dividends, even though the audience was primarily not native English-speakers. It gave an energy to the script, and everything was understandable to the audience.

One of the so-called problems about this play is the sudden change in *Valentine* toward the end, forgiving *Protheus* for his attempted ravishing of *Silvia* and his general deceitfulness. Our actor on this occasion was Richard Jacobs, and he puzzled about the gear change in his last speech. He was told, of course, that it was his job as actor to give a convincing theatrical reason for the observed change.

In his first scene he came on stage wearing a rather overlarge crucifix that stayed with him all the way through. At the end, when the words demanded he forgive *Protheus*, very reluctantly and tightly holding his crucifix, he did so. The convinced Christian grudgingly giving the necessary forgiveness made perfect sense of the lines, and of the moment—and was solved by the actor from his own text, as it so often is.

Protheus is forcing himself onto *Silvia*, with her fiance *Valentine* hiding nearby:

PROTHEUS:
Ile force thee yeeld to my desire.
VALENTINE:
Ruffian: let goe that rude uncivill touch,
Thou friend of an ill fashion.
PROTHEUS:
Valentine.
VALENTINE:
Thou common friend, that's without faith or love,
For such is a friend now: treacherous man,
Thou hast beguil'd my hopes; nought but mine eye
Could have perswaded me: now I dare not say
I have one friend alive; thou wouldst disprove me:
Who should be trusted, when ones right hand
Is perjured to the bosome? *Protheus*
I am sorry I must never trust thee more,
But count the world a stranger for thy sake:
The private wound is deepest: oh time, most accurst:
'Mongst all foes that a friend should be the worst?
PROTHEUS:
My shame and guilt confounds me:
Forgive me *Valentine*: if hearty sorrow
Be a sufficient Ransome for offence,
I tender't heere: I doe as truely suffer,
As ere I did commit.

VALENTINE:

> Then I am paid:
> And once againe, I doe receive thee honest;
> Who by Repentance is not satisfied,
> Is nor of heaven, nor earth; for these are pleas'd:
> By Penitence th'Eternalls wrath's appeas'd:
> And that my love may appeare plaine and free,
> All that was mine, in *Silvia*, I give thee.

Needless to say, the women onstage were less forgiving in their attitude, and this perhaps is one of the messages of the play, of how fickle men can be in matters of love. *Julia* takes off her disguise and confronts her love *Protheus*:

JULIA:

> Oh *Protheus*, let this habit make thee blush.
> Be thou asham'd that I have tooke upon me,
> Such an immodest rayment; if shame live
> In a disguise of love?
> It is the lesser blot modesty findes,
> Women to change their shapes, then men their minds.

At which, the entire Arab audience went "Ahhh," and the thrill was that this obscure play was completely clear to them, and we had done it without "helping" out with an interpretation, but just doing the play as written.

Cymbeline, September 1999

Our third presentation at Shakespeare's Globe—and as it turned out our last—was this great rambling play of the late period, and far too long to be presented within our time slot at the Globe. I had often wondered about how the plays would be cut, and thought that to cut whole chunks of a scene would mean that all the actors would have to stand around with their Cue Scripts, changing and altering in a way that would be bound to lead to errors. Instead, I told my actors that cuts were necessary, that they were to cut their own lines, and that the only rule was they had to <u>leave their existing cue lines alone</u>. We were thus able fairly painlessly to cut over four hundred lines from the play, bring it in on time, and yet have actors working from Cue Scripts not being confused. I feel we had again by practical means come across a theatrical truth of how they must have tackled the very same problems all those years ago.

The play is full of all sorts of theatrical changes and devices, the main one being:

> *JUPITER DESCENDS IN THUNDER AND LIGHTNING, SITTING UPPON AN EAGLE:*
> *HEE THROWES A THUNDER-BOLT.*

The Platt of Cymbeline

An OSC Presentation for Shakespeare's Globe, London
at 7:30 pm on Monday 6th September, 1999

I-1: Enter two Gentlemen: (ADRIAN O'DONNELL; BRYAN TORFEH). Exeunt.

I-2: Enter the Queene: (JUDITH PARIS), Posthumus: (PHILIP BIRD), and Imogen: (JULIETTE GRASSBY). Exit Queene. To them the Queene. Exit Queene. Imogen and Posthumus exchange a ring and a bracelet. Enter Cymbeline: (NICHOLAS DAY), and Lords: (ADRIAN O'DONNELL; MICHAEL PALMER; BRYAN TORFEH). Exit Posthumus. Enter Queene. Exit Cymbeline and Lords. Then enter Pisanio with Letters: (DAVID HALL). Exeunt.

I-3: Enter Clotten: (JONATHAN ROBY), and two Lords: (ADRIAN O'DONNELL; BRYAN TORFEH). Exeunt.

I-5: Enter Philario, Iachimo: (GRAHAM POUNTNEY; CALLUM COATES), a Frenchman, a Dutchman, and a Spaniard: (SCOTT AINSLIE; SONIA RITTER; SARAH HOWE). Enter Posthumus. He wagers his ring. Exeunt.

I-6: Enter Queene, Ladies: (HEATHER TRACY; ANDREA NEWLAND), and Cornelius: (CRISPIN HARRIS). Exit Ladies. Cornelius gives the Queene a drug. Enter Pisanio. Exit Cornelius. The Queene drops the box, which Pisanio picks up. Exit Pisanio. Enter Pisanio, and Ladies, carrying flowers. Exit Queene and Ladies. Exit Pisanio.

I-7: Enter Imogen alone. Enter Pisanio, and Iachimo, with Letters from Posthumus which he gives to Imogen. She reads the Letter. Exit Pisanio. Exeunt.

II-1: Enter Clotten, and the two Lords. Exit Clotten. Exeunt.

II-2: Enter Imogen, in her Bed with book and candle, and Helen: (SARAH FINCH), the Trunke being in the room. Imogen Sleepes. Exit the Lady. Then Iachimo from the Trunke. He notes down details, and removes her bracelet. Clocke strikes three. Iachimo returns to the Trunke. Exit the Bed and Trunke. Close the door.

II-3: Enter Clotten, and Lords. Enter Musitians: (HANNAH JACKSON; PATRICK CRUMLY). Song: "Hearke, hearke, the Larke". Exit Musicians. Then enter Cymbeline, and Queene. To them, a Messenger: (MICHAEL PALMER). Exeunt, manet Clotten. He knocks on the door. Enter Helen. Clotten gives her gold. Enter Imogen. Then exit the Lady. To Imogen, Pisanio. Exit Imogen and Pisanio. Exit Clotten. Open the door.

II-4: Enter Posthumus, and Philario. Enter Iachimo, with Letters for Posthumus. He shows Imogen's bracelet, wins the wager, and is given Posthumus' ring. Exit Posthumus. Exeunt. Then enter Posthumus. Exit Posthumus.

III-1: Enter in State, Cymbeline, Queene, Clotten, and Lords: (CRISPIN HARRIS; ADRIAN O'DONNELL; BRYAN TORFEH) and Ladies at one doore, and at another, Caius Lucius: (STEPHEN NEALON), and Attendants: (SCOTT AINSLIE; MICHAEL PALMER). Exeunt.

III-2: Enter Pisanio reading of a Letter from Posthumus. Enter Imogen. Pisanio gives her another Letter from Posthumus, which she reads. Exeunt.

III-3: Close the Curtain. Enter Belarius, Guiderius, and Arviragus from the Cave: (DANIEL HOPKINS; SONIA RITTER; SARAH HOWE). Exeunt Guiderius and Arviragus to go hunting. Exit Belarius.

!II-4: Enter Pisanio and Imogen. He gives her Posthumus' Letter, which she reads. She draws his sword. She throws away Posthumus' Letters kept in her breast. He gives her the small box. Exeunt.

III-5: Enter Cymbeline, Queene, Clotten, Lucius with letters, and Lords. Exit Lucius, and Lords. Enter a Messenger: (MICHAEL PALMER). Exit Cymbeline and Messenger. Exit Clotten. Enter Queene. Enter Pisanio. He gives Posthumus' Letter to Clotten, who gives him his purse. Exit Pisanio. Enter Pisanio with Posthumus' clothes. Exit Clotten. Exit Pisanio.

III-6: Enter Imogen alone, dressed as a page. Exit Imogen to the Cave, with her sword drawn.

III-7: Enter Belarius, Guiderius, and Arviragus, with dead game. Enter Imogen from the Cave. She offers them money. Exeunt to the Cave.

III-8: Enter two Roman Senators: (ANDREA NEWLAND; HEATHER TRACY) with letters, and Tribunes: (SARAH FINCH; MICHAEL PALMER). Exeunt.

IV-1: Enter Clotten alone, wearing the clothes of Posthumus. Exit Clotten.

IV-2: Enter Belarius, Guiderius, Arviragus, and Imogen from the Cave. Imogen swallows the drug. Exit Imogen to the Cave. Enter Clotten. Exeunt Belarius and Arviragus. Guiderius and Clotten Fight and Exeunt. Then enter Belarius and Arviragus. Enter Guiderius with the head of Clotten. Exit Guiderius. Exit Arviragus to the Cave. Enter Guiderius. Solemn Musick. Enter Arviragus, with Imogen dead, bearing her in his Armes. Exit Belarius. Song: "Feare no more the heate o'th'Sun". Enter Belarius with the headless body of Clotten. He places it next to Imogen, they strew flowers on them, and Exeunt. Imogen awakes. She faints onto the headless body. Enter Lucius with letters, Captaines: (SCOTT AINSLIE; ANDREA NEWLAND; SARAH FINCH), and a Soothsayer: (MICHAEL PALMER). Exeunt with the body. Open the curtain.

IV-3: Enter Cymbeline, Lords, and Pisanio. Exeunt, manet Pisanio. Exit Pisanio.

IV-4: Enter Belarius, Guiderius, and Arviragus. Exeunt.

V-1: Enter Posthumus alone, with a bloody cloth. He takes off his Roman clothes. Exit Posthumus.

V-2: Enter Lucius, Iachimo, and the Romane Army: (SCOTT AINSLIE; SARAH FINCH; ANDREA NEWLAND) at one doore: and Cymbeline and the Britaine Army: (MICHAEL PALMER; JONATHAN ROBY; HEATHER TRACY) at another: Leonatus Posthumus following like a poore Souldier. They march over, and goe out. Then enter again in Skirmish Iachimo and Posthumus: he vanquisheth and disarmeth Iachimo, and then leaves him. Exit Iachimo. The Battaile continues, the Britaines fly, Cymbeline is taken: Then enter to his rescue, Belarius, Guiderius, and Arviragus. Enter Posthumus, and seconds the Britaines. They Rescue Cymbeline, and Exeunt. Then enter Lucius, Iachimo and Imogen. Exeunt.

V-3: Enter Posthumus. He resumes his Roman clothes. Enter two British Captaines: (JONATHAN ROBY; MICHAEL PALMER). Enter Cymbeline, Belarius, Guiderius, Arviragus, Pisanio, Romane Captives: (SCOTT AINSLIE; SARAH FINCH; ANDREA NEWLAND), and two Gaolers: (BRYAN TORFEH; ADRIAN O'DONNELL). The Captaines present Posthumus to Cymbeline, who delivers him over to the Gaolers. Exeunt all but Posthumus and Gaolers.

V-4: The Gaolers manacle Posthumus, and Exeunt. He sleepes. Solemne Musicke. Enter (as in an Apparition) Sicillius Leonatus: (CRISPIN HARRIS), Father to Posthumus, an old man, attyred like a warrior, leading in his hand an ancient Matron: (JUDITH PARIS) (his wife, and Mother to Posthumus) with Musicke before them. Then, after other Musicke, followes the two young Leonati: (HEATHER TRACY; ANDREA NEWLAND) (Brothers to Posthumus) with wounds as they died in the warrs. They circle Posthumus round as he lies sleeping. Jupiter descends in Thunder and Lightning: (GRAHAM POUNTNEY), sitting upon an Eagle: (SCOTT AINSLIE; SARAH FINCH): hee throwes a Thunder-bolt. The Ghostes fall on their knees. Jupiter drops a Tablet, which they place on Posthumus' breast. Jupiter Ascends, the Eagle exits. The Ghosts Vanish. Posthumus reads the Tablet. To him, the First Gaoler. To them, a messenger: (MICHAEL PALMER). They knock off his manacles. Exeunt.

I remember reading a learned discussion about whether the original Globe had one or two pulleys in the heavens, since there was only evidence for one, but surely the *Jupiter* would turn and swing if there was only a single pulley. This is the sort of thing that was written about, while not a word was said about how they had rehearsed. I felt that the one pulley should be used, and (as with all my experiments) we would see what happened.

When it came to the day of performance, we had hired an aerial firm to install the necessary lowering equipment, and told them our requirements. To my horror, they had installed two pulleys, when I had asked specifically for one. "Well," I was told, "if you only have one, then *Jupiter* will spin around and not face the front."

This concept of "front" drives me mad. The Globe is in essence a theatre in the round, with audience and groundlings on three sides, and the nobles in the Lords room completing the circle. So wherever *Jupiter* faces, he will be facing some of the audience, and in fact be facing front. The single line installed, and *Jupiter* lowered in, I wondered how long it would take for him to be hauled up again:

JUPITER:
> Mount Eagle, to my Palace Christalline.
> *JUPITER ASCENDS.*

SICILLIUS LEONATUS:
> He came in Thunder, his Celestiall breath
> Was sulphurous to smell: the holy Eagle
> Stoop'd, as to foote us: his Ascension is
> More sweet then our blest Fields: his Royall Bird
> Prunes the immortall wing, and cloyes his Beake,
> As when his God is pleas'd.

ALL:
> Thankes Jupiter.

SICILLIUS LEONATUS:
> The Marble Pavement clozes, he is enter'd
> His radiant Roofe: Away, and to be blest
> Let us with care performe his great behest.

The men in the heavens started pulling him upward at his cue, and the actors spoke their lines, and—yes—they were closing the trap after his ascended body exactly as the last lines were being said. The play was written for that space, so it should not be surprising, but it was very rewarding.

The audience reaction was more rewarding still. I had wondered why and what this moment of theatre was about, and had assumed it was a solemn moment. But when *Jupiter* started to be lowered, the audience began to laugh, and as he slowly spun around, giving to whomever he could his grave lines, the merriment increased, and I found it to be one of those regular comic letting-off-steam moments that Shakespeare so often puts into his plays. (To be told that this was theatrically wrong, because the characters in *Cymbeline* would be in awe of *Jupiter*, and so this should be a solemn moment, completely missed the point that to the <u>people of the time</u> (who were Christians), an appeal to a pagan God would and could be funny, since they "knew" that it was an invalid prayer.)

During the Burbadge, I was arranging who should bring on the bed that *Imogen* sleeps on—the Globe had kindly lent us their big four-poster. I heard myself commanding that the bed be brought down to the hot spot, so that everyone in the audience could see it, and then had a theatrical flash of putting a rostrum onto the top of the four-poster, and bingo: there was the balcony for *Romeo and Juliet*, as well as the walls of Harfleur for *King John*, the battlements for *Richard the Second*, and the walls for *Anthonie, and Cleopatra*. Such an arrangement—a portable balcony—would allow a theatrical company to play any play anywhere, for where the balcony would be for a *Romeo and Juliet* at the Globe would be where it was when the play was being done at the Great Hall at Hampton Court, at a Lord's mansion in the country, or in the courtyard of an inn. I had always wondered how the original actors would have coped with having to change their staging/acting relationships with all the very different buildings they would have performed in, and here I saw in practice how a consistency and theatrical practicality would allow them to go anywhere with this universal bit of scenery.

All the actors were wearing our basic "Elizabethan" costume, with extra bits of Roman togas or British skins thrown on top, and the whole thing looked very good.

When *Clotten* the idiot son first appears, Editors often give (aside) to many of the speeches:

FIRST LORD:
 Sir, I would advise you to shift a shirt. The
 violence of action hath make you reek as a sacrifice.
 Where air comes out, air comes in. There's none abroad
 so wholesome as that you vent.
CLOTTEN:
 If my shirt were bloody, then to shift it. Have I
 hurt him?
SECOND LORD:
 (aside) No, faith, not so much as his patience.
FIRST LORD:
 Hurt him? His body's a passable carcass if he
 be not hurt. It is a throughfare for steel if he be not
 hurt.
SECOND LORD:
 (aside) His steel was in debt—it went o'th'
 backside the town.

CLOTTEN:

The villain would not stand me.

SECOND LORD:

(aside) No, but he fled forward still, toward
your face.

But the Folio puts it like this:

ENTER CLOTTEN, AND TWO LORDS.

FIRST GENTLEMAN:

Sir, I would advise you to shift a Shirt; the Violence of Action hath make you reek as a Sacrifice: where
ayre comes out, ayre comes in: There's none abroad so
wholesome as that you vent.

CLOTTEN:

If my Shirt were bloody, then to shift it.
Have I hurt him?

SECOND GENTLEMAN:

No faith: not so much as his patience.

FIRST GENTLEMAN:

Hurt him? His bodie's a passable Carkasse if he bee
not hurt. It is a through-fare for Steele if it be not hurt.

SECOND GENTLEMAN:

His Steele was in debt, it went o'th'Backe-side the
Towne.

CLOTTEN:

The Villaine would not stand me.

SECOND GENTLEMAN:

No, but he fled forward still, toward your face.

FIRST GENTLEMAN:

Stand you? you have Land enough of your owne:
But he added to your having, gave you some ground.

SECOND GENTLEMAN:

As many Inches, as you have Oceans (Puppies.)

CLOTTEN:

I would they had not come betweene us.

SECOND GENTLEMAN:

So would I, till you had measur'd how long a Foole
you were upon the ground.

CLOTTEN:

And that shee should love this Fellow, and refuse mee.

SECOND GENTLEMAN:

If it be a sin to make a true election, she is damn'd.

FIRST GENTLEMAN:

Sir, as I told you alwayes: her Beauty and her Braine
go not together. Shee's a good signe, but I have seene
small reflection of her wit.

SECOND GENTLEMAN:

She shines not upon Fooles, least the reflection
Should hurt her.

CLOTTEN:

Come, Ile to my Chamber: would there had
beene some hurt done.

SECOND GENTLEMAN:

I wish not so, unlesse it had bin the fall of an Asse,
which is no great hurt.

CLOTTEN:

You'l go with us?

FIRST GENTLEMAN:

Ile attend your Lordship.

CLOTTEN:

Nay come, let's go together.

SECOND GENTLEMAN:

Well my Lord.

    EXEUNT.

I had often wondered how an actor would know <u>which</u> of their lines should be asides, since the Folio does not give them, but in this case, the actor, not "<u>knowing</u>" the lines were asides, gave them directly to *Clotten*. *Clotten*, not having any reply to the extreme rudeness given to him by his *Second Gentleman*, could only get more and more puzzled, and the <u>effect</u> of this was to make *Clotten* even more stupid—a very clever theatrical device, completely ruined if any of the actors had given any of the lines as "asides." We had found this worked very well with *Thurio* in *The Two Gentlemen of Verona*, and it worked equally well here.

When *Iachimo* came out of the trunk hidden in *Imogen*'s bedroom, the whole audience started to shout to warn her, and he had to come down to them to shush them and get on with his speech:

IACHIMO:

The Crickets sing, and mans ore-labor'd sense
Repaires it selfe by rest: Our *Tarquine* thus
Did softly presse the Rushes, ere he waken'd
The Chastitie he wounded. *Cytherea,*

How bravely thou becom'st thy Bed; fresh Lilly,
And whiter then the Sheetes: that I might touch,
But kisse, one kisse. Rubies unparagon'd,
How deerely they doo't: 'Tis her breathing that
Perfumes the Chamber thus: the Flame o'th'Taper
Bowes toward her, and would under-peepe her lids.

The Globe is a wonderful place for discovering about playing the text, for here the audience is always equally lit with the actors—simulating daylight. There is no divide between the actors in artificial light and the audience sitting in the darkness. This leads soliloquies to be debates between the character and the audience, and they always play best when directed straight to the audience's eyes, not delivered to some invisible person hovering above their heads.

The second result is that the soliloquies no longer have to be taken as a character's innermost thoughts. They are simply a debate with the audience, and sometimes I am convinced that the soliloquy is <u>not</u> what the character believes but what he wants the audience to believe. Do we believe *Iago* seriously thinks his wife has been bedded by *Othello*? Or is he simply trying to get the audience to join him in his poor opinion of *Othello*:

IAGO:
That *Cassio* loves her, I do well beleev't:
That she loves him, 'tis apt, and of great Credite.
The Moore (howbeit that I endure him not)
Is of a constant, loving, Noble Nature,
And I dare thinke, he'le prove to *Desdemona*
A most deere husband. Now I do love her too,
Not out of absolute Lust, (though peradventure
I stand accomptant for as great a sin)
But partely led to dyet my Revenge,
For that I do suspect the lustie Moore
Hath leap'd into my Seate. The thought whereof,
Doth (like a poysonous Minerall) gnaw my Inwardes:
And nothing can, or shall content my Soule
Till I am eeven'd with him, wife, for wife.
Or fayling so, yet that I put the Moore,
At least into a Jelouzie so strong
That judgement cannot cure. Which thing to do,
If this poore Trash of Venice, whom I trace
For his quicke hunting, stand the putting on,
Ile have our *Michael Cassio* on the hip,
Abuse him to the Moore, in the right garbe

(For I feare *Cassio* with my Night-Cape too)
Make the Moore thanke me, love me, and reward me,
For making him egregiously an Asse,
And practising upon his peace, and quiet,
Even to madnesse. 'Tis heere: but yet confus'd,
Knaveries plaine face, is never seene, till us'd.

I had some problems at first with the part of *Guiderius*, for in the verse sessions I could not find a lot of help for the actress, although there was plenty of evidence for *Arviragus*. Then I saw that there was a complete contrast between the two brothers, as their scene with *Imogen* shows:

CUE SCRIPT FOR GUIDERIUS

ENTER·BELARIUS, GUIDERIUS, AND ARVIRAGUS.

_____ that keep'st thy selfe.
I am throughly weary.

_____ strong in appetite.
There is cold meat i'th'Cave, we'l brouz on that
Whil'st what we have kill'd, be Cook'd.

_____ Heere were a Faiery.
What's the matter, Sir?

_____ for the Provider.
Money? Youth.

_____ bid him welcome.
Were you a woman, youth,
I should woo hard, but be your Groome in honesty:
I bid for you, as I do buy.

_____ at some distresse.
Would I could free't.

_____ as thou wilt speake it.
Pray draw neere.

_____ I pray draw neere.
            EXEUNT.

Terse, straightforward language, but a great contrast to that of his brother:

CUE SCRIPT FOR ARVIRAGUS

ENTER BELARIUS, GUIDERIUS, AND ARVIRAGUS.

_____ am throughly weary.
I am weake with toyle, yet strong in appetite.

_____ Money? Youth.

All Gold and Silver rather turne to durt,
As 'tis no better reckon'd, but of those
Who worship durty Gods.

_____ as I do buy.

Ile make't my Comfort
He is a man, Ile love him as my Brother:
And such a welcome as I'ld give to him
(After long absence) such is yours. Most welcome:
Be sprightly, for you fall 'mongst Friends.

_____ Would I could free't.

Or I, what ere it be,
What paine it cost, what danger: Gods!

_____ Pray draw neere.

The Night to'th'Owle,
And Morne to th'Larke lesse welcome.

_____ Thankes Sir.

I pray draw neere.
        EXEUNT.

Flowery language, full of images and metaphors, so a very different performance came from it. I realize that my searching for clues in *Guiderius*'s lines, and not finding any, <u>was</u> the clue: he is straightforward, and a little boring perhaps.

For the end of the play, I had been worrying about how the actors tended to slow down in Act Five, and I concluded that in this play the audience knows everything by the end. The only people who do not know are the characters, and in particular *Cymbeline* himself. I therefore made all the actors have a speed verse nurse session, and I assured them that although <u>they</u> might worry about the audience's not understanding the plot, and be tempted to go slowly so everyone can follow what is going on, the audience would be well ahead of them all the time, and so they should play it all at lightning speed.

Well, they did, and that finale was about the best we have ever done. The audience rolled with laughter at the realizations going on onstage, and when the *Soothsayer* rattled off his final speech, it brought the house down, it not being a speech usually considered so entertaining:

LUCIUS:
    Read, and declare the meaning.
SOOTHSAYER:
    Reades.
    When as a Lyons whelpe, shall to himselfe unknown, with-
    out seeking finde, and bee embrac'd by a peece of tender

Ayre: And when from a stately Cedar shall be lopt branches,
which being dead many yeares, shall after revive, bee joynted to
the old Stocke, and freshly grow, then shall Posthumus end his
miseries, Britaine be fortunate, and flourish in Peace and Plen-
tie.
Thou *Leonatus* art the Lyons Whelpe,
The fit and apt Construction of thy name
Being *Leonatus*, doth import so much:
The peece of tender Ayre, thy vertuous Daughter,
Which we call *Mollis Aer*, and *Mollis Aer*
We terme it *Mulier*; which *Mulier* I divine
Is this most constant Wife, who even now
Answering the Letter of the Oracle,
Unknowne to you unsought, were clipt about
With this most tender Aire.

It was a tremendous end to a great show, with the packed house going off having delighted in such entertainment, and a lot of the actors having had <u>no</u> idea they were going to be in a play with such varied moments, *Jupiter* flying in and all. One person not
enjoying the proceedings was the Globe's artistic director, who felt that it was too trivial
an interpretation, and our subsequent application to play our first tragedy, *Romeo and
Juliet,* on the Globe stage the next year was turned down.

Hamlet (abridged), June 2000

We had been invited to present an abridged *Hamlet,* and so we did the main soliloquies
together with selected scenes, linked with a narrative, and played it to an audience in a
walled garden at The Bothy in north London.

I deal with the *Polonius/Laertes/Ophelia* scene and the changes between *you* and *thee*
in the MODES OF ADDRESS section. An interesting insight into getting character from a
Cue Script is that of *Reynoldo*. Here it is:

CUE SCRIPT FOR REYNOLDO

ENTER POLONIUS, AND REYNOLDO.

_____ notes *Reynoldo.*

I will my Lord.

_____ Of his behaviour.

My Lord, I did intend it.

_____ marke this *Reynoldo?*

I, very well my Lord.

_____ and liberty.

As gaming my Lord.

_____ may goe so farre.

My Lord that would dishonour him.

_____ generall assault.

But my good Lord.

_____ should you doe this?

I my Lord, I would know that.

_____ man and Country.

Very good my Lord.

_____ where did I leave?

At closes in the consequence:
At friend, or fo, and Gentleman.

_____ me, have you not?

My Lord I have.

_____ you; fare you well.

Good my Lord.

_____ inclination in your selfe.

I shall my Lord.

_____ plye his Musicke.

Well, my Lord.
    EXIT.

As you can see—as an actor could so easily see—every single line has the word *Lord* in it but one, and so <u>that</u> is the line that would be said differently. How differently? Try anything, especially the thing that you feel rather than think. In fact, this is the moment when *Polonius* has forgotten what he was saying, and has asked *Reynoldo* to prompt him, but the actor does not need to know why: he already knows that the line is to be done in a different manner.

I suppose the most famous speech of all—*To be, or not to be, that is the Question:*—was given great poignancy by having *Ophelia* onstage, as is indicated in the script. Brendan Fleming played it as if he did not know she was there, but Emma Bown certainly listened and reacted to the speech, which made her *O what a Noble minde is heere o're-throwne?* all the more moving.

Hamlet's soliloquy was particularly interesting when he came across *Claudius* praying:

HAMLET:
    Now might I do it pat, now he is praying,
    And now Ile doo't, and so he goes to Heaven,
    And so am I reveng'd: that would be scann'd,
    A Villaine killes my Father, and for that
    I his foule Sonne, do this same Villaine send
    To heaven. Oh this is hyre and Sallery, not Revenge.

A lot of Editors add stage instructions about when he gets his sword out, when he puts it away, but the above is, of course, what is in the Folio. Since *Claudius* is onstage, if *Hamlet* were to stand above him, waving a sword about, the audience may wonder why on earth *Claudius* does not notice. By letting the actor act this just from the words—he came on with his sword, wondered about killing *Claudius*, and then came

---

The Platt of The Tragedie of Hamlet (abridged)
by William Shakespeare
An OSC Presentation for Summer 2000 @ The Bothy
at 4:00 pm on Sunday 25th June, 2000

I-1: Enter Barnardo and Francisco: (SIMON PURSE; MICHAEL PALMER), two Centinels. Enter Horatio and Marcellus: (BRENDAN FLEMING; KATHRYN HARE). Exit Francisco. Enter Ghost: (STEPHEN NEALON). Exit Ghost. <u>Ends</u>. *Enter Ghost againe. The cocke crowes. Exit Ghost. Exeunt.*

I-2: Enter Claudius King of Denmark: (), with Letters, Gertrude the Queene: (), Hamlet (dressed in black): (), Polonius, Laertes: (), and his Sister Ophelia: (), Lords, Attendants: (). Enter to the Court, Voltemand and Cornelius: (). Exit Voltemand and Cornelius. Exeunt. <u>Manet Hamlet</u>: (MICHAEL PALMER). To him, Horatio, Barnardo, and Marcellus: (BRENDAN FLEMING; SIMON PURSE; KATHRYN HARE). Exeunt, manet Hamlet. Exit Hamlet.

I-3: Enter Laertes and Ophelia. Enter Polonius. Exit Laertes. Exeunt.

I-4: Enter Hamlet, Horatio, Marcellus: (MICHAEL PALMER; BRENDAN FLEMING; KATHRYN HARE). **A florish of trumpets and 2 peeces goes off for the King's celebration:** (AUDIENCE). Enter Ghost: (STEPHEN NEALON). Ghost beckons Hamlet. Exeunt Hamlet and Ghost. Exeunt.

I-5: Enter Ghost and Hamlet. Exit Ghost. Horatio and Marcellus speak within, then enter to Hamlet. Ghost cries under the Stage. Exeunt.

II-1: Enter Polonius, and Reynoldo his servant: (). Polonius gives him money and notes. Exit Reynoldo. <u>Manet Polonius</u>: (STEPHEN NEALON), enter Ophelia: (KATHRYN HARE). Exeunt.

II-2: Enter King, Queene, Rosincrance and Guildensterne: () cum aliis: (). Exeunt Rosincrance and Guildensterne, enter Polonius. Exit Polonius. Enter Polonius, and Voltemand and Cornelius, with Letters. Exeunt Ambassadors. Polonius reads out Hamlet's letter. To Polonius, Hamlet reading on a booke. Exeunt King and Queene. Enter Rosincrance and Guildensterne, exit Polonius. Flourish for the Players. Enter Polonius. Enter foure or five Players: (). Exit Polonius with some of the Players: (). Exeunt, <u>Manet Hamlet</u>: (MICHAEL PALMER). Exit Hamlet.

III-1: Enter King, Queene, Polonius, Ophelia, Rosincrance, Guildensterne, and Lords: (). Exeunt Rosincrance and Guildensterne. <u>Manet King, Queene, Polonius, Ophelia</u>: (SIMON PURSE; SARAH HARVEY; STEPHEN NEALON; KATHRYN HARE). Exit the Queene. Polonius gives Ophelia a book. Exeunt King and Polonius. Enter Hamlet: (BRENDAN FLEMING). Ophelia gives him letters. Exit Hamlet. Enter King and Polonius. Exeunt.

Interval.

III-2: Enter Hamlet, and two or three of the Players: (SARAH HARVEY; SIMON PURSE; AUDIENCE). Exit Players. <u>Ends</u>. *Enter Polonius, Rosincrance and Guildensterne. Exit Polonius. Exeunt Rosincrance and Guildensterne. Enter Horatio. Enter King, Queene, Polonius, Ophelia, Rosincrance, Guildensterne and some other Lords attendant: () with his Guard carrying torches: (). Danish March. Sound a Flourish. Hoboyes Play. The dumbe shew enters: (). Exeunt Players. Enter Prologue: (). Enter two players; King and his Queene: Gonzago and Baptista: (). Player King sleepes. Exit Player Queene. Enter Player Lucianus: (). Lucianus powres the poyson in his eares. Exeunt, manet Hamlet and Horatio. Enter Rosincrance and Guildensterne. Enter one Player with a Recorder: (). To Hamlet, Polonius. Exit Polonius. Exeunt, manet Hamlet. Exit Hamlet.*

III-3: Enter King, Rosincrance and Guildensterne. <u>Manet King</u>: (STEPHEN NEALON), to him Polonius: (SIMON PURSE). Exit Polonius. Enter Hamlet armed: (BRENDAN FLEMING). Exit Hamlet. Exit King.

III-4: Enter Queene and Polonius: (SARAH HARVEY; SIMON PURSE). Hamlet calls within: (MICHAEL PALMER), Polonius hides. To the Queene, Hamlet. Hamlet killes Polonius. Hamlet shows Gertrude two pictures. Enter Ghost: (BRENDAN FLEMING). Exit Ghost. <u>Ends</u>. *Exit Hamlet tugging in Polonius, to the Queene, the King. Enter Rosincrance and Guildensterne. Exeunt Gentlemen: Rosincrance and Guildensterne. Exeunt King and Queene.*

III-5: Enter Hamlet. Rosincrance and Guildensterne shout within. Enter Rosincrance and Guildensterne. Hamlet runs off, Rosincrance and Guildensterne following.

III-6: Enter King. To him, Rosincrance. Enter Hamlet close attended by Guildensterne. Exit Rosincrance, to find the dead body of Polonius. Exit Hamlet. Exit Guildensterne following. Exit King.

IV-1: Enter Fortinbras: () and an Armie: (). Exeunt Fortinbras and soldiers.

IV-2: Enter Queene and Horatio: (SARAH HARVEY; SIMON PURSE). Enter Ophelia distracted: (KATHRYN HARE), she sings. Enter King: (STEPHEN NEALON). Exit Ophelia. Exit Horatio. <u>Ends</u>. *A noise within, enter a Messenger: (). Noise within, enter Laertes. A noise within: "Let her come in.", enter Ophelia. Exit Ophelia. Exeunt.*

IV-3: Enter Horatio, with an Attendant: (). To Horatio a Saylor: () with a letter from Hamlet. Horatio reads the letter. Exeunt.

IV-4: Enter King and Laertes. Enter a Messenger: (), with Letters. Exit Messenger. Claudius reads Hamlet's letter. <u>Manet Claudius and Laertes</u>: (STEPHEN NEALON; MICHAEL PALMER). Enter Queene: (SARAH HARVEY). Exit Laertes. Exeunt King and Queene.

away from him, talking to the audience, <u>already</u> having decided not to kill the king—the soliloquy came over as justification, as if the debate was already over. And when I asked the actor why he had done it that way, he simply said that was the way that best made sense to him, and it certainly made sense with the audience. The Editors also change this "foule Sonne" in the Folio to the "sole sonne" of the Quarto, but I see no

---

The Platt of The Tragedie of Hamlet (abridged)
by William Shakespeare
An OSC Presentation for Summer 2000 @ The Bothy
at 4:00 pm on Sunday 2nd July, 2000

I-1: Enter Barnardo and Francisco: (SIMON PURSE; MICHAEL PALMER), two Centinels. Enter Horatio and Marcellus: (BRENDAN FLEMING; EMMA BOWN). Exit Francisco. Enter Ghost: (NICHOLAS DAY). Exit Ghost. Ends. *Enter Ghost againe. The cocke crowes. Exit Ghost. Exeunt.*

I-2: Enter Claudius King of Denmark: (), with Letters, Gertrude the Queene: (), Hamlet (dressed in black): (), Polonius, Laertes: (), and his Sister Ophelia: (), Lords, Attendants: (). Enter to the Court, Voltemand and Cornelius: (). Exit Voltemand and Cornelius. Exeunt. Manet Hamlet: (MICHAEL PALMER). To him, Horatio, Barnardo, and Marcellus: (BRENDAN FLEMING; SIMON PURSE; EMMA BOWN). Exeunt, manet Hamlet. Exit Hamlet.

I-3: Enter Laertes and Ophelia. Enter Polonius. Exit Laertes. Exeunt.

I-4: Enter Hamlet, Horatio, Marcellus: (MICHAEL PALMER; BRENDAN FLEMING; EMMA BOWN). **A florish of trumpets and 2 peeces goes off for the King's celebration:** (AUDIENCE). Enter Ghost: (NICHOLAS DAY). Ghost beckons Hamlet. Exeunt Hamlet and Ghost. Exeunt.

I-5: Enter Ghost and Hamlet. Exit Ghost. Horatio and Marcellus speak within, then enter to Hamlet. Ghost cries under the Stage. Exeunt.

II-1: Enter Polonius, and Reynoldo his servant: (). Polonius gives him money and notes. Exit Reynoldo. Manet Polonius: (NICHOLAS DAY), enter Ophelia: (EMMA BOWN). Exeunt.

II-2: Enter King, Queene, Rosincrance and Guildensterne: () cum aliis: (). Exeunt Rosincrance and Guildensterne. Exit Polonius. Enter Polonius, and Voltemand and Cornelius, with Letters. Exeunt Ambassadors. Polonius reads out Hamlet's letter. To Polonius, Hamlet reading on a Booke. Exeunt King and Queen. Enter Rosincrance and Guildensterne, exit Polonius. Flourish for the Players. Enter Polonius. Enter foure or five Players: (). Exit Polonius with some of the Players: (). Exeunt, Manet Hamlet: (MICHAEL PALMER). Exit Hamlet.

III-1: Enter King, Queene, Polonius, Ophelia, Rosincrance, Guildensterne, and Lords: (). Exeunt Rosincrance and Guildensterne. Manet King, Queene, Polonius, Ophelia: (STEPHEN NEALON; CHRISTINE OZANNE; NICHOLAS DAY; EMMA BOWN). Exit the Queene. Polonius gives Ophelia a book. Exeunt King and Polonius. Enter Hamlet: (BRENDAN FLEMING). Ophelia gives him letters. Exit Hamlet. Enter King and Polonius. Exeunt.

Interval.

III-2: Enter Hamlet, and two or three of the Players: (CHRISTINE OZANNE; SIMON PURSE; AUDIENCE). Exit Players. Ends. *Enter Polonius, Rosincrance and Guildensterne. Exit Polonius. Exeunt Rosincrance and Guildensterne. Enter Horatio. Enter King, Queene, Polonius, Ophelia, Rosincrance, Guildensterne and some other Lords attendant: () with his Guard carrying torches: (). Danish March. Sound a Flourish. Hoboyes Play. The dumbe shew enters: (). Exeunt Players. Enter Prologue: (). Enter two players; King and his Queene: Gonzago and Baptista: (). Player King sleepes. Exit Player Queene. Enter Player Lucianus: (). Lucianus powres the poyson in his eares. Exeunt, manet Hamlet and Horatio. Enter Rosincrance and Guildensterne. Enter one Player with a Recorder: (). To Hamlet, Polonius. Exit Polonius. Exeunt, manet Hamlet. Exit Hamlet.*

III-3: Enter King, Rosincrance and Guildensterne. Exeunt Rosincrance and Guildensterne. Manet King: (NICHOLAS DAY), to him Polonius: (STEPHEN NEALON). Exit Polonius. Enter Hamlet armed: (BRENDAN FLEMING). Exit Hamlet. Exit King.

III-4: Enter Queene and Polonius: (CHRISTINE OZANNE; STEPHEN NEALON). Hamlet calls within: (MICHAEL PALMER), Polonius hides. To the Queene, Hamlet. Hamlet killes Polonius. Hamlet shows Gertrude two pictures. Enter Ghost: (BRENDAN FLEMING). Exit Ghost. Ends. *Exit Hamlet tugging in Polonius, to the Queene, the King. Enter Rosincrance and Guildensterne. Exeunt Gentlemen: Rosincrance and Guildensterne. Exeunt King and Queene.*

III-5: Enter Hamlet. Rosincrance and Guildensterne shout within. Enter Rosincrance and Guildensterne. Hamlet runs off, Rosincrance and Guildensterne following.

III-6: Enter King. To him, Rosincrance. Exit Rosincrance, to find the dead body of Polonius. Exit Hamlet. Exit Guildensterne following. Exit King.

IV-1: Enter Fortinbras: () and an Armie: (). Exeunt Fortinbras and soldiers.

IV-2: Enter Queene and Horatio: (CHRISTINE OZANNE; SIMON PURSE). Enter Ophelia distracted: (EMMA BOWN), she sings. Enter King: (NICHOLAS DAY). Exit Ophelia. Exit Horatio. Ends. *A noise within, enter a Messenger: (). Noise within, enter Laertes. A noise within: "Let her come in.", enter Ophelia. Exit Ophelia. Exeunt.*

IV-3: Enter Horatio, with an Attendant: (). To Horatio a Saylor: () with a letter from Hamlet. Horatio reads the letter. Exeunt.

IV-4: Enter King and Laertes. Enter a Messenger: (), with Letters. Exit Messenger. Claudius reads Hamlet's letter. Manet Claudius and Laertes: (NICHOLAS DAY; MICHAEL PALMER). Enter Queene: (CHRISTINE OZANNE). Exit Laertes. Exeunt King and Queene.

good reason to change, and it plays well with *Hamlet* being disgusted with himself at this point in the play.

The famous "mad" scene when *Ophelia* comes on was, I had thought, a bit of a problem. How would the actress play it? In performance, it was quite wonderful, and talking to me afterward, she said it was very simple, you did not act "mad," you just acted the words he had given you, and if that <u>came over</u> as mad, well, that was the audience's perception, <u>her</u> job was to make each bit of her line make sense, and be willing to radically change between lines. She was able to play it so well because she was not limited by being consistent:

ENTER OPHELIA *DISTRACTED*.

OPHELIA:
Where is the beauteous Majesty of Denmark.

GERTRUDE:
How now *Ophelia*?

OPHELIA:
How should I your true love know from another one?
By his Cockle hat and staffe, and his Sandal shoone.

GERTRUDE:
Alas sweet Lady: what imports this Song?

OPHELIA:
Say you? Nay pray you marke.
He is dead and gone Lady, he is dead and gone,
At his head a grasse-greene Turfe, at his heeles a stone.
ENTER KING.

GERTRUDE:
Nay but *Ophelia.*

OPHELIA:
Pray you marke.
White his Shrow'd as the Mountaine Snow.

The *There is a willow* scene, when *Gertrude* brings *Laertes* news of his sister's death, threw up some interesting insights. The speech itself is illogical: Do we imagine that *Gertrude* was standing by watching *Ophelia* drown, to report back so accurately what happened? Anyway, when *Laertes* is told his sister is drowned, his reply is not why or how, but *Drown'd. Oh Where?*:

GERTRUDE:
There is a Willow growes aslant a Brooke,
That shewes his hore leaves in the glassie streame:
There with fantasticke Garlands did she come,
Of Crow-flowers, Nettles, Daysies, and long Purples,

That liberall Shepheards give a grosser name;
But our cold Maids doe Dead Mens Fingers call them:
There on the pendant boughes, her Coronet weeds
Clambring to hang; an envious sliver broke,
When downe the weedy Trophies, and her selfe,
Fell in the weeping Brooke, her cloathes spred wide,
And Mermaid-like, a while they bore her up,
Which time she chaunted snatches of old tunes,
As one incapable of her owne distresse,
Or like a creature Native, and indued
Unto that Element: but long it could not be,
Till that her garments, heavy with her drinke,
Pul'd the poore wretch from her melodious buy,
To muddy death.

Gertrude played it as if she were making it up, making up a pretty package of half-truths, as well as quite bawdy images, to pacify *Laertes*, who had burst onto the stage wanting revenge for his father's death. Before this, *Claudius* had taken great pains to calm *Laertes* down, and now this. When *Laertes* stormed offstage again, *Claudius* was really peeved with his wife:

CLAUDIUS:
Let's follow, *Gertrude*:
How much I had to doe to calme his rage?
Now feare I this will give it start againe;
Therefore let's follow.

And so he too went offstage, thwarted by *Gertrude* trying to do what he had already done, and only inflaming *Laertes* more.

Of course, the play of *Hamlet* includes the famous instructions to the actors, and it is worth putting them here, since if you read them knowing the actors were preparing the plays the way discussed in this book, then they become even more interesting and perceptive:

HAMLET:
Speake the Speech I pray you, as I pronounc'd
it to you trippingly on the Tongue: But if you mouth it,
as many of your Players do, I had as live the Town-Cryer
had spoke my Lines: Nor do not saw the Ayre too much
your hand thus, but use all gently; for in the verie Torrent, Tempest, and (as I may say) the Whirle-winde of
Passion, you must acquire and beget a Temperance that

may give it Smoothnesse. O it offends mee to the Soule,
to see a robustious Pery-wig-pated Fellow, teare a Passion to tatters, to verie ragges, to split the eares of the
Groundlings: who (for the most part) are capeable of
nothing, but inexplicable dumbe shewes, and noise: I could
have such a Fellow whipt for o're-doing Termagant: it
out-*Herod's Herod*. Pray you avoid it.

FIRST PLAYER:

I warrant your Honor.

HAMLET:

Be not too tame neyther: but let your owne
Discretion be your Tutor. Sute the Action to the Word,
the Word to the Action, with this speciall observance:
That you ore-stop not the modestie of Nature; for any
thing so over-done, is from the purpose of Playing, whose
end both at the first and now, was and is, to hold as 'twer
the Mirrour up to Nature; to shew Vertue her owne
Feature, Scorne her owne Image, and the verie Age and
Bodie of the Time, his forme and pressure. Now, this
over-done, or come tardie off, though it make the unskil-
full laugh, cannot but make the Judicious greeve; The
censure of the which One, must in your allowance o're-
way a whole Theater of Others. Oh, there bee Players
that I have seene Play, and heard others praise, and that
highly (not to speake it prophanely) that neyther having
the accent of Christians, nor the gate of Christian, Pagan,
or Norman, have so strutted and bellowed, that I have
thought some of Natures Jouerney-men had made men,
and not made them well, they imitated Humanity so ab-
hominably.

FIRST PLAYER:

I hope we have reform'd that indifferently with
us, Sir.

HAMLET:

O reforme it altogether. And let those that
play your Clownes, speake no more then is set downe for
them. For there be of them, that will themselves laugh,
to set on some quantitie of barren Spectators to laugh
too, though in the meane time, some necessary Question
of the Play be then to be considered: that's Villanous, and
shewes a most pittifull Ambition in the Foole that uses
it. Go make you readie.

EXIT PLAYERS.

Who else but an actor could have written these lines? This leads us to an interesting insight onto the vexed (to the unenlightened) Who Wrote Shakespeare? debate.

There was a delightful program on UK television that gave equal time to the three alternative suspects who self-appointed experts think ought to have written the works of Shakespeare: Marlowe, Bacon, and Oxford. Supporters of each had twenty minutes to make their case, and groups of clever amateur sleuths all argued for their preferred candidate. The only certainty at the end of the program was that, at the very least, two of the groups of experts were completely wrong.

Actually, I am convinced that all three groups are wrong.

The question of authorship only strongly arose in the last century, and it is interesting that the rise of alternative theories exactly corresponded with the rise of the detective story, with its belief that minute clues can lead amateurs to out-think the traditional police force. Much is made of the fact that we do not have a lot of written evidence about Shakespeare from Stratford-upon-Avon. Yet we know far more about him than any other son of a sixteenth-century glover.

Because of the breadth of his knowledge, a case is made that a boy from the English countryside could not know of all the court practices, foreign countries, and human life that Shakespeare displays. I have read articles showing that he had great knowledge of medicine, therefore he must have been a doctor; he knew about the ways of the court, therefore he must have been a courtier; he knew about foreign places and habits, therefore he must have been a traveler; he knew a great deal about the Jewish faith, therefore he must have been a Jew.

Actually, I believe that his work shows one main thing, shining through all his words and works: he had an unprecedented knowledge of theatre and theatricality and knew the job of an actor better than any other contemporary writer. To my mind, this makes Shakespeare of Stratford-upon-Avon the sole candidate.

Working from Shakespearean Cue Scripts is one thing, working from Cue Scripts written by others from that period is another. I have presented Cue Script performances from *No Help No Wit Like a Woman* by Middleton; *Edward the Third* by Anonymous (all right, some believe parts of it may be by Shakespeare); *Woodstock* by Anonymous; and *Edward the Second* by Christopher Marlowe. Some of these were at the Drama Studio London, and I was approached by the embarrassed staff, who asked me to desist. Since the students had only a limited time in their training, surely they should be challenged with the best texts, rather than these inferior ones. And I think they were right: there is a quantifiable difference between the acting information given to the performer by Shakespeare and that given by his contemporaries.

All his plays work stunningly well without need for further interpretation or analysis, and the individual characterizations are matchless. Cue Script presentations from other authors work all right, but the acting results are thinner and less satisfying.

Anyway, anyone who has worked in theatre will know that for a group of actors to keep a secret for over forty years while one of their own pretends to be the author of their most popular successes is an impossibility. With his plays being in the repertoire for many years, it would soon have become apparent to the other members of the company if one of their fellow actors was not the author of them, and the evidence from letters and diaries of the time shows that the backbiting and gossip so beloved of our modern show business journalists were just as prevalent then.

Or as Mark Twain should have put it: "If Shakespeare did not write those plays, it was another fellow with the same name."

Romeo and Juliet, July 2000

Working at the Globe, I had become convinced that the balcony there was in fact not used for acting purposes. We know that lords and important patrons would sit up there to watch a play, and that the center of the balcony gives the best view. To reserve this space for actors or—as in most of the Globe performances—for musicians seems a woeful use of prime space. I cannot imagine my Lord Pembroke sitting to one side while the best view in the theatre is taken up by a trumpet player.

A scene being acted on the Globe's balcony is hard for all the audience to see. For its third season the Globe Company, realizing the difficult sightlines, moved the center of the balcony forward. This by no means helped the scene played there (*Cleopatra* hauling up *Anthony*), made the side balcony views impossible for some of those sitting there, and interfered with anything lowered from the heavens.

To play *Romeo and Juliet* you need a balcony—and if you are to tour the play around, you will need a balcony for those arenas which do not have a convenient balcony of their own. When the Royal Shakespeare Company brought its famous *Romeo and Juliet* with Ian McKellan and Judi Dench to London, it had to install closed-circuit cameras so the audience tucked in at the back of the stalls could see the action on the balcony.

As I said in the *Cymbeline* section, I have come to the conclusion that the Elizabethans had a touring balcony cum truck that was used for <u>all</u> their structures: the balcony for *Romeo and Juliet*; the walls for the *Citizen* in *King John*—and for *Arthur* to jump to his death; the walls from which *Richard the Second* descends; and so on. I had such a balcony, roughly made, standing about 1 meter (about three feet) high, for our presentation in Jordan.

Our balcony needed to be moved, so four actors would move it as it changed from being part of *Capulet*'s house, to the first balcony where *Romeo* woos *Juliet*, to the balcony scene from which *Romeo* jumps and from which *Juliet* must come down to talk with her mother, and finally for the tomb itself at the end. My actors were enjoined—as always—to keep the play going, so that when the words of one scene ended, the words of the next began; and so I discovered more about the play than I could have imagined.

I have recorded in THE FOLIO section the lack of the Prologue in the First Folio version of the play, but I have always been puzzled about the retention of the second Soliloquy. In performance, as the scene changers moved the balcony downstage to get ready for the first balcony scene—and it could not have been moved earlier as the stage had to be clear for the *Capulet* scene with its dancing—the second Soliloquy began; ah, it was to cover the scene change!

The Platt of The Tragedie of Romeo and Juliet
by William Shakespeare
An OSC Presentation on the Artimes Steps at the Jerash Festival, Jordan on Saturday 29th July, 2000

I-1: Enter Sampson and Gregory: (LEWIS HANCOCK; SARAH HARVEY), with Swords and Bucklers, of the house of Capulet. Enter Abraham and Balthazar: (RICHARD JACOBS; SARAH HOWE), of the house of Mountague. Enter Benvolio at one doore and Tibalt at another: (DANIEL HOPKINS; CALLUM COATES). They all Fight. Enter Officer and Citizen: (SIMON PURSE; SCOTT AINSLIE) with Clubs. Enter old Capulet in his Gowne, and his wife, with a sword: (NICHOLAS DAY; CHRISTINE OZANNE). Enter old Mountague, and his wife, with a sword: (RICHARD BURNIP; MARIANNE MARCH). Enter Prince Eskales, with his Traine: (STEPHEN NEALON; CAROLYN JONES). Exeunt, manet Mountague, his wife, Benvolio. Enter Romeo: (JONATHAN ROBY). Exeunt Mountague and his wife. Exeunt.

I-2: Enter Capulet, Countie Paris: (ADRIAN O'DONNELL), and the Clowne Peter: (LEWIS HANCOCK). Capulet gives Peter the list. Exeunt Capulet and Paris. Enter Benvolio and Romeo. Romeo reads the Letter. Exit Peter. Exeunt.

I-3: Enter Capulet's Wife and Nurse: (CAROLYN JONES). To them, Juliet: (EMMA BOWN). To them, a Serving man: (SARAH HARVEY). Exit Serving man. Exeunt.

I-4: Enter Romeo, Mercutio: (SCOTT AINSLIE), Benvolio, and Masker: (RICHARD JACOBS). They march about the Stage. Set Truck, and 1st Serving man comes forth with his napkin: (LEWIS HANCOCK), enter Serving Man to Capulet: (SIMON PURSE). Enter Capulet, 2nd Capulet: (RICHARD BURNIP), Paris, Lady Capulet, Juliet, Nurse, all the Guests and Gentlewomen: (STEPHEN NEALON; SARAH HARVEY; SARAH HOWE; MARIANNE MARCH) to the Maskers. Musicke playes: and the dance. Exit Tibalt. Exeunt, manet Juliet and the Nurse. One cals within, Juliet. Exeunt. Set Truck.

II-1: Enter Chorus: (STEPHEN NEALON). Exit Chorus, enter Romeo alone. Enter Benvolio, with Mercutio, Romeo hides. Exeunt Benvolio and Mercutio. Enter Juliet on the balcony. Nurse cals within. Exit Juliet. Enter Juliet againe. Exit Juliet. Exit Romeo. Set Truck.

II-2: Enter Frier alone: (RICHARD JACOBS) with a basket and herbs. Enter Romeo. Exeunt.

II-3: Enter Benvolio and Mercutio. Enter Romeo. Enter Nurse and her man Peter. Exit Mercutio and Benvolio. Exeunt.

II-4: Enter Juliet. Enter Nurse. Exeunt.

II-5: Enter Frier and Romeo. Enter Juliet. Exeunt.

III-1: Enter Mercutio, Benvolio, and Balthazar. Enter Tybalt, and others: (LEWIS HANCOCK; SARAH HARVEY). Enter Romeo. They make to fight. Exit Tybalt and men. Benvolio and Balthazar carry off Mercutio. Enter Benvolio. Enter Tybalt. Romeo and Tybalt fight, Tybalt falles. Exit Romeo, enter Officer and Citizen: (ADRIAN O'DONNELL). Enter Prince, old Montague, Capulet, their Wives and all: (LEWIS HANCOCK; SARAH HARVEY; SARAH HOWE). Exeunt.

Interval.

III-2: Enter Juliet alone. Enter Nurse with cords. Juliet gives the Nurse a ring. Exeunt.

III-3: Enter Frier and Romeo. Enter Nurse within, and knockes. Enter Nurse. Nurse gives a ring to Romeo. Exit Nurse. Exeunt. Set Truck.

III-4: Enter old Capulet, his Wife and Paris. Exeunt.

III-5: Enter Romeo and Juliet aloft. Enter Nurse. Exit Nurse, Romeo climbs down. Exit Romeo. Enter Mother. Enter Capulet and Nurse. Exit Capulet. Exit Mother. Exeunt. Set Truck.

IV-1: Enter Frier and Countie Paris. Enter Juliet, with a knife. Exit Paris. Frier gives Juliet a violl. Exeunt.

IV-2: Enter Father Capulet, Mother, Nurse, and Serving men: (LEWIS HANCOCK; MARIANNE MARCH; SIMON PURSE). Exeunt Serving men. Enter Juliet. Exeunt Juliet and Nurse. Exeunt. Set Bed.

IV-3: Enter Juliet and Nurse. Enter Mother. Exeunt Nurse and Mother. Juliet drinks the violl, and falls upon the bed. Enter Lady of the House with keys, and Nurse. Enter old Capulet. Exit Lady and Nurse. Enter Serving men: (LEWIS HANCOCK; MARIANNE MARCH; SIMON PURSE) with spits, and logs, and baskets. Play Musicke, exeunt Serving men. Enter Nurse. Exit Nurse. Enter Mother. Enter Father. Enter Frier and the Countie and Musician: (SARAH HARVEY). Exeunt, manet Nurse and Musician. Exeunt. Strike Bed.

V-1: Enter Romeo. Enter Romeo's man Balthazar. Exit Man. Enter Apothecarie: (SCOTT AINSLIE). Romeo buys poison from him with gold. Exeunt.

V-2: Enter Frier John: (DANIEL HOPKINS) to Frier Lawrence. Enter Frier Lawrence. Frier John returns the Letter. Exit Frier John. Exit Frier Lawrence. Set Truck and Tomb.

V-3: Enter Paris and his Page: (MARIANNE MARCH), with Torch and flowers. Page whistles. Enter Romeo, and Balthazar, with torch, Mattocke, and iron crow. Romeo gives him a Letter. Romeo opens the Tomb, and fights Paris. Exit Page. Paris is killed. Romeo drags the body into the Tomb, drinks the poison, and dies. Enter Frier with Lanthorne, Crow and Spade. Exeunt Frier and Balthazar. Juliet awakes. Enter Page and Watch: (CALLUM COATES). Juliet kills herself with Romeo's dagger. Enter Romeo's Man and 2nd Watch: (SIMON PURSE). Enter Frier, and another Watchman: (LEWIS HANCOCK), with Mattocke and Spade. Enter the Prince. Enter Capulet and his wife. Enter the Mountague. Exeunt.

Finis.

Shakespeare

Verse Nurses:	SIMON PURSE; PATRICK TUCKER
Costumes:	ELLIE COCKERILL
Fights:	RICHARD BURNIP
Book-Holder:	SIMON PURSE
Presenter:	PATRICK TUCKER

CHORUS:

Now old desire doth in his death bed lie,

And yong affection gapes to be his Heire,

The Platt of The Tragedie of Romeo and Juliet
by William Shakespeare
An OSC Presentation on the Artimes Steps at the Jerash Festival, Jordan
on Sunday 30th July, 2000

I-1: Enter Sampson and Gregory: (LEWIS HANCOCK; SARAH HARVEY), with Swords and Bucklers, of the house of Capulet. Enter Abraham and Balthazar: (RICHARD JACOBS; EMMA BOWN), of the house of Mountague. Enter Benvolio at one doore and Tibalt at another: (DANIEL HOPKINS; CALLUM COATES). They all Fight. Enter Officer and Citizen: (SIMON PURSE; SCOTT AINSLIE) with Clubs. Enter old Capulet in his Gowne, and his wife, with a sword: (NICHOLAS DAY; CHRISTINE OZANNE). Enter old Mountague, and his wife, with a sword: (RICHARD BURNIP; MARIANNE MARCH). Enter Prince Eskales, with his Traine: (STEPHEN NEALON; CAROLYN JONES). Exeunt, manet Mountague, his wife, Benvolio. Enter Romeo: (JONATHAN ROBY). Exeunt Mountague and his wife. Exeunt.

I-2: Enter Capulet, Countie Paris: (ADRIAN O'DONNELL), and the Clowne Peter: (LEWIS HANCOCK). Capulet gives Peter the list. Exeunt Capulet and Paris. Enter Benvolio and Romeo. Romeo reads the Letter. Exit Peter. Exeunt.

I-3: Enter Capulet's Wife and Nurse: (CAROLYN JONES). To them, Juliet: (SARAH HOWE). To them, a Serving man: (SARAH HARVEY). Exit Serving man. Exeunt.

I-4: Enter Romeo, Mercutio: (SCOTT AINSLIE), Benvolio, and Masker: (RICHARD JACOBS). They march about the Stage. Set Truck, and 1st Serving man comes forth with his napkin: (LEWIS HANCOCK), enter Serving Man to Capulet: (SIMON PURSE). Enter Capulet, 2nd Capulet: (RICHARD BURNIP), Paris, Lady Capulet, Juliet, Nurse, all the Guests and Gentlewomen: (STEPHEN NEALON; EMMA BOWN; SARAH HARVEY; MARIANNE MARCH) to the Maskers. Musicke playes: and the dance. Exit Tibalt. Exeunt, manet Juliet and the Nurse. One cals within, Juliet. Exeunt. Set Truck.

II-1: Enter Chorus: (STEPHEN NEALON). Exit Chorus, enter Romeo alone. Enter Benvolio, with Mercutio, Romeo hides. Exeunt Benvolio and Mercutio. Enter Juliet on the balcony. Nurse cals within. Exit Juliet. Enter Juliet againe. Exit Juliet. Exit Romeo. Set Truck.

II-2: Enter Frier alone: (RICHARD JACOBS) with a basket and herbs. Enter Romeo. Exeunt.

II-3: Enter Benvolio and Mercutio. Enter Romeo. Enter Nurse and her man Peter. Exit Mercutio and Benvolio. Exeunt.

II-4: Enter Juliet. Enter Nurse. Exeunt.

II-5: Enter Frier and Romeo. Enter Juliet. Exeunt.

III-1: Enter Mercutio, Benvolio, and Balthazar. Enter Tybalt, and others: (LEWIS HANCOCK; SARAH HARVEY). Enter Romeo. They make to fight. Exit Tybalt and men. Benvolio and Balthazar carry off Mercutio. Enter Benvolio. Enter Tybalt. Romeo and Tybalt fight, Tybalt falles. Exit Romeo, enter Officer and Citizen: (ADRIAN O'DONNELL). Enter Prince, old Montague, Capulet, their Wives and all: (EMMA BOWN; LEWIS HANCOCK; SARAH HARVEY). Exeunt.

Interval.

III-2: Enter Juliet alone. Enter Nurse with cords. Juliet gives the Nurse a ring. Exeunt.

III-3: Enter Frier and Romeo. Enter Nurse within, and knockes. Enter Nurse. Nurse gives a ring to Romeo. Exit Nurse. Exeunt. Set Truck.

III-4: Enter old Capulet, his Wife and Paris. Exeunt.

III-5: Enter Romeo and Juliet aloft. Enter Nurse. Exit Nurse, Romeo climbs down. Exit Romeo. Enter Mother. Enter Capulet and Nurse. Exit Capulet. Exit Mother. Exeunt. Set Truck.

IV-1: Enter Frier and Countie Paris. Enter Juliet, with a knife. Exit Paris. Frier gives Juliet a violl. Exeunt.

IV-2: Enter Father Capulet, Mother, Nurse, and Serving men: (LEWIS HANCOCK; MARIANNE MARCH; SIMON PURSE). Exeunt Serving men. Enter Juliet. Exeunt Juliet and Nurse. Exeunt. Set Bed.

IV-3: Enter Juliet and Nurse. Enter Mother. Exeunt Nurse and Mother. Juliet drinks the violl, and falls upon the bed. Enter Lady of the House with keys, and Nurse. Enter old Capulet. Exit Lady and Nurse. Enter Serving men: (LEWIS HANCOCK; MARIANNE MARCH; SIMON PURSE) with spits, and logs, and baskets. Play Musicke, exeunt Serving men. Enter Nurse. Exit Capulet. Enter Mother. Enter Father. Enter Frier and the Countie and Musician: (SARAH HARVEY). Exeunt, manet Nurse and Musician. Exeunt. Strike Bed.

V-1: Enter Romeo. Enter Romeo's man Balthazar. Exit Man. Enter Apothecarie: (SCOTT AINSLIE). Romeo buys poison from him with gold. Exeunt.

V-2: Enter Frier John: (DANIEL HOPKINS) to Frier Lawrence. Enter Frier Lawrence. Frier John returns the Letter. Exit Frier John. Exit Frier Lawrence. Set Truck and Tomb.

V-3: Enter Paris and his Page: (MARIANNE MARCH), with Torch and flowers. Page whistles. Enter Romeo, and Balthazar, with torch, Mattocke, and iron crow. Romeo gives him a Letter. Romeo opens the Tomb, and fights Paris. Exit Page. Paris is killed. Romeo drags the body into the Tomb, drinks the poison, and dies. Enter Frier with Lanthorne, Crow and Spade. Exeunt Frier and Balthazar. Juliet awakes. Enter Page and Watch: (CALLUM COATES). Juliet kills herself with Romeo's dagger. Enter Romeo's Man and 2nd Watch: (SIMON PURSE). Enter Frier, and another Watchman: (LEWIS HANCOCK), with Mattocke and Spade. Enter the Prince. Enter Capulet and his wife. Enter Mountague. Exeunt.

Finis.

Shakespeare
original
company

Verse Nurses:	SIMON PURSE; PATRICK TUCKER
Costumes:	ELLIE COCKERILL
Fights:	RICHARD BURNIP
Book-Holder:	SIMON PURSE
Presenter:	PATRICK TUCKER

That faire, for which Love gron'd for and would die,
With tender *Juliet* matcht, is not not faire.
Now *Romeo* is beloved, and Loves againe,
A like bewitched by the charme of lookes:
But to his foe suppos'd he must complaine,
And she steale Loves sweet bait from fearefull hookes:
Being held a foe, he may not have accesse
To breath such vowes as Lovers use to sweare,
And she as much in Love, her meanes much lesse,
To meete her new Beloved any where:
But passion lends them Power, time, meanes to meete,
Temp'ring extremities with extreame sweete.

When they had to move the balcony back, there was *Frier Lawrence* with his poetic entrance *The gray ey'd morne*—but as a near repeat of what *Romeo* had just said, this was already known to the audience and, again, a successful cover for the scene change:

ROMEO:
> Would I were sleepe and peace so sweet to rest,
> The gray ey'd morne smiles on the frowning night,
> Checkring the Easterne Clouds with streakes of light,
> And darknesse fleckel'd like a drunkard reeles,
> From forth dayes pathway, made by *Titans* wheeles.
> Hence will I to my ghostly Friers close Cell,
> His helpe to crave, and my deare hap to tell.
> > *EXIT.*
> > *ENTER FRIER ALONE WITH A BASKET.*

FRIER LAWRENCE:
> The gray ey'd morne smiles on the frowning night,
> Checkring the Easterne Cloudes with streaks of light:
> And fleckled darknesse like a drunkard reeles,
> From forth daies path, and *Titans* burning wheeles:
> Now ere the Sun advance his burning eye,
> The day to cheere, and nights danke dew to dry,
> I must upfill this Osier Cage of ours,
> With balefull weedes, and precious Juiced flowers,

Oh yes, the Editors remove these lines, believing they are a misprint, because they are a repeat of what the *Frier* is about to say. But look at them, they are not the same, and if they were just a compositor putting it down twice, why would they be so different? In performance it came over that there was a link between *Romeo* and the *Frier*—perhaps *Romeo* had heard this poem or saying before from the *Frier*, or even the other way round. The Bad Quarto of 1597 does not have this, but the Good Quarto of 1599 does have these repeated but not similar four lines.

The move of the balcony for the farewell scene of *Romeo and Juliet* happened as *Capulet* repeated the plot talking with *Paris*, and it was removed during *Paris*'s entrance with the *Frier* prior to *Juliet*'s coming on.

Juliet's bed was set as she talked with her *Nurse* about what to wear, and her "dead" body on the bed was taken off as the musicians finished their scene and *Romeo* came on in Mantua—including a wonderful frisson as he talked of dreaming about *Juliet* finding him dead, and we see her body being carried offstage.

The last big scene change necessary is to bring on the tomb—and for this I decided that the tomb area needed to be different from the rest of the stage area, that there were two acting spaces needed: outside and inside the tomb. I asked the actors therefore to treat the balcony truck as the entrance to the tomb, through which they had to stoop to get in. *Juliet* preset on her slab also had to be brought in, and I was loath to let all this happen when *Paris* was starting the scene. However, to keep the pace up, this is what I asked him to do, and again the performance experience showed us that *Paris*'s first speech—telling his *Page* where to go, and to whistle if anyone comes—was just a fill-in while the scenery was moved into position.

The sheer practicality of performance seems to be stitched into these plays; it is what you might expect, but it is always a revelation and surprise to me just how theatrically proved these pieces are.

When *Juliet* finds she has been rejected by both her mother and father in wanting to get out of her marriage to *Paris*, this is what happens next:

JULIET:
> O God!
> O Nurse, how shall this be prevented?
> My Husband is on earth, my faith in heaven,
> How shall that faith returne againe to earth,
> Unlesse that Husband send it me from heaven,
> By leaving earth? Comfort me, counsaile me:
> Alacke, alacke, that heaven should practise stratagems
> Upon so soft a subject as my selfe.
> What saist thou? hast thou not a word of joy?
> Some comfort Nurse.

NURSE:
> Faith here it is,
> *Romeo* is banished, and all the world to nothing,
> That he dares nere come backe to challenge you:
> Or if he do, it needs must be by stealth.
> Then since the case so stands as now it doth,
> I thinke it best you married with the Countie,
> O hee's a Lovely Gentleman:
> *Romeo*s a dish-clout to him: an Eagle Madam
> Hath not so greene, so quicke, so faire an eye
> As *Paris* hath, beshrow my very heart,
> I thinke you are happy in this second match,
> For it excels your first: or if it did not,

Your first is dead, or 'twere as good he were,
As living here and you no use of him.
NURSE:

JULIET:

Speakest thou from thy heart?
NURSE:

And from my soule too,
Or else beshrew them both.
JULIET:

Amen.
NURSE:

What?
JULIET:

Well, thou hast comforted me marve'lous much,
Go in, and tell my Lady I am gone,
Having displeas'd my Father, to *Lawrence* Cell,
To make confession, and to be absolv'd.
NURSE:

Marrie I will, and this is wisely done.
JULIET:

Auncient damnation, O most wicked fiend!
It is more sin to wish me thus forsworne,
Or to dispraise my Lord with that same tongue
Which she hath prais'd him with above compare,
So many thousand times? Go Counsellor,
Thou and my bosome henceforth shall be twaine:
Ile to the Frier to know his remedie,
If all else faile, my selfe have power to die.
    EXEUNT.

Now, all Editors send the *Nurse* off before *Juliet's* condemnation of her, and change the final *EXEUNT* to *EXIT*, but as always I was intrigued to see what happened if we played it as per. The results were wonderful.

The *Nurse*, having given what she thought was good advice, is about to leave when she receives that harsh speech from *Juliet*, including the threat of suicide. From this moment on, the *Nurse* does not say another word to *Juliet*, despite their closeness. When *Juliet* returns from *Frier Lawrence's* cell, she notes it, but says nothing to her. *Juliet* goes off to bed with the *Nurse* getting clothes ready for the morrow, but again no words. When they are in her bed chamber, the mother says goodnight to her, but not the *Nurse*.

When the *Nurse* comes in to wake her up, she has a lot of words to say before she admits that *Juliet* is dead. My actress Carolyn Jones, because she had been onstage to hear *Juliet's* threat of suicide, played the scene as if she knew very early on that her beloved

Juliet was dead and she was telling those awful bawdy jokes about her and *Paris* in a desperate attempt to put off the moment when she had to acknowledge her death. It played superbly and made perfect sense of leaving the *Nurse* on stage at that earlier scene. It also made the "wake up" scene so much easier to play, rather than having the *Nurse* talk of waking her up and fuss about until the moment of discovery. By playing that she already had dreadful suspicions about *Juliet*, the *Nurse* was better able to accuse the parents with *She's dead* when they arrive onstage. It was a marvelous piece of theatre.

Mercutio does not fight *Tybalt*. That is how the play is written in the Folio. *Mercutio* and *Tybalt* square off against each other, but there is no fight indicated. There <u>is</u> a fatal fight between *Romeo* and *Tybalt*:

ROMEO:
  Draw *Benvolio*, beat downe their weapons:
  Gentlemen, for shame forbeare this outrage,
  Tibalt, *Mercutio*, the Prince expresly hath
  Forbidden bandying in *Verona* streetes.
  Hold *Tybalt*, good *Mercutio*.
      EXIT TYBALT.

And then later on in the scene:

TYBALT:
  Thou wretched Boy that didst consort him here,
  Shalt with him hence.
ROMEO:
  This shall determine that.
      THEY FIGHT. TYBALT FALLES.

When we performed this scene, all sorts of good theatrical discoveries came about. For a start, it made *Benvolio's* description of what had happened (the description that directors use to choreograph the fight from and so give *Benvolio* the problem of saying that which the audience knows already) a knowing falsehood. The *Prince* is about to pronounce on *Romeo*—death or banishment—and *Benvolio* goes to a grand description of what had gone on:

BENVOLIO:
  Tybalt here slaine, whom *Romeo's* hand did slay,
  Romeo that spoke him faire, bid him bethinke
  How nice the Quarrell was, and urg'd withall
  Your high displeasure: all this uttered,
  With gentle breath, calme looke, knees humbly bow'd
  Could not take truce with the unruly spleene

Of *Tybalts* deafe to peace, but that he Tilts
With Peircing steele at bold *Mercutio's* breast,
Who all as hot, turnes deadly point to point,
And with a Martiall scorne, with one hand beates
Cold death aside, and with the other sends
It back to *Tybalt*, whose dexterity
Retorts it: *Romeo* he cries aloud,
Hold Friends, Friends part, and swifter then his tongue,
His aged arme, beats downe their fatall points,
And twixt them rushes, underneath whose arme,
An envious thrust from *Tybalt*, hit the life
Of stout *Mercutio*, and then *Tybalt* fled.
But by and by comes backe to *Romeo*,
Who had but newly entertained Revenge,
And too't they goe like lightning, for ere I
Could draw to part them, was stout *Tybalt* slaine:
And as he fell, did *Romeo* turne and flie:
This is the truth, or let *Benvolio* die.

Reading this, you can see that it is <u>not</u> what happened—there <u>was</u> no *Hold Friends, Friends part* from *Romeo*—but *Benvolio* is doing his best to put a good slant on the day's doing, trying to prevent *Romeo*'s being sentenced to death.

My *Benvolio* discovered that this must also apply to his speech to *Mountague* at the beginning of the play telling what had happened in the first scene's fight:

BENVOLIO:
Heere were the servants of your adversarie,
And yours close fighting ere I did approach,
I drew to part them, in the instant came
The fiery *Tibalt*, with his sword prepar'd,
Which as he breath'd defiance to my eares,
He swong about his head, and cut the windes,
Who nothing hurt withall, hist him in scorne.
While we were enterchanging thrusts and blowes,
Came more and more, and fought on part and part,
Till the Prince came, who parted either part.

This again can be seen not to be exactly what went on, and so the actor playing *Benvolio* realized that this character was a dissembler, a politician—and he was thrilled at being so enabled in his performance.

With no fight, what happened to make the play work? In performance, *Tybalt* and *Mercutio* circled each other, then *Tybalt* aimed a quick blow at *Mercutio* and exited. It was so quick, so undramatic, that it was barely seen, and so *Mercutio*, having to die with no big fight, no dramatic end, made his lines as noble and dramatic as possible. It played so well, with the character trying to give himself a noble end, and it also worked well dramatically, since the only real drama is in the fight where *Romeo* kills *Tybalt*, not the *Tybalt-Mercutio* one. For more Folio and Quarto thoughts affecting *Romeo*, see Appendix 3.

We had now performed comedies, history, romance—and now a tragedy. The use of a Book-Holder for a tragedy—with the audience hearing and seeing a prompter during a serious play—had had no detrimental effect on the presentation. It just meant that the actors took their prompts simply, rather than making jokes of them as they tended to do when playing a comedy. In each of these differing styles of play, the way of working produced original and valid theatrical results. In comedies, the use of the Book-Holder or prompter tended to be comical and add to the humor of the evening, but in the other plays the use was as unobtrusive as the conductor of a concert bringing in the oboes, or cuing the singer when to sing. We had tested the theories in all forms of Shakespeare, and at all times they had held up, and helped to make the plays both accessible and entertaining to an audience.

Romeo and Juliet and A Midsommer Nights Dreame, September 2000

We had been asked to present some productions at the Elmbridge Arts Festival, a small celebration in south London, and I decided that we should of course show our wonderful *Romeo and Juliet* in the UK, and they had also asked for *A Midsommer Nights Dreame*.

It was interesting to see how the cast would fare, having performed *Romeo and Juliet* so recently. Although we had to have a few replacements for those actors no longer available, the cast maintained the freshness and inspiration of the Jordan performance. Just as the actors would add some things from knowledge of their previous outing, so other bits would go as they no longer seemed appropriate. Those who call themselves our regular audience found it enchanting, and urged us to do more.

We had two changes of cast, with a new *Nurse* and a new *Paris*, and although they played the roles very differently from the Jordan cast, the poignancy and effect of the play were in no way diminished.

For the presentation of *A Midsommer Nights Dreame*, because we had done the play several times before and because there were so few female parts in *Romeo and Juliet*, I decided that we should do the play as a Boys' Company presentation, with an all-female cast. I was so busy that the whole experiment, including workshops on playing men, was handed over to Simon Purse, who is responsible for our discovery of all these wonderful insights.

I had over the years found that actresses playing boys roles brought a fascinating slant to them, and I knew that it was completely authentic for a company of boy actors to play in those far-off days; there was even a record of a boy playing old men so successfully that Ben Jonson wrote a poem about him:

WEEP with me all you that read
This little story;
And know for whom a tear you shed
Death's self is sorry.

The Platt of The Tragedie of Romeo and Juliet
by William Shakespeare
*An OSC Presentation in the Marquee for the Elmbridge Arts Festival 2000
on Friday 29th September, 2000*

I-1: Enter Sampson and Gregory: (LEWIS HANCOCK; SALLY WOODFIELD), of the house of Capulet. Enter Abraham and Balthazar: (RICHARD JACOBS; EMMA BOWN), of the house of Mountague. Enter Benvolio at one doore and Tibalt at another: (DANIEL HOPKINS; CALLUM COATES). They all Fight. Enter Officer and Citizen: (JOANNA HARTE; STEPHEN NEALON) with Clubs. Enter old Capulet in his Gowne, and his wife: (NICHOLAS DAY; CHRISTINE OZANNE). Enter old Mountague, and his wife, with a sword: (RICHARD BURNIP; MARIANNE MARCH). Enter Prince Eskales, with his Traine: (GRAHAM POUNTNEY; BRYAN TORFEH). Exeunt, manet Mountague, his wife, Benvolio. Enter Romeo: (JONATHAN ROBY). Exeunt Mountague and his wife. Exeunt.

I-2: Enter Capulet, Countie Paris: (MICHAEL PALMER), and the Clowne Peter: (LEWIS HANCOCK). Capulet gives Peter the list. Exeunt Capulet and Paris. Enter Benvolio and Romeo. Romeo reads the Letter. Exit Peter. Exeunt.

I-3: Enter Capulet's Wife and Nurse: (JULIETTE GRASSBY). To them, Juliet: (SARAH HOWE). To them, a Serving man: (SALLY WOODFIELD). Exit Serving man. Exeunt.

I-4: Enter Romeo, Mercutio: (SCOTT AINSLIE), Benvolio, and Masker: (RICHARD JACOBS). They march about the Stage. Set Truck, and 1st Serving man comes forth with his napkin: (LEWIS HANCOCK), enter Serving Men to Capulet: (JOANNA HARTE; GRAHAM POUNTNEY). Enter Capulet, 2nd Capulet: (RICHARD BURNIP), Paris, Lady Capulet, Juliet, Nurse, all the Guests and Gentlewomen: (STEPHEN NEALON; EMMA BOWN; MARIANNE MARCH; SALLY WOODFIELD) to the Maskers. Musicke playes: and the dance. Exit Tibalt. Exeunt, manet Juliet and the Nurse. One cals within, Juliet. Exeunt. Set Truck.

II-1: Enter Chorus: (SIMON PURSE). Exit Chorus, enter Romeo alone. Enter Benvolio, with Mercutio, Romeo hides. Exeunt Benvolio and Mercutio. Enter Juliet on the balcony. Nurse cals within. Exit Juliet. Enter Juliet againe. Exit Juliet. Exit Romeo. Set Truck.

II-2: Enter Frier alone: (RICHARD JACOBS) with a basket and herbs. Enter Romeo. Exeunt.

II-3: Enter Benvolio and Mercutio. Enter Romeo. Enter Nurse and her man Peter. Exit Mercutio and Benvolio. Exeunt.

II-4: Enter Juliet. Enter Nurse. Exeunt.

II-5: Enter Frier and Romeo. Enter Juliet. Exeunt.

III-1: Enter Mercutio, Benvolio, and Balthazar. Enter Tybalt, and others: (LEWIS HANCOCK; SALLY WOODFIELD). Enter Romeo. Exit Tybalt and men. Benvolio and Balthazar carry off Mercutio. Enter Benvolio. Enter Tybalt. Romeo and Tybalt fight, Tybalt falles. Exit Romeo, enter Officer and Citizen: (STEPHEN NEALON). Enter Prince, Montague, Capulet, their Wives and all: (EMMA BOWN; LEWIS HANCOCK; BRYAN TORFEH; SALLY WOODFIELD). Exeunt.

Interval.

III-2: Enter Juliet alone. Enter Nurse with cords. Juliet gives the Nurse a ring. Exeunt.

III-3: Enter Frier and Romeo. Enter Nurse within, and knockes. Enter Nurse. Nurse gives the ring to Romeo. Exit Nurse. Exeunt. Set Truck.

III-4: Enter old Capulet, his Wife and Paris. Exeunt.

III-5: Enter Romeo and Juliet aloft. Enter Nurse. Exit Nurse, Romeo climbs down. Exit Romeo. Enter Mother. Enter Capulet and Nurse. Exit Capulet. Exit Mother. Exeunt. Set Truck.

IV-1: Enter Frier and Countie Paris. Enter Juliet, with a knife. Exit Paris. Frier gives Juliet a violl. Exeunt.

IV-2: Enter Father Capulet, Mother, Nurse, and Serving men: (JOANNA HARTE; LEWIS HANCOCK; MARIANNE MARCH; GRAHAM POUNTNEY; SALLY WOODFIELD). Exeunt Serving men. Enter Juliet. Exeunt Juliet and Nurse. Exeunt. Set Bed.

IV-3: Enter Juliet and Nurse. Enter Mother. Exeunt Nurse and Mother. Juliet drinks the violl, and falls upon the bed. Enter Lady of the House with keys, and Nurse. Enter old Capulet. Exit Lady and Nurse. Enter Serving men with spits, and logs, and baskets. Play Musicke, exeunt Serving men. Enter Nurse. Exit Capulet. Enter Mother. Enter Father. Enter Frier and the Countie and Musicians: (BRYAN TORFEH; SALLY WOODFIELD). Exeunt, manet Nurse and Musicians. Exeunt. Strike Bed.

V-1: Enter Romeo. Enter Romeo's man Balthazar. Exit Man. Enter Apothecarie: (STEPHEN NEALON). Romeo buys poison from him with gold. Exeunt.

V-2: Enter Frier John: (DANIEL HOPKINS). Enter Frier Lawrence. Frier John returns the Letter. Exit Frier John. Exit Frier Lawrence. Set Truck and Tomb.

V-3: Enter Paris and his Page: (MARIANNE MARCH), with Torch and flowers. Page whistles. Enter Romeo, and Balthazar, with torch, Mattocke, and iron crow. Romeo gives him a Letter. Romeo opens the Tomb, and fights Paris. Exit Page. Paris is killed. Romeo drags the body into the Tomb, drinks the poison, and dies. Enter Frier with Lanthorn, Crow and Spade. Exeunt Frier and Balthazar. Juliet awakes. Enter Page and Watch: (CALLUM COATES). Juliet kills herself with Romeo's dagger. Enter Romeo's Man and 2nd Watch: (JOANNA HARTE). Enter Frier, and another Watchman: (LEWIS HANCOCK), with Mattocke and Spade. Enter the Prince. Enter Capulet and his wife. Enter Mountague. Exeunt.

Finis.

Shakespeare
original
company

Verse Nurses:	SIMON PURSE; PATRICK TUCKER
Costumes:	ELLIE COCKERILL
Fights:	RICHARD BURNIP
Book-Holder:	SIMON PURSE
Presenter:	PATRICK TUCKER

'Twas a child that so did thrive
In grace and feature
As Heaven and Nature seem'd to strive
Which own'd the creature.

The Platt of A Midsommer Nights Dreame
by William Shakespeare
*An OSC Boys' Company Presentation in the Marquee for the Elmbridge Arts Festival
on Saturday 30th September, 2000*

I-1 Enter Theseus, Duke of Athens: (TESS DIGNAN), with his bride-to-be Hippolita Queene of the Amazons: (KATHRYN HARE). To them, Egeus: (CHRISTINE OZANNE), and his daughter Hermia: (SALLY WOODFIELD), and Lysander, and Demetrius: (JULIETTE GRASSBY; ANDREA NEWLAND). Lysander and Demetrius stand forth. Exeunt all but Lysander and Hermia. To them Helena: (JOANNA HARTE). Exit Hermia. Exit Lysander. Exit Helena.

I-2 Enter Quince the Carpenter, Snug the Joyner, Bottome the Weaver, Flute the bellowes-mender, Snout the Tinker, and Starveling the Taylor: (JENNIFER BURGESS; TOR CLARK; NATASHA TAMAR; EMMA BOWN; KALI PEACOCK; MARIANNE MARCH). Quince gives out the scrolls. Exeunt.

II-1 Enter a Fairie at one doore: (HELEN PUNT), and Robin Goodfellow, known as Pucke, at another: (SARAH HOWE). Enter the King of Fairies, Oberon: (DEBORAH BLAKE) at one doore, and the Queen of Fairies, Tytania: (SARAH FINCH) at another with her traine: (TOR CLARK; MARIANNE MARCH; KALI PEACOCK). Exeunt the Queen with her traine. Exit Pucke. Enter Demetrius, Helena following him, the King being invisible. Exit Demetrius, Helena following. To the King, Pucke with the flower. Exeunt.

II-2 Enter the Queen of Fairies, with her traine. They sing her to sleep, and exit. To the Queene, Oberon. He puts a charm on her eyes. Exit Oberon. Enter Lysander and Hermia. They sleep. Enter Pucke, who puts a charm on Lysander, and exits. Enter Demetrius and Helena running. Exit Demetrius. Lysander wakes. Exit Helena. Lysander rejects his old love Hermia and exits. Hermia wakes and exits.

III-1 Enter the Mechanicals: (JENNIFER BURGESS; TOR CLARK; NATASHA TAMAR; EMMA BOWN; KALI PEACOCK; MARIANNE MARCH). Enter Robin. Exit Bottome. Pucke follows him to put on the Asse head. Enter Piramus with the Asse head, and Pucke. The Clownes all exit. Exit Pucke. To Bottome, Snout and Quince, who exit. Alone, Bottome sings. Tytania wakes. To the Queene her fairies Peasblossome, Cobweb, Moth, Mustard-seede: (HELEN PUNT; TOR CLARK; MARIANNE MARCH; KALI PEACOCK). Exeunt.

III-2 Enter the King of Pharies, Oberon, solus. To him Pucke. Enter Demetrius and Hermia. Exit Hermia. Demetrius lies down and sleeps. Exit Pucke. Oberon puts a charm on Demetrius' eye. To Oberon, Pucke. Enter Lysander and Helena. Demetrius wakes. To them Hermia. Exeunt Lysander and Demetrius. Exit Helena, chased off by Hermia. Exit Oberon. Enter Lysander led by Pucke. Enter Demetrius led by Pucke. Exeunt Demetrius and Pucke. Lysander shifts places, lies down and sleeps. Enter Pucke leading Demetrius, who lies down and sleeps. Enter Helena, who sleeps. Enter Hermia, who sleeps. Pucke removes the charm from Lysander. The lovers sleep all the Act. Exit Pucke.

IV-1 Enter Queene of Fairies and Clowne and fairies, with Oberon hiding behind. Musicke. Tytania and Bottome sleep. Enter Pucke. Oberon removes the charm from Tytania. Tytania awakes. Musick, and Pucke removes the Asse head from Bottome. Exeunt Oberon, Pucke and Tytania, the sleepers lying still. The Fairies sing the song, and exeunt. Winde horns. Enter Theseus, Egeus, Hippolita, for a hunt. Hornes, and they wake. Shout within, they all start up. Exit the Duke and Lords. Exit the lovers. Bottome awakes, and exits.

IV-2 Enter Quince, Flute, Snout and Starveling. To them, Snug. To them Bottome, and all exeunt.

V-1 Enter Theseus, Hippolita, and Egeus. To them the lovers, Lysander, Demetrius, Hermia and Helena.

The Play: Flourish of trumpets. Enter the Prologue, Quince. Enter Piramus, Thisbie, Wall, Moone-shine, Lyon: (NATASHA TAMAR; EMMA BOWN, KALI PEACOCK, MARIANNE MARCH, TOR CLARK). Exit all but Wall. Enter Piramus, enter Thisbie. Exeunt Piramus and Thisbie, and exit Wall. Enter Lyon and Moone-shine carrying lanthorne, bush and with his dog. Enter Thisbie. Lyon roars and Thisbie exits, dropping her mantle. Lyon bites the mantle and exits. Enter Piramus, with his sword, who sees the mantle, stabs himself and dies. Exit Moone-shine, enter Thisbie, who sees Piramus, stabs herself and dies.

Bottome and Flute dance a Burgomaske. Exeunt. Enter Pucke with his broome. Enter the King and Queene of Fairies, with their traines. They sing and dance. Pucke speaks the Epilogue.

Interval

Finis.

Costumes   ELLIE COCKERILL
Verse Nurse and Book-Holder   SIMON PURSE

Years he number'd scarce thirteen
When Fates turn'd cruel
Yet three fill'd zodiacs had he been
The stage's jewel;
And did act (what now we moan)
Old men so duly
As sooth the Parcae thought him one
He play'd so truly.
So by error to his fate
They all consented;
But viewing him since alas too late!
They have repented;
And have sought to give new birth
In baths to steep him;
But being so much too good for earth
Heaven vows to keep him.

Assembling a company of actresses to put on the play, I started to investigate what happens when women play men, and in particular why it is often unsuccessful.

I remembered that when I had gone to the theatre to see a girl play a boy—whether it was a *Viola*, an *Imogen*, or a *Rosalind*, no one would ever be convinced by the boy disguise. Even in my own presentations, I realized that the actresses playing men always showed some feminine elements, especially in the hair, so that the audience would know it was really a girl. Looking back, I remembered that in every case an actress playing or impersonating a boy always left some curl, some fringe, or some moment when their cap came off so luxurious hair cascaded over their shoulders. This applies across the board, so even in the recent successful film *Boys Don't Cry*, Hilary Swank <u>still</u> sported a hairstyle that had a girlish feminine fringe.

I then recalled seeing a play in New York where I and the rest of the audience were completely fooled by an actress we all thought was a man in Act One, but was later revealed to be a woman. She had an absolutely convincing man's hairdo, and it was one of the very rare occasions that I had seen this carried out with complete success.

Investigating hair, I found out that this is a very powerful area—so powerful that many societies or religions demand that their women cover up all their hair in public. I asked my actresses to investigate acting with tight caps or slicked back hair, and suddenly it became apparent how often a woman touches her hair, refers to it, and uses it in her interface with the world. I had recently seen an all-female production of *Richard the Third*, and even then not a single actress wore a man's hairstyle. In conversation afterward, every one of them had a good excuse or reason why they had to have that fringe, that bow in the hair, and that silky smooth look. Ponytails were worn female style (halfway up the head) rather than male style (at the nape of the neck).

My actresses, practicing in the workshops organized by Simon, all followed this style, and the result was an extraordinary evening of theatre. The competition and secret battle between *Theseus* and *Hippolita* was very clear—and very funny. The lovers were as good, and as funny, as I have ever seen, and the *Mechanicals* were a joy (*Starveling* even sporting a hairy chest wig—there was a first).

The real revelation was that a company of actresses, working away from the influence of actors, did not compete with one another, and were tremendously cooperative. They felt that they were not so much adding any masculine qualities as excising their feminine ones—and that was the message of changing their hairstyles. They found that when walking around with their hair in a masculine style, they would often have impulses to touch or adjust their hair, and it was removing those elements that made them such successful "men." No one tried to be masculine, and by playing it in a neutral way, they found that they needed and played the text even more, and with less competition came more honesty.

In other words, they all felt that by peeling away their femininity, they assumed masculinity. They were not as afraid of being physical as they can be in a mixed sex production, because they need not be worried about their fellow actors taking it further, the way a lot of male actors do.

Powerful conclusions from a wonderful experiment, and one that the audience really loved. The knowledge that here was a company of supportive actors made the audience as warm as I have known and brought this ten-year experiment to a logical conclusion. Our next task is to get a longer run of plays, or even of emulating the Elizabethans, and doing six different plays in one week. Now there is challenge that would be as irresistible as it would be expensive.

Sarah Howe capped a wonderful year with us by giving her *Pucke* (following her *Ophelia* and *Juliet*), and when it came to the spell part, she performed a little song and dance:

ENTER PUCKE. THEY SLEEPE.
PUCKE:
    Through the Forrest have I gone,
    But *Athenian* finde I none,
    One whose eyes I might approve
    This flowers force in stirring love.
    Night and silence: who is heere?
    Weedes of *Athens* he doth weare:
    This is he (my master said)
    Despised the *Athenian* maide:
    And heere the maiden sleeping sound,
    On the danke and durty ground.
    Pretty soule, she durst not lye
    Neere this lacke-love, this kill-curtesie.
    Churle, upon thy eyes I throw

All the power this charme doth owe:
When thou wak'st, let love forbid
Sleepe his seate on thy eye-lid.
So awake when I am gone:
For I must now to *Oberon*.
    EXIT.

When afterward I asked her why, she explained that she had changed from speaking in regular iambic pentameters to a different beat here, and so thought it should also be performed differently. A simple answer—and a lovely theatrical result.

One thing did happen in getting the play ready, and that was they did prepare a bit of the play—the difficult bit. We had up to Elmbridge put on six performances of *A Midsommer Nights Dreame* in three different presentations, and at each performance the lovers had had difficulty coming in with their lines during the *Piramus and Thisby* section at the end. Because we knew that this was going to be a problem, Simon had the girls run over these particular lines beforehand—and a final thought came to me.

In modern theatre we carefully rehearse everything, and try to guess which bits would be most difficult, and put most effort into those. We in the OSC had often thought that there was going to be a particularly difficult bit (the last scene in *Cymbeline* springs to mind) but in performance had found that it was another scene entirely that had had a few problems. What we found ourselves doing for this Boys' Company presentation was to rehearse <u>in retrospect</u>; that is, only go over those bits that, by performance, have proved to be a problem. So perhaps they did go over those very things that <u>by performance</u> they found to be tricky theatrically—that, or have the playwright rewrite them so that a company coming to it could easily perform it under the existing original conditions.

To prepare those parts of a play which are known to be difficult would be an obvious choice for them to make, and again would throw a spotlight on our underlining passion, that plays were to be performed, that actors would perform them, and that it was the experience of the actors from performance that informed any reworking, not an advance guess by nonactors.

ACTORS' RESPONSES

By now you know about my reactions to this work, and this approach, but what about those who actually have to go onstage without a safety net? Without the usual comfort blankets of given moves, approved characterizations, and bits of stage business? What do the actors who have taken part in these presentations think about it? Can we allow the reactions of the performers to be part of the evidence?

Actors in the UK

Philip Bird (*Marcellus; Angelo; Launce; Orlando; King John; Orsino; Posthumus*)

What is strange is that when you play ordinarily in the theatre there's a sort of <u>us and them</u> feeling with the audience. With this one they were friends; they were as much part of the production as we were. Patrick Tucker peels away the patina of footnotes and guesswork which has crusted and clouded the text over the last 400 years. The verse is revealed clean and shining, and as an actor one feels once again directly in touch with the words Shakespeare wrote.

Elizabeth Counsell (*Luciana; Portia; Tytania; Edmund*)

I think it was one of the most joyous evenings I've ever had in the theatre, ever.

Meg Davies (*Isabella; Tytania; Adriana; Portia; Hippolita*)

Going back to the First Folio is like seeing colour television for the first time and realising why you want to watch colour from now on and not black and white any more.

Nicholas Day (*Bottome; Shylocke; Polonius; Malvolio; Cymbeline; Capulet*)

It works for the actor; it works for the audience. That's all that matters.

Sarah Howe (*Sheriffe; Sebastian; Speed; Arviragus; Juliet; Pucke*)

Learning how to work from a Cue Script can revolutionize the way an actor thinks about the work. Personally, it made me question everything I had previously clung on to as necessary for creating a character: building a history; finding physical characteristics; discussing relationships with other characters; analyzing what other characters say about you. I learned that all of those things (if one still chooses to use them) start and end with the only piece of evidence there is—the text. And that the more clues a writer gives an actor, the richer and more detailed the performance can be.

So, to remove any of those clues in the name of "regularization" is akin to stripping Beethoven's compositions of their pianissimo's or fortissimo's in order to allow the musician to find them for herself. Rather than restricting the performer, clues in the text allow freedom and choice.

Michael Maloney (*Second Brother; Hamlet*)

Patrick Tucker provides the modern actor with a system and a technique that enables the player to understand the power of verse. It is simple, tried, tested and has truth. I have found it to be a foundation for all my classical acting in the last ten years. My only regret is that I and many other actors did not arrive at it ten years before that!

Christine Ozanne
(*Book-Holder; First Fairy; Starveling; Gertrude; Lady Capulet; Egeus*)

It is interesting that we should use the phrase "Verse Nursing," because there is something about the OSC process that resembles alternative medicine. You know, you try all the recognised traditional approaches first, then you find a treatment which unlocks new thoughts and seems to cure the problem.

Such remarks as "It's like light bulbs going on"; "I always felt there was something I was missing"; "It's so obvious, once you've learned the scoring in the text"; and "It demystifies Shakespeare"; are common among our actors, and their enjoyment of discovery is reflected in the audiences' continual enthusiastic delight, which we trust was the original intention of William Shakespeare himself.

Sonia Ritter (*Nerrissa; Hermia; Julia; Isabella; Richard; Lady Macbeth; Pucke; Abbesse; Rosalind; Constance; Maria; Guiderius*)

I am an avid reader of what are called "whodunits." I have often wondered why. It has occurred to me that it is because the long convoluted and difficult journey that a detective or amateur sleuth takes is not a long way from the journey the actor makes when trying to create a role from a text. Like a detective, the actor simply cannot follow any fancy or personal idea of a character: he must first and foremost study the text—the evidence.

For years I was led to believe that Shakespeare's texts were inaccurate, full of errors which would lead me astray as an innocent consumer of the plays. I was supposed to be thankful that worthy scholars through the ages had rendered these poor manuscripts into something I might, just might manage to interpret for an audience—if I worked hard.

Then I met Patrick Tucker. He threw a First Folio text at me (it was *Imogen* in *Cymbeline*—a speech that had got me into the Royal Shakespeare Company) and barked "just do it." I was on the road to Damascus. For eight years now I have mined the jewels of the Folio. I trust that the men who printed it were closer to the soul of Elizabethan and Jacobean theatre than we are today. They smelt and saw it at its birth, and savoured its magical qualities, which were essentially and magnificently aural.

I found that I did not need to sink into a morass of technical or psychological detail that can dog the textual editor. There is visual and visceral muscularity in the way the early scripts are written that demands that I respond first and foremost to the architecture of the words and their myriad aural relationships. The script is more like a musical score. Allowing the physical sound and texture of the words to affect me first, before arguing with myself or anyone else about their meaning, is a brave and thrilling thing. As for textual comprehension, that is, what it means, I have found it coming upon me without effort, suddenly illuminated by trusting the text to speak for itself, creating a terrific marriage of poetic musicality and meaning.

The OSC does not rehearse in the modern sense of the word. This means that I am thrown back onto the text as if it were a map. And behold! A set of guidelines (some call them rules but I don't like that—rules lead to pedantry) are there helping me to move about the stage. I find I am devising on the spot a theatrical dance with fellow actors that springs from textual knowledge and good stagecraft.

Cue Scripts help to eliminate endless procrastination about the play. Revelations in performance are frequently spectacular. To me the greatest are when the sheer performance begins to throw you yourself into the emotions of the character. Yet there is no chance of becoming complacent or self-indulgent. In fact the challenge is to remain sharp and open to what is happening around you, that the unforseen may liberate your creativity further.

My work with the OSC had made me fastidious about speaking text. Every vowel and consonant, punctuation mark and size of letter is a possible key to how (not just why) I vocalize the words—ACT them—that is, create the character. The delight of performing obscure poetry, difficult verse drama or even strangely enough very bad television scripts has increased beyond measure.

I am equipped to explore what is written in front of me with much the same curiosity and hunger as any detective or amateur sleuth, sifting with delicate assurance through the evidence that they have to solve the crime. I have found a new joyful fearlessness in my approach to acting work.

Jonathan Roby (*Laertes; Rutland; Lysander; Flute; Dromio; Silvius; Aguecheek; Dauphin; Launce; Clotten; Romeo*)

Working for the Original Shakespeare Company is the most exciting, frightening, and ultimately rewarding experience I have found on stage because it allows, even demands, that the actor takes responsibility for their entire performance. Careful study of Shakespeare's texts can give clues to the playing of a role but the character on stage is as individual and unique as the actor himself. The personal, spontaneous reactions of the actor on stage become entwined with the reactions of the character to each moment in the play, so the audience see "real" surprise, confusion, or joy. The audience share these moments and in the unravelling of the story, which creates a wonderful relationship between actors and audience. I have often felt that the audience have been "with me" sharing in my journey through the play (especially when I have been acting in plays that I know less well).

I have a print of a painting which shows a man walking a tightrope which he is creating for himself from a ball of string in his hands. The string is only attached to a building at one end but somehow the tightrope stays beneath his feet. Being on stage in an OSC production is like being this tightrope walker: logic says something shouldn't be possible, but it is happening right in front of your eyes.

Hugh Walters (*Egeus; Quince; Duke; Old Gobbo; Arragon; Tutor; Duncan*)

I do it (OSC work) because I find it the most liberating and exciting way of doing Shakespeare. Also I feel, curiously enough, closer to what Shakespeare had intended us to do than in any other form of Shakespeare performance I have been engaged in and I've been engaged in quite a lot.

I only know my part of the story and I'm about to discover what the story is at exactly the same time as the audience, and that gives an excitement and a freshness to one's responses; it gives a spontaneity that, normally, you simply don't have.

Actors in Canada

Ted Atherton (*Oliver; Hortensio; Lucentio*)

Playing *Oliver* in Patrick Tucker's *As you Like it* at the Du Maurier World Stage Festival was a revelation but also, in some ways, a reminder of what I already knew; that the works of Shakespeare are naturally accessible. Presented by actors who are themselves exhilarated by the possibilities of the language, they cannot help but compel the imagination. Our audiences went absolutely berserk.

But they went crazy, I think, not because that what we were doing was like a dog walking on its hind legs, (i.e., "It is not done well; but you are surprised to find it done at all." Samuel Johnson), but because the actors were quite openly sharing the play and themselves. Doing that, we created a community. In the shared enactment and active witnessing of events which we communally recognized as reflecting some kind of human truth, we acknowledged and celebrated our common humanity. And I think that's what theatre is supposed to do.

Sally Cahill (*Curtis; Widdow; Bianca*)

There is a great freedom in structure. A world of possibilities in process and discipline. I feel this process came alive and was most magical when we <u>did</u> serve the <u>play</u>, hit our cues, served the text. And within that perimeter there was an incredible feeling of freedom.

For me, realizations and sudden bursts of inspiration came practically as I was stepping onto the stage and we all continued to create as we went along—it was incredible fun. I think this kind of work needs actors who have a good mix of discipline, care, and audacity. Thanks for taking the handcuffs off me, Patrick and Christine.

Robert Dodds (*Le Beau; Silvius; Pedant; Hortensio*)

Patrick Tucker's approach to Shakespeare brings a vitality and immediacy to the theatre that is quite extraordinary. His technique for analysing text is just that; analysing—looking for what the author (and we have a rather good one in Shakespeare) ACTUALLY intended to be played, not what we think he intended or what we have preconceived from past performances. This leads to an openness in performance which yields remarkable theatre. What at first glance appears to be a "tragic" and "serious" scene can turn out to be quite humorous—but always with purpose because that is what the author intended!! Patrick Tucker's approach always guarantees an exciting time in the theatre!

In a strong field, I think the best reason to make use of Patrick Tucker's approach to Shakespeare is that it asks actors, in a logical and practical way, to do the impossible. I suspect this has always been the most direct way to good theatre.

Torri Higginson (*Widdow; Bianca; Curtis*)

What every actor strives for is that moment of truth, to create the moment of discovery for the audience. With this process there is no way to avoid it. The moment of discovery is as truthful for you as it is for the audience.

Seana McKenna (*Rosalind*)

Just a note to thank you for the adventure—goes to show, no matter what the weather, tame or tempestuous—that Shakespeare's map will guide you, if you know north from south. Thank you both—I've gleaned much. And yes—actually had FUN! Spontaneity always does that, it seems. Take good care—Hope we cross paths again.

Lauren Piech (*Biondello; Haberdasher; Widdow*)

I love this work. I have never been so petrified. I have never been so happy and playful. My needs are hard to meet. I want so much to do work that is truly alive and where you cannot lie. Your pals on stage have no choice but to deal with you. The great feeling of looking up and really knowing you're connecting with someone you're sure you're breathing together.

I think it's important to serve the characters well and recognize that Shakespeare's people are so incredibly real. Even when you have only a dozen lines, there are enough clues to flush them out and make them whole—and this is easier to do in this work. What you decide, what you go with is embraced by the company and thus you can really hook in. I also think it's important to tell the story—this is the priority. I thank you so much for your support and confidence that has allowed me to fly. I would do this work again in a second. It has been a wonderful experience.

Actors in Australia

Isobel Kirk (*Tytania; Snout*)

After some demoralising experiences in mainstream theatre where rehearsals were self-conscious beasts, it was very exciting and liberating to be able to take responsibility for the performance and the thrill of being BIG BIG BIG.

Susie Lindeman (*Hermia*)

The experience of performing Hermia on the first night was like a gift of freedom—challenge—flight. With no "inner dialogue" telling me where,—when to reach a certain "pre-determined" point, no inner eye watching, checking, or directing my performance on an outer level, I, as actor, was enabled to feel completely in the moment, completely in the circumstance and processes created by Shakespeare. It really did feel to be directed by the lines, the words and images inspiring me, rather than a designer/director's vision of "his" Shakespeare.

Patrick told us he wanted us actors as "co-creators" and that very sensation has empowered me and I think will continue to do so.

Amelia Longhurst (*Pucke*)

I developed a severe migraine by the end of the show and found it difficult to bow. Could the smiling, clapping audience have possibly enjoyed the performance that I had <u>no</u> control over? Yep. They sure did.

Veronica Neave (*Hermia*)

There is a <u>monster</u> at large now streaming through my body. How dare you come and emancipate him and then leave me with the consequences—However he feels very nice inside me.

Greta Scacchi (*Helena, Tytania*)

My experiences of the OSC, both from the audience and as a player, have been illuminating, exhilarating and sometimes hysterical. Patrick has uncovered simple guidelines to disentangle much of the obscurity in the text and provide actors with practical tools to make their path lighter and clearer. The result is entertainment more varied, witty, and spontaneous than we usually associate with the Bard today, and a convincing key to the broad popularity of Shakespeare in his time.

Julie Shearer (*Hermia; Tytania*)

I've said it before and I'll say it again, I never felt so ALIVE! That's why I do this, follow this tortuous path. How could you not long to act when you know this pure, adrenaline direct line between you and your fellow players and THE CROWD!

Jeanette Taylor (*Helena*)

I have always known in my heart that the text is THE THING. The words, chosen, the structure of the sentences—they always seemed/felt to me to be the most important thing—Ever since I began acting my heart has sank at every director or actor who has dared to cut a text or ignore the punctuation or not even bother to speak the words written—how do they ever presume they know more, or better than, the writer? What a joy to meet two people who demand that you rely on the text (and nothing else!) Who ask for you to simply attend to, and respect Shakespeare's words. As an actor I've felt I need to know exactly where I was to move at every moment <u>before</u> I got on that stage. No so! I had my words and my ears and my brave fellow actors—and it was enough! Something else carried me along during the performance. I was freed from getting it right or wrong—I felt like a little kid playing joyfully. I have never felt this on stage before. <u>Never!</u> And talking to the audience—seeing their eyes—I got energy from them—when I talked to <u>them</u>, asked <u>them</u> questions <u>I</u> understood what I was saying. This is what it means to share a night in the theatre—SHARING.

Lastly—yes lastly! I am so grateful that Patrick and Christine didn't allow me to lean on them—"You choose" is a phrase I will treasure forever—"It's in the text!" is another. When I did that it's almost like having this great big genius at your back gently guiding you through. So how is it possible to go wrong when William Shakespeare is whispering directions in your ear?

THE SECRETS

Prose and Poetry

When you first look at a piece, you need to find out if it is in prose or poetry before planning what to do with it.

To begin with, a simple definition:

Prose is where each line uses up all the space available, and just runs on to the next line when it runs out of space. Capitals are in the usual places, at the start of a sentence and for proper names:

SHYLOCKE:
To baite fish withall, if it will feede nothing
else, it will feede my revenge; he hath disgrac'd me, and
hindred me halfe a million, laught at my losses, mockt at
my gaines, scorned my Nation, thwarted my bargaines,
cooled my friends, heated mine enemies, and what's the
reason? I am a *Jewe*: Hath not a *Jew* eyes? hath not a
Jew hands, organs, dementions, sences, affections, passi-
ons, fed with the same foode, hurt with the same weapons, subject to the same diseases, healed by the same
meanes, warmed and cooled by the same Winter and
Sommer as a Christian is: if you pricke us doe we not
bleede? if you tickle us, doe we not laugh? if you poison
us doe we not die? and if you wrong us shall we not revenge? if we are like you in the rest, we will resemble you
in that. If a *Jew* wrong a *Christian*, what is his humility,
revenge? If a *Christian* wrong a *Jew*, what should his sufferance be by Christian example, why revenge? The vil-
lanie you teach me I will execute, and it shall goe hard
but I will better the instruction.

Poetry is where each line begins with a capital letter, and the length of the line is determined by the type of poetry being used (in Shakespeare's case, the vast ma-jority of it being in iambic pentameters):

HAMLET:
>   To be, or not to be, that is the Question:
>   Whether 'tis Nobler in the minde to suffer
>   The Slings and Arrowes of outragious Fortune,
>   Or to take Armes against a Sea of troubles,
>   And by opposing end them: to dye, to sleepe
>   No more; and by a sleepe, to say we end
>   The Heart-ake, and the thousand Naturall shockes
>   That Flesh is heyre too? 'Tis a consummation
>   Devoutly to be wish'd. To dye to sleepe,
>   To sleepe, perchance to Dreame; I, there's the rub,
>   For in that sleepe of death, what dreames may come,
>   When we have shuffel'd off this mortall coile,
>   Must give us pawse. There's the respect
>   That makes Calamity of so long life:
>   For who would beare the Whips and Scornes of time,
>   The Oppressors wrong, the poore mans Contumely,
>   The pangs of dispriz'd Love, the Lawes delay,
>   The insolence of Office, and the Spurnes
>   That patient merit of the unworthy takes,
>   When he himselfe might his *Quietus* make
>   With a bare Bodkin? Who would these Fardles beare
>   To grunt and sweat under a weary life,
>   But that the dread of something after death,
>   The undiscovered Countrey, from whose Borne
>   No Traveller returnes, Puzels the will,
>   And makes us rather beare these illes we have,
>   Then flye to others that we know not of.
>   Thus Conscience does make Cowards of us all,
>   And thus the Native hew of Resolution
>   Is sicklied o're, with the pale cast of Thought,
>   And enterprizes of great pith and moment,
>   With this regard their Currants turne away,
>   And loose the name of Action. Soft you now,
>   The faire *Ophelia*? Nimph, in thy Orizons
>   Be all my sinnes remembred.

Having now worked out which you are dealing with, what _is_ the difference from an acting/interpretive point of view?

Some characters, such as *King Richard the Second*, only speak in poetry. Some, such as *Dogberry*, only in prose. This in itself is a guide to the nature of their characters and the degree to which their natures are "heightened," or even to the degree to which both are educated. The really interesting notes come when a character speaks both in prose and in poetry.

Consider for example the character of *Beatrice* in *Much Adoe about Nothing*. She speaks only in prose, until the point in the play where she hides in the arras, and overhears *Hero* and *Ursula* speaking of *Benedicke*'s "love" for her. After they leave, she comes forward and for the first time in the play speaks in poetry:

> *EXEUNT HERO AND URSULA.*
>
> BEATRICE:
>> What fire is in mine eares? can this be true?
>> Stand I condemn'd for pride and scorne so much?
>> Contempt, farewell, and maiden pride, adew,
>> No glory lives behinde the backe of such.
>> And *Benedicke,* love on, I will requite thee,
>> Taming my wilde heart to thy loving hand:
>> If thou dost love, my kindenesse shall incite thee
>> To binde our loves up in a holy band.
>> For others say thou dost deserve, and I
>> Beleeve it better then reportingly.
>>> *EXIT.*

This is not an insignificant moment in the play, and I suggest that the change from prose to poetry, so easily seen by an actor working from a Cue Script, is a clue to the state of mind, and change of mind, of the character.

This is seen even more plainly in the first encounter between *Olivia* and *Viola* in *Twelfe Night*, which I have discussed earlier under that play's OSC production.

Sometimes, the gear change is the other way. The *Duke* in *Measure, For Measure* speaks nothing but poetry, until he in his turn hides in the arras, and overhears the searing scene between *Isabella* and her brother *Claudio*, when she tells him she would rather he lost his life than she her virginity. When the *Duke* reenters the scene, he speaks in prose for the first time. Again, an actor would find this clue and act on the significance of that change, for a case can be made for arguing that this is indeed when the *Duke* as a character changes, and decides he must interfere with the political situation that he had set up.

Another nice example is in *The Merchant of Venice*, where *Jessica, Clowne,* and *Lorenzo* all speak in prose, but once the *Clowne* leaves the stage, the husband and wife speak to each other only in poetry:

> JESSICA:
>> Nay, you need not feare us *Lorenzo, Launcelet*
>> and I are out, he tells me flatly there is no mercy for mee
>> in heaven, because I am a Jewes daughter: and hee saies

you are no good member of the common wealth, for
in converting Jewes to Christians, you raise the price
of Porke.

LORENZO:

I shall answere that better to the Commonwealth, than you can the getting up of the Negroes bel-
lie: the Moore is with childe by you *Launcelet*?

CLOWNE:

It is much that the Moore should be more then
reason: but if she be lesse then an honest woman, shee is
indeed more then I tooke her for.

LORENZO:

How everie foole can play upon the word, I
thinke the best grace of witte will shortly turne into silence, and discourse grow commendable in none onely
but Parrats: goe in sirra, bid them prepare for dinner?

CLOWNE:

That is done sir, they have all stomacks?

LORENZO:

Goodly Lord, what a witte-snapper are you,
then bid them prepare dinner.

CLOWNE:

That is done to sir, onely cover is the word.

LORENZO:

Will you cover than sir?

CLOWNE:

Not so sir neither, I know my dutie.

LORENZO:

Yet more quarreling with occasion, wilt thou
shew the whole wealth of thy wit in an instant; I pray
thee understand a plaine man in his plaine meaning: goe
to thy fellowes, bid them cover the table, serve in the
meat, and we will come in to dinner.

CLOWNE:

For the table sir, it shall be serv'd in, for the
meat sir, it shall bee covered, for your comming in to
dinner sir, why let it be as humors and conceits shall go-
verne.

    EXIT CLOWNE.

LORENZO:

O deare discretion, how his words are suted,
The foole hath planted in his memory

An Armie of good words, and I doe know
A many fooles that stand in better place,
Garnisht like him, that for a tricksie word
Defie the matter: how cheer'st thou *Jessica*,
And now good sweet say thy opinion,
How dost thou like the Lord *Bassiano's* wife?

JESSICA:
Past all expressing, it is very meete
The Lord *Bassanio* live an upright life
For having such a blessing in his Lady,
He findes the joyes of heaven heere on earth,
And if on earth he doe not meane it, it
Is reason he should never come to heaven?

So poetry is when the character is heightened, or is in a heightened state—a state we all know about when writing poetry to our loved one, and is a good example of complex language, which is dealt with next.

Simple and Complex

Shakespeare knows how to be straightforward, as *Macbeth* is addressed by his *Lady*:

LADY MACBETH:
Give me the Daggers:

or as *Hamlet* says to *Gertrude* in her bedroom:

HAMLET:
Now Mother, what's the matter?

All pretty straightforward, so we see that if you have a straightforward speech, then be straightforward about it. If however you have a complicated speech, then perhaps something else is going on.

Think about a romantic encounter—maybe your own—that starts with two strangers meeting each other, goes through the embarrassments of getting to know each other, going out on dates, finding accommodations with each other, ending up with the blissful union of two like souls in a wonderful marriage. And how do they speak to each other at each stage?

At first the language would be a simple and friendly "How do you do?" or "Would you like to go to the movies?" As the relationship progresses, the language will get altogether more complicated: "I am awfully afraid I am getting rather fond of you." How strange to couple the word "awful" with "fond"—but in fact this is a true reflection of the relationship, for they are not really sure what the relationship is or where it is going, and the actual emotion between them is probably somewhere on the line between "awful" and "fond." Only when the couple are sure of each other, and of themselves, can they come up with the simplicity of "I love you."

Shakespeare uses exactly the same techniques, giving simple statements where it is warranted, and complex statements when the person is struggling to express a complex feeling or message.

Sometime back in the UK there was a train crash, and a railway official was being interviewed on television as to why the accident had happened, since it was known that the trains were equipped with two-way radios and should have been warned of the danger on the track. He replied, "Although our systems are terrestrial, the topography was against us." (Translation: the trains were in a valley and could not pick up the radio message.) Now here the individual was concentrating <u>not</u> on giving information but on appearing important, perhaps being sure to give away nothing that might bring criticism onto his firm—in other words, a truly Shakespearean reply where the <u>structure</u> of the language gives valuable <u>acting</u> notes as to what is called the subtext.

That is in fact a wonderful acting note for approaching Shakespeare: the subtext is in the structure of the language.

Those struggling to express themselves with wit and humor, with metaphors and clever language, are struggling to express a complex feeling, and we go wrong if we take a complex speech and just say it simply, just as we go wrong if we take a very simple speech and give it all sorts of complicated interpretations or emotion.

Here is a good example of characters switching from one to another:

ENTER ROMEO AND JULIET ALOFT.

JULIET:
    Wilt thou be gone? It is not yet neere day:
    It was the Nightingale, and not the Larke,
    That pier'st the fearefull hollow of thine eare,
    Nightly she sings on yond Pomgranet tree,
    Beleeve me Love, it was the Nightingale.

> She starts speaking simply, but then gets really complicated.

ROMEO:
    It was the Larke the Herauld of the Morne:
    No Nightingale: looke Love what envious streakes
    Do lace the severing Cloudes in yonder East:
    Nights Candles are burnt out, and Jocond day
    Stands tipto on the mistie Mountaines tops,
    I must be gone and live, or stay and die.

> He starts complicated, but ends with the simplest and most sincere *I must be gone and live, or stay and die.*

JULIET:
    Yond light is not daylight, I know it I:
    It is some Meteor that the Sun exhales,

> She continues in her complicated, overblown style, but ends with the simple *Therefore stay yet, thou need'st not to be gone.*

To be to thee this night a Torch-bearer,
And light thee on thy way to *Mantua*.
Therefore stay yet, thou need'st not to be gone.

ROMEO:
Let me be tane, let me be put to death,
I am content, so thou wilt have it so.
Ile say yon gray is not the mornings eye,
'Tis but the pale reflex of *Cinthias* brow.
Nor that is not the Larke whose noates do beate
The vaulty heaven so high above our heads,
I have more care to stay, then will to go:
Come death, and welcome, *Juliet* wills it so.
How ist my soule, lets talke, it is not day.

> He now is on his complicated form of words. Do we think that they are both unwilling to face up to the reality of parting, and are covering up their real emotions with clever words?

JULIET:
It is, it is, hie hence be gone away:
It is the Larke that sings so out of tune,
Straining harsh Discords, and unpleasing Sharpes.
Some say the Larke makes sweete Division;
This doth not so: for she divideth us.
Some say, the Larke and loathed Toad change eyes,
O now I would they had chang'd voyces too:
Since arme from arme that voyce doth us affray,
Hunting thee hence, with Hunts-up to the day,
O now be gone, more light and it light growes.

> She finally faces up to the truth, and speaks simply, but then quickly goes back into her florid style.

A good tip is to play simple lines straight to the other actor, and take the complicated ones away. This is what we do in real life after all, when we face up to each other with "What do you mean?" and avert each other's gaze when going into "I am afraid I am going to play the bad uncle, I feel a real heel, as I have to tell you some rather embarrassing news."

These are further examples of where Shakespeare's language structure matches that of our real lives. When people are in great grief, they will pen memorial poems in local newspapers; when in love, they will write poetry of all qualities; it seems we need poetry when we are in a heightened state, remembering a great emotion.

The worlds of Shakespeare's words and our own are not so very far apart or alien to each other.

Modes of Address

Both in French and in German, there is a difference between the first person intimate (*tu*; *du*) and the first person formal (*vous*; *Sie*). Spoken English used to have such a distinction in the use of *thee* and *you*. It is no longer in general use today, but in the Elizabethan days, it was—and when we find these differences in Shakespeare's work, they are indeed guides and helps to the situation, and how the actor should respond to them, and are our next valuable secret.

Take, for example, the confrontation between *Lady Capulet* and *Juliet* concerning the proposed marriage between her and *Paris*. As she is persuading *Juliet*, *Lady Capulet* uses the more intimate *thou/thee*, but when *Juliet* rejects her proposal, *Lady Capulet* switches to the more formal *you/yours*:

LADY CAPULET:

Find thou the meanes, and Ile find such a man.
But now Ile tell thee joyfull tidings Gyrle.

Lady Capulet starts by addressing her with *thou*, and as *Gyrle*.

JULIET:

And joy comes well, in such a needy time,
What are they, beseech your Ladyship?

Juliet replies with *your* and *Ladyship*.

LADY CAPULET:

Well, well, thou hast a carefull Father Child?
One who to put thee from thy heavinesse,
Hath sorted out a sudden day of joy,
That thou expects not, nor I lookt not for.

Her mother stays with *thou* but changes to *Child*.

JULIET:

Madam in happy time, what day is this?

Now she still uses the formal *Madam*.

LADY CAPULET:

Marry my Child, early next Thursday morne,
The gallant, young, and Noble Gentleman,
The Countie *Paris* at Saint *Peters* Church,
Shall happily make thee a joyfull Bride.

The reply is still with *Child*, and *thee*.

JULIET:

Now by Saint *Peters* Church, and *Peter* too,
He shall not make me there a joyfull Bride.
I wonder at this hast, that I must wed
Ere he that should be Husband comes to woe:
I pray you tell my Lord and Father Madam,
I will not marrie yet, and when I doe, I sweare
It shall be *Romeo*, whom you know I hate
Rather then *Paris*. These are newes indeed.

Juliet is still using the formal *you* with the formal *Madam*.

LADY CAPULET:

Here comes your Father, tell him so your selfe,
And see how he will take it at your hands.

The mother loses patience, and uses the more distant *your* with her daughter.

ENTER CAPULET AND NURSE.

Again in the scene in *Hamlet* between *Polonius* and his son *Laertes*, and then with his daughter *Ophelia*, he addresses *Laertes* first as *you*, but then changes to the more intimate *thou*, but keeps to the more distant *you* all the way through the scene with his daughter.

LAERTES:

Oh, feare me not.

ENTER POLONIUS.

I stay too long; but here my Father comes:

A double blessing is a double grace;

Occasion smiles upon a second leave.

POLONIUS:

Yet heere *Laertes*? Aboord, aboord for shame,

The winde sits in the shoulder of your saile,

And you are staid for there: my blessing with you;

And these few Precepts in thy memory,

See thou Character. Give thy thoughts no tongue,

Nor any unproportion'd thought his Act:

Be thou familiar; but by no meanes vulgar:

The friends thou hast, and their adoption tride,

Grapple them to thy Soule, with hoopes of Steele:

But doe not dull thy palme, with entertainment

Of each unhatch't, unfledg'd Comrade. Beware

Of entrance to a quarrell: but being in

Bear't that th'opposed may beware of thee.

Give every man thine eare; but few thy voyce:

Take each mans censure; but reserve thy judgement:

Costly thy habit as thy purse can buy;

But not exprest in fancie; rich, not gawdie:

For the Apparell oft proclaimes the man.

And they in France of the best ranck and station,

Are of a most select and generous cheff in that.

Neither a borrower, nor a lender be;

For lone oft loses both it selfe and friend:

And borrowing duls the edge of Husbandry.

This above all; to thine owne selfe be true:

And it must follow, as the Night the Day,

Thou canst not then be false to any man.

Farewell: my Blessing season this in thee.

LAERTES:

Most humbly doe I take my leave, my Lord.

POLONIUS:

The time invites you, goe, your servants tend.

Polonius starts speaking to his son with *your* and *you*, but then when he gives him advice, switches to the more personal *thy*.

Laertes addresses his father with the formal *my Lord*.
And now *Polonius* uses *you*, maybe indicating that this bit is more public than the *thee* speeches.

LAERTES:

Farewell *Ophelia*, and remember well

What I have said to you.

OPHELIA:

Tis in my memory lockt,

And you your selfe shall keepe the key of it.

LAERTES:

Farewell.

EXIT LAERTES.

POLONIUS:

What ist *Ophelia* he hath said to you?

> *Polonius* only uses *you* to his daughter.

OPHELIA:

So please you, somthing touching the Lord *Hamlet*.

POLONIUS:

Marry, well bethought:

Tis told me he hath very oft of late

Given private time to you; and you your selfe

Have of your audience beene most free and bounteous.

If it be so, as so tis put on me;

And that in way of caution: I must tell you,

You doe not understand your selfe so cleerely,

As it behoves my Daughter, and your Honour.

What is betweene you, give me up the truth?

OPHELIA:

He hath my Lord of late, made many tenders

Of his affection to me.

> *Ophelia* uses the formal *My Lord* to her father all the way through the scene.

This change in address is equally important when studying what each character calls each other. In a modern world, we know if someone is being familiar with us (using our first name) or being distant (using our last). All through the plays of Shakespeare the title or style of address used can minutely graph the changing relationships in a scene.

Looking back again at the *Romeo and Juliet* example, you can now see that *Lady Capulet* addresses her daughter in the sequence: *Gyrle; Child; Child*. In reply, *Juliet* calls her mother: *Ladyship; Madam; Madam*. Again, the differences are always of interest to a performer or interpreter, and often give the very variety that they expect, but thought that they had to provide from background research and rehearsal, rather than finding that it is already in the script.

A final example, of where the gear changes are within the very same speech, from *The First Part of Henry the Fourth*. Can you think of what the instruction to the actor playing *Hotspurre* may be, arguing with his wife, *Lady Percie,* that she should stay at home? Examine the changes between *you* and *thee*:

HOTSPURRE:

Come, wilt thou see me ride?	He starts with *thou*
And when I am a horsebacke, I will sweare	
I love thee infinitely. But hearke you *Kate*,	Continues with *thee*, but sud-
I must not have you henceforth, question me,	denly changes to *you*
Whether I go: nor reason whereabout.	
Whether I must, I must: and to conclude,	
This Evening must I leave thee, gentle *Kate*.	Back to *thee*, but the very
I know you wise, but yet no further wise	next line is again back to *you*.
Then *Harry Percies* wife. Constant you are,	
But yet a woman: and for secrecie,	
No Lady closer. For I will beleeve	
Thou wilt not utter what thou do'st not know,	And now the more intimate
And so farre wilt I trust thee, gentle *Kate*.	*thou* and *thee* to end with.

Iambic Pentameters

They sound difficult and academic, but all it means is five lots of di-dum, so that a standard line will go:

Di-dum, di-dum, di-dum, di-dum, di-dum.

There are ten bits, and five feet, in the line. If there are more than ten bits, and the last bit is a "di," making it eleven bits, then that means it has a feminine ending:

Di-dum, di-dum, di-dum, di-dum, di-dum, di.

If there are twelve bits, and the extra two bits are a di-dum, then it is called an Alexandrine:

Di-dum, di-dum, di-dum, di-dum, di-dum, di-dum.

If they do not go di-dum but dum-di, it is called a trochaic foot, and the effect is to change the regularity, and to give you an acting note that all is not as straightforward as it was.

Whatever you call them, iambic pentameter or five di-dums, they are there to help you. The poetry should be used, not all jumbled up as if it were written in prose. To run lines on and ignore the poetry is to ignore one of the clearest clues given to an actor, for in poetry, line endings secure emphasis for terminal words or syllables.

Take for example the famous speech by *Hermione* from *The Winters Tale*:

HERMIONE:
> Since what I am to say, must be but that
> Which contradicts my Accusation, and
> The testimonie on my part, no other
> But what comes from my selfe, it shall scarce boot me
> To say, Not guiltie: mine Integritie
> Being counted Falsehood, shall (as I expresse it)
> Be so receiv'd. But thus, if Powres Divine
> Behold our humane Actions (as they doe)
> I doubt not then, but Innocence shall make
> False Accusation blush, and Tyrannie
> Tremble at Patience.

Most actors will approach it from a sense of what the speech is about, and will follow it according to the punctuation only, speaking it approximately like this:

HERMIONE:
> Since what I am to say,
> must be but that Which contradicts my Accusation,
> and The testimonie on my part,
> no other But what comes from my selfe,
> it shall scarce boot me To say, Not guiltie:
> mine Integritie Being counted Falsehood,
> shall (as I expresse it) Be so receiv'd.
> But thus, if Powres Divine Behold our humane Actions (as they doe)
> I doubt not then, but Innocence shall make False Accusation blush,
> and Tyrannie Tremble at Patience.

However, a lot of time and trouble was taken by one William Shakespeare to write it all in verse, and by following a simple but significant rule—of choosing the last "dum" of a line wherever it may come—a totally different speech emerges (I have put the last "dum" of each line into bold):

HERMIONE:
> Since what I am to say, must be but **that**
> Which contradicts my Accusation, **and**
> The testimonie on my part, no **other**
> But what comes from my selfe, it shall scarce **boot** me
> To say, Not guiltie: mine **Integrite**
> Being counted Falsehood, shall (as I **expresse** it)
> Be so receiv'd. But thus, if Powres **Divine**

Behold our humane Actions (as they **doe**)
I doubt not then, but Innocence shall **make**
False Accusation blush, and Tyrannie
Tremble at Patience. You (my Lord) best **know**
(Whom least will seeme to doe so) my past **life**
Hath beene as continent, as chaste, as **true,**
As I am now unhappy; which is **more**
Then Historie can patterne, though de**vis'd,**
And play'd, to take Spectators. For be**hold** me,
A Fellow of the Royall Bed, which **owe**
A Moitie of the Throne: a great Kings **Daugh**ter,
The Mother to a hopefull Prince, here **stand**ing
To prate and talke for Life, and Honor, **fore**
Who please to come, and heare. For Life, I **prize** it
As I weigh Griefe (which I would spare:) For **Hon**or,
'Tis a derivative from me to **mine,**
And onely that I stand for. I ap**peale**
To your owne Conscience (Sir) before *Polixenes*
Came to your Court, how I was in your **grace,**
How merited to be so: Since he **came,**
With what encounter so uncurrant, **I**
Have strayn'd t'appeare thus; if one jot be**yond**
The bound of Honor, or in act, or **will**
That way enclining, hardned be the **hearts**
Of all that heare me, and my neer'st of **Kin**
Cry fie upon my Grave.

The choice goes to the final "dum," and sometimes in this speech the line ends with a dum-di-di (<u>that</u> is called an anapest), which is why the bold has gone where it has.

To break up a speech into bite-sized chunks is just what we do with our natural speech, where we speak in bursts, rather than pour out a continuous torrent of words, and the average size of the burst in our Anglo-Saxon–based language is, yes, you are right, an iambic pentameter.

We know that French, for example, takes more bits to express the same idea as English, as a sign I saw at Toronto airport put it:

TAXI PICKUP ON ARRIVALS LEVEL ONLY
TAXIS: PRISE EN CHARGE Á L'ÉTAGE DES ARRIVÉES SEULEMENT

So it will come as no surprise that the basic verse line in a French play is twelve bits, or an Alexandrine, as the French need more bits to express the same idea.

The <u>use</u> of the verse has the remarkable effect of making the whole more natural and believable. It is a question not of making the verse naturalistic by avoiding it but of fully incorporating it into the performance.

If Shakespeare, then, ends the thought in the middle of a line, if there is a period or full stop there, the modern tendency is to give a pause, to allow the new thought to develop and reveal itself. I believe, however, that if Shakespeare wants you to pause, he tells you to do so with a half-line, and therefore if he ends a thought midline, if he gives you a <u>midline ending</u>, then he is giving you the instruction to "get on with it," that he is telling you precisely <u>not</u> to pause (otherwise he would have given you that needed half-line).

Have a look at the scene between *Angelo* and *Isabella* from *Measure, For Measure*, and I have written in the changes that can be seen from the verse structure itself, including some wonderful <u>midline endings</u>:

ANGELO:
   Your Brother is a forfeit of the Law,
   And you but waste your words.   6 bits in the line.

ISABELLA:
   Alas, alas: She has 4 bits, so must come
   Why all the soules that were, were forfeit once,   in on cue (6 + 4 = 10).
   And he that might the vantage best have tooke,
   Found out the remedie: how would you be,
   If he, which is the top of Judgement, should
   But judge you, as you are? Oh, thinke on that,   Midline ending drives her on.
   And mercie then will breathe within your lips
   Like man new made.   4 bits here.

ANGELO:
   Be you content, (faire Maid)   6 bits here, so he comes in on
                                                        cue.

   It is the Law, not I, condemne your brother,   A feminine ending—so the
   Were he my kinsman, brother, or my sonne,   end of the word *brother* is
                                                        weakened.

   It should be thus with him: he must die to morrow.   3 iambic feet; 3 trochaic
                                                        feet—irregular verse for the
                                                        moment when *Angelo* confirms
                                                        the death sentence.

ISABELLA:
   To morrow? oh, that's sodaine,   7 bits on this line, 4 bits on
   Spare him, spare him: the next: two half-lines are
                                                        <u>not</u> one single line but an in-
                                                        dication of a pause—maybe a
                                                        pause for stage business as *Is-*
                                                        abella realizes she must fight
                                                        for her brother's life.

Hee's not prepar'd for death; even for our kitchins
We kill the fowle of season: shall we serve heaven
With lesse respect then we doe minister
To our grosse selves? good, good my Lord, bethink you;
Who is it that hath di'd for this offence?
There's many have committed it.

And now she herself goes into irregular verse, perhaps showing her inner turmoil.

A feminine ending, to throw the focus onto the word bethink.

The varying verse lines and structure give the actors major clues as to both their gear changes and their delivery of each line. It is almost as if the author has scored the piece the way a composer will score a piece of music, but then this makes sense when we remember that Shakespeare was writing for very time-pressed actors, and needed to give them as much help as possible.

Lineage

The next clue is in the format of the lines themselves. If the line is only a half-line and the next character has a half-line, then that is a note to come in on cue and not to pause. If there is a half-line not completed by another, or one in the middle of a speech, then that is a note to pause—usually for some "business." In other words, Shakespeare used these half-lines to communicate pauses to his actors; to join them all up (as modern Editors sometimes do) is to obliterate essential acting notes.

So perhaps this section should be under THE FOLIO SECRETS, but the fact remains that in modern edited texts there are still great examples of half-lines:

HAMLET:
O what a rogue and peasant slave am I!
Is it not monstrous that this player here,
But in a fiction, in a dream of passion,
Could force his soul so to his own conceit
That from her working all his visage wann'd,
Tears in his eyes, distraction in his aspect,
A broken voice, and his whole function suiting
With forms to his conceit? And all for nothing!
For Hecuba!
What's Hecuba to him, or he to her,
That he should weep for her? What would he do
Had he the motive and the cue for passion
That I have? He would drown the stage with tears,
And cleave the general ear with horrid speech,
Make mad the guilty and appal the free,
Confound the ignorant, and amaze indeed

The very faculties of eyes and ears.
Yet I,
A dull and muddy-mettled rascal, peak
Like John-a-dreams, unpregnant of my cause,
And can say nothing—no, not for a king,
Upon whose property and most dear life
A damn'd defeat was made. Am I a coward?
Who calls me villain, breaks my pate across,
Plucks off my beard and blows it in my face,
Tweaks me by the nose, gives me the lie i'th'throat
As deep as to the lungs—who does me this?
Ha!

When my colleague Michael Maloney played the Prince in a conventional production of *Hamlet*, one of the highlights was this speech, where in the middle of it he leapt into the grave trap, and then popped his head back out again. It was a lovely piece of theatre, and afterward I asked him why he did it. "You told me to" was the reply. I confessed that I had no recollection of any such thing, but he reminded me that he was applying the "half-line" rule, so after *For Hecuba!* he thought he would fill up the half-line with this exit and reentrance to the stage.

If, as you can see, Shakespeare knows how to give you a pause by using a half-line, then if he does <u>not</u> give you a half-line, you do not pause. But what about all those lovely pauses that actors use to put in all sorts of moods and expressions? Actors will always give themselves excuses for a nice juicy pause, but they are like money—use too many of them up, and they lose effectiveness. Put your expressions into your <u>language</u>, keep it all going (your audience will thank you for the shorter evening), and leave the pauses to the man who put them in in the first place, knows where they are, and <u>where they are not</u>.

Verbal Conceits

This is a general term I learned from John Barton when I was his assistant director at the RSC, that he uses for all those bits which are not quite straightforward, and they all have the effect of "underlining" certain words and so bring the actor to a quicker and better understanding of what they are doing.

Musicians have been known to join the orchestra pit for a performance of a musical, never having read or heard the music to be played before. They look at the notes, and get as much from them as possible as they accompany *Cats* or *Phantom of the Opera*, getting a little extra interpretive information as they do it from the way it sounds and the way the conductor valiantly tries to keep it all together. This process is known as "putting in a dep (or deputy)" and is the closest modern equivalent I can find to being an Elizabethan Cue Script actor (with the Book-Holder being the conductor, of course).

The fact that the words alliterate or assonate with others, or have rhymes at the end of a line (which should be played as rhymes), shows that the character being played wants to indulge in particular verbal conceits at this moment.

Take for example the scene from *King Richard the Second* when his courtiers are discussing his plight. I have written down certain of the conceits:

BUSHY:

The winde sits faire for newes to go to Ireland,
But none returnes: For us to levy power
Proportionable to th'enemy, is all impossible.

Bushy in his first speech uses the alliteration on *p*: power/proportional/impossible.

GREENE:

Besides our neerenesse to the King in love,
Is neere the hate of those love not the King.

Greene is using wordplay on the words *near* and *love*.

BAGOT:

And that's the wavering Commons, for their love
Lies in their purses, and who so empties them,
By so much fils their hearts with deadly hate.

Bagot in his turn makes a pun on the word *lyes*, which means either *resting* or *telling of untruths*.

BUSHY:

Wherein the king stands generally condemn'd.

Another alliteration for *Bushy* with *king* and *condemn'd*.

BAGOT:

If judgement lye in them, then so do we,
Because we have beene ever neere the King.

More puns from *Bagot* on *lye*.

GREENE:

Well: I will for refuge straight to Bristoll Castle,
The Earle of Wiltshire is alreadie there.

Here *Greene* is completely straightforward.

BUSHY:

Thither will I with you, for little office
Will the hatefull Commons performe for us,
Except like Curres, to teare us all in peeces:
Will you go along with us?

A simile for *Bushy*.

BAGOT:

No, I will to Ireland to his Majestie:
Farewell, if hearts presages be not vaine,
We three here part, that nev'r shall meete againe.

Assonance between *I* and *Ireland* and a complicated or overblown word *presages* show *Bagot* to be in a complicated (shifty?) mood.

BUSHY:

That's as Yorke thrives to beate back *Bullinbroke.*

Tremendous alliteration, three *b*s in a row: *beate back Bullinbroke.*

GREENE:

Alas poore Duke, the taske he undertakes
Is numbring sands, and drinking Oceans drie,
Where one on his side fights, thousands will flye.

Greene goes into metaphors and the rhyme of *drie* and *flye.*

BUSHY:

    Farewell at once, for once, for all, and ever.

    Well, we may meete againe.

BAGOT:

    I feare me never.

      EXIT.

One final rhyme of *ever* and *never*.

As you can see, each of the characters has a different form of verbal conceit, giving different clues as to the type of person the character is.

These actors would be playing many different parts over a short period of time, maybe even with the same sort of plot, and they would need obvious and quick "instructions" from the author as to how they should play them, and what was going on. Verbal conceits are a vital part of this communication.

Incidentally, the *Bushy, Bagot,* and *Greene* scene when played gives the audience no clue as to who is who. It would have been so easy to include lines such as *Aye, My Lord Bagot.* or *What thinkest thou, my Lord Greene?* I believe that this is quite intentional on Shakespeare's part, that he was deliberately not letting us know who was who, or what was what, so that we the audience would be seeing the disintegration of the court in general, not just the conversation between three named members of his retinue.

Here is a list of the main verbal conceits, with examples illustrating which ones they are (I am indebted to Maureen Clarke of New York for her insight into separations). In each case, the verbal conceit brings to the actor's attention something specific:

1. Rhyme

Wrath-kindled Gentlemen be rul'd by me:

Let's purge this choller without letting blood:

This we prescribe, though no **Physition**,

Deepe malice makes too deepe **incision**.

Forget, forgive, conclude, and be **agreed**,

Our Doctors say, This is no time to **bleed**.

Good Unckle, let this end where it **begun**,

Wee'l calme the Duke of Norfolke; you, your **son**.

      Richard: King Richard the Second

The rhymes are really quite childish; it could even be an acting note that *Richard* is using such condescending wordplay.

To woe your lady: yet a barrefull **strife**,

Who ere I woe, my selfe would be his **wife**.

      Viola: Twelfe Night

Viola here is using a rhyming couplet—often used at the end of a scene. One theory is that it alerted offstage actors that the end of the scene was upon them and their next scene was about to begin.

2. Alliteration

Stand you a-while aloofe. *Cesario*,
Thou knowst no lesse, but all: I have unclasp'd
To thee the booke even of my **secret soule**.
Therefore good youth, addresse thy gate unto her,
Be not deni'de accesse, stand at her doores,
And tell them, there thy **fixed foot** shall grow
Till thou have audience.

Orsino: Twelfe Night

The alliteration brings attention to this bit of *Orsino*'s
speech.

Be it lawfull that I invocate thy Ghost,
To heare the Lamentations of poore *Anne*,
Wife to thy *Edward*, to thy **slaughtred Sonne**,
Stab'd by the **selfesame** hand that made these wounds.
Loe, in these windowes that let forth thy life,
I powre the helplesse Balme of my poore eyes.
O cursed be the **hand** that made these **holes**:
Cursed the **Heart**, that **had** the **heart** to do it:
Cursed the **Blood**, that let this blood from hence:
More direfull hap betide that hated Wretch
That makes us wretched by the death of thee,
Then I can **wish** to **Wolves**, to Spiders, Toades,
Or any creeping venom'd thing that lives.
If ever he have Childe, Abortive be it,
Prodigeous, and untimely brought to light,
Whose ugly and unnaturall Aspect
May fright the hopefull Mother at the view,
And that be Heyre to his unhappinesse.
If ever he have Wife, let her be **made**
More miserable by the death of him,
Then I am made by my young Lord, and thee.

Lady Anne: Richard the Third

Lady Anne's speech is just
packed with verbal conceits—
I have just picked out the alliterations. This of course is
the argument that she therefore cannot be so upset if she
is capable of such clever and
conscious wordplay. Trying to
play this scene in tears, and
saying this clever language,
defeats all who try it.

It is better to play a clever
woman, the one drawn so
clearly in this speech, who
seems a powerful crowd
manipulator.

3. Assonance

O what a **Noble** minde is heere **o're-throwne**?
The Courtiers, **Soldiers**, Schollers: Eye, tongue, sword,
Th'expectansie and **Rose** of the faire State,
The glasse of Fashion, and the **mould** of Forme,
Th'**observ'd** of all **Observers**, quite, quite downe.

The same argument can be
used on *Ophelia*, whose
speech here is quite artificial
and aware, not the simple
outpouring of a heartbroken
young girl. We often impose

Have I of Ladies most **deject** and **wretched**,
That **suck'd** the **Honie** of his Musicke **Vowes**:
Now see that **Noble**, and **most** Soveraigne **Reason**,
Like **sweet** Bels jangled out of tune, and harsh,
That unmatch'd Forme and Feature of **blowne** youth,
Blasted with extasie. **Oh woe** is **me**,
T'have **seene** what I have **seene**: see what I **see**.

Ophelia: Hamlet

on these clever speeches simple solutions, and then wonder
why the audience cannot work
out what is going on.

If **Musicke** be the **food** of Love, play on,

Orsino: Twelfe Night

The start of the play has these
certain words "picked out."
Incidentally, note that the
first line does <u>not</u> end in a full
stop or period, but is the start
of a continuing argument.

4. Repeated Words

Set downe, set downe your honourable load,
If Honor may be shrowded in a Herse;
Whil'st I a-while obsequiously lament
Th'untimely fall of Vertuous Lancaster.

Lady Anne: Richard the Third

And why should *Lady Anne* repeat these words? What acting
note can she find to justify repeating? Maybe that the pall-
bearers did not hear her the
first time? That they cannot
believe she wants to put the
coffin down in the middle of
the street? All good interesting stuff, and the interpretation is coming from the <u>text</u>,
not the <u>context</u>.

What's this? what's this? is **this** her fault, or mine?
The Tempter, or the Tempted, who sins most? ha?

Angelo: Measure, For Measure

The repeat of these words
brings us to wonder what *this*
is? His change of heart
brought about by meeting
Isabella? Change of mind?
Change of state of arousal?

5. Simile

A simile is "like" something.

A blanke my Lord: she never told her love,
But let concealment **like a worme i'th'budde**
Feede on her damaske cheeke: she pin'd in thought,
And with a greene and yellow melancholly,
She sate **like Patience on a Monument**,
Smiling at greefe.

Viola: Twelfe Night

6. Metaphor

Live you the **Marble-brested Tirant** still.
But this your Minion, whom I know you love,
And whom, by heaven I sweare, I tender deerely,
Him will I teare out of that cruell eye,
Where he **sits crowned** in his masters spight.
Come boy with me, my thoughts are ripe in mischiefe:
Ile sacrifice the **Lambe** that I do love,
To spight a **Ravens heart within a Dove**.

Orsino: Twelfe Night

A metaphor is when you say it "is" something.

7. Clever Words

How will this fadge? My master loves her deerely,
And I (poore monster) fond as much on him:
And she (mistaken) seemes to dote on me:
What will become of this? As I am **man**,
My state is desperate for my maisters love:
As I am **woman** (now alas the day)
What thriftlesse sighes shall poore *Olivia* breath?
O time, thou must untangle this, **not** I,
It is too hard a **knot** for me t'unty.

Viola: Twelfe Night

Hath kill'd the flocke of all affections else
That **live** in her. When **Liver**, Braine, and Heart,
These soveraigne thrones,

Orsino: Twelfe Night

Viola uses clever words here as she addresses the audience (see Soliloquies in the Checklist for more).

She makes a pun on *man* and *woman*—or is it *woe man*? And another pun on *not* and *knot*; these indicate to the actress what sort of mood and attitude to associate with *Viola*.

A rather forced cleverness for the pun between *live* and *liver*.

8. Separations

Now is the Winter of our Discontent,
Made gloriou<u>s S</u>ummer by thi<u>s S</u>on of Yorke:

Richard: Richard the Third

The fourth Sonne, *Yor<u>ke c</u>laymes it from the third:

Warwicke: The second Part of Henry the Sixt

Separations are those words which, when put together, might blur into one word. I believe that Shakespeare is deliberately making the actor <u>choose</u> the second word, so instead of saying *thisson of Yorke*, he must say *this* (little pause) *son of Yorke*. This gives a little extra "picking out" for the word, and my actors find it very useful for refining the sense and attitude.

Verbal conceits are your key to unlocking so many speeches and scenes.

Obedience to the Text

Or: do what you are told by the author.

It is so easy to get into the habit of doing what you think you ought to, or of thinking that the play needs you to solve its problems, that to go in for simple obedience can be quite a shock—and shockingly revealing. I have outlined many times by now the value of playing what is written down for you. Here are a few more examples.

In *Much adoe about Nothing*, *Hero* and *Ursula* are planning to tease *Beatrice* by "accidentally" letting her think that *Benedicke* is in love with her:

HERO:

> Good *Margaret* runne thee to the parlour,
> There shalt thou finde my Cosin *Beatrice*,
> Proposing with the Prince and *Claudio*,
> Whisper her eare, and tell her I and *Ursula*,
> Walke in the Orchard, and our whole discourse
> Is all of her, say that thou over-heardst us,
> And bid her steale into the pleached bower,
> Where hony-suckles ripened by the sunne,
> Forbid the sunne to enter: like favourites,
> Made proud by Princes, that advance their pride,
> Against that power that bred it, there will she hide her,
> To listen our purpose, this is thy office,
> Beare thee well in it, and leave us alone.

MARGARET:

> Ile make her come I warrant you presently.
> > *EXIT.*

HERO:

> Now *Ursula*, when *Beatrice* doth come,
> As we do trace this alley up and downe,
> Our talke must onely be of *Benedicke*,
> When I doe name him, let it be thy part,
> To praise him more then ever man did merit,
> My talke to thee must be how *Benedicke*
> Is sicke in love with *Beatrice*: of this matter,
> Is little *Cupids* crafty arrow made,
> That onely wounds by heare-say: now begin,
> > *ENTER BEATRICE.*
> For looke where *Beatrice* like a Lapwing runs
> Close by the ground, to heare our conference.

URSULA:

> The pleasant'st angling is to see the fish

Cut with her golden ores the silver streame,
And greedily devoure the treacherous baite:
So angle we for *Beatrice*, who even now,
Is couched in the wood-bine coverture,
Feare you not my part of the Dialogue.

HERO:

Then go we neare her that her eare loose nothing,
Of the false sweete baite that we lay for it:
No truely *Ursula*, she is too disdainfull,
I know her spirits are as coy and wilde,
As Haggerds of the rocke.

URSULA:

But are you sure,
That *Benedicke* loves *Beatrice* so intirely?

Now it is very simple: the author has told the two girls to walk up and down as they talk of *Benedicke*, so that *Beatrice* in the arbor will have to pop up and down as they pass and re-pass her hiding place; yet in many productions they just stand still, with *Beatrice* hopping from place to place trying to get close to them. As written, the scene plays extremely well. Why change it?

Again, in *Julius Cæsar* when *Portia* confronts her husband *Brutus*, she is told very precisely where her injury is:

PORTIA:

If this were true, then should I know this secret.
I graunt I am a Woman; but withall,
A Woman that Lord *Brutus* tooke to Wife:
I graunt I am a Woman; but withall,
A Woman well reputed: *Cato's* Daughter.
Thinke you, I am no stronger then my Sex
Being so Father'd, and so Husbanded?
Tell me your Counsels, I will not disclose 'em:
I have made strong proofe of my Constancie,
Giving my selfe a voluntary wound
Heere, in the Thigh: Can I beare that with patience,
And not my Husbands Secrets?

Yet I have seen this injury being placed everywhere from the knees to the ankles, and only rarely near those wifely parts that perhaps is the point of this sad speech, where she is trying to connect with her husband, using the last vestiges of her womanly attractions.

In the sleepwalking scene in *Macbeth*, the *Doctor* is instructed by the *Gentlewoman*:

GENTLEWOMAN:

Neither to you, nor any one, having no witnesse
to confirme my speech.

ENTER LADY, WITH A TAPER.

Lo you, heere she comes: This is her very guise, and upon my life fast asleepe: observe her, stand close.

DOCTOR:

How came she by that light?

GENTLEWOMAN:

Why it stood by her: she ha's light by her continually, 'tis her command.

DOCTOR:

You see her eyes are open.

GENTLEWOMAN:

I but their sense are shut.

Yet in most productions the *Doctor* and *Gentlewoman* will hide far away from *Lady Macbeth*, even though the *Doctor* has indeed been told to *stand close*, and the *Gentlewoman* is able to see of her eyes that *their sense are shut*. Having the *Doctor* so close makes the scene all the more terrifying, as the sleepwalking *Lady Macbeth* walks past and by them as they take notes and talk about her quite openly.

If ever there are Lords or Soldiers mentioned, then of course they should come on and, moreover, be part of the scene. Those on stage should use them, like *Viola* must use the *Saylors* at the start of the play, or the *Duke* and *Rosalind* and *Celia* each in turn must use the *Lords* onstage with them as they argue about banishment. It also means that if these extras are not mentioned, then they should not appear upon the stage. If they were needed, they would be there.

The same of course applies to directors. Watching a recent *Julius Cæsar*, and seeing *Cæsar* stabbed on the top step, totter down to the next step where he was stabbed again, seeing this repeated all the way to the bottom, where *Cassius* threw him upon a reluctant *Brutus's* dagger, I wondered what the original text might indicate:

CASKA:

Speake hands for me.

THEY STAB CÆSAR.

CÆSAR:

Et Tu Brute?—Then fall *Cæsar.*

DYES.

CINNA:

Liberty, Freedome; Tyranny is dead,
Run hence, proclaime, cry it about the Streets.

It all reads very quickly, all very untheatrically, all very like the quick way President John F. Kennedy was taken from our midst. How wonderful if it were played that way, that the destruction of a great man should be so simple, so sudden. I wonder if that was the original intention?

THE FOLIO

Folios and Quartos

CORUS:
Two housholds both alike in dignitie,
(In fair *Verona* where we lay our Scene)

Thus begins one of the most popular of Shakespeare's plays—back then as well as to-day—*Romeo and Juliet*. Or rather, that is the way it begins in the good Quarto version, printed in 1599. In the Folio, printed in 1623, this passage is omitted. How strange that the Folio, introduced by two of Shakespeare's own acting company—who themselves must have acted in the play many, many times—should not accurately present the start of *Romeo and Juliet*. How incompetent of Heminge and Condell, in a volume presented in honor of its dead author, to allow the start of one of his masterpieces to be inaccurate.

Hmmm. . . .

Back in the 1950s, a brand new musical by Leonard Bernstein was being tried out in the provinces. It was choreographed by the great Jerome Robbins, and although it was getting good reviews on the road, it was not yet a smash hit. A play doctor was sent for, who after watching the production in Philadelphia, pronounced that the opening number—a dance routine—should be cut. They protested to him that this was the very best work of Robbins, but were sternly told that if you started the production with such a number, that outlined all the plot and conclusion of the show, there would be nowhere for the production to go. So they cut the opening number of *West Side Story*, the number that was the theatricalization of the opening prologue of *Romeo and Juliet*, and the show went on to become the classic musical we now know it to be.

Hmmm. . . .

I believe that this only echoed what happened when the play of *Romeo and Juliet* was first presented: that the audience enjoys the play more if they are <u>not</u> told at the beginning that all will end in death. They can still hope and believe that all might turn out well in the end. And this leads to the thought that the Folio version of the plays is what they finally found themselves presenting in the theatre of the time, the version that in fact played best. In other words, the omission of the Prologue is what the original company found made the play work best.

Applying this thought to the play of *Hamlet* reveals that the Quarto version is indeed longer than the Folio—which would make sense if you found you had a wonderful play but the audience found it a bit too long. You also find that the soliloquy

HAMLET:
How all occasions doe informe against me,
And spur my dull revenge. What is a man
If his chiefe good and market of his time
Be but to sleepe and feede, a beast, no more:

is not in the Folio (the above is from the Second Quarto).

I puzzled over this, thinking that we ought to give to the audience all the *Hamlet* soliloquies. But I also checked with actors who have played *Hamlet*, and found no great desire to retain this speech. As one of them put it to me, he thought that by this time in the play, *Hamlet* was indeed on the edge of madness, and then he had to cool himself down to deliver this rather logical speech, and leaving out the speech would make the arc of his performance more complete.

I realize that there are many different relationships between the Quarto and the Folio versions, far too complex for me to go into here, so I shall just say that to perform the Folio version, or even the Quarto version, will get you closer to what the original intention may have been, but to work from a conflation of the two versions will almost certainly drown and miss certain vital theatrical messages. See Appendix 3.

At the front of the Folio is an introduction by two members of the company that worked over all those years with Shakespeare himself. In this, they tell of their mission, and how they are bringing this book out as a tribute to him. I find it hard to believe that they who were so close to the text, who of all people in the world would know the value of these scripts, and would know the difficulty of working with inferior scripts, would carelessly let a multitude of mistakes litter the printed page.

To the great Variety of Readers.

rom the most able, to him that can but spell: There you are number'd. We had rather you were weighd. Especially, when the fate of all Bookes depends upon your capacities: and not of your heads alone, but of your purses. Well! It is now publique, and you wil stand for your priviledges wee know: to read, and censure. Do so, but buy it first. That doth best commend a Booke, the Stationer saies. Then, how odde soever your braines be, or your wisedomes, make your licence the same, and spare not. Judge your six-pen'orth, your shillings worth, your five shillings worth at a time, or higher, so you rise to the just rates, and welcome. But, what ever you do, Buy. Censure will not drive a Trade,

or make the Jacke go. And though you be a Magistrate of wit, and sit on the Stage at *Black-Friers*, or the *Cocke-pit*, to arraigne Playes dailie, know, these Playes have had their triall alreadie, and stood out all Appeales; and do now come forth quitted rather by a Decree of Court, then any purchas'd Letters of commendation.

It had bene a thing, we confesse, worthie to have bene wish'd, that the Author himselfe had liv'd to have set forth, and overseen his owne writings; But since it hath bin ordain'd otherwise, and he by death departed from that right, we pray you do not envie his Friends, the office of their care, and paine, to have collected and publish'd them; and so to have publish'd them, as where (before) you were abus'd with diverse stolne, and surreptitious copies, maimed, and deformed by the frauds and stealthes of injurious impostors, that expos'd them: even those, are now offer'd to your view cur'd, and perfect of their limbes; and all the rest, absolute in their numbers, as he conceived them. Who, as he was a happie imitator of Nature, was a most gentle expresser of it. His mind and hand went together: And what he thought, he uttered with that easinesse, that wee have scarse received from him a blot in his papers. But it is not our province, who onely gather his works, and give them you, to praise him. It is yours that reade him. And there we hope, to your divers capacities, you will finde enough, both to draw, and hold you: for his wit can no more lie hid, then it could be lost. Reade him, therefore; and againe, and againe: And if then you doe not like him, surely you are in some manifest danger, not to understand him. And so we leave you to other of his Friends, whom if you need, can bee your guides: if you neede them not, you can leade your selves, and others. And such Readers we wish him.

John Heminge.
Henrie Condell.

Although they say *worthie to have bene wish'd, that the Author himselfe had liv'd to have set forth, and overseen his owne writings;* it is probably fortunate that Shakespeare himself did <u>not</u> prepare his own works for publication, and maybe change his works to be more like "literature," the way Ben Jonson did when he prepared his own collected "Works." It is also important to remember that these were workingmen of the theatre, who would know the difference between brilliant scripts and ordinary ones. I myself know very well the difference in directing a screenplay by a wonderful writer like Jimmy McGovern and having to cope with one written by some less-gifted author. I trust that Heminge and Condell, as members of that theatre company, would know better than most what a difference it was acting one of William's scripts, and would have made sure that those elements they found useful would make their way into print.

I know that to give huge authority to the Folio is an extreme view, and that there are many obvious errors in it, but the trouble is that when you start changing it, you start changing those things that to you seem obvious but to an actor may be a very valuable and worthwhile piece of evidence. Do not forget, this text is the only lifeline to a nonrehearsed or nondirected actor, and so each bit of information is crucial and important. I confirm to you again that a favorite party trick of mine is to have an actor recite a speech—any speech, one that perhaps the actor has performed at the highest level of our profession—and then let me guide the actor into doing the First Folio version of it. In all cases, at every event, workshop, conference, and of course scene study I have worked on, the First Folio version always plays better. Not sometimes, not almost, but always performs better.

If the Folio were so full of errors, then just sometimes an actor would give an inferior performance when made to do what the Folio has set down rather than a careful Editor, but I have yet to have that experience. One of the Editors touched on this, when he commented that although the Folio was "carelessly printed," it was surprisingly accurate on the "'d" or "ed" endings—this is where a word either has the end of it pronounced "glanc'd" or "glanced" according to the needs of the verse. Modern Editors tend to print it "glanced" or "glancèd"—but, as noted, the Folio is very reliable on this, and the devil in me thinks that if it so accurate on this matter, maybe it is also more accurate than suspected in other places.

My Folio journey itself started in 1980 when I was directing, in a quite normal way, a tour of *The Merchant of Venice*. I had read a wonderful book about text: *Shakespeare's Producing Hand* by Richard Flatter, and was applying some of the ideas from there: in particular, the idea that a half-line followed by a half-line indicated that you should come in on cue, but a half-line unfulfilled by any other line was Shakespeare's way of telling you that you should pause. This appealed to the almost dead physicist in me, and I was applying it with gusto.

I reached an impasse in the scene where *Morrocho* is choosing one of the caskets, because this is what the actor was faced with:

> *Por.* There, take it, prince; and if my form lie there,
> Then I am yours. *[He unlocks the golden casket.]*
>   *Mor.* O hell! what have we here?
> A carrion death, within whose empty eye
> There is a written scroll. I'll read the writing.
> *[Reads.] All that glisters is not gold;*

My actor with, I noted, a rather malicious smile, pointed out that he could not in fact come in on cue with his half-line, because although *Portia* has spoken a half-line herself, he had to take the key, open the box, get out the skull, and look at it before replying to her line, and this was not possible in a flash, the way I had asked him. There was another text of the play in the room, and I looked at that:

Por.   There take it prince, and if my form lie there
Then I am yours! *[He unlocks the golden casket.]*
Mor.   O hell! what have we here?
    A carrion Death, within whose empty eye
    There is a written scroll,—I'll read the writing.
        All that glisters is not gold,

The only changes were in the additional exclamation marks, which did not look too promising an explanation. I was about to tell my actor that this "come in on cue" rule worked on <u>most</u> occasions (a usual director's response), when I found in my bag another copy of the play, that contained the Folio text:

Por.   There take it Prince, and if my forme lye there
Then I am yours.
    Mor.   O hell! what have we here, a carrion death,
Within whose emptie eye there is a written scroule;
Ile reade the writing.
        All that glisters is not gold,

I was amazed and aghast: the very problem was solved not by analysis and thought but by the simple expedient of going back to the original text. As you can see, the Folio had an unfulfilled half-line for *Portia* to speak, giving *Morrocho* plenty of time to do his stage business. There is also a final unfulfilled half line *Ile reade the writing,* which gives *Morrocho* time to unwind the scroll before reading it.

After the production, when I was able to reread all the scripts of the play I could find, I noticed that every single edition of Shakespeare makes this "improvement" to the text; I presume that an Editor long ago took one look at it, saw a half-line followed by two full lines followed by a half-line, and thought that if they "moved them all up half a line" they would regularize it. And so they have, and every Editor has followed them, and yet I guarantee that every actor that has ever played the part of *Morrocho* has had to, wanted to, pause after *Portia* gives him the key.

I cannot emphasize enough what a strange thought this is: every Editor changes the lineage from the First Folio, and every actor subsequently without knowing it changes it back to the way it was originally written. It was this moment above all that gave me the incentive to <u>start</u> with the Folio text, and only move from it when I found it was not actable.

Again, working on *Anthonie, and Cleopatra*, I found that the very first entrance of *Cleopatra* went like this:

ALEXAS:
Lo now, if it lay in their hands to make mee a

Cuckold, they would make themselves Whores, but
they'ld doo't.

    ENTER CLEOPATRA.

ENOBARBUS:

Hush, heere comes *Anthony.*

CHARMIAN:

Not he, the Queene.

CLEOPATRA:

Save you, my Lord.

ENOBARBUS:

No Lady.

So the Editors change her entrance to after the *Anthony* line, because "they would obviously have seen that it was not Anthony but Cleopatra." It could be irony (and plays
very well as such) that the court sees *Cleopatra* as taking on *Anthony's* mantle—after all,
they do also wear each other's clothes, and the Folio entrance, as I have found and
recorded so often, performs remarkably well.

As you can see from the rest of these pages, this approach has brought forward
many, many goodies and ideas.

For an example where editors take a bit of a Quarto text, and push it into the middle
of a Folio text to create something Shakespeare never wrote, see Appendix 3.

THE FOLIO SECRETS

Well, it cannot be a secret to you that I have found a lot of theatrical insights through the use of the Folio text, and here follow some specific areas that have been helpful.

For reasons that I am not completely sure of, putting the Folio forward as a valid text seems to make some people very angry—shouting, even, that I am completely wrong and that the Folio is riddled with errors and not an authentic text to work from. My reply that it always works for me does not cut any ice.

I am well aware that there are some mistakes in the Folio; for example, in *A Midsommer Nights Dreame* the word is at one time spelt *Mehcanical*. As I have stated elsewhere in this book, the problem of correcting the Folio is where to stop. I have no proof that the text was closely supervised by the actors John Heminge and Henrie Condell, except that I find the Folio a very actor-friendly piece of work. Even if the punctuation, spelling, and capitalization were only the opinion of the seventeenth-century printer, or the infamous Compositor E that is used to justify "correcting" whole swathes of text, the person who set these words in type was still closer to the original than we are.

If you twisted my arm, and asked me if I really believed that the Folio is correct in every variation, I would reply no, but that if it is actable, then it is worth trying, and anyway, with my actors striding out onstage with nothing to guide them except the text, I find that using the "original" text allows them to act and make theatrical decisions with great confidence. Sometimes actors will feel there is an error in their lines, and I then encourage them to change it to what an Editor has found to be a "better" solution, thinking that here at least the Folio has shown itself to be mistaken. Then at a later time, other actors will find that the same piece works just fine as printed, and they do not want a change at all.

So if it does not work for you, change it—but do not change it for everyone, for all time. Studying the Variorum of *Romeo and Juliet*, for example, you will find that for the line *That run-awayes eyes may wincke* there are thirty pages of discussion, and thirty-nine different alternatives suggested for the word *run-awayes*, and that is only up to 1871, so to change anything permanently to the word of your choice will simply be adding to the lengthening list of possibilities (although I think the original is quite good enough, and none of my *Juliet*s have had a problem acting it).

As for how Editors can, with the best intentions in the world, make changes that do not help a text, let me tell you about Winston Churchill, and one of his famous speeches, given during World War II on June 18, 1940.

WINSTON CHURCHILL:

Upon this battle depends the survival of Christian civilization. Upon it depends our own British life and the long continuity of our institutions and our Empire. The whole fury and might of the enemy must very soon be turned on us. Hitler knows that he will have to break us in this island or lose the war. If we can stand up to him all Europe may be free, and the life of the world may move forward into broad, sunlit uplands, but if we fail then the whole world, including the United States, and all that we have known and cared for, will sink into the abyss of a new dark age made more sinister, and perhaps more prolonged, by the lights of a perverted science. Let us therefore brace ourselves to our duty and so bear ourselves that if the British Commonwealth and Empire lasts for a thousand years men will still say: "This was their finest hour."

Reading it, one tries to get a feeling of how he might have said it, when he was the only weapon left to the British. I found the above in a UK book of speeches, but in an American book I found the following:

WINSTON CHURCHILL:

On this battle depends the survival of Christian civilization.

Upon it depends our own British life and the long continuity of our institutions and our empire. The whole fury and might of the enemy must very soon be turned upon us. Hitler knows he will have to break us in this island or lose the war.

If we can stand up to him all Europe may be freed and the life of the world may move forward into broad sunlit uplands; but if we fail, the whole world, including the United States and all that we have known and cared for, will sink into the abyss of a new dark age made more sinister and perhaps more prolonged by the lights of a perverted science.

Let us therefore brace ourselves to our duty and so bear ourselves that if the British Commonwealth and Empire last for a thousand years, men will still say "This was their finest hour."

Now, the layout is different, giving a different feel to the speech, and it is not quite the same in its punctuation and capitalization. I thought I preferred the American version until I found in the published Churchill papers, the original text that he typed out himself, prior to delivering the speech:

WINSTON CHURCHILL:

Upon this battle depends the
  survival of Christian civilization.

Upon it depends our own British life
  and the long continuity of our
    institutions, and our Empire.

The whole fury and might of the enemy
  must very soon be turned on us.

Hitler knows that he will have to break
  us in this Island, or lose the war.

If we can stand up to him,
  all Europe may be freed,
    and the life of the world
      may move forward into the
        broad and sunlit uplands.

But if we fail,
  then the whole world,
    including the United States,
      and all that we have known and cared for,
      will sink into the abyss of a
        new Dark Age
          made more sinister and
            perhaps more prolonged by
              the lights of perverted Science.

Let us therefore brace ourselves to
  our duty, and so bear ourselves that
    if the British Empire and
      Commonwealth lasts for a
        thousand years, men will still say,
        'This was their finest hour'.

Now this version I know how to perform, the writer's voice speaks out in the layout he wrote it in, a layout he used just to help himself when he was delivering the speech. It is a performer's script, not a literary script, and the parallel with our Mr. Shakespeare is obvious, because he too wrote for those who were to perform the lines, not for those who were to read them.

We have now been told that during the war Churchill himself was too busy to repeat this speech he had made to Parliament, and so had an actor to read the speech when it was broadcast on the BBC, imitating his delivery. Does this suggest why he might have written it out in the way he did—to help the actor perform it correctly?

For the record, compared with the original, the UK version makes the following amendments:

11 changes in punctuation;
5 capitals removed;
5 words changed or added.

And the American version is equally "edited":

8 changes in punctuation;
6 capitals removed;
8 words changed or added.

Hooray for Editors! Or perhaps not, for although their motives with Shakespeare are of course well intentioned, when it comes to editing a performance script, you can so easily change it from what is most useful to something that is grammatically "correct," and therefore less helpful to the performer, just as they "edited" Winston.

Folio Capitalization

In the Folio Facsimile, a lot of the words are capitalized. When it is edited, the Editors as a matter of course remove most of them, deciding to "regularize" the situation.

When I inspected the First Folio, I suspected that the capitalizations were not in fact as random as previously thought, but could reflect an actor's intonation and stress. Since the plays were written to be acted, not read as literature, then those words which appear so capitalized start to produce interesting results. I know all the arguments about different compositors having different habits of capitalization, but look at the following.

Consider the famous speech of *Mark Antony*, where for ease of observation I have made bold all the words in capitals (apart from the first word in each verse line, of course), and used a modern edited text:

ANTONY:
Friends, **Romans**, countrymen, lend me your ears!
I come to bury **Caesar**, not to praise him.
The evil that men do lives after them,
The good is oft interred with their bones;
So let it be with **Caesar**. The noble **Brutus**

Hath told you **Caesar** was ambitious;
If it were so, it was a grievous fault,
And grievously hath **Caesar** answer'd it.
Here, under leave of **Brutus** and the rest
(For **Brutus** is an honorable man,
So are they all, all honorable men),
Come I to speak in **Caesar's** funeral.
He was my friend, faithful and just to me;
But **Brutus** says he was ambitious,
And **Brutus** is an honorable man.
He hath brought many captives home to **Rome**,
Whose ransoms did the general coffers fill;
Did this in **Caesar** seem ambitious?
When that the poor have cried, **Caesar** hath wept;
Ambition should be made of sterner stuff:
Yet **Brutus** says he was ambitious:
And **Brutus** is an honorable man.
You all did see that on the **Lupercal**
I thrice presented him a kingly crown,
Which he did thrice refuse. Was this ambition?
Yet **Brutus** says he was ambitious,
And sure he is an honorable man.
I speak not to disprove what **Brutus** spoke,
But here I am to speak what I do know.
You all did love him once, not without cause;
What cause withholds you then to mourn for him?
O judgement! thou art fled to brutish beasts,
And men have lost their reason. Bear with me,
My heart is in the coffin there with **Caesar**,
And I must pause till it come back to me.

And now the same speech, treated the same way of bolding all the words in capitals, but with the text from the Folio:

ANTHONY:
Friends, **Romans**, **Countrymen**, lend me your ears:
I come to bury *Cæsar*, not to praise him:
The evill that men do, lives after them,
The good is oft enterred with their bones,
So let it be with *Cæsar*. The **Noble** *Brutus*,
Hath told you *Cæsar* was **Ambitious**:
If it were so, it was a greevous **Fault**,

And greevously hath *Cæsar* answer'd it.
Heere, under leave of *Brutus*, and the rest
(For *Brutus* is an **Honourable** man,
So are they all; all **Honourable** men)
Come I to speake in *Cæsars* **Funerall**.
He was my **Friend**, faithfull, and just to me;
But *Brutus* sayes, he was **Ambitious**,
And *Brutus* is an **Honourable** man.
He hath brought many **Captives** home to **Rome**,
Whose **Ransomes**, did the generall **Coffers** fill:
Did this in *Cæsar* seeme **Ambitious**?
When that the poore have cry'de, *Cæsar* hath wept:
Ambition should be made of sterner stuffe,
Yet *Brutus* sayes, he was **Ambitious**:
And *Brutus* is an **Honourable** man.
You all did see, that on the *Lupercall*,
I thrice presented him a **Kingly Crowne**,
Which he did thrice refuse. Was this **Ambition**?
Yet *Brutus* sayes, he was **Ambitious**:
And sure he is an **Honourable** man.
I speake not to disproove what *Brutus* spoke,
But heere I am, to speake what I do know;
You all did love him once, not without cause,
What cause with-holds you then, to mourne for him?
O **Judgement**! thou art fled to brutish **Beasts**,
And **Men** have lost their **Reason**. Beare with me,
My heart is in the **Coffin** there with *Cæsar*,
And I must pawse, till it come backe to me.

There are, in addition to the removal of most of the capitalization, 24 changes of punctuation in the 35 lines.

Reading through the speech, picking out the words in capitals—the words I have made bold—gives a whole sense of the shape and drive of the speech. Look at the **Brutus, Ambitious, Brutus, Honourable** sequence that occurs three times. The capitalization turns out to be a guide to the acting of the piece, not just a piece of irrelevant Elizabethan printing practice; the capitals seem to be stepping-stones helping actors get through a wonderful speech, when they have had little time to prepare for it.

Taking another well-known speech, and bolding the capitals, in a modern version, gives:

PORTIA:
The quality of mercy is not strain'd,

It droppeth as the gentle rain from heaven
Upon the place beneath. It is twice blest:
It blesseth him that gives and him that takes.
'Tis mightiest in the mightiest, it becomes
The throned monarch better than his crown.
His scepter shows the force of temporal power,
The attribute to awe and majesty,
Wherein doth sit the dread and fear of kings;
But mercy is above this sceptered sway,
It is enthroned in the hearts of kings,
It is an attribute to **God** himself;
And earthly power doth then show likest **God's**
When mercy seasons justice. Therefore, **Jew,**
Though justice be thy plea, consider this,
That in the course of justice, none of us
Should see salvation. We do pray for mercy,
And that same prayer doth teach us all to render
The deeds of mercy. I have spoke thus much
To mitigate the justice of thy plea,
Which if thou follow, this strict court of **Venice**
Must needs give sentence 'gainst the merchant there.

Compare the words chosen and picked out in capitals in the Folio text:

PORTIA:
The quality of mercy is not strain'd,
It droppeth as the gentle raine from heaven
Upon the place beneath. It is twice blest,
It blesseth him that gives, and him that takes,
'Tis mightiest in the mightiest, it becomes
The throned **Monarch** better then his **Crowne.**
His **Scepter** shewes the force of temporall power,
The attribute to awe and **Majestie,**
Wherein doth sit the dread and feare of **Kings:**
But mercy is above this sceptred sway,
It is enthroned in the hearts of **Kings,**
It is an attribute to **God** himselfe;
And earthly power doth then shew likest **Gods**
When mercie seasons **Justice.** Therefore **Jew,**
Though **Justice** be thy plea, consider this,
That in the course of **Justice,** none of us
Should see salvation: we do pray for mercie,

And that same prayer, doth teach us all to render
The deeds of mercie. I have spoke thus much
To mittigate the justice of thy plea:
Which if thou follow, this strict course of **Venice**
Must needes give sentence 'gainst the **Merchant** there.

One of the more interesting observations is that the word *mercy*, which appears five times, is not capitalized at all, whereas all the images of God and Country—and "Jew" (an insult then, as now)—were. Reading it—or better still speaking it—with these capitals delivers a different interpretation to the "received" wisdom that this is a great plea for mercy.

In the final analysis, no one knows if the capitalization was what the actors' script would have had, but my work with actors reveals that it <u>always</u> gives useful and valuable acting notes to the performer. Even if the capitalization was a whim of the compositor—and the more work I do with the original script the more I find this difficult to believe—then at least it is an Elizabethan's choice of which word to highlight with the use of the capital, and therefore someone close to the original performance.

Folio Lineage

Here are some examples of how the original lineage compares with that changed by latecomers. See if you think the older or the newer version is better:

This is the famous *Enobarbus* speech from *Anthonie, and Cleopatra* as seen in the Folio:

ENOBARBUS:
  I will tell you,
  The Barge she sat in, like a burnisht Throne
  Burnt on the water: the Poope was beaten Gold,
  Purple the Sailes: and so perfumed that
  The Windes were Love-sicke.
  With them the Owers were Silver,
  Which to the tune of Flutes kept stroke, and made
  The water which they beate, to follow faster;
  As amorous of their strokes. For her owne person,
  It beggerd all discription, she did lye
  In her Pavillion, cloth of Gold, of Tissue,
  O're-picturing that Venus, where we see
  The fancie out-worke Nature. On each side her,
  Stood pretty Dimpled Boyes, like smiling Cupids,
  With divers coulour'd Fannes whose winde did seeme,

To glove the delicate cheekes which they did coole,
And what they undid did.

And now a modern "edited" version:

ENOBARBUS:
    I will tell you.
    The barge she sat in, like a burnished throne
    Burned on the water. The poop was beaten gold;
    Purple the sails, and so perfumed that
    The winds were love-sick with them. The oars were silver,
    Which to the tune of flutes kept stroke, and made
    The water which they beat to follow faster,
    As amorous of their strokes. For her own person,
    It beggared all description. She did lie
    In her pavilion—cloth of gold, of tissue—
    O'er-picturing that Venus where we see
    The fancy outwork nature. On each side her
    Stood pretty dimpled boys, like smiling Cupids,
    With divers-colored fans whose wind did seem
    To glow the delicate cheeks which they did cool,
    And what they undid did.

The Editor has removed the half-lines by pushing two lines together to make a whole one (albeit one with twelve syllables), but for an actor it is much better to play the speech as it appears in the Folio. This means that *Enobarbus* ends the thought on *The Windes were Love-sicke*. And then, in the pause that follows, realizes that the others listening to him are spellbound—and so he starts afresh (and this speech is the first time in the play he speaks in poetry). All the actors I have worked with on these passages prefer the Folio text as an acting guide; still, the editions I have studied follow these "corrections."

When I was working on *Anthonie, and Cleopatra*, I found that there was some very interesting information in the way *Cæsar* changed from poetry to prose and back again, but alas it had been edited out of the modern version most of us have easy access to. The lines in **bold** are the ones that modern Editors change from prose to poetry, even though the lines cannot be made to be regular:

ANTHONY:
    You do mistake your busines, my Brother never
    Did urge me in his Act: I did inquire it,
    And have my Learning from some true reports
    That drew their swords with you, did he not rather
    Discredit my authority with yours,

And make the warres alike against my stomacke,
Having alike your cause. Of this, my Letters
Before did satisfie you. If you'l patch a quarrell,
As matter whole you have to make it with,
It must not be with this.

CÆSAR:

**You praise your selfe, by laying defects of judge-
ment to me: but you patcht up your excuses.**

ANTHONY:

Not so, not so:
I know you could not lacke, I am certaine on't,
Very necessity of this thought, that I
Your Partner in the cause 'gainst which he fought,
Could not with gracefull eyes attend those Warres
Which fronted mine owne peace. As for my wife,
I would you had her spirit, in such another,
The third oth'world is yours, which with a Snaffle,
You may pace easie, but not such a wife.

ENOBARBUS:

**Would we had all such wives, that the men
might go to Warres with the women.**

ANTHONY:

So much uncurable, her Garboiles (*Cæsar*)
Made out of her impatience: which not wanted
Shrodenesse of policie to: I greeving grant,
Did you too much disquiet, for that you must,
But say I could not helpe it.

CÆSAR:

I wrote to you, when rioting in Alexandria you
Did pocket up my Letters: and with taunts
Did gibe my Misive out of audience.

ANTHONY:

Sir, he fell upon me, ere admitted, then:
Three Kings I had newly feasted, and did want
Of what I was i'th'morning: but next day
I told him of my selfe, which was as much
As to have askt him pardon. Let this Fellow
Be nothing of our strife: if we contend
Out of our question wipe him.

CÆSAR:

**You have broken the Article of your oath,
which you shall never have tongue to charge me with.**

LEPIDUS:

    Soft *Cæsar.*

ANTHONY:

    No *Lepidus*, let him speake,

    The Honour is Sacred which he talks on now,

    Supposing that I lackt it: but on *Cæsar*,

    The Article of my oath.

CÆSAR:

    To lend me Armes, and aide when I requir'd

    them, the which you both denied.

ANTHONY:

    Neglected rather:

    And then when poysoned houres had bound me up

    From mine owne knowledge, as neerely as I may,

    Ile play the penitent to you. But mine honesty,

    Shall not make poore my greatnesse, nor my power

    Worke without it. Truth is, that *Fulvia*,

    To have me out of Egypt, made Warres heere,

    For which my selfe, the ignorant motive, do

    So farre aske pardon, as befits mine Honour

    To stoope in such a case.

LEPIDUS:

    'Tis Noble spoken.

Now the interesting thing is that the <u>actors</u> in my production were quite happy to swing from poetry to prose, as their characters changed mood and attitude toward them, but it was the Editors who wanted to smooth everything out, to standardize things—as if consistency were ever the mark of a real live person. It was as if when opposed by *Anthony*, *Cæsar* sulked by only muttering back at him in prose, getting back to poetry when the scene developed.

I was lecturing on Shakespeare to a group of nuns (don't ask), and I found myself saying "Is there any question you have always wanted to ask about his plays?" One nun spoke up that she had been teaching *Romeo and Juliet* for over twenty years, and had always had to tell her students that the *Queene Mab* speech by *Mercutio* was a great piece of poetry, but she had never seen the greatness in it. I consulted my Folio, and gave her the glad tidings that the speech is, in fact, in prose—it is the modern Editors that put it into poetry, although they have to change a few words to get it to fit. Here are the first three lines:

O then I see Queene Mab hath beene with you:
She is the Fairies Midwife, and she comes in shape no bigger than Agat-stone, on the fore-finger of an Alderman,

And all the rest of it is in prose, except for the last four lines,

MERCUTIO:
    This is the hag, when Maides lie on their backs,
    That presses them, and learnes them first to beare,
    Making them women of good carriage:
    This is she.

My nun laughed at this, since the only bit of poetry in the Folio version was the bit she always had to leave out, as it was considered too rude for her students.

Folio Punctuation

First of all, the punctuation—the original punctuation is, I believe, crucial, for it defines where the individual thoughts end. Working from the First Folio—for the punctuation there is, I am certain, an actor's punctuation—I insist all of it should be obeyed.

It is plain to see that Editors give themselves total permission to change the Folio punctuation. What is not so clear at first are the changes that this makes to the intention and meaning of a speech.

Each speech should be looked at to find the full stops or periods. The words before each one are usually what this thought is about, and all the preceding lines lead up to this concluding thought. The Folio punctuation divides the speeches into actor thoughts; these are not necessarily grammatical or even logical, but they are actable. Care should be taken not to "end-stop," that is, to end each line of poetry as if it were the end of a thought.

Consider *Pucke*'s description of what he has done in *A Midsommer Nights Dreame*:

PUCKE:
    My Mistris with a monster is in love,
    Neere to her close and consecrated bower,
    While she was in her dull and sleeping hower,
    A crew of patches, rude Mechanicals,
    That worke for bread upon *Athenian* stals,
    Were met together to rehearse a Play,
    Intended for great *Theseus* nuptiall day:
    The shallowest thick-skin of that barren sort,
    Who *Piramus* presented, in their sport,
    Forsooke his Scene, and entred in a brake,
    When I did him at this advantage take,
    An Asses nole I fixed on his head.
    Anon his *Thisbie* must be answered,

And forth my Mimmick comes: when they him spie,
As Wilde-geese, that the creeping Fowler eye,
Or russet-pated choughes, many in sort
(Rising and cawing at the guns report)
Sever themselves, and madly sweepe the skye:
So at his sight, away his fellowes flye,
And at our stampe, here ore and ore one fals;
He murther cries, and helpe from *Athens* cals.
Their sense thus weake, lost with their fears thus strong,
Made senselesse things begin to do them wrong.
For briars and thornes at their apparell snatch,
Some sleeves, some hats, from yeelders all things catch,
I led them on in this distracted feare,
And left sweete *Piramus* translated there:
When in that moment (so it came to passe)
Tytania waked, and straightway lov'd an Asse.

Looking at the punctuation, it is easy to see that *Pucke*'s thought goes right through
from the beginning to *An Asses nole I fixed on his head.*, which would be what he is so
anxious to tell.

Compare the speech with a modern edited version:

PUCK:
My mistress with a monster is in love.
Near to her close and consecrated bower
While she was in her dull and sleeping hour
A crew of patches, rude mechanicals
That work for bread upon Athenian stalls,
Were met together to rehearse a play
Intended for great Theseus' nuptial day.
The shallowest thickskin of that barren sort,
Who Piramus presented, in their sport
Forsook his scene and entered in a brake,
When I did him at this advantage take.
An ass's nole I fixèd on his head.
Anon his Thisbe must be answerèd,
And forth my mimic comes. When they him spy—
As wild geese that the creeping fowler eye,
Or russet-pated choughes, many in sort,
Rising and cawing at the gun's report,
Sever themselves and madly sweep the sky—
So, at his sight, away his fellows fly,

And at our stamp here o'er and o'er one falls.
He 'Murder' cries, and help from Athens calls.
Their sense thus weak, lost with their fears thus strong,
Made senseless things begin to do them wrong.
For briers and thorns at their apparel snatch;
Some sleeves, some hats—from yielders all things catch.
I led them on in this distracted fear,
And left sweet Piramus translated there;
When in that moment, so it came to passe,
Titania waked and straightway loved an ass.

So this Editor has divided the speech up into *ten* separate thoughts—as opposed to the Folio's *four* thoughts—and has actually increased the acting difficulty, let alone obscured the thoughts of *Pucke*. The beginning becomes a series of statements, rather than building a story up to the glory of *Pucke*'s use of the ass's head.

I have never forgotten the words of the English actor Ian Richardson to me when discussing performing Shakespeare: "Whenever I have a problem with a speech, I go back to the First Folio, for that is an <u>actor's</u> punctuation, and I find it helps me every time."

Here is a modern version of *Macbeth*'s soliloquy. So you can see what has happened, I am putting a space after each full stop—the end of each thought—so you can see what the speech has been made into:

MACBETH:
She should have died hereafter.

There would have been a time for such a word.

Tomorrow, and tomorrow, and tomorrow
Creeps in this petty pace from day to day
To the last syllable of recorded time,
And all our yesterdays have lighted fools
The way to dusty death.
                              Out, out, brief candle.

Life's but a walking shadow, a poor player
That struts and frets his hour upon the stage,
And then is heard no more.
                              It is a tale
Told by an idiot, full of sound and fury,
Signifying nothing.

And now the version you will find in the Folio (with the same pointing out of thoughts'
ends):

MACBETH:
    She should have dy'de heereafter;
    There would have beene a time for such a word:
    To morrow, and to morrow, and to morrow,
    Creepes in this petty pace from day to day,
    To the last Syllable of Recorded time:
    And all our yesterdayes, have lighted Fooles
    The way to dusty death.
                     Out, out, breefe Candle,
    Life's but a walking Shadow, a poore Player,
    That struts and frets his houre upon the Stage,
    And then is heard no more.
                  It is a Tale
    Told by an Ideot, full of sound and fury
    Signifying nothing.

As can be seen, the original has a sweep of thought and feeling up to *to dusty death.*, but
the edited version breaks it up into smaller, more trivial ones, leading to *have died hereafter.*, *such a word.*, and only then *to dusty death.*

In the preface to a modern edited *Anthonie and Cleopatra* (the Arden Edition, M.R.
Rilky, 1954), the Editor writes:

Since Case's edition (the first Arden edition 1906) first appeared a great deal
more attention had been paid to the punctuation of the early Quarto and First
Folio texts than had been paid by early editors, who felt themselves free to play
any old Harry they chose with the original punctuation . . .

I think therefore that in the punctuation of the early texts we have, pretty certainly, at least "playhouse" punctuation, and very possibly a great deal of Shakespeare's own. If this is so, it means that no modern editor can neglect the Q and F
punctuation. I should go further, and be prepared to say that no editor can desert
it without very careful consideration, and if he does, does so at his peril . . .

"For these reasons I have in the text which follows retained an unusually high
proportion of the F punctuation . . . "

In the edition that follows these high aims, the Editor in 3,014 lines of text makes
<u>1,466</u> changes in punctuation (including the addition of 217 exclamation points and
with the removal of just one).

These changes in punctuation change not just meaning but the whole thrust of a moment. Consider when *Malvolio* finally leaves the court of *Olivia*, having been humiliated and falsely imprisoned. Every modern edition will print his final words as *I'll be reveng'd on the whole packe of you!* But here in the Folio it is:

FABIAN:

    Good Madam heare me speake,
    And let no quarrell, nor no braule to come,
    Taint the condition of this present houre,
    Which I have wondred at. In hope it shall not,
    Most freely I confesse my selfe, and *Toby*
    Set this device against *Malvolio* heere,
    Upon some stubborne and uncourteous parts
    We had conceiv'd against him. *Maria* writ
    The Letter, at sir *Tobyes* great importance,
    In recompence whereof, he hath married her:
    How with a sportfull malice it was follow'd,
    May rather plucke on laughter then revenge,
    If that the injuries be justly weigh'd,
    That have on both sides past.

OLIVIA:

    Alas poore Foole, how have they baffel'd thee?

FESTE:

    Why some are borne great, some atchieve great-
    nesse, and some have greatnesse throwne upon them. I
    was one sir, in this Enterlude, one sir *Topas* sir, but that's
    all one: By the Lord Foole, I am not mad: but do you re-
    member: Madam, why laugh you at such a barren rascall,
    and you smile not he's gag'd: and thus the whirlegigge
    of time, brings in his revenges.

MALVOLIO:

    Ile be reveng'd on the whole packe of you?
      EXIT MALVOLIO.

Changing the question mark to an exclamation point is changing the interpretation. And the excuse that the Elizabethans used both bits of punctuation interchangeably is unproven. I find that the real support for the Folio punctuation comes from performance, where *Malvolio* starts his exit with a threat, realizes that he is outnumbered, and leaves us laughing at the deflation of his pomposity.

Of course, such things are personal interpretations, but the original punctuation works <u>theatrically</u>, an aspect too often neglected in changing the Folio text.

Some speeches seem very opaque and difficult precisely <u>because</u> the Editor has changed them from the Folio. Consider for example the Folio start of *Measure, For Measure* when the *Duke* makes his first, convoluted speech:

DUKE:
> Of Government, the properties to unfold,
> Would seeme in me t'affect speech and discourse,
> Since I am put to know, that your owne Science
> Exceedes (in that) the lists of all advice
> My strength can give you: Then no more remaines
> But that, to your sufficiency, as your worth is able,
> And let them worke: The nature of our People,
> Our *Cities Institutions*, and the Termes
> For Common Justice, y'are as pregnant in
> As Art, and practise, hath inriched any
> That we remember: There is our Commission,
> From which, we would not have you warpe; call hither,
> I say, bid come before us *Angelo*:
> What figure of us thinke you, he will beare.
> For you must know, we have with speciall soule
> Elected him our absence to supply;
> Lent him our terror, drest him with our love,
> And given his Deputation all the Organs
> Of our owne powre: What thinke you of it?

This is rather unintelligible, and seems to need the punctuation changes that appear in all edited versions:

DUKE:
> Of government the properties to unfold
> Would seem in me t'affect speech and discourse,
> Since I am put to know that your own science
> Exceeds in that the lists of all advice
> My strength can give you. Then no more remains
> But this: to your sufficiency, as your worth is able,
> And let them work. The nature of our people,
> Our city's institutions, and the terms
> For common justice, you're as pregnant in
> As art and practice hath enriched any
> That we remember.
> *He gives Escalus papers.*

> There is our commission,
> From which we would not have you warp.
> *To a lord.*
>   Call hither,
> I say bid come before us, Angelo.
>   *EXIT LORD.*
> *To Escalus.* What figure of us think you he will bear?
> For you must know we have with special soul
> Elected him our absence to supply,
> Lent him our terror, dress'd him with our love,
> And given his deputation all the organs
> Of our own power. What think you of it?

However, when given this piece by an actor who was having difficulty in understanding and performing it, I asked him to act the Folio version. "But it does not make sense." "Then that is your acting note."

When <u>performed</u>, the Folio version suddenly takes off and makes perfect sense, as the *Duke* rambles along with several <u>unfinished</u> sentences—understandable, as the actor, having performed the Folio version, now told me, in someone who was breaking the bad news to his deputy (*Escalus*) that *Angelo* and not he was getting the preferment.

This has happened to me twice on the same speech. An actor preparing the role of *Duke* for the San Diego Globe contacted me specifically because of his confusion over the first speech. And I went over the same ground: "Then the confusion <u>is</u> your acting note." He acted the Folio's seeming illogical structure and came to the same conclusion, that the *Duke* was prevaricating while trying to tell *Escalus* the bad news.

One last thought about punctuation. There is a famously incorrectly punctuated piece, *Peter Quince's* Introduction to the play at the end of *A Midsommer Nights Dreame*, that is punctuated incorrectly for the humor of the audience's hearing someone get it all wrong. How do the Editors cope with this? They either print the piece exactly as in the Folio or make one or two changes.

However, in the preceding ten lines they make ten changes, in the <u>next</u> ten lines they make ten changes, and they are saying in effect that the original compositor got the original bad punctuation right but all the right punctuation wrong! Interestingly enough, the Quarto has almost point for point the same punctuation as the Folio for this whole passage.

Here is the piece in the original:

THESEUS:
>   The kinder we, to give them thanks for nothing
>   Our sport shall be, to take what they mistake;
>   And what poore duty cannot doe, noble respect
>   Takes it in might, not merit.

Where I have come, great Clearkes have purposed
To greete me with premeditated welcomes;
Where I have seene them shiver and looke pale,
Make periods in the midst of sentences,
Throttle their practiz'd accent in their feares,
And in conclusion, dumbly have broke off,
Not paying me a welcome. Trust me sweete,
Out of this silence yet, I pickt a welcome:
And in the modesty of fearfull duty,
I read as much, as from the ratling tongue
Of saucy and audacious eloquence.
Love therefore, and tongue-tide simplicity,
In least, speake most, to my capacity.

EGEUS:

So please your Grace, the Prologue is addrest.

THESEUS:

Let him approach.

FLORISH. TRUMPET.

ENTER THE PROLOGUE. QUINCE.

PROLOGUE:

If we offend, it is with our good will.
That you should thinke, we come not to offend,
But with good will. To shew our simple skill,
That is the true beginning of our end.
Consider then, we come but in despight.
We do not come, as minding to content you,
Our true intent is. All for your delight,
We are not heere. That you should here repent you,
The Actors are at hand; and by their show,
You shall know all, that you are like to know.

THESEUS:

This fellow doth not stand upon points.

LYSANDER:

He hath rid his Prologue, like a rough Colt: he
knowes not the stop. A good morall my Lord. It is not
enough to speake, but to speake true.

HIPPOLITA:

Indeed hee hath plaid on his Prologue, like a
childe on a Recorder, a sound, but not in government.

THESEUS:

His speech was like a tangled chaine: nothing
impaired, but all disordered. Who is next?

TAWYER WITH A TRUMPET BEFORE THEM.
ENTER PYRAMUS AND THISBY, WALL, MOONE-SHINE, AND LYON.

PROLOGUE:

    Gentles, perchance you wonder at this show,
    But wonder on, till truth make all things plaine.
    This man is *Piramus*, if you would know;
    This beauteous Lady, *Thisby* is certaine.
    This man, with lyme and rough-cast, doth present
    Wall, that vile wall, which did these lovers sunder:
    And through walls chink (poor soules) they are content
    To whisper. At the which, let no man wonder.
    This man, with Lanthorne, dog, and bush of thorne,
    Presenteth moone-shine. For if you will know,
    By moone-shine did these Lovers thinke no scorne
    To meet at *Ninus* toombe, there, there to wooe:
    This grizy beast (which Lyon hight by name)
    The trusty *Thisby*, comming first by night,
    Did scarre away, or rather did affright:
    And as she fled, her mantle she did fall;
    Which Lyon vile with bloody mouth did staine.
    Anon comes *Piramus*, sweet youth and tall,
    And findes his *Thisbies* Mantle slaine;
    Whereat, with blade, with bloody blamefull blade,
    He bravely broacht his boiling bloudy breast,
    And *Thisby*, tarrying in Mulberry shade,
    His dagger drew, and died. For all the rest,
    Let *Lyon, Moone-shine, Wall*, and Lovers twaine,
    At large discourse, while here they doe remaine.

    EXIT ALL BUT WALL.

And now, in the modern "regularized" version, with all changes to the Folio punctuation indicated with underlining (_):

THESEUS:

    The kinder we, to give them thanks for nothing_.
    Our sport shall be_to take what they mistake;
    And what poor duty cannot do, noble respect
    Takes it in might, not merit.
    Where I have come, great clerks have purposed
    To greet me with premeditated welcomes;
    Where I have seen them shiver and look pale,
    Make periods in the midst of sentences,

Throttle their practic'd accent in their fears,
And in conclusion_dumbly have broke off,
Not paying me a welcome. Trust me_, sweet,
Out of this silence yet_I pickt a welcome_;
And in the modesty of fearful duty_
I read as much_as from the rattling tongue
Of saucy and audacious eloquence.
Love_, therefore, and tongue-tied simplicity_
In least_speake most, to my capacity.

PHILOSTRATE:

So please your Grace, the Prologue is address'd.

DUKE:

Let him approach.

> FLOURISH. TRUMPETS.
>
> ENTER THE PROLOGUE. QUINCE.

PROLOGUE:

If we offend, it is with our good will.
That you should think, we come not to offend,
But with good will. To show our simple skill,
That is the true beginning of our end.
Consider then, we come but in despite.
We do not come, as minding to content you,
Our true intent is. All for your delight_
We are not here. That you should here repent you,
The actors are at hand; and_, by their show,
You shall know all, that you are like to know.

THESEUS:

This fellow doth not stand upon points.

LYSANDER:

He hath rid his prologue_like a rough colt_; he
knows not the stop. A good moral_, my lord_: it is not
enough to speak, but to speak true.

HIPPOLITA:

Indeed he hath play'd on this prologue_like a
child on a recorder —— a sound, but not in government.

THESEUS:

His speech was like a tangled chaine_; nothing
impair'd, but all disorder'd. Who is next?

> ENTER WITH A TRUMPET BEFORE THEM PIRAMUS AND THISBY,
> WALL, MOONE-SHINE, AND LYON.

PROLOGUE:

Gentles, perchance you wonder at this show_;

But wonder on till truth make all things plain.
This man is Piramus, if you would know;
This beauteous lady Thisby is certain.
This man, with lime and rough-cast, doth present
Wall, that vile Wall, which did these lovers sunder ;
And through Wall's chink, poor soules, they are content
To whisper. At the which let no man wonder.
This man, with lantern, dog, and bush of thorn,
Presenteth Moonshine ; for if you will know,
By moonshine did these lovers think no scorn
To meet at Ninus' tomb, there, there to woo .
This grizzly beast, which Lion hight by name,
The trusty Thisby, coming first by night,
Did scare away, or rather did affright ;
And as she fled, her mantle she did fall,
Which Lion vile with bloody mouth did stain.
Anon comes Piramus, sweet youth and tall,
And finds his trusty Thisby's mantle slain;
Whereat, with blade, with bloody blameful blade,
He bravely broach'd his boiling bloody breast ;
And Thisby, tarrying in mulberry shade,
His dagger drew, and died. For all the rest,
Let Lion, Moonshine, Wall, and lovers twain
At large discourse, while here they do remain.
    EXIT.

I have found that comparing Editors with the Folio, the more famous the play, the more changes they make, whereas the less well known plays are printed in much closer versions to the "original." Do we really believe that the original compositors were meticulous with, say, the *Henry the Sixt* plays, but needed to be corrected on almost every line for a famous play like *Hamlet*?

Now, do the changes to the *Piramus and Thisby* make it easier to act, or easier to understand? I hope by now you are realizing that the original text has more to offer than you had been led to believe, and that is no more apparent than in the case of which words were printed in Capitals, and which not.

Folio Spelling

At least with the spelling in the First Folio, there are some Editors who go along with the original spelling, at least as far as the pronunciation of dialects is concerned. Here are the various regional speakers in *Henry the Fift*:

ENTER MAKMORRICE, AND CAPTAINE JAMY.

GOWER:

Here a comes, and the Scots Captaine, Captaine
Jamy, with him.

WELCH:

Captaine *Jamy* is a marvellous falorous Gentleman, that is certain, and of great expedition and knowledge in th'aunchiant Warres, upon my particular knowledge of his directions: by *Cheshu* he will maintaine his
Argument as well as any Militarie man in the World, in
the disciplines of the Pristine Warres of the Romans.

SCOT:

I say gudday, Captaine *Fluellen*.

WELCH:

Godden to your Worship, good Captaine
James.

GOWER:

How now Captaine *Mackmorrice*, have you
quit the Mynes? have the Pioners given o'er?

IRISH:

By Chrish Law tish ill done: the Worke ish
give over, the Trompet sound the Retreat. By my Hand
I sweare, and my fathers Soule, the Worke ish ill done:
it ish give over: I would have blowed up the Towne,
so Chrish save me law, in an houre. O tish ill done, tish ill
done: by my Hand tish ill done.

WELCH:

Captaine *Mackmorrice*, I beseech you now,
will you voutsafe me, looke you, a few disputations with
you, as partly touching or concerning the disciplines of
the Warre, the Roman Warres, in the way of Argument,
looke you, and friendly communication: partly to satisfie
my Opinion, and partly for the satisfaction, looke you, of
my Mind: as touching the direction of the Militarie discipline, that is the Point.

SCOT:

It sall be vary gud, gud feith, gud Captens bath,
and I sall quit you with gud leve, as I may pick occasion:
that sall I mary.

IRISH:

It is no time to discourse, so Chrish save me:
the day is hot, and the Weather, and the Warres, and the

King, and the Dukes: it is no time to discourse, the Town
is beseech'd: and the Trumpet call us to the breech, and
we talke, and be Chrish do nothing, tis shame for us all:
so God sa' me tis shame to stand still, it is shame by my
hand: and there is Throats to be cut, and Workes to be
done, and there ish nothing done, so Christ sa' me law.

SCOT:

By the Mes, ere theise eyes of mine take themselves to slomber, ayle de gude service, or Ile ligge i'th'
grund for it; ay, or goe to death: and Ile pay't as valo-
rously as I may, that sal I suerly do, that is the breff and
the long: mary, I wad full faine heard some question
tween you tway.

WELCH:

Captaine *Mackmorrice*, I thinke, looke you,
under your correction, there is not many of your Nation.

IRISH:

Of my Nation? What ish my Nation? Ish a
Villaine, and a Basterd, and a Knave, and a Rascall. What
ish my Nation? Who talkes of my Nation?

WELCH:

Looke you, if you take the matter otherwise
then is meant, Captaine *Mackmorrice*, peradventure I
shall thinke you doe not use me with that affabilitie, as in
discretion you ought to use me, looke you, being as good
a man as your selfe, both in the disciplines of Warre, and
in the derivation of my Birth, and in other particula-
rities.

IRISH:

I doe not know you so good a man as my selfe:
so Chrish save me, I will cut off your Head.

GOWER:

Gentlemen both, you will mistake each other.

SCOT:

A, that's a foule fault.

A PARLEY.

GOWER:

The Towne sounds a Parley.

WELCH:

Captaine *Mackmorrice*, when there is more

better oportunitie to be required, looke you, I will be
so bold as to tell you, I know the disciplines of Warre:
and there is an end.

    EXIT.

This original Folio spelling is for the most part kept by the modern Editors, for they see correctly that the spelling gives the regional accent to the performance.

However, elsewhere, they make many changes—some of them positively harmful to the sense of the Folio.

The spelling in the Folio is of more significance than just the sounds of early English dialects, and cannot just be laid to the vagaries of an early compositor. Looking at the reading of the letter by *Ferdinand* interrupted by *Costard* in *Loves Labour's lost*, one might wonder at the incompetence of the early compositor who was so inconsistent with the spelling of the simple word *me*:

FERDINAND:

So it is besieged with sable coloured melancholie, I
did commend the blacke oppressing humour to the most whole-
some Physicke of thy health-giving ayre: And as I am a Gen-
tleman, betooke my selfe to walke: the time When? about the
sixt houre, When beasts most grase, birds best pecke, and men
sit downe to that nourishment which is called supper: So much
for the time When. Now for the ground Which? which I
meane I walkt upon, it is ycliped, Thy Parke. Then for the
place Where? where I meane I did encounter that obscene and
most preposterous event that draweth from my snow-white pen
the ebon coloured Inke, which heere thou viewest, beholdest,
survayest, or seest. But to the place Where? It standeth
North North-east and by East from the West corner of thy
curious knotted garden; There did I see that low spiri-
ted Swaine, that base Minow of thy myrth, (Clown. Mee?)
that unletered small knowing soule, (Clow Me?) *that shallow*
vassall (Clow. Still mee?) *which as I remember, hight Co-*
stard, *(Clow.* O me) *sorted and consorted contrary to thy e-*
stablished proclaymed Edict and Continet, Cannon: Which
with, O with, but with this I passion to say wherewith:
CLOWNE:
With a Wench.

So *Costard* in order says: *Mee*; *Me*; *Still mee*; *O me*. Modern editions, of course, change all the vagaries in the spelling to the standardized *me*. However, when an actor speaks these original lines, the Folio spelling gives them differing ways of stressing the *me* from a quick snapped one to a long-drawn-out one: the variations in the spelling turn out to be precise scoring for the acting (and understanding) of the lines.

The spelling itself was yet another acting note, useful for anyone acting or analyzing the part of *Costard*, and not visible to anyone studying an edited text: it had been regularized away. Elizabethan spelling was much more phonetic than ours, and the best golden rule is to say it the way it is spelled. For example, when *Capulet* meets up with *Old capulet (Second Capulet)* in *Romeo and Juliet*, the modern Editor will present the scene thus:

CAPULET:
> Nay, sit, nay, sit, good cousin Capulet,
> For you and I are past our dancing days.
> How long is't now since last yourself and I
> Were in a masque?

CAPULET'S COUSIN:
> By'r Lady, thirty years.

CAPULET:
> What, man, 'tis not so much, 'tis not so much.
> 'Tis since the nuptial of Lucentio,
> Come Pentecost as quickly as it will,
> Some five-and-twenty years; and then we masqued.

CAPULET'S COUSIN:
> 'Tis more, 'tis more. His son is elder, sir.
> His son is thirty.

CAPULET:
> Will you tell me that?
> His son was but a ward two years ago.

A simple interaction between the two that adds not a lot to the sequence, and in fact is often cut from a production, saving as it does the salary of *Capulet's Cousin*, since this is the only scene he is in.

Whereas the Folio spells it all out differently:

CAPULET:
> Nay sit, nay sit, good Cozin *Capulet,*
> For you and I are past our dauncing daies:
> How long 'ist now since last your selfe and I
> Were in a Maske?

SECOND CAPULET:
> Berlady thirty yeares.

CAPULET:
> What man: 'tis not so much, 'tis not so much,

'Tis since the Nuptiall of *Lucentio,*
Come Pentecost as quickely as it will,
Some five and twenty yeares, and then we Maskt.
SECOND CAPULET:
'Tis more, 'tis more, his Sonne is elder sir:
His Sonne is thirty.
CAPULET:
Will you tell me that?
His Sonne was but a Ward two yeares agoe.

Here, the response of *Second Capulet* is *Berlady,* and speaking all his speeches the way they are written (with nearly every word containing an "r" sound) tends to give the character of *Second Capulet* a country "burr" to his voice. He comes over as a little old country gentleman. But if that is his background—and class—it can throw a much larger light on the background and class of *Capulet* himself (nouveau riche?), and perhaps explain why he is so outraged when his daughter refuses to marry the aristocrat *Paris.*

Here in the Folio, where no Editor has interfered with some of the words and perhaps obscured what was the original intent, these things can be read, and acted on.

UNDERSTANDING
THROUGH ACTING

It is not necessary for you to <u>be</u> an actor to understand what is going on in Shake-speare's language, but understanding how an actor thinks and works is a great help. I have tried in these pages to show how through performance my understanding of the original texts has grown and developed simply by putting an actor's point of view onto the words and the situations an original actor would have found when presenting these plays to audiences in Renaissance times.

When asked if I am writing for those with an academic approach or an acting one, the answer is of course for both, since both are inextricably linked by the fact that these words were written for actors in the first place. But with these new insights and thoughts a whole world of new understanding can be brought onto these famous lines whether you are able or intend to act them, or plan to use these ideas to unlock greater depths in this most fascinating of all playwrights' thoughts, ideas, and practices.

There is a small parting of the ways here, for if you want to know more about the nitty-gritty of the world of Shakespeare's theatre, with proper researched examples and careful analysis, then I can do no better than point you in the direction of Dr. Tiffany Stern's groundbreaking book *Rehearsal from Shakespeare to Sheridan*.

If you really want to act out the ideas and thoughts, then what follows is a purely practical accumulation of thoughts and ideas that have arisen out of the ten years of per-formances that the Original Shakespeare Company has put on. And the best way of stat-ing them is to set out the Checklist that is given to all new recruits to the Company when they have shown their abilities and are starting on the journey that begins with workshop presentations, continues through public demonstrations and workshops, and culminates in the final proof and climactic joy of a full-length public performance.

Because we work from the First Folio, some of the notes here refer strictly to that, but whatever text you have access to, the hints here will be of help to you.

Note: The "Bing-Bong Machine" is simply that whenever an actor in their verse nurs-ing session puts in a period or full stop that does not belong, they end-stop. In other words, I call out "Bing-Bong!" as a friendly way of pointing out that they have not yet acted the punctuation correctly. (Yes, sometimes when they ignore the end of a sentence, and do not act the period that <u>is</u> there, I have been known to go: "Bong-Bing!")

Never believe that you are too stupid or not well educated enough to understand or perform Shakespeare. His actors were, in some cases, taken from the very bottom of society, and if <u>they</u> could manage to act them well, then so can we all today.

Here it is, a mixture of what has already been set out in this book, and practical theatre procedures.

THE OSC CHECKLIST

A. Text

1. Always remember to <u>theatricalize</u> the difference between prose and poetry. The bigger the gear change you put in (physical change is <u>always</u> a valid way of showing this), the easier it is for the audience to understand that a change has happened— and this is what Shakespeare intended when he made the initial poetry/prose change.

2. The form of address indicates status and relationship. To go from *thee* to *you* is a precise gauge to the way the relationship is changing at that moment: *you* can indicate a more distant relationship, *thee* a more intimate one—some of you find that to vary the distance between each other according to which one you are using is also helpful to the acting. <u>These changes are always interesting, and always consistent— so go with them—and make them physical!</u>

3. Titles and styles of address <u>and how they change</u> are also concrete clues as to attitude and mood. *My gracious Lord* (deep bow) is a different attitude from *Sir* (nod of head); *Uncle* (friendly contact) is a different relationship and attitude from *Sovereign* (kneel) and from *My Liege* (complete obeisance to the floor). *Farewell* could indicate a hug or handclasp/shake; <u>no</u> adornment could indicate a bald statement, with no bows or scrapes—putting a change into a physical form makes it easier for your fellow actors to react.

4. Do not forget that the original spelling (such as *hee, mee,* etc.) always adds information as to the strength of the thoughts.

5. The First Folio spelling of some words can be a little confusing: *I* (can often) = aye; *Ile* = I'll; *then* (can often) = than; *divel* = devil; *shew* = show; *onely* = only; *sodaine* = sudden; *do's* = does; *hast* = haste; and *sound* or *swound* = swoon.

6. Do not make complex speeches (or bits of speeches) simple and sincere; anyone expressing themselves with wit, humor, double entendres, and so forth, is someone struggling to express a complex feeling. A simple rule of thumb is to deliver a simple speech straight to the other character, and to go for a walk on a complex one.

7. A pause (an unfulfilled half-line) is usually a pause for business, not just a cessation of talking. <u>Do</u> something—even if it means rushing offstage and rapidly returning. Similarly, if a thought ends at the end of one line, then the new thought starting on the next line should be just that—a new thought, so do not stay with the mood and attitude of what has just been said.

8. A half-line at the start of a speech is NOT a cue to pause, but a clue that your line joins with someone else's (so you must come in smack on cue). A half-line at the end of a speech is NOT a cue to pause, but a clue that the next person is going to come in with lines smack on cue. Only a half-line elsewhere is a pause (if Shakespeare makes it blindingly clear it is a pause, it is; if not, <u>not</u>). An isolated half-line is often a clue for stage business.

9. Be true to your own text—and be aware that Shakespeare often sends you in an unexpected direction. An example of this is how many speeches do <u>not</u> build to a climax at the end, but have it some two-thirds of the way through.

10. <u>Asides</u> are never printed in First Folio text, so it is up to you to identify which lines might be asides and to make the appropriate acting choices. Many of the asides added by Editors to their texts are <u>wrong</u>!

11. If you have information that you suspect no one else has (*Hang off thou cat, thou bur*), and you need others to cooperate with you, then get help from your fellow actor in the Burbadge time. Remember, it could be intentional that you speak of something that is <u>not</u> happening.

12. <u>The final double iamb of your speech is like a "baton" that you pass on to the next speaker</u>: it is <u>that actor's</u> cue. These <u>final words belong to the Company, not to you.</u> Remember, the wrong cue can lead to a major hiccough, so any breaking up of those final words will be confusing to your fellow actors. If you find that the final cue words also appear somewhere else in your speech, deliver them so as not to confuse the next speaker, unless you think that the similar final cue is <u>intended</u> to get the other actor to try to come in with their line.

13. A <u>Watchword</u> is the cue for someone else's entrance. Make sure it is delivered so that it can be heard offstage. These will be confirmed during verse nursing sessions.

B. Lines and Preparation

1. <u>There is no substitute for learning your lines early</u>. Many a potentially wonderful OSC performance has been undermined by inadequate learning. Prose will take you longer to learn than poetry.

2. Learn your main chunks or long speeches first; do not neglect the final act, which tends to suffer from "tired" learning.

3. Learn each cue as part of your speech, then memorize the next cue following each speech. This means when you have finished a speech, your next cue is already ready in your mind.

4. In verse nursing sessions, the lines ought to be learned by the second session. There should be at least one day off between sessions, and between a verse session and the performance. The final verse nursing session (third?) should be a <u>speed run</u>.

5. The Bing-Bong Machine does <u>not</u> mean you must rush everything; it means you have stopped a <u>thought</u>, and the solution is <u>not</u> to rush on but to keep the thought going (and you can even breathe and pause as well). There is no necessary connec-

tion between breathing and delivering a long thought (oh no, there <u>is not</u>!). You can snatch or top up a breath without ending a thought.

6. A good way of learning your lines is to write the cue words on one side of a card and the full speech on the other. A friend can give you the cue and prompt you from the card, or you can look at the cue words, see if you remember the speech, and then turn it over to see how accurate you were. You can even shuffle the pack of cards to see if you can remember the speeches out of logical order!

7. Beware of putting on accents and funny voices—they tend to shout of an imposition. Of all the accents and lisps used in past OSC productions, <u>most</u> of them have been a cop-out from the acting problems presented, and have <u>not</u> helped the play or fellow actors.

8. Keep your scroll on you for those offstage reminder moments (and remember to arrange to have a pocket in your costume to carry it in). A scroll reduced in size is valuable.

C. Props and Costumes

1. The elements of costume are up to you, but should be inspired by your text and augment your performance. With power comes responsibility—do <u>not</u> get trapped into the cuteness of wearing a costume to surprise or amuse your fellow actors. A servant can be dressed in many ways (a french pastry cook, a Victorian gardener, an English butler), but dressing as a lumberjack is confusing, and not true to the text.

2. <u>Do not wear clumpy, noisy shoes in performance!</u>

3. The OSC will provide all the necessary (scripted) props, letters, and so forth, needed for a production. If you want something other than what is provided, fine: you get or make it.

4. Choose your own costume accessories, and get your own properties, as much as possible. They are there to augment your performance, and you know better than any designer what your character needs.

5. <u>ALL</u> actresses playing men, boys, or women disguised as men want to go on stage with a feminine hairstyle. The silhouette/look <u>MUST</u> be masculine (you don't need the gruff voice, the wide strides—just the correct hair <u>and</u> makeup, i.e., facial hair, lip lines and a touch of mascara).

D. Design

1. Our aim is to empower the actor, which is why we work as we do, with Cue Scripts and the First Folio. Therefore, it makes sense to carry this one step further into the area of design, and work in a way that Shakespeare's actors probably did.

2. We never work with a conventional set, but use what is found, that is, the pillars and painting at the Globe, or existing ruins in Jerash. We have a prompt desk, a truck, and a few pieces of furniture. We have indications as to nationality—just

flags on poles in colors that show allegiance. We also have some rather wonderful crowns and basic armor. Beyond this, props are character specific: your character, your specification. The same goes for frocks.

3. The OSC wardrobe has a colorful collection of basic tudor-ish outfits (style of, not copy of). Doublet and hose, bodice and skirt. Some tailored to particular actors, but with tweaks here and there, everyone can be accommodated. We have undershirts and rough peasant-type gear. As we do different pieces, we add in "specials" like cardinal's robes, but with a little imagination, they can become other things. A company member at the time of Shakespeare would, we understand, have been provided with a basic outfit and then expected to characterize it, so that's our rule.

4. You do not, however, have to do this on your own. We work with everyone on how to do it; there is quite a lot of reference available and lots of things in the costume store that can be adapted—just add imagination. If a character has a piece of costume mentioned in the text or has an obvious status symbol, cloak, gloves, headwear, and so forth, then we provide it or it is a joint effort, sometimes in a workshop situation, otherwise one-to-one. Footwear is always a problem. Everyone is encouraged to raid Charity shops and Granny's attic.

5. We think we all feel that putting the effort in beyond the text enhances the performance and enables everyone to understand a little more about the problems and parameters faced by the design team in ordinary circumstances. Anyone daunted by this should have a word with those company members who are particularly into design and research.

E. Burbadge Time

1. Before each major presentation, we will have a "Burbadge time." This is where all the entrances and exits are assigned and agreed. The actors can also decide what bits of the play/presentation need to be clarified or worked out.

2. A useful part of Burbadge is for the cast to stand in their family groups, so that everybody can see and understand the relationships in the upcoming performance.

3. All actors will have the opportunity to raise anything that troubles them, or is seen as a potential problem for the performance.

4. Burbadge time <u>must</u> include a vocal testing of the venue, where all actors try out their voices (not of course doing any of their actual part) with the others listening and reacting to the vocal level. Even if the Presenter thinks that a vocal check is not necessary, <u>do it</u>!

5. We have found that actors telling each other what business they intend to do is not a constructive idea unless it directly affects others; the danger is of actors indicating to others how they would like the scene to be played, and this can be inhibiting.

6. Looking at the Book-Keeper's backstage prompt script beforehand, to check the pattern of text in patter scenes and one-liners, can be of immense help.

F. Book-Holder (Onstage)

1. The Book-Holder (the prompter) is the master, not servant, of the production. When wanting or taking a prompt, catch the eye of the prompter and <u>keep in character and in mood</u>. If the Book-Holder gives a prompt, it must be followed: there may have been an incorrect final words cue, or vital text may have been missed.
2. When taking a prompt, <u>do not repeat the line from the beginning</u>—just pick up and continue.
3. Looking at the Book-Holder as you start a speech can give you confirmation that you are embarking on the correct lines.
4. If you want to pause in a speech, it must be agreed with the Book-Holder; otherwise you will get an unwanted prompt (how else will they know you are pausing and not drying?).
5. The bell will start the play, and resume it after an interval. A bell rung in the middle of a scene means that someone has missed an entrance, and is to alert those offstage.

G. Book-Keeper (Backstage)

1. Use the Book-Keeper backstage to get you ready for a scene, so you do not have to use up valuable theatrical energy straining to get ready for your entrance. If you want to start your entrance away from the stage to get on in a run, arrange this beforehand with the Book-Keeper.
2. The Book-Keeper is <u>not</u> the stage manager who runs errands for you; the Book-Keeper is there to stand you by for your entrances. <u>You</u> are still responsible for entering at the correct cue words.
3. The Book-Keeper has many other backstage responsibilities, such as cuing musicians, so do not burden the person with things <u>you</u> should take responsibility for.

H. Moves and Staging

1. If you know whom you are speaking to, clearly make the identification for the audience and fellow actors. Talking across other characters confuses everyone. Crossing over to the person you are speaking to often helps—and in a traverse theatre you should keep on walking to create another nice long diagonal.
2. Traverse theatre arrangements means that everyone can easily speak an aside at any moment, since there is always some audience near you.
3. For proscenium productions cheating eyelines <u>is</u> sometimes necessary, and the listeners and nonspeakers in a scene should discipline themselves to move <u>downstage</u> and so be in a good position to receive speeches and help the speaker to be seen by the audience.
4. Long diagonals are necessary, as they allow the audience to see at least one of a pair

of actors working together. Where appropriate, keep your distance; this will also allow your vocal projection to appear more natural.

5.   If other actors are not in the best place for you, it is quite allowed for you, gently, to take them to a better one by a firm grip on the elbow. You can also "invite" them to rest by propelling them onto a bench, if you know you have a long speech that would benefit from having such an attentive and close listener. Therefore, if you find yourself upstaged, do not just blame your fellow artists, but blame yourself for not having moved them to where they would contribute better to your scene.

6.   Never "cheat" by talking over your shoulder to the other person. It is very insulting to those members of the audience who happen to be sitting behind the other person and wonder why you do not want to face them. Let your shoulders face the person you are speaking to.

I. Exits and Entrances

1.   Be careful never to leave the stage before your designated exit line. You can make any number of false exits according to what you hear, or indicate offstage for someone else to enter, but your job is to stay on until you get your cue line to leave.

2.   On an entrance with a line, it should be spoken as your foot hits the stage floor. Do not wait for other actors to clear before you speak, although you can wait for a fanfare to finish.

3.   Avoid those "*who comes here?*" lines given to one entrance with the next actor coming on in the opposite direction. It should <u>never</u> be played as a gag—it looks <u>and is</u> cheap, and the problem should have been solved in Burbadge time (if you have such a line, with no entrance marked in your script, then you <u>know</u> that those offstage are waiting for your line before they can enter). Do not wait for an entrance before you say your line unless your script tells you to do so.

J. Gesture and Business

1.   If you hear your name mentioned, give an acknowledgment by a slight move, bow, or the like. It may be important for the speaker to know exactly <u>who</u> is playing the person they are talking about. Similarly, if you know who you are talking to, <u>catch their eye</u> at least once as you mention their name.

2.   Suit the word to the action, and the action to the word. This can be criticized as "illustrating," but it is *Hamlet's* advice to the Players, and <u>he</u> should know—so: illustrate!

3.   Preplanned business must be forfeited if it is not responded to by the other actors on stage. <u>Do not block your fellow actor's ideas</u>. If you do not agree with what they do, <u>go along with it</u> and <u>then</u> change it to what you would prefer.

4.   If a fellow actor is upstaging you with business, costumes, or properties during your

lines, and you consider this to be inappropriate, you are entirely within your rights to stop or change them. When you are speaking, you have the power to govern what the audience looks at, so if there is a distraction, either incorporate it into your performance or get rid of it.

5. We <u>like</u> and use you for your acting instincts, not your intellect. <u>Your biggest acting enemy is your in-built wish to be logical!</u> Your next biggest enemy is the wish to be consistent. Remember, only be consistent if the <u>lines</u> are consistent; if they vary, <u>you</u> should vary.

K. Pace

1. <u>Come in on cue</u> with each speech. <u>DO NOT</u> put pauses in before you speak (neither the audience nor your fellow actors know who is to speak next, so the audience is uncertain where to look). Once you start a speech, <u>then</u> you can put in business <u>with</u> your lines (and not in between speeches).

2. Pace in a first performance is usually too slow—especially at the beginning. Do not forget that Shakespeare will repeat important information, so you do not have to slow down to make sure the audience gets every bit of it: they can wait until the plot is repeated by another character.

3. Beware of picking up each other's pace, and getting slower and slower. If in doubt, top your fellow actor—do not choose to come in under, either in pace or tone.

4. Have an awareness of the function of your part. It is the comic's job to get laughs, and the job of those at the start of the play to set the scene. Putting in funny business in an exposition scene holds up the whole play, and leaves the audience exhausted.

5. Bear in mind that what to you is a wonderful moment may be at the end of a very long evening both for your audience and your fellow actors! By Act Five, the audience know everything; only the characters on stage do not know the whole picture. Explanations are therefore only telling the audience what they already know, so they are interested in the reactions to the information, not in having the information slowly and carefully explained. Act Five should therefore be done at <u>lightning speed</u>!

L. Style and Mood

1. Don't adopt an attitude before you come on. Always allow the audience to witness the gear changes that define attitude (and you will find that this is what Shakespeare has indeed done in your lines).

2. Be careful not to pick up the other characters' style and mood. They are getting their information from their own lines, and there are many cases of two different characters having been given entirely differently styles for the same scene.

3. Let <u>your</u> discoveries, sudden understandings, even confusions be your <u>character's</u> as

well, and let them show. Shakespeare frequently puts the actor—you—into the same situation as the character, and all you need to do is reveal your feelings and thoughts to be perfectly in character and theatrically valid.

4. Remember, servants and the like do not know if they are in a comedy or a tragedy—they just do their thing from the text (and so should you!)

M. Audience

1. All soliloquies should be delivered directly to the audience's eyes. A soliloquy is direct contact with the audience—and is <u>not</u> the character's innermost thoughts; some characters <u>lie</u> in their soliloquies, or at least exaggerate in order to impress or persuade their audience, just as they do with other characters in the play.

2. Never forget that we are sharing the excitement and discoveries with an audience. So if in doubt, give it out to them. We have all failed if anything good (a discovery, a new interpretation, a wonderful insight) is not also shared by our audience. After all, they are the ones who paid to come in.

3. Because the performances are in a lit auditorium, all lip shapes need to be carefully outlined to help the audience hear you. This means men as well as women ought to wear light makeup and lipstick.

4. Vary where you speak from in order to satisfy all parts of the audience.

N. Shakespeare's Globe

1. Never act in the "Valley of Death" (the space between the two pillars).

2. When you stage yourself below the pillars, face <u>upstage</u>. Facing out to the groundlings is to address the cheapest seats, and insult the higher payers who are sitting in the side seats. The groundlings get more than enough for their £5, so give your back to them, and your face to the £20 sides. <u>The very worst staging is to have two actors below the pillars talking to each other, and so excluding a good third of the audience.</u>

3. Break up a long speech by addressing all four sides of the house (and particularly give "lordly" lines to those sitting in the balcony above the stage).

4. Walking round the outside of the pillars is a good way of indicating a different area, and sitting on the inside of the pillars (even in the Valley of Death) is a good place to listen.

5. It is not a good plan to go back up to the loft to change costumes (two people got caught out in *Cymbeline*, and missed an entrance because of this).

O. Last word

1. All your gear changes <u>belong to the Company, not to you</u>. They enable your fellow actors to know how to relate to you, so the clearer (the bigger) the better. A half done clue is bad acting; a completely committed clear theatricalized clue is magic!

2. Everything you do must be to help the play go forward, and to share the story with the audience. Funny walks, costumes, extravagant pauses for funny business all have their place, but should never be at the expense of the whole project, and <u>must be rooted in the text you were given</u>.

3. If in doubt, DO IT! (After all, when will you next be allowed to walk on stage without all that burden of moves, prepared stage business, and a director's expectation of you?)

4. The <u>Original Shakespeare Company</u> is determined to get you out of the "actor-as-victim" frame of mind, so do not allow anything to drag you back to that way of performing. The plays were written for you the actors. <u>So act them</u>!

EPILOGUE

I had finished this book, and sent the well-overdue manuscript off to my long-suffering editor in New York, when I received this e-mail from Richard Cordery, who had been so memorable as *Dromio of Syracuse* in our very first OSC presentation, and the wonderful double of *Pucke* and *Shylocke* for our presentations in Neuss, and was preparing an RSC production:

Just a brief note to wish you and Christine well and to share with you my continuing enthusiasm for the work you introduced me to. It is tricky writing this with our new production still to open (one doesn't want to tempt fate) but I want you to know that not a day goes by, not a rehearsal do I attend, and not a performance have I given where the magic that you revealed to me about Shakespeare's scripts does not loom large. I don't proselytize, and am still amazed by the dullness of so many people who should know better, but many of our (splendid) cast have sought me out on the quiet to ask "What is the secret of your appearing so clear in what you are saying? You seem to make it up as you go along."

I've loaded the folio versions onto the company's computer and these are often accessed by the cast and a full folio version is always in rehearsal.

However, this is not to say that they then approach their work any differently. Alas, too many want to use it only when they have a problem. And too often, much too often, they disregard the most obvious clues; such as the informal "Thy" as opoposed to the formal "You," or the encouragement to be close to someone on "This dagger" and apart on "That sword" or the folio punctuation, or the lineation. I could go on, but you know the howlers better than me. I continue to be amazed at their stubborn refusal to "give in" wholeheartedly to the folio, that they will cherry pick those aspects which suit them and their ideas of the scene/character, and reject wonderful clues which might alter their pre-judged view of the play.

But essentially the approach you helped me obtain gives me a certainty in rehearsals and a confidence in performance. I feel that I am not likely to flounder helplessly when Shakespeare himself is offering the advice. And for that I thank you (and him).

As ever,
Richard

I had no idea when I started my journey all those years ago that the results would be so rewarding, and that to explore original theatre practices would bring out the sort of response seen in the lovely letter from Richard: to be giving back to the actors the responsibility for acting.

Genealogical Table from Henry II to Edward III

Reigns of the English Kings for this period:		Reigns of the French Kings for this period:	
Henry II	1154–1189	Philip II	1180–1223
Richard I	1189–1199	Louis VIII	1223–1226
John	1199–1216	Louis IX	1226–1270
Henry III	1216–1272	Philip III	1270–1285
Edward I	1272–1307	Philip IV	1285–1314
Edward II	1307–1327	Louis X	1314–1316
Edward III	1327–1377	John I	1316
		Philip V	1316–1322
		Charles IV	1322–1328

Notes

CONSTANCE, supported by France, is pressing the claim of her son for the throne of England against that of KING JOHN. The conflict is over who has precedence—the son of a King, or the son of an elder brother.

The solution is to arrange a marriage between one from the English side BLANCH, and one from the French one, the Dauphin LEWIS. This was only one of a great number of inter-marriages between the two sides over the years.

Plantagenet

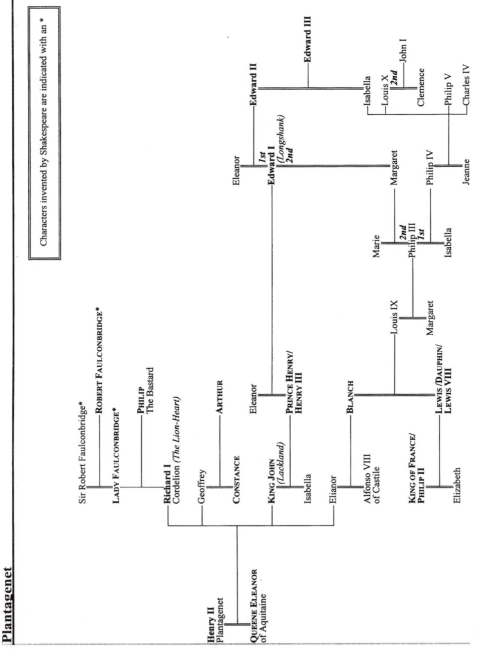

Characters invented by Shakespeare are indicated with an *

APPENDIX 2

Genealogical Table from Edward III to James I

The characters appearing in the plays of Shakespeare are marked thus: **RICHARD II**:*a*, with the letter indicating which play they are in.

Reigns of the English Kings and Queens for this period:		Reigns of the French Kings for this period:	
Edward III	1327–1377	Charles IV	1322–1328
Richard II	1377–1399	Philip VI	1328–1350
Henry IV	1399–1413	John II	1350–1364
Henry V	1413–1422	Charles V	1364–1380
Henry VI	1422–1461	Charles VI	1380–1422
Edward IV	1461–1470	Charles VII	1422–1461
Henry VI	1470–1471	Louis XI	1461–1483
Edward IV	1471–1483	Charles VIII	1483–1498
Edward V	1483	Louis XII	1498–1515
Richard III	1483–1485	Francis I	1515–1547
Henry VII	1485–1509	Henry II	1547–1559
Henry VIII	1509–1547	Francis II	1559–1560
Edward VI	1547–1553	Charles IX	1560–1574
Lady Jane Gray	1553	Henry III	1574–1589
Mary I	1553–1558	Henry IV	1589–1610
Elizabeth I	1558–1603	Louis XIII	1610–1643
James I	1603–1625		

Notes

REIGNIER:*e*, father of **MARGARET OF ANJOU**:*e:f:g:h*, was himself the brother of the Queen of **CHARLES VII**:*e*.

Margaret Beauford's (Countesse Richmond) second husband was Stafford, second son to **BUCKINGHAM**:*f*; and her third husband was **DERBY**, who later became **STAN-LEY**:*h*. This was why **EARL RICHMOND**:*g:h* referred to him as "Father in Law" (he was actually his step-father), and he referred to "thy Brother, tender *George*" to the Earl (they were half brothers).

BUCKINGHAM:*h* was forced to marry the sister of **LADY GRAY**:*g:h*, and so was very anti the house of Woodvile, and a natural ally of **RICHARD OF GLOUCESTER**:*f:g:h*.

The Wars of the Roses

EDWARD III had seven sons, and the eldest—the Black Prince—died before his father. This meant that his son, RICHARD II:*a*, although no son of a King, became King—but all his jealous uncles <u>were</u> sons of a King. Richard had to resign his throne to BULLING-BROOKE:*a:b:c*, the son of JOHN OF GAUNT:*a*, Duke of Lancaster and Edward's fourth son. He took the title of HENRY IV. *(The life and death of King Richard the Second).*

The **Yorkes**, descendants of the fifth son, felt that <u>they</u> should inherit the crown because they had married into the line of the third son, through his daughter Phillipa. The resulting Civil War was known as the **Wars of the Roses**. *(The First, Second, and Third Parts of Henry the Sixt).*

The youngest of **Yorke**:*e:f:g*'s sons, RICHARD DUKE OF GLOUCESTER:*f:g:h*, reputedly found his way to the throne by having his brother CLARENCE:*g:h*, and his cousins PRINCE EDWARD:*g:h* and RICHARD:*h* killed (the "Princes in the Tower"). HENRY TUDOR:*g:h*, Earl of Richmond and a distant descendant of the **Lancasters**, defeated RICHARD in battle, married ELIZABETH the descendant of the **Yorkes**, united the country, founded the House of **Tudor**, and called himself HENRY VII. *(The Tragedy of Richard the Third, with the Landing of Earle Richmond, and the Battell at Bosworth Field).*

Because the **Tudors** had a debatable claim to the Throne, they did all they could to prevent other claimants to the Crown arising and to secure it for the Tudors in the long term—hence HENRY VIII's persistent efforts to get a son. (This would perhaps be an influence on Tudor playwrights to portray non-Tudor Kings as corrupt and evil?)

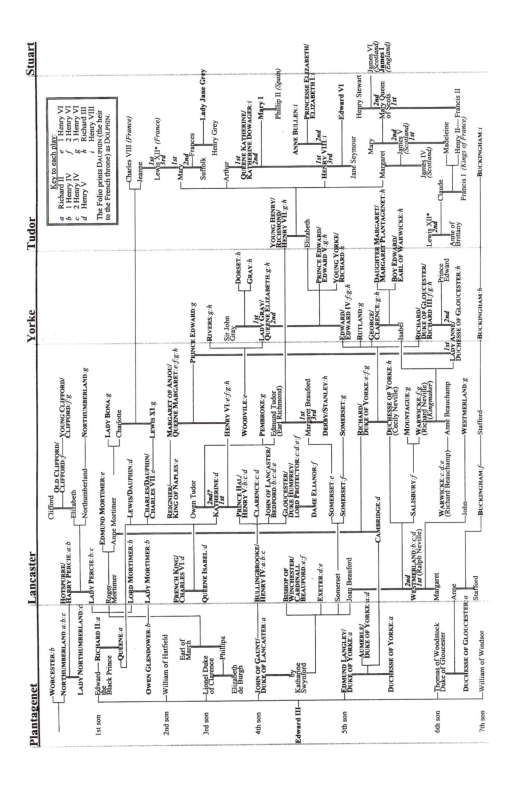

Romeo and his stars

> Pardon me Sir, that am the Meſſenger of ſuch bad tidings.
> Rom: Is it euen ſo? then I defie my Starres.

First Quarto 1957

> O pardon me for bringing theſe ill newes,
> Since you did leaue it for my office Sir.
> Rom. Is it euen ſo?
> Then I denie you Starres.

Second Quarto 1599

> O pardon me for bringing theſe ill newes,
> Since you did leaue it for my office ſir.
> Rom. Is it in ſo? then I denie you ſtarres.

First Folio 1623

Notes

The First (Bad) Quarto has   defie my
The Second Quarto, Third Quarto, and First Folio have   denie you
The Fifth Quarto, Second, Third and Fourth Folios have   deny you

All Editors seem to take one word from the Bad Quarto, *defie,* and insert it into the one of the other versions, making a line that there is not a scintilla of evidence that Shakespeare ever wrote:

Kittredge: (1940)	Is it e'en so?	Then I defy you, stars!
Riverside: (1974)	Is it e'en so?	Then I defy you, stars!
Arden: (1979)	Is it e'en so?	Then I defy you, stars!
Oxford: (1986)	Is it e'en so?	Then I defy you, stars.

BIBLIOGRAPHY

TEXTS

The First Folio of Shakespeare: The Norton Facsimile
  Ed. Charlton Hinman (Paul Hamlyn, New York, 1996)
The First Folio Speeches for Men
The First Folio Speeches for Women
  Patrick Tucker and Christine Ozanne (Oberon Books/LAMDA, London 1997)
Shakespeare Cue Scripts for the Classroom: General Selection; Duologues
  Patrick Tucker and Christine Ozanne (LAMDA/OSC, 1998)
The Shakespeare's Globe Acting Editions *(22 plays now available)*
  Ed. Patrick Tucker and Michael Holden (M.H. Publications, London, 1990+)
The Paperback Folio Series
  Ed. Simon Purse, Bryan Torfeh, and Patrick Tucker (Paperback Folio, 1999)

WORDS AND VERSE

The Actor and His Text
  Cicely Berry (Harrap, 1987)
How Poetry Works
  Philip Davies Roberts (Penguin, 1986)
The Riverside Shakespeare: General Introduction
  Harry Levin (Houghton Mifflin, Boston, 1974)
Shakespeare Lexicon & Quotation Dictionary
  Alexander Schmidt (2 vols., Dover reprint; New York, 1971)
Shakespeare's Bawdy
  Eric Partridge (E. P. Dutton, New York, [1948] 1969)
Shakespeare's Imagery
  Carolyn Spurgeon (Cambridge University, [1935] 1971)
Shakespeare's Names: A Pronouncing Dictionary
  Helge Kökeritz (Yale University, 1974)
Shakespeare's Wordplay
  M. M. Mahood (Methuen, London, [1957] 1979)

THEATRICALIZATION

The Genius of Shakespeare
  Jonathan Bate (Picador, 1997)
Playing Shakespeare
  John Barton (Methuen, London, 1984)

Prefaces to Shakespeare
   H. Granville Barker (Batsford, 1958)
Shakespeare's Producing Hand (out of print, but invaluable)
   Richard Flatter (W. W. Norton, New York, 1948)
Shakespeare's Stagecraft
   J. L. Styan (Cambridge University, [1967] 1971)

LIFE AND TIMES OF SHAKESPEARE AND THE GLOBE

Documents of the Rose Playhouse
   Ed. Carol Rutter (Manchester University Press, 1984)
Early English Stages
   Glynne Wickham (Columbia University Press, 1972)
Nothing Like the Sun (a novel)
   Anthony Burgess (Penguin, 1973)
Shakespeare at the Globe
   Bernard Beckerman (Macmillan Company, New York, 1962)
William Shakespeare
   Andrew Gurr (HarperCollins, 1995)

REHEARSAL

Rehearsal from Shakespeare to Sheridan
   Tiffany Stern (Clarendon Press, Oxford, 2000)

VIDEOS

Forge Productions taped *The Comedie of Errors* at The Mermaid Theatre in 1991, and our two performances of *A Midsommer Nights Dreame* in Jordan in 1997.

Alan Butland, freelance archive recordist, videotaped our Workshop Season event for Shakespeare's Globe in September 1995, and the special "Pillars and Staging" Workshop in October 1995, for the Globe Video Archive.

He also taped our three presentations of *As you Like it; King John; Cymbeline* at Shakespeare's Globe in 1997, 1998, and 1999, as well as some of our preparations and Burbadge time for them.

He also taped our Lecture/Demonstration on *Hamlet* at Cambridge University in May 2000, and our Elmbridge Arts Festival's *Romeo and Juliet* and *A Midsommer Nights Dreame*, in September 2000, including both the Burbadge times.

INTERNET

The website for the Original Shakespeare Company gives further details of their productions and contacts: www.oscuk.com.

The First Folio text can be found at: etext.lib.virginia.edu/shakespeare/folio.

INDEX

Patrick Tucker

He started by taking a degree in Physics from the University of London, and then went to America to take an MFA in Theatre Directing at Boston University. Since his first professional production in 1968, he has directed over 130 plays in all forms of theatre, from weekly repertory to the Royal Shakespeare Company. He has also directed more than 150 television programs, ranging from plays for the BBC, most recently episodes of *Casualty*, to many episodes of Liverpool's own soap opera *Brookside*.

Internationally, he has also directed plays and musicals in Australia, Canada, Germany, Israel, Kenya, South Africa, South Korea, and the United States, as well as giving his workshops on Shakespeare, directing, and screen acting.

He is the vice chairman of the Artistic Directorate of the International Shakespeare Globe Centre, which has rebuilt the Globe on the south bank of the Thames in London, and he founded and runs the Original Shakespeare Company with Christine Ozanne.

If you think these ideas are a little strange, you should read his *Secrets of Screen Acting*, also published by Routledge.